New Theory and Applications of Nonlinear Analysis, Fractional Calculus and Optimization

New Theory and Applications of Nonlinear Analysis, Fractional Calculus and Optimization

Guest Editor

Wei-Shih Du

MDPI

Basel • Beijing • Wuhan • Barcelona • Belgrade • Novi Sad • Cluj • Manchester

Guest Editor
Wei-Shih Du
Department of Mathematics
National Kaohsiung Normal University
Kaohsiung
Taiwan

Editorial Office
MDPI AG
Grosspeteranlage 5
4052 Basel, Switzerland

This is a reprint of the Special Issue, published open access by the journal *Axioms* (ISSN 2075-1680), freely accessible at: https://www.mdpi.com/journal/axioms/special_issues/J93COO0KLN.

For citation purposes, cite each article independently as indicated on the article page online and as indicated below:

Lastname, A.A.; Lastname, B.B. Article Title. *Journal Name* **Year**, *Volume Number*, Page Range.

ISBN 978-3-7258-5113-3 (Hbk)
ISBN 978-3-7258-5114-0 (PDF)
https://doi.org/10.3390/books978-3-7258-5114-0

Contents

About the Editor

Wei-Shih Du

Wei-Shih Du is a Full Professor of Mathematics in the Department of Mathematics, National Kaohsiung Normal University, Kaohsiung 824004, Taiwan. His main research interests include nonlinear analysis and its applications, fixed point theory and its applications, variational principles and inequalities, iterative methods for nonlinear mappings, optimization theory, equilibrium problems, and fractional calculus theory.

Preface

This Special Issue of *Axioms* paid greater attention to the new originality and real-world applications of nonlinear analysis, fractional calculus, their optimization, and their applications. It is well known that nonlinear analysis has widespread and significant applications in many areas at the core of many branches of pure and applied mathematics and modern science. The rapid development of fractional calculus and its applications over the past thirty years or more has led to a number of scholarly essays on the importance of its promotion and application. Over the past eighty years, optimization problems have been intensively studied, and many scholars have developed various feasible methods with which to analyze the convergence of algorithms and find approximate solutions. The Guest Editor has made every effort to ensure the success of this Special Issue and we hope that these efforts will be rewarded. Following a comprehensive review process, per the journal's policy and guidelines, 10 research papers have been included in this Special Issue. These articles demonstrate the profound impact and widespread applications of nonlinear analysis, fractional calculus, and optimization in applied mathematics and modern science. We would like to express our heartfelt appreciation to all authors and reviewers who contributed to this Special Issue. It was with the enthusiasm and spirit of the authors and reviewers that we could make this Special Issue an extraordinary success.

We are confident that the contributions to this Special Issue provide new insights into several important issues while, at the same time, providing new research problems or avenues that undoubtedly exceed our original aim. We also hope that researchers and practitioners find these papers interesting and inspirational for future research work in these exciting areas. Finally, we would like to express our sincere thanks to the Editorial team and the reviewers of *Axioms*, particularly the Editor-in-Chief, Prof. Dr. Humberto Bustince, and the Assistant Editors, for their great support throughout the editing process of our Special Issue.

Wei-Shih Du
Guest Editor

axioms

MDPI

Editorial

Editorial Conclusion for the Special Issue "New Theory and Applications of Nonlinear Analysis, Fractional Calculus and Optimization"

Wei-Shih Du

Department of Mathematics, National Kaohsiung Normal University, Kaohsiung 82444, Taiwan; wsdu@mail.nknu.edu.tw

Nonlinear analysis has widespread and significant applications in many areas at the core of many branches of pure and applied mathematics and modern science, including nonlinear ordinary and partial differential equations, critical point theory, functional analysis, fixed point theory, nonlinear optimization, fractional calculus, variational analysis, convex analysis, dynamical system theory, mathematical economics, data mining, signal processing, control theory, and many more. For more details, we refer readers to [1–7] and the references cited therein. The rapid development of fractional calculus and its applications during the past thirty years or more has led to a number of scholarly essays on the importance of its promotion and application in physical chemistry, probability and statistics, electromagnetic theory, financial economics, biological engineering, electronic networks, and so forth. Almost all areas of modern science and engineering have been influenced by the theory of fractional calculus. Due to the complexity of the various problems that arise in nonlinear analysis, fractional calculus and optimization, it is not always easy to find exact solutions, which often leads researchers to resort to approximate solutions. Over the past eighty years, optimization problems have been intensively studied, and many scholars have developed various feasible methods with which to analyze the convergence of algorithms and find approximate solutions. For more details about these subjects, we refer readers to research monographs [8–16].

This Special Issue paid greater attention to the new originality and real-world applications of nonlinear analysis, fractional calculus, optimization and their applications. Following a comprehensive review process as per the journal's policy and guidelines, 10 research papers have been included in this Special Issue and are listed as follows:

(i). Gao, L.; Yu, G.; Han, W. Optimality Conditions of the Approximate Efficiency for Nonsmooth Robust Multiobjective Fractional Semi-Infinite Optimization Problems. *Axioms* **2023**, *12*, 635. https://doi.org/10.3390/axioms12070635

Summary: *In this paper, the authors study new optimality conditions and establish saddle point theorems for robust approximate quasi-weak efficient solutions for a nonsmooth uncertain multiobjective fractional semi-infinite optimization problem (NUMFP).*

(ii). Huang, H.; Došenović, T.; Rakić, D.; Radenović, S. Fixed Point Results in Generalized Menger Probabilistic Metric Spaces with Applications to Decomposable Measures. *Axioms* **2023**, *12*, 660. https://doi.org/10.3390/axioms12070660

Summary: *This manuscript offers new fixed-point theorems in generalized Menger probabilistic metric spaces. Moreover, the authors provide some nontrivial examples and interesting applications to illustrate the superiority of the results obtained.*

(iii). Sun, Z.-Y.; Guo, B.-N.; Qi, F. Determinantal Expressions, Identities, Concavity, Maclaurin Power Series Expansions for van der Pol Numbers, Bernoulli Numbers, and Cotangent. *Axioms* **2023**, *12*, 665. https://doi.org/10.3390/axioms12070665

Summary: *This article mainly has the following innovations and contributions:*

- *Four determinantal expressions for van der Pol numbers;*
- *Two new identities for the Bernoulli numbers and van der Pol numbers;*
- *The increasing properties and concavity of a function involving the cotangent function;*
- *Two alternative Maclaurin power series expansions of a function involving the cotangent function;*
- *The coefficients of the Maclaurin power series expansions are expressed in terms of specific Hessenberg determinants whose elements contain the Bernoulli numbers and binomial coefficients.*

(iv). Lv, W.; Tian, L. Pricing of Credit Risk Derivatives with Stochastic Interest Rate. *Axioms* **2023**, *12*, 782. https://doi.org/10.3390/axioms12080782

Summary: *In this article, the authors generalize the conventional reduced-form credit risk model for a credit default swap market to deal with a credit derivative pricing problem using the martingale approach.*

(v). Chegloufa, N.; Chaouchi, B.; Kostić, M.; Du, W.-S. On the Study of Pseudo $\mathcal{S}$-Asymptotically Periodic Mild Solutions for a Class of Neutral Fractional Delayed Evolution Equations. *Axioms* **2023**, *12*, 800. https://doi.org/10.3390/axioms12080800

Summary: *The authors investigate the existence and uniqueness of pseudo $\mathcal{S}$-asymptotically periodic mild solutions for a class of neutral fractional evolution equations with finite delay by applying the fractional powers of closed linear operators, the semigroup theory and some classical fixed-point theorems.*

(vi). Jiang, B.; Huang, H.; Radenović, S. Common Fixed Point of (ψ, β, L)-Generalized Contractive Mapping in Partially Ordered b-Metric Spaces. *Axioms* **2023**, *12*, 1008. https://doi.org/10.3390/axioms12111008

Summary: *This manuscript provides new coincidences and common fixed points in four mappings satisfying (ψ, β, L)-generalized contractive conditions in partially ordered b-metric spaces, which generalize some recent results in the existing literature.*

(vii). Fedorov, V.E.; Plekhanova, M.V.; Melekhina, D.V. On Local Unique Solvability for a Class of Nonlinear Identification Problems. *Axioms* **2023**, *12*, 1013. https://doi.org/10.3390/axioms12111013

Summary: *In this paper, the authors study nonlinear identification problems for evolution differential equations, solved with respect to the highest-order Dzhrbashyan–Nersesyan fractional derivative. Applying the contraction mappings theorem, the authors establish the unique local solvability of the nonlinear identification problems.*

(viii). Xie, T.; Li, M. Finite-Time Stability of Impulsive Fractional Differential Equations with Pure Delays. *Axioms* **2023**, *12*, 1129. https://doi.org/10.3390/axioms12121129

Summary: *In this article, the authors introduce a novel concept of the impulsive delayed Mittag–Leffler-type vector function, which improved and generalized the Mittag–Leffler matrix function. The position of the pulse point in this paper is arbitrary, which renders the research more universal. Using the relationship between the Riemann–Liouville fractional derivative and the Caputo fractional derivative, the authors establish new finite-time stability results of impulsive fractional differential delay equations.*

(ix). Raza, N.; Fadel, M.; Du, W.-S. New Summation and Integral Representations for 2-Variable (p, q)-Hermite Polynomials. *Axioms* **2024**, *13*, 196. https://doi.org/10.3390/axioms13030196

Summary: *This manuscript offers various new features of two-variable (p, q)-Hermite polynomials, such as diffusion equation, differential equations, integral and summation representations.*

(x). Özger, F.; Temizer Ersoy, M.; Ödemiş Özger, Z. Existence of Solutions: Investigating Fredholm Integral Equations via a Fixed-Point Theorem. *Axioms* **2024**, *13*, 261. https://doi.org/10.3390/axioms13040261

Summary: *The main purpose of this article is to investigate the existence conditions for the solutions of the nonlinear quadratic Fredholm integral equations of the form*

$$\chi(l) = \varrho(l) + \chi(l)\int_p^q k(l,z)(V\chi)(z)dz$$

in the space $C_\omega[p,q]$, where ω is a modulus of continuity, χ is the unknown function to be determined, V is a given operator, and ϱ, k are two given functions.

In this Editorial, we express our heartfelt appreciation to all authors and reviewers who contributed to this Special Issue. It was with the enthusiasm and spirit of the authors and reviewers that we could make this Special Issue an extraordinary success. The 27 authors of these 10 papers are listed below:

Belkacem Chaouchi (see v);	Naceur Chegloufa (see v);
Tatjana Došenović (see ii);	Wei-Shih Du (see v, ix);
Merve Temizer Ersoy (see x);	Mohammed Fadel (see ix);
Vladimir E. Fedorov (see vii);	Liu Gao (see i);
Bai-Ni Guo (see iii);	Wenyan Han (see i);
Huaping Huang (see ii, vi);	Binghua Jiang, (see vi);
Marko Kostić (see v);	Mengmeng Li (see viii);
Wujun Lv (see iv);	Daria V. Melekhina (see vii);
Faruk Özger (see x);	Zeynep Ödemiş Özger (see x);
Marina V. Plekhanova (see vii);	Feng Qi (see iii);
Stojan Radenović (see ii, vi);	Dušan Rakić (see ii);
Nusrat Raza (see ix);	Zhen-Ying Sun (see iii);
Linlin Tian (see iv);	Guolin Yu (see i);
Tingting Xie (see vii).	

The published contributions to this Special Issue can be divided according to the following scheme considering their main purposes:

- Nonlinear analysis (see ii, iii, v, vii, viii, ix, x);
- Fractional calculus (see v, vi, vii, viii);
- Optimization and analytic number theory (see i, iii, iv).

We hope that researchers and practitioners find these papers interesting and inspirational for future research work in these exciting areas. We also believe that the contributions to this Special Issue provide new insights on several important issues while, at the same time, providing new research problems or avenues that undoubtedly exceed our original aim. Finally, we would like to express our sincere thanks to the Editorial team and the reviewers of *Axioms*, particularly the Editor-in-Chief, Prof. Dr. Humberto Bustince, and the assistant editors, for their great support throughout the editing process of our Special Issue.

Author Contributions: Conceptualization, W.-S.D.; methodology, W.-S.D.; software, W.-S.D.; validation, W.-S.D.; formal analysis, W.-S.D.; investigation, W.-S.D.; writing-original draft preparation, W.-S.D.; writing-review and editing, W.-S.D.; visualization, W.-S.D.; supervision, W.-S.D.; project administration, W.-S.D. All authors have read and agreed to the published version of the manuscript.

Funding: Wei-Shih Du is partially supported by grant No. NSTC 112-2115-M-017-002 of the National Science and Technology Council of the Republic of China.

Institutional Review Board Statement: Not applicable.

Informed Consent Statement: Not applicable.

Data Availability Statement: Data are contained within the article.

Conflicts of Interest: The authors declare no conflicts of interest.

References

1. Hyers, D.H.; Isac, G.; Rassias, T.M. *Topics in Nonlinear Analysis and Aapplications*; World Scientific: Singapore, 1997.
2. Takahashi, W. *Nonlinear Functional Analysis*; Yokohama Publishers: Yokohama, Japan, 2000.
3. Reich, S.; Zaslavski, A.J. *Genericity in Nonlinear Analysis*; Developments in Mathematics; Springer: New York, NY, USA, 2014.
4. Zaslavski, A.J. *Approximate Solutions of Common Fixed Point Problems*; Springer Optimization and Its Applications; Springer: Cham, Switzerland, 2016.
5. Du, W.-S. On some nonlinear problems induced by an abstract maximal element principle. *J. Math. Anal. Appl.* **2008**, *247*, 391–399. [CrossRef]
6. Du, W.-S. Critical point theorems for nonlinear dynamical systems and their applications. *Fixed Point Theory Appl.* **2010**, *2010*, 246382. [CrossRef]
7. Du, W.-S. Existence and uniqueness of zeros for vector-valued functions with K-adjustability convexity and their applications. *Mathematics* **2019**, *7*, 809. [CrossRef]
8. Podlubny, I. *Fractional Differential Equations*; Academic Press: San Diego, CA, USA, 1999.
9. Kilbas, A.A.; Srivastava, H.M.; Trujillo, J.J. *Theory and Applications of Fractional Differential Equations*; North-Holland Mathematics Studies; Elsevier Science B.V.: Amsterdam, The Netherlands, 2006; Volume 204.
10. Diethelm, K. *The Analysis of Fractional Differential Equations*; Lecture Notes in Mathematics; Springer: Berlin/Heidelberg, Germany, 2010.
11. Kostić, M. *Abstract Volterra Integro-Differential Equations*; CRC Press: Boca Raton, FL, USA, 2015.
12. Luc, D.T. *Theory of Vector Optimization, Lecture Notes in Economics and Mathematical Systems*; Springer: Berlin/Heidelberg, Germany, 1989; Volume 319.
13. Chen, G.Y.; Huang, X.X.; Yang, X.Q. *Vector Optimization*; Springer: Berlin/Heidelberg, Germany, 2005.
14. Hadjisavvas, N.; Komlosi, S.; Schaible, S. (Eds.) Generalized Convexity and Generalized Derivatives. In *Handbook of Generalized Convexity and Generalized Monotonicity*; Kluwer Academic Publishers: Norwell, MA, USA, 2005; pp. 421–464.
15. Göpfert, A.; Tammer, C.; Riahi, H.; Zălinescu, C. *Variational Methods in Partially Ordered Spaces*; Springer: New York, NY, USA, 2003.
16. Jahn, J. *Vector Optimization Theory, Applications, and Extensions*; Springer: Berlin/Heidelberg, Germany, 2011.

axioms

MDPI

Article

Optimality Conditions of the Approximate Efficiency for Nonsmooth Robust Multiobjective Fractional Semi-Infinite Optimization Problems

Liu Gao [1], Guolin Yu [1,*] and Wenyan Han [2]

1 School of Mathematics and Information Science, North Minzu University, Yinchuan 750021, China; gaoliu@nmu.edu.cn
2 School of Mathematics and Statistics, Ningxia University, Yinchuan 750021, China; hanwenyan@nmu.edu.cn
* Correspondence: guolin_yu@126.com or yuguolin@nmu.edu.cn

Abstract: This paper is devoted to the investigation of optimality conditions and saddle point theorems for robust approximate quasi-weak efficient solutions for a nonsmooth uncertain multiobjective fractional semi-infinite optimization problem (NUMFP). Firstly, a necessary optimality condition is established by using the properties of the Gerstewitz's function. Furthermore, a kind of approximate pseudo/quasi-convex function is defined for the problem (NUMFP), and under its assumption, a sufficient optimality condition is obtained. Finally, we introduce the notion of a robust approximate quasi-weak saddle point to the problem (NUMFP) and prove corresponding saddle point theorems.

Keywords: multiobjective semi-infinite optimization; approximate solution; generalized convexity; optimality conditions; saddle point

1. Introduction

Recently, much attention had been paid to semi-infinite optimization problems; see [1–3]. Specially, multiobjective semi-infinite optimization refers to finding values of decision variables that give the optimum of more than one objective, and many interesting results have been presented in [4] and the references therein. Moreover, fractional optimization is a ratio of two functions, and it is widely used in the fields of information technology, resource allocation and engineering design; see [5–8]. It is worth noting that in many practical problems the objective or constraint functions to optimization models are nonsmooth and are affected by various uncertain information. Therefore, it is meaningful to investigate nonsmooth uncertain optimization problems; see [9–11]. Robust optimization [12,13] is one of the powerful tools to deal with optimization problems with data uncertainty. The aim of the robust optimization approach is to find the worst-case solution, which is immunized against the data uncertainty to optimization problems. However, most of solutions obtained by numerical algorithms are approximate solutions. In these situations, the study of approximate solutions is very significant from both the theoretical aspect and practical application. This paper intends to investigate the properties of a problem (NUMFP) with respect to approximate quasi-weak efficient solutions by the robust approach.

Optimality conditions and saddle point theorems are two important contents of nonsmooth optimization problems. The subdifferential is a powerful tool to characterize optimality conditions. For a nonsmooth multiobjective optimization problem, Caristi et al. [14] and Kabgani et al. [15] investigated optimality conditions of weakly efficient solutions by using the Michel–Penot subdifferential and convexificator, respectively. Chuong [5] obtained optimality theorems for robust efficient solutions to a nonsmooth multiobjective fractional optimization problem based on the Mordukhovich subdifferential. It is important to mention that the Clarke subdifferential has attracted much attention because of its good properties [16]. Fakhar et al. [17] constructed optimality conditions and saddle point theorems of robust efficient solutions for a nonsmooth multiobjective optimization problem by utilizing the Clarke subdifferential. The purpose of this article is to examine optimality conditions and saddle point theorems of robust approximate quasi-weak efficient solutions for a problem (NUMFP) under the Clarke subdifferential. Moreover, Lee et al. [18] employed a separation theorem to established necessary conditions for approximate solutions. Chen et al. [19] used a generalized alternative theorem to obtain necessary optimality conditions for weakly robust efficient solutions. It is worth noting that the Gerstewitz's function is an important nonlinear scalar function, which plays a significant role in solving optimization problems due to its good properties, such as convexity, positive homogeneity and continuity; see [20,21]. This paper will use the Gerstewitz's function to examine a necessary optimality condition of robust approximate quasi-weak efficient solutions for a problem (NUMFP).

In addition, convexity and its generalization play an important role in establishing sufficient optimality conditions of optimization problems. In this paper, we will define a class of approximate (pseudo quasi) convex functions for the objective and constraint functions of a problem (NUMFP) and establish a sufficient optimality condition and saddle point theorems for robust approximate quasi-weak efficient solutions under their assumptions.

This paper is organized as follows. Section 2 provides some basic concepts and lemmas, which will be used in the subsequent sections. In Section 3, we establish optimality conditions for robust approximate quasi-weak efficient solutions to a problem (NUMFP). In Section 4, we introduce the concept of a robust approximate quasi-weak saddle point to a problem (NUMFP) and prove corresponding saddle point theorems.

2. Preliminaries

Throughout this paper, $\mathbb{N}$ and $\mathbb{R}^n$ stand for the set of natural numbers and n-dimensional Euclidean space, respectively. $\mathbb{B}(\bar{x}, r)$ denotes the open ball with center $\bar{x} \in \mathbb{R}^n$ and radius $r > 0$; $\mathbb{B}$ represents the closed unit ball of $\mathbb{R}^n$. The inner product in $\mathbb{R}^n$ is denoted by $\langle x, y \rangle$ for any $x,\ y \in \mathbb{R}^n$. We set

$$\mathbb{R}^n_+ = \{x = (x_1, \cdots, x_n) \in \mathbb{R}^n \mid x_i \geq 0, i = 1, \cdots, n\},$$

$$\mathbb{R}^n_{++} = \{x = (x_1, \cdots, x_n) \in \mathbb{R}^n \mid x_i > 0, i = 1, \cdots, n\},$$

and utilize the following symbols to represent an order relation in $\mathbb{R}^n$:

$$x < y \Leftrightarrow y - x \in \mathbb{R}^n_{++},$$

$$x \leqq y \Leftrightarrow y - x \in \mathbb{R}^n_+.$$

Let $C \subset \mathbb{R}^n$ be a nonempty subset and int$C$, cl$C$ and co$C$ stand for the interior, the closure, and the convex hull of C, respectively. The Clarke contingent cone and normal cone to C at point $\bar{x} \in \mathbb{R}^n$ are defined, respectively, by the following (see [16]):

$$T(C, \bar{x}) = \{y \in \mathbb{R}^n \mid \forall x_n \in C, x_n \to \bar{x}, \forall t_n \to 0, \exists y_n \to y,\ \ s.t.\ \ x_n + t_n y_n \in C, \forall n \in \mathbb{N}\},$$

$$N(C, \bar{x}) = \{\xi \in \mathbb{R}^n \mid \langle \xi, y \rangle \leq 0,\ \forall y \in T(C, \bar{x})\}.$$

The conical convex hull (see [22]) of the set C is defined as

$$\text{pos}(C) = \{y \in \mathbb{R}^n \mid \exists l \in \mathbb{N}\ s.t.\ y = \sum_{i=1}^{l} \lambda_i y_i,\ \lambda_i \geq 0,\ y_i \in C,\ i = 1, \cdots, l\}.$$

Let $F : \mathbb{R}^n \to \mathbb{R}^m$. F is said to be locally Lipschitz at $\bar{x} \in \mathbb{R}^n$ if there exist constant $L > 0$ and $r > 0$ such that

$$\| F(x_1) - F(x_2) \| \leq L \| x_1 - x_2 \|, \ \forall x_1, x_2 \in \mathbb{B}(\bar{x}, r).$$

If F is locally Lipschitz at x for any $x \in \mathbb{R}^n$, then F is called locally Lipschitz mapping. Particularly, for a real value locally Lipschitz function $f : \mathbb{R}^n \to \mathbb{R}$ ($\mathbb{R}$ denotes real number), the Clarke generalized directional derivative of f at $\bar{x} \in \mathbb{R}^n$ in the direction $d \in \mathbb{R}^n$ is given by (see [16])

$$f(\bar{x}; d) = \limsup_{y \to \bar{x}, t \to 0^+} \frac{f(y + td) - f(y)}{t},$$

and the Clarke subdifferential (see [16]) of f at $\bar{x}$ is denoted by

$$\partial f(\bar{x}) = \{\xi \in \mathbb{R}^n \mid f(\bar{x}; d) \geq \langle \xi, d \rangle, \ \forall d \in \mathbb{R}^n\}.$$

Let $C \subset \mathbb{R}^n$ be a nonempty subset, and the indicator function of C is defined as

$$\delta_C(x) = \begin{cases} 0, & x \in C, \\ +\infty, & x \notin C. \end{cases}$$

It is pointed out in [16] that

$$\partial \delta_C(\bar{x}) = N(C, \bar{x}), \ \forall \bar{x} \in C.$$

The following lemmas characterize some properties of the Clarke subdifferential.

Lemma 1 ([16]). Let $f, h : \mathbb{R}^n \to \mathbb{R}$ be locally Lipschitz at $\bar{x} \in \mathbb{R}^n$. Then, the following applies:

(i) $\partial f(\bar{x})$ is nonempty compact convex;
(ii) for any $t \in \mathbb{R}$, $\partial f(t\bar{x}) = t\partial f(\bar{x})$;
(iii) $\partial(f + h)(\bar{x}) \subset \partial f(\bar{x}) + \partial h(\bar{x})$;
(iv) if f attains a local minimum at $\bar{x}$, then $0 \in \partial f(\bar{x})$.

Lemma 2 ([16]). Let $f, h : \mathbb{R}^n \to \mathbb{R}$ be locally Lipschitz at $\bar{x} \in \mathbb{R}^n$, and $h(\bar{x}) \neq 0$. Then, $\frac{f}{h}$ is also locally Lipschitz at $\bar{x}$, and

$$\partial(\frac{f}{h})(\bar{x}) \subset \frac{h(\bar{x})\partial f(\bar{x}) - f(\bar{x})\partial h(\bar{x})}{(h(\bar{x}))^2}.$$

Lemma 3 ([16]). Let $F : \mathbb{R}^n \to \mathbb{R}^m$ be locally Lipschitz at $\bar{x} \in \mathbb{R}^n$ and $f : \mathbb{R}^m \to \mathbb{R}$ be locally Lipschitz at $F(\bar{x})$. Then,

$$\partial(f \circ F)(\bar{x}) \subset \mathrm{cl}(\mathrm{co}(\bigcup_{\Lambda \in \partial f(F(\bar{x}))} \partial(\Lambda \circ F)(\bar{x}))).$$

Next, we give a scalar function, which will play an essential role in the proof of optimality conditions in Section 3.

Definition 1 ([20]). *Let $C \subset \mathbb{R}^n$ be a pointed closed convex cone, $\bar{e} \in intC \neq \emptyset$. The Gerstewitz's function $\Psi_{\bar{e}} : \mathbb{R}^n \to \mathbb{R}$ is defined as*

$$\Psi_{\bar{e}}(y) = inf\,\{t \in \mathbb{R} \mid y \in t\bar{e} - C\}, \ y \in \mathbb{R}^n.$$

Some properties of the Gerstewitz's function are summarized in the following Lemma 4.

Lemma 4 ([20]). Let $C \subset \mathbb{R}^n$ be a pointed closed convex cone, $\bar{e} \in \text{int}C \neq \emptyset$. Then, the following applies:

(i) $\Psi_{\bar{e}}$ is continuous and locally a Lipschitz function;
(ii) $\Psi_{\bar{e}}(y) \leq t \Leftrightarrow y \in t\bar{e} - C$;
(iii) $\Psi_{\bar{e}}(y) \geq t \Leftrightarrow y \notin t\bar{e} - \text{int}C$;
(iv) $\partial\Psi_{\bar{e}}(y) = \{\lambda \in C^* \mid \langle \lambda, y \rangle = \Psi_{\bar{e}}(y)\}$;
(v) $\partial\Psi_{\bar{e}}(y) \subset C^* \backslash \{0\}$,

where $C^* = \{\lambda \in \mathbb{R}^n \mid \langle \lambda, y \rangle \geq 0, \forall y \in C\}$ represents the dual cone of C.

Lemma 5 ([22]). Let $\{C_i \mid i \in I\}$ be an arbitrary collection of nonempty convex sets in $\mathbb{R}^n$ and K be the convex cone generated by the union of the collection. Then, every nonzero vector of K can be expressed as a nonnegative linear combination of n or fewer linearly independent vectors, each belonging to a different C_i.

Let T be a nonempty and arbitrary index set. Considering the following *nonsmooth uncertain multiobjective fractional semi-infinite optimization problem* (NUMFP)

$$\text{(NUMFP)} \quad \begin{cases} \min & \frac{f(x)}{h(x)} = \left(\frac{f_1(x)}{h_1(x)}, \cdots, \frac{f_l(x)}{h_l(x)}\right), \\ \text{s.t.} & g_t(x, v_t) \leq 0, \ \forall t \in T, \end{cases}$$

where v_t and $t \in T$, are uncertain parameters from the uncertainty set $V_t \subset \mathbb{R}^p$, $t \in T$. f_i, h_i : $\mathbb{R}^n \to \mathbb{R}$, $h_i(x) \neq 0$, $i = 1, \cdots, l$, $g_t : \mathbb{R}^n \times V_t \to \mathbb{R}$, f_i, h_i, g_t are locally Lipschitz functions, and the uncertainty map $V : T \rightrightarrows \mathbb{R}^p$ is defined as $V(t) := V_t$.

We consider the robust counterpart of the problem (NUMFP) as follows:

$$\text{(NRMFP)} \quad \begin{cases} \min & \frac{f(x)}{h(x)} = \left(\frac{f_1(x)}{h_1(x)}, \cdots, \frac{f_l(x)}{h_l(x)}\right), \\ \text{s.t.} & g_t(x, v_t) \leq 0, \ \forall v_t \in V_t, \ t \in T, \end{cases}$$

where the feasible set of the problem (NRMFP) is denoted by

$$\mathcal{F} := \{x \in \mathbb{R}^n \mid g_t(x, v_t) \leq 0, \ \forall v_t \in V_t, \ t \in T\}.$$

Definition 2. *Let $\varepsilon = (\varepsilon_1, \cdots, \varepsilon_l) \in \mathbb{R}^l_+$. $\bar{x} \in \mathcal{F}$ is called a robust quasi-weak ε-efficient solution of the problem (NUMFP) if $\bar{x}$ is a quasi-weak ε-efficient solution of the problem (NRMFP); that is,*

$$\frac{f(x)}{h(x)} - \frac{f(\bar{x})}{h(\bar{x})} + \varepsilon\|x - \bar{x}\| \notin -\mathbb{R}^l_{++}, \ \forall x \in \mathcal{F}.$$

Remark 1. *When $\varepsilon = 0$, the quasi-weak ε-efficient solution degrades into the weak efficient solution in [8].*

3. Optimality Conditions

In this section, we will establish necessary and sufficient optimality conditions for the quasi-weak ε-efficient solutions to the problem (NRMFP). We begin with the following constraint qualification.

Definition 3 ([23]). *For $x \in \mathbb{R}^n$, let $\Pi(x) := \{(t, v) \in gphV \mid g_t(x, v) = 0\}$ and*

$$\Delta(x) := \bigcup_{(t,v) \in \Pi(x)} \partial_x g_t(x, v),$$

where $gphV := \{(t, v) \in T \times \mathbb{R}^p \mid v \in V(t)\}$.

Definition 4 ([16]). *Let $\bar{x} \in \mathcal{F}$. The Basic Constraint Qualification (BCQ) holds at $\bar{x}$ if $N(\mathcal{F}, \bar{x}) \subset pos(\Delta(\bar{x}))$.*

Next, we present a necessary optimality condition for the quasi-weak ε-efficient solutions to the problem (NRMFP) by using the properties of the Gerstewitz's function.

Theorem 1. *In problem (NRMFP), let $\varepsilon = (\varepsilon_1, \cdots, \varepsilon_l) \in \mathbb{R}^l_+$. If $\bar{x} \in \mathcal{F}$ is a quasi-weak ε-efficient solution of the problem (NRMFP) and the BCQ holds at $\bar{x}$, then there exist $\bar{\alpha} = (\bar{\alpha}_1, \cdots, \bar{\alpha}_l) \in \mathbb{R}^l_+ \setminus \{0\}$, $\bar{\lambda}_i = \frac{\bar{\alpha}_i}{h_i(\bar{x})}$, $i = 1, \cdots, l$, $\bar{\mu} = (\bar{\mu}_1, \cdots, \bar{\mu}_n) \in \mathbb{R}^n_+$ and $(\bar{t}_j, \bar{v}_j) \in gphV$, $j = 1, \cdots, n$, such that*

$$0 \in \sum_{i=1}^{l} \bar{\lambda}_i (\partial f_i(\bar{x}) - \frac{f_i(\bar{x})}{h_i(\bar{x})} \partial h_i(\bar{x})) + \sum_{j=1}^{n} \bar{\mu}_j \partial_x g_{\bar{t}_j}(\bar{x}, \bar{v}_j) + \sum_{i=1}^{l} \bar{\alpha}_i \varepsilon_i \mathbb{B}, \tag{1}$$

$$\bar{\mu}_j g_{\bar{t}_j}(\bar{x}, \bar{v}_j) = 0, \ \forall j = 1, \cdots, n. \tag{2}$$

Proof. Since $\bar{x}$ is a quasi-weak ε-efficient solution of the problem (NRMFP), we obtain

$$\frac{f(x)}{h(x)} - \frac{f(\bar{x})}{h(\bar{x})} + \varepsilon \|x - \bar{x}\| \notin -\mathbb{R}^l_{++}, \ \forall x \in \mathcal{F}.$$

Let $H(x) = (\frac{f(x)}{h(x)} - \frac{f(\bar{x})}{h(\bar{x})} + \varepsilon\|x - \bar{x}\|)$, by Lemma 4 (iii), then we obtain

$$\Psi_{(\bar{e})}(H(x)) \geq 0, \quad \forall x \in \mathcal{F}.$$

As $\bar{x} \in \mathcal{F}$, thus,

$$\Psi_{(\bar{e})}(H(\bar{x})) \geq 0. \tag{3}$$

Note that $H(\bar{x}) = 0$, then $H(\bar{x}) \in -\mathbb{R}^l_+$, and it follows from Lemma 4 (ii) that

$$\Psi_{(\bar{e})}(H(\bar{x})) \leq 0,$$

together with (3), and then we have

$$\Psi_{(\bar{e})}(H(\bar{x})) = 0.$$

Therefore,

$$\Psi_{(\bar{e})}(H(x)) \geq \Psi_{(\bar{e})}(H(\bar{x})) = 0, \quad \forall x \in \mathcal{F},$$

and this means that $\bar{x}$ is a local minimizer of $\Psi_{(\bar{e})} \circ H(x)$ on $\mathcal{F}$, and $\bar{x}$ is also a local minimizer of $\Psi_{(\bar{e})} \circ H(x) + \delta_{\mathcal{F}}(x)$ on $\mathcal{F}$. By Lemma 1 (iii), we obtain

$$0 \in \partial(\Psi_{(\bar{e})} \circ H + \delta_{\mathcal{F}})(\bar{x}) \subset \partial(\Psi_{(\bar{e})} \circ H)(\bar{x}) + \partial\delta_{\mathcal{F}}(\bar{x}). \tag{4}$$

Due to

$$\partial\delta_{\mathcal{F}}(\bar{x}) = N(\mathcal{F}; \bar{x}),$$

combined with (4), we arrive at

$$0 \in \partial(\Psi_{(\bar{e})} \circ H)(\bar{x}) + N(\mathcal{F}; \bar{x}).$$

Since $H(x)$ is locally Lipschitz at $\bar{x}$ and $\Psi_{(\bar{e})}$ is locally Lipschitz at $H(\bar{x})$, it follows from Lemma 3 that

$$\partial(\Psi_{(\bar{e})} \circ H)(\bar{x}) \subset \mathrm{cl}(\mathrm{co}(\bigcup_{\Lambda \in \partial\Psi_{(\bar{e})}(H(\bar{x}))} \partial(\Lambda \circ H)(\bar{x}))).$$

According to Lemma 4 (v), there exists $\bar{\alpha} = (\bar{\alpha}_1, \cdots, \bar{\alpha}_l) \in \partial\Psi_{(\bar{e})}(H(\bar{x})) \subset \mathbb{R}^l_+ \backslash \{0\}$ such that

$$\begin{aligned} 0 &\in \mathrm{cl}(\mathrm{co}(\partial(\bar{\alpha} \circ H)(\bar{x}))) + N(\mathcal{F}; \bar{x}) \\ &= \mathrm{cl}(\mathrm{co}(\partial(\bar{\alpha} \circ (\frac{f(\cdot)}{h(\cdot)} - \frac{f(\bar{x})}{h(\bar{x})} + \varepsilon\| \cdot - \bar{x}\|)(\bar{x}))) + N(\mathcal{F}; \bar{x}) \\ &\subset \mathrm{cl}(\mathrm{co}(\partial(\bar{\alpha} \circ (\frac{f}{h}))(\bar{x}) + \langle \bar{\alpha}, \varepsilon \rangle \mathbb{B})) + N(\mathcal{F}; \bar{x}). \end{aligned}$$

From Lemma 1 (i), it leads to

$$\begin{aligned} 0 &\in \partial(\bar{\alpha} \circ (\frac{f}{h}))(\bar{x}) + \langle \bar{\alpha}, \varepsilon \rangle \mathbb{B} + N(\mathcal{F}; \bar{x}) \\ &= \sum_{i=1}^{l} \bar{\alpha}_i \partial(\frac{f_i}{h_i})(\bar{x}) + \sum_{i=1}^{l} \bar{\alpha}_i \varepsilon_i \mathbb{B} + N(\mathcal{F}; \bar{x}). \end{aligned}$$

According to Lemma 2, we obtain

$$0 \in \sum_{i=1}^{l} \frac{\bar{\alpha}_i}{h_i(\bar{x})}(\partial f_i(\bar{x}) - \frac{f_i(\bar{x})}{h_i(\bar{x})}\partial h_i(\bar{x})) + \sum_{i=1}^{l} \bar{\alpha}_i \varepsilon_i \mathbb{B} + N(\mathcal{F}; \bar{x}).$$

Since the BCQ holds, it leads to

$$0 \in \sum_{i=1}^{l} \frac{\bar{\alpha}_i}{h_i(\bar{x})}(\partial f_i(\bar{x}) - \frac{f_i(\bar{x})}{h_i(\bar{x})}\partial h_i(\bar{x})) + \sum_{i=1}^{l} \bar{\alpha}_i \varepsilon_i \mathbb{B} + \mathrm{pos}(\triangle(\bar{x})).$$

By Lemma 5, there exist $p \leq n$, $\bar{\mu} = (\bar{\mu}_1, \cdots, \bar{\mu}_p) \in \mathbb{R}^p_+$ and $(\bar{t}_j, \bar{v}_j) \in \Pi(\bar{x})$, $j = 1, \cdots, p$ such that

$$0 \in \sum_{i=1}^{l} \frac{\bar{\alpha}_i}{h_i(\bar{x})}(\partial f_i(\bar{x}) - \frac{f_i(\bar{x})}{h_i(\bar{x})}\partial h_i(\bar{x})) + \sum_{j=1}^{p} \bar{\mu}_j \partial_x g_{\bar{t}_j}(\bar{x}, \bar{v}_j) + \sum_{i=1}^{l} \bar{\alpha}_i \varepsilon_i \mathbb{B}. \tag{5}$$

Let $\frac{\bar{\alpha}_i}{h_i(\bar{x})} = \bar{\lambda}_i$. If $p = n$, then (1) and (2) hold due to $(\bar{t}_j, \bar{v}_j) \in \Pi(\bar{x})$, $j = 1, \cdots, p$. When $p < n$, we take multipliers $\bar{\mu}_{p+1} = \cdots = \bar{\mu}_n = 0$ in (5) to obtain the desired result and complete the proof. □

Remark 2. *In studies [18,19], the necessary optimality conditions were obtained by utilizing a separation theorem and an alternative theorem, respectively. Different from [18,19], the necessary optimality condition of the above Theorem 1 is directly proved by using the properties of the Gerstewitz's function. However, if $\varepsilon = 0$ and T is a finite index set, then Theorem 1 of this paper will reduce to Theorem 1 in [8].*

Before we establish a sufficient optimality condition of quasi-weak ε-efficient solutions for the problem (NRMFP), we next introduce the following two kinds of generalized convexities for the objective and constraint functions of the problem (NRMFP).

Definition 5. *In the problem (NRMFP), (f, h, g) is called an approximate convex function at $\bar{x} \in \mathcal{F}$ if for any $x \in \mathcal{F}$, $\xi_i \in \partial f_i(\bar{x})$, $\eta_i \in \partial h_i(\bar{x})$, $i = 1, \cdots, l$, $(t_j, v_j) \in gphV$, and $\delta_j \in \partial_x g_{t_j}(\bar{x}, v_j)$, $j = 1, \cdots, n$, such that*

$$\frac{f_i(x)}{h_i(x)} - \frac{f_i(\bar{x})}{h_i(\bar{x})} \geq \frac{1}{h_i(\bar{x})}(\langle \xi_i, x - \bar{x} \rangle - \frac{f_i(\bar{x})}{h_i(\bar{x})}\langle \eta_i, x - \bar{x} \rangle),\ i = 1, \cdots, l,$$

$$g_{t_j}(x, v_j) - g_{t_j}(\bar{x}, v_j) \geq \langle \delta_j, x - \bar{x} \rangle,\ j = 1, \cdots, n.$$

Here is an example of an approximate convex function.

Example 1. *In the problem (NRMFP), let* $f_i,\ h_i : \mathbb{R} \to \mathbb{R}, i = 1,2,\ g : \mathbb{R} \times V_t \to \mathbb{R},\ t \in T = [0,1],\ v \in V_t = [2-t, 2+t],\ (t,v) \in gphV$, *and*

$$\frac{f(x)}{h(x)} = (\frac{f_1(x)}{h_1(x)}, \frac{f_2(x)}{h_2(x)}) = (\frac{x^2+2x}{3}, \frac{2x^2}{x^2+1}),$$

$$g_t(x,v) = 2tx^2 - vx.$$

By a simple calculation, we obtain $\mathcal{F} = [0, \frac{1}{2}]$. *Let* $\bar{x} = 0 \in \mathcal{F}$, *then we have* $\partial f_1(\bar{x}) = \{2\},\ \partial f_2(\bar{x}) = \{0\},\ \partial h_1(\bar{x}) = \{0\},\ \partial h_2(\bar{x}) = \{0\}$, *and* $\partial_x g_t(\bar{x}, v) = \{-v\}$. *For any* $x \in \mathcal{F},\ \xi_i \in \partial f_i(\bar{x}),\ \eta_i \in \partial h_i(\bar{x}),\ i = 1,2,\ \delta \in \partial_x g_t(\bar{x}, v)$, *since*

$$\frac{f_1(x)}{h_1(x)} - \frac{f_1(\bar{x})}{h_1(\bar{x})} = \frac{x^2+2x}{3} \geq \frac{2x}{3} = \frac{1}{h_1(\bar{x})}(\langle \xi_1, x-\bar{x}\rangle - \frac{f_1(\bar{x})}{h_1(\bar{x})}\langle \eta_1, x-\bar{x}\rangle),$$

$$\frac{f_2(x)}{h_2(x)} - \frac{f_2(\bar{x})}{h_2(\bar{x})} = \frac{2x^2}{x^2+1} \geq 0 = \frac{1}{h_2(\bar{x})}(\langle \xi_2, x-\bar{x}\rangle - \frac{f_2(\bar{x})}{h_2(\bar{x})}\langle \eta_2, x-\bar{x}\rangle),$$

$$g_t(x,v) - g_t(\bar{x}, v) = 2tx^2 - vx \geq -vx = \langle \delta, x - \bar{x}\rangle.$$

We obtain an approximate convex function (f,h,g) *at* $\bar{x} = 0$.

Definition 6. *In the problem (NRMFP), let* $\varepsilon = (\varepsilon_1, \cdots, \varepsilon_l) \in \mathbb{R}^l_+$. (f,h,g) *is called an approximate pseudo/quasi-convex function at* $\bar{x} \in \mathcal{F}$ *if for any* $x \in \mathcal{F},\ \xi_i \in \partial f_i(\bar{x}),\ \eta_i \in \partial h_i(\bar{x}),\ i = 1, \cdots, l,\ (t_j, v_j) \in gphV$, *and* $\delta_j \in \partial_x g_{t_j}(\bar{x}, v_j),\ j = 1, \cdots, n$, *such that*

$$\frac{1}{h_i(\bar{x})}(\langle \xi_i, x-\bar{x}\rangle - \frac{f_i(\bar{x})}{h_i(\bar{x})}\langle \eta_i, x-\bar{x}\rangle) + \varepsilon_i\|x-\bar{x}\| \geq 0 \Rightarrow \frac{f_i(x)}{h_i(x)} - \frac{f_i(\bar{x})}{h_i(\bar{x})} + \varepsilon_i\|x-\bar{x}\| \geq 0,$$

$$g_{t_j}(x, v_j) - g_{t_j}(\bar{x}, v_j) \leq 0 \Rightarrow \langle \delta_j, x-\bar{x}\rangle \leq 0.$$

Remark 3. *Clearly, if* (f,h,g) *is an approximate convex function at* $\bar{x} \in \mathcal{F}$, *then* (f,h,g) *is an approximate pseudo/quasi-convex function at* $\bar{x} \in \mathcal{F}$; *conversely, it is not true (see the following Example 2).*

Example 2. *In problem (NRMFP), let* $f_i, h_i : \mathbb{R} \to \mathbb{R}, i = 1,2$,

$$\frac{f(x)}{h(x)} = (\frac{f_1(x)}{h_1(x)}, \frac{f_2(x)}{h_2(x)}),$$

where

$$f_1(x) = x^4 + x,\ h_1(x) = 2,\ f_2(x) = x^2,\ h_2(x) = x^4 + 1,$$

$g : \mathbb{R} \times V_t \to \mathbb{R}, t \in T = [1,3],\ v \in V_t = [1, 3+t],\ (t,v) \in gphV$,

$$g_t(x,v) = -x^2 - 2vt.$$

Through a clear calculation, we obtain $\mathcal{F} = \mathbb{R}$. *Taking* $\bar{x} = 0 \in \mathcal{F},\ \varepsilon = (1,2)$, *we obtain* $\partial f_1(\bar{x}) = \{1\},\ \partial f_2(\bar{x}) = \{0\},\ \partial h_1(\bar{x}) = \{0\},\ \partial h_2(\bar{x}) = \{0\}$ *and* $\partial_x g_t(\bar{x}, v) = \{0\}$. *For any* $x \in \mathcal{F},\ \xi_i \in \partial f_i(\bar{x}),\ \eta_i \in \partial h_i(\bar{x}),\ i = 1,2$, *and* $\delta \in \partial_x g_t(\bar{x}, v)$, *since*

$$\frac{1}{h_1(\bar{x})}(\langle \xi_1, x-\bar{x}\rangle - \frac{f_1(\bar{x})}{h_1(\bar{x})}\langle \eta_1, x-\bar{x}\rangle) + \varepsilon_1\|x-\bar{x}\| = \frac{x}{2} + |x| \geq 0$$
$$\Rightarrow \frac{f_1(x)}{h_1(x)} - \frac{f_1(\bar{x})}{h_1(\bar{x})} + \varepsilon_1\|x-\bar{x}\| = \frac{x^4+x}{2} + |x| \geq 0,$$

$$\frac{1}{h_2(\bar{x})}(\langle\xi_2, x-\bar{x}\rangle - \frac{f_2(\bar{x})}{h_2(\bar{x})}\langle\eta_2, x-\bar{x}\rangle) + \varepsilon_2\|x-\bar{x}\| = 2|x| \geq 0$$

$$\Rightarrow \frac{f_2(x)}{h_2(x)} - \frac{f_2(\bar{x})}{h_2(\bar{x})} + \varepsilon_2\|x-\bar{x}\| = \frac{x^2}{x^4+1} + 2|x| \geq 0,$$

$$g_t(x,v) - g_t(\bar{x},v) = -x^2 \leq 0 \Rightarrow \langle\delta, x-\bar{x}\rangle = 0 \leq 0.$$

We obtain (f,h,g), an approximate pseudo/quasi-convex function, at $\bar{x}=0$. However, for $x \in \mathcal{F}\backslash\{0\}$ and $\delta \in \partial_x g_t(\bar{x},v)$, one has

$$g_t(x,v) - g_t(\bar{x},v) = -x^2 \not\geq 0 = \langle\delta, x-\bar{x}\rangle.$$

Therefore, (f,h,g) is not an approximate convex function at $\bar{x}=0$.

The following Theorem 2 presents a sufficient optimality condition for the quasi-weak ε-efficient solutions to the problem (NRMFP).

Theorem 2. *In problem (NRMFP), let $\varepsilon = (\varepsilon_1, \cdots, \varepsilon_l) \in \mathbb{R}^l_+$ and (f,h,g) be an approximate pseudo/quasi-convex function at $\bar{x} \in \mathcal{F}$. If there exist multipliers $\bar{\alpha} = (\bar{\alpha}_1, \cdots, \bar{\alpha}_l) \in \mathbb{R}^l_+\backslash\{0\}$, $\bar{\mu} = (\bar{\mu}_1, \cdots, \bar{\mu}_n) \in \mathbb{R}^n_+$ and $(\bar{t}_j, \bar{v}_j) \in gphV$, such that (1) and (2) hold, then $\bar{x}$ is a quasi-weak ε-efficient solution of the problem (NRMFP).*

Proof. It follows from (1) that there exist $\bar{\xi}_i \in \partial f_i(\bar{x})$, $\bar{\eta}_i \in \partial h_i(\bar{x})$, $\bar{\delta}_j \in \partial_x g_{\bar{t}_j}(\bar{x},\bar{v}_j)$ and $\bar{b}_i \in \mathbb{B}$, such that

$$0 = \sum_{i=1}^{l}\bar{\lambda}_i(\bar{\xi}_i - \frac{f_i(\bar{x})}{h_i(\bar{x})}\bar{\eta}_i) + \sum_{j=1}^{n}\bar{\mu}_j\bar{\delta}_j + \sum_{i=1}^{l}\bar{\alpha}_i\varepsilon_i\bar{b}_i.$$

Due to $\bar{b}_i \in \mathbb{B}$, for any $x \in \mathcal{F}$, $\langle\bar{b}_i, x-\bar{x}\rangle \leq \|x-\bar{x}\|$, we obtain

$$\langle\sum_{i=1}^{l}\bar{\lambda}_i(\bar{\xi}_i - \frac{f_i(\bar{x})}{h_i(\bar{x})}\bar{\eta}_i) + \sum_{j=1}^{n}\bar{\mu}_j\bar{\delta}_j, x-\bar{x}\rangle + \sum_{i=1}^{l}\bar{\alpha}_i\varepsilon_i\|x-\bar{x}\| \geq 0.$$

This is equivalent to

$$\langle\sum_{i=1}^{l}\bar{\lambda}_i(\bar{\xi}_i - \frac{f_i(\bar{x})}{h_i(\bar{x})}\bar{\eta}_i), x-\bar{x}\rangle + \sum_{i=1}^{l}\bar{\alpha}_i\varepsilon_i\|x-\bar{x}\| \geq -\langle\sum_{j=1}^{n}\bar{\mu}_j\bar{\delta}_j, x-\bar{x}\rangle. \tag{6}$$

When $\bar{\mu}_j = 0$, $\langle\sum_{j=1}^{n}\bar{\mu}_j\bar{\delta}_j, x-\bar{x}\rangle = 0$. If $\bar{\mu}_j \neq 0$, from (2), we derive

$$g_{\bar{t}_j}(x,\bar{v}_j) \leq g_{\bar{t}_j}(\bar{x},\bar{v}_j) = 0.$$

Since (f,h,g) is an approximate pseudo/quasi-convex function at $\bar{x}$, for $\bar{\delta}_j \in \partial_x g_{\bar{t}_j}(\bar{x},\bar{v}_j)$, we have

$$\langle\bar{\delta}_j, x-\bar{x}\rangle \leq 0. \tag{7}$$

Combining with (6) and (7), we obtain

$$\langle\sum_{i=1}^{l}\bar{\lambda}_i(\bar{\xi}_i - \frac{f_i(\bar{x})}{h_i(\bar{x})}\bar{\eta}_i), x-\bar{x}\rangle + \sum_{i=1}^{l}\bar{\alpha}_i\varepsilon_i\|x-\bar{x}\| \geq 0. \tag{8}$$

Conversely, suppose that $\bar{x}$ is not a quasi-weak ε-efficient solution of the problem (NRMFP). Then, there exists $\hat{x} \in \mathcal{F}$ such that

$$\frac{f(\hat{x})}{h(\hat{x})} - \frac{f(\bar{x})}{h(\bar{x})} + \varepsilon\|\hat{x}-\bar{x}\| \in -\mathbb{R}^l_{++},$$

which implies that

$$\frac{f_i(\hat{x})}{h_i(\hat{x})} - \frac{f_i(\bar{x})}{h_i(\bar{x})} + \varepsilon_i\|\hat{x} - \bar{x}\| < 0,\ i = 1, \cdots, l.$$

Since (f, h, g) is an approximate pseudo/quasi-convex at $\bar{x}$, for $\bar{\xi}_i \in \partial f_i(\bar{x})$, and $\bar{\eta}_i \in \partial h_i(\bar{x})$, $i = 1, \cdots, l$, we obtain

$$\frac{1}{h_i(\bar{x})}(\langle \bar{\xi}_i, \hat{x} - \bar{x}\rangle - \frac{f_i(\bar{x})}{h_i(\bar{x})}\langle \bar{\eta}_i, \hat{x} - \bar{x}\rangle) + \varepsilon_i\|\hat{x} - \bar{x}\| < 0,\ i = 1, \cdots, l.$$

Noticing that $\bar{\alpha} \in \mathbb{R}^l_+ \backslash \{0\}$, $\frac{\bar{\alpha}_i}{h_i(\bar{x})} = \bar{\lambda}_i$, $i = 1, \cdots, l$, we arrive at

$$\langle \sum_{i=1}^{l} \bar{\lambda}_i(\bar{\xi}_i - \frac{f_i(\bar{x})}{h_i(\bar{x})}\bar{\eta}_i), \hat{x} - \bar{x}\rangle + \sum_{i=1}^{l} \bar{\alpha}_i\varepsilon_i\|\hat{x} - \bar{x}\| < 0,$$

which contradicts (8). Hence, $\bar{x}$ is a quasi-weak ε-efficient solution to the problem (NRMFP). □

4. Saddle Point Theorems

In this section, we establish saddle point theorems of quasi-weak ε-efficiency. We first give the definition of a quasi ε-weak saddle point for the problem (NRMFP).

Let $\bar{x} \in \mathcal{F}$, $\bar{\alpha} = (\bar{\alpha}_1, \cdots, \bar{\alpha}_l) \in \mathbb{R}^l_+ \backslash \{0\}$, $e = (1, \cdots, 1) \in \mathbb{R}^l_+$, $\mu = (\mu_1, \cdots \mu_n) \in \mathbb{R}^n_+$ and $v = (t_j, v_j) \in \text{gph}V$, $j = 1, \cdots, n$. The Lagrangian function of the problem (NRMFP) is defined as

$$\mathcal{L}(x, \bar{\alpha}, \mu, v) = (\mathcal{L}_1(x, \bar{\alpha}, \mu, v), \cdots, \mathcal{L}_l(x, \bar{\alpha}, \mu, v)),$$

where

$$\mathcal{L}(x, \bar{\alpha}, \mu, v) = \bar{\alpha}(\frac{f(x)}{h(x)} - \frac{f(\bar{x})}{h(\bar{x})}) + \frac{1}{l}\sum_{j=1}^{n} \mu_j g_{t_j}(x, v_j)e, \tag{9}$$

$$\mathcal{L}_i(x, \bar{\alpha}, \mu, v) = \bar{\alpha}_i(\frac{f_i(x)}{h_i(x)} - \frac{f_i(\bar{x})}{h_i(\bar{x})}) + \frac{1}{l}\sum_{j=1}^{n} \mu_j g_{t_j}(x, v_j),\ i = 1, \cdots, l.$$

Definition 7. *In the problem (NRMFP), let* $\varepsilon = (\varepsilon_1, \cdots, \varepsilon_l) \in \mathbb{R}^l_+$*.* $(\bar{x}, \bar{\alpha}, \bar{\mu}, \bar{v}) \in \mathcal{F} \times (\mathbb{R}^l_+ \backslash \{0\}) \times \mathbb{R}^n_+ \times gphV$ *is said to be a quasi* ε*-weak saddle point if*

$$\mathcal{L}(x, \bar{\alpha}, \bar{\mu}, \bar{v}) + \varepsilon\|x - \bar{x}\| - \mathcal{L}(\bar{x}, \bar{\alpha}, \bar{\mu}, \bar{v}) \notin -\mathbb{R}^l_{++},\quad \forall x \in \mathcal{F}, \tag{10}$$

$$\mathcal{L}(\bar{x}, \bar{\alpha}, \mu, v) - \varepsilon\|\mu - \bar{\mu}\| \leqq \mathcal{L}(\bar{x}, \bar{\alpha}, \bar{\mu}, \bar{v}),\quad \forall \mu \in \mathbb{R}^n_+,\ v \in gphV. \tag{11}$$

The following example is presented to illustrate Definition 7.

Example 3. *In the problem (NRMFP), let* f_i, $h_i : \mathbb{R} \to \mathbb{R}$, $i = 1, 2$, $g : \mathbb{R} \times V_t \to \mathbb{R}$, $t \in T = [0, 1)$*, and* $v \in V_t = [2 - t, 2 + t]$*. Define*

$$\frac{f(x)}{h(x)} = (\frac{f_1(x)}{h_1(x)}, \frac{f_2(x)}{h_2(x)}) = (\frac{x^2}{2}, \frac{2x}{x+1}),$$

$$g_t(x, v) = -tx - vx.$$

Via calculation, we obtain $\mathcal{F} = [0, +\infty)$. *For any* $(x, \bar{\alpha}, \mu, v) \in \mathcal{F} \times (\mathbb{R}^2_+ \backslash \{0\}) \times \mathbb{R}_+ \times gphV$, *the Lagrangian function of the problem (NRMFP) is*

$$\mathcal{L}(x, \bar{\alpha}, \mu, v) = (\bar{\alpha}_1(\frac{x^2}{2} - \frac{\bar{x}^2}{2}) + \frac{1}{2}\mu(-tx - vx), \bar{\alpha}_2(\frac{2x}{x+1} - \frac{2\bar{x}}{\bar{x}+1}) + \frac{1}{2}\mu(-tx - vx)).$$

Let $\bar{x} = 0 \in \mathcal{F}$, $\varepsilon = (\varepsilon_1, \varepsilon_2) = (1, 1)$, $\bar{\alpha} = (\bar{\alpha}_1, \bar{\alpha}_2) = (\frac{1}{2}, \frac{1}{2})$, $\bar{\mu} = 1$ *and* $\bar{v} = 2 - t$. *It is easy to obtain*

$$\mathcal{L}(x, \bar{\alpha}, \bar{\mu}, \bar{v}) = (\frac{x^2}{4} - x, \frac{x}{x+1} - x), \quad \mathcal{L}(\bar{x}, \bar{\alpha}, \bar{\mu}, \bar{v}) = (0, 0),$$

$$\mathcal{L}(\bar{x}, \bar{\alpha}, \mu, v) = (0, 0).$$

Hence,

$$\mathcal{L}(x, \bar{\alpha}, \bar{\mu}, \bar{v}) + \varepsilon\|x - \bar{x}\| - \mathcal{L}(\bar{x}, \bar{\alpha}, \bar{\mu}, \bar{v}) = (\frac{x^2}{4}, \frac{x}{x+1}) \notin -\mathbb{R}^2_{++}, \quad \forall x \in \mathcal{F},$$

$$\mathcal{L}(\bar{x}, \bar{\alpha}, \mu, v) - \varepsilon\|\mu - \bar{\mu}\| = -\varepsilon|\mu - 1| \leqq \mathcal{L}(\bar{x}, \bar{\alpha}, \bar{\mu}, \bar{v}), \quad \forall \mu \in \mathbb{R}_+, \ v \in gphV.$$

The above result is seen in the following Figures 1 and 2. Therefore, $(\bar{x}, \bar{\alpha}, \bar{\mu}, \bar{v})$ *is a quasi* ε*-weak saddle point of the problem (NRMFP).*

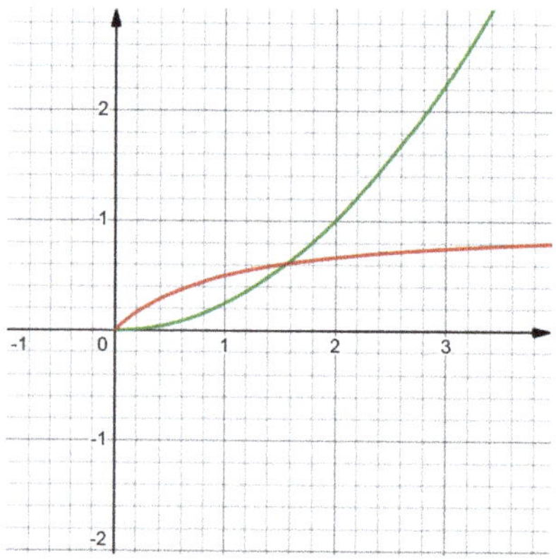

Figure 1. The illustration of $\mathcal{L}(x, \bar{\alpha}, \bar{\mu}, \bar{v}) + \varepsilon\|x - \bar{x}\| - \mathcal{L}(\bar{x}, \bar{\alpha}, \bar{\mu}, \bar{v})$.

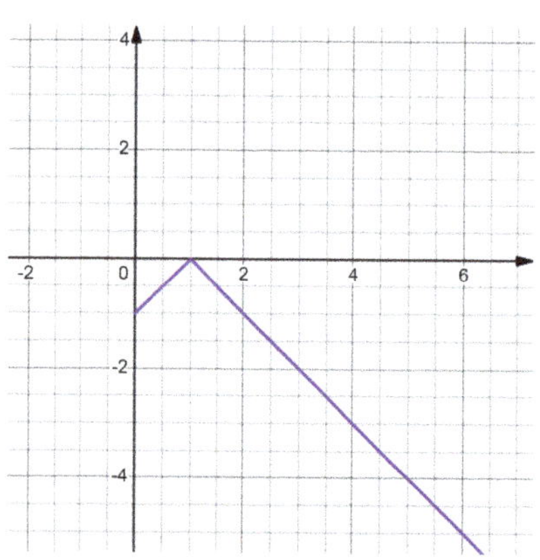

Figure 2. The illustration of $\mathcal{L}(\bar{x}, \bar{\alpha}, \mu, v) - \varepsilon\|\mu - \bar{\mu}\|$.

Theorem 3. *In the problem (NRMFP), suppose that* $\bar{x} \in \mathcal{F}$ *is a quasi-weak* ε*-efficient solution of the problem (NRMFP) and Theorem 1 is satisfied. If* (f, h, g) *is an approximate convex function at* $\bar{x}$*, then* $(\bar{x}, \bar{\alpha}, \bar{\mu}, \bar{v}) \in \mathcal{F} \times (\mathbb{R}^l_+ \backslash \{0\}) \times \mathbb{R}^n_+ \times gphV$ *is a quasi* $\bar{\alpha}\varepsilon$*-weak saddle point, where* $\bar{\alpha}\varepsilon = (\bar{\alpha}_1\varepsilon_1, \cdots \bar{\alpha}_l\varepsilon_l)$.

Proof. Firstly, we verify (10) holds. Since $\bar{x}$ is a quasi-weak ε-efficient solution of the NRMFP, it follows from Theorem 1 that

$$0 \in \sum_{i=1}^{l} \bar{\lambda}_i(\partial f_i(\bar{x}) - \frac{f_i(\bar{x})}{h_i(\bar{x})}\partial h_i(\bar{x})) + \sum_{j=1}^{n} \bar{\mu}_j \partial_x g_{\bar{t}_j}(\bar{x}, \bar{v}_j) + \sum_{i=1}^{l} \bar{\alpha}_i \varepsilon_i \mathbb{B},$$

$$\bar{\mu}_j g_{\bar{t}_j}(\bar{x}, \bar{v}_j) = 0, \ \forall j = 1, \cdots, n.$$

Therefore, there exist $\bar{\xi}_i \in \partial f_i(\bar{x})$, $\bar{\eta}_i \in \partial h_i(\bar{x})$, $\bar{\delta}_j \in \partial_x g_{\bar{t}_j}(\bar{x}, \bar{v}_j)$, and $\bar{b}_i \in \mathbb{B}$ such that

$$0 = \sum_{i=1}^{l} \bar{\lambda}_i(\bar{\xi}_i - \frac{f_i(\bar{x})}{h_i(\bar{x})}\bar{\eta}_i) + \sum_{j=1}^{n} \bar{\mu}_j \bar{\delta}_j + \sum_{i=1}^{l} \bar{\alpha}_i \varepsilon_i \bar{b}_i.$$

Due to $\bar{b}_i \in \mathbb{B}$, for $x \in \mathcal{F}$, $\langle \bar{b}_i, x - \bar{x} \rangle \leq \|x - \bar{x}\|$, we have

$$\langle \sum_{i=1}^{l} \bar{\lambda}_i(\bar{\xi}_i - \frac{f_i(\bar{x})}{h_i(\bar{x})}\bar{\eta}_i) + \sum_{j=1}^{n} \bar{\mu}_j \bar{\delta}_j, x - \bar{x} \rangle + \sum_{i=1}^{l} \bar{\alpha}_i \varepsilon_i \|x - \bar{x}\| \geq 0. \tag{12}$$

Suppose that $(\bar{x}, \bar{\alpha}, \bar{\mu}, \bar{v})$ is not a quasi ε-weak saddle point of the problem (NRMFP); then, there exists $\hat{x} \in \mathcal{F}$ such that

$$\mathcal{L}(\hat{x}, \bar{\alpha}, \bar{\mu}, \bar{v}) + \bar{\alpha}\varepsilon\|\hat{x} - \bar{x}\| - \mathcal{L}(\bar{x}, \bar{\alpha}, \bar{\mu}, \bar{v}) \in -\mathbb{R}^l_{++}.$$

From (9), we deduce

$$\bar{\alpha}(\frac{f(\hat{x})}{h(\hat{x})} - \frac{f(\bar{x})}{h(\bar{x})}) + \frac{1}{l}\sum_{j=1}^{n} \bar{\mu}_j(g_{\bar{t}_j}(\hat{x}, \bar{v}_j) - g_{\bar{t}_j}(\bar{x}, \bar{v}_j))e + \bar{\alpha}\varepsilon\|\hat{x} - \bar{x}\| \in -\mathbb{R}^l_{++}.$$

Thus,

$$\bar{\alpha}_i(\frac{f_i(\hat{x})}{h_i(\hat{x})} - \frac{f_i(\bar{x})}{h_i(\bar{x})}) + \frac{1}{l}\sum_{j=1}^{n} \bar{\mu}_j(g_{\bar{t}_j}(\hat{x}, \bar{v}_j) - g_{\bar{t}_j}(\bar{x}, \bar{v}_j)) + \bar{\alpha}_i\varepsilon_i\|\hat{x} - \bar{x}\| < 0, \ i = 1, \cdots, l. \tag{13}$$

Since (f, h, g) is an approximate convex function at $\bar{x}$, there exist $\bar{\xi}_i \in \partial f_i(\bar{x})$, $\bar{\eta}_i \in \partial h_i(\bar{x})$ and $\bar{\delta}_j \in \partial_x g_{\bar{t}_j}(\bar{x}, \bar{v}_j)$ such that

$$\frac{f_i(\hat{x})}{h_i(\hat{x})} - \frac{f_i(\bar{x})}{h_i(\bar{x})} \geq \frac{1}{h_i(\bar{x})}(\langle \bar{\xi}_i, \hat{x} - \bar{x} \rangle - \frac{f_i(\bar{x})}{h_i(\bar{x})}\langle \bar{\eta}_i, \hat{x} - \bar{x} \rangle), \ i = 1, \cdots, l,$$

$$g_{\bar{t}_j}(\hat{x}, \bar{v}_j) - g_{\bar{t}_j}(\bar{x}, \bar{v}_j) \geq \langle \bar{\delta}_j, \hat{x} - \bar{x} \rangle, \ j = 1, \cdots, n.$$

Let $\frac{\bar{\alpha}_i}{h_i(\bar{x})} = \bar{\lambda}_i$, $i = 1, \cdots, l$, and then together with (13) we have

$$\bar{\lambda}_i \langle (\bar{\xi}_i - \frac{f_i(\bar{x})}{h_i(\bar{x})}\bar{\eta}_i), \hat{x} - \bar{x} \rangle + \frac{1}{l}\langle \sum_{j=1}^{n} \bar{\mu}_j \bar{\delta}_j, \hat{x} - \bar{x} \rangle + \bar{\alpha}_i\varepsilon_i\|\hat{x} - \bar{x}\| < 0, \ i = 1, \cdots, l.$$

Then, we obtain

$$\langle \sum_{i=1}^{l} \bar{\lambda}_i(\bar{\xi}_i - \frac{f_i(\bar{x})}{h_i(\bar{x})}\bar{\eta}_i), \hat{x} - \bar{x} \rangle + \langle \sum_{j=1}^{n} \bar{\mu}_j \bar{\delta}_j, \hat{x} - \bar{x} \rangle + \sum_{i=1}^{l} \bar{\alpha}_i\varepsilon_i\|\hat{x} - \bar{x}\| < 0,$$

which contradicts (12).

Next, we prove (11) holds. Since $\bar{\mu}_j g_{\bar{t}_j}(\bar{x}, \bar{v}_j) = 0$, for any $\mu_j \geq 0$, $(t_j, v_j) \in (\text{gph}V)$, $i = 1, \cdots, l$, we have $\mu_j g_{t_j}(\bar{x}, v_j) \leq 0$; hence,

$$\sum_{j=1}^{n} \bar{\mu}_j g_{\bar{t}_j}(\bar{x}, \bar{v}_j) - \sum_{j=1}^{n} \mu_j g_{t_j}(\bar{x}, v_j) \geq 0.$$

That is,

$$-\bar{\alpha}\varepsilon\|\mu_j - \bar{\mu}_j\| \leqq (0, \cdots, 0) \leqq \bar{\alpha}(\frac{f(\bar{x})}{h(\bar{x})} - \frac{f(\bar{x})}{h(\bar{x})}) + \frac{1}{l}\sum_{j=1}^{n} \bar{\mu}_j g_{\bar{t}_j}(\bar{x}, \bar{v}_j)e - \bar{\alpha}(\frac{f(\bar{x})}{h(\bar{x})} - \frac{f(\bar{x})}{h(\bar{x})}) - \frac{1}{l}\sum_{j=1}^{n} \mu_j g_{t_j}(\bar{x}, v_j)e,$$

which implies that

$$\mathcal{L}(\bar{x}, \bar{\alpha}, \mu, v) - \bar{\alpha}\varepsilon\|\mu_j - \bar{\mu}_j\| \leqq \mathcal{L}(\bar{x}, \bar{\alpha}, \bar{\mu}, \bar{v}).$$

The next Theorem 4 shows that a quasi $\bar{\alpha}\varepsilon$-weak saddle point is a quasi-weak ε-efficient solution of the problem (NRMFP). □

Theorem 4. *In the problem (NRMFP), if $(\bar{x}, \bar{\alpha}, \bar{\mu}, \bar{v}) \in \mathcal{F} \times \mathbb{R}^l_{++} \times \mathbb{R}^n_+ \times gphV$ is a quasi $\bar{\alpha}\varepsilon$-weak saddle point and $\bar{x}$ is an optimal solution of the problem* $\max \sum_{j=1}^{n} \bar{\mu}_j g_{\bar{t}_j}(x, \bar{v}_j)$, *then $\bar{x}$ is a quasi-weak ε-efficient solution, where $\bar{\alpha}\varepsilon = (\bar{\alpha}_1\varepsilon_1, \cdots \bar{\alpha}_l\varepsilon_l)$.*

Proof. Since $(\bar{x}, \bar{\alpha}, \bar{\mu}, \bar{v})$ is a quasi $\bar{\alpha}\varepsilon$-weak saddle point of the problem (NRMFP), it follows from (10) that

$$\bar{\alpha}(\frac{f(x)}{h(x)} - \frac{f(\bar{x})}{h(\bar{x})}) + \frac{1}{l}\sum_{j=1}^{n} \bar{\mu}_j g_{\bar{t}_j}(x, \bar{v}_j)e + \bar{\alpha}\varepsilon\|x - \bar{x}\| - \bar{\alpha}(\frac{f(\bar{x})}{h(\bar{x})} - \frac{f(\bar{x})}{h(\bar{x})}) - \frac{1}{l}\sum_{j=1}^{n} \bar{\mu}_j g_{\bar{t}_j}(\bar{x}, \bar{v}_j)e \notin -\mathbb{R}^l_{++}, \ \forall x \in \mathcal{F}. \tag{14}$$

Because $\bar{x}$ is an optimal solution of the problem $\max \sum_{j=1}^{n} \bar{\mu}_j g_{\bar{t}_j}(x, \bar{v}_j)$, it holds that

$$\sum_{j=1}^{n} \bar{\mu}_j g_{\bar{t}_j}(x, \bar{v}_j) - \sum_{j=1}^{n} \bar{\mu}_j g_{\bar{t}_j}(\bar{x}, \bar{v}_j) \leq 0, \ \forall x \in \mathcal{F}. \tag{15}$$

Together with (14) and (15), we obtain

$$\bar{\alpha}(\frac{f(x)}{h(x)} - \frac{f(\bar{x})}{h(\bar{x})}) + \bar{\alpha}\varepsilon\|x - \bar{x}\| \notin -\mathbb{R}^l_{++}, \ \forall x \in \mathcal{F}.$$

Note that $\bar{\alpha} \in \mathbb{R}^l_{++}$, and we obtain

$$(\frac{f(x)}{h(x)} - \frac{f(\bar{x})}{h(\bar{x})}) + \varepsilon\|x - \bar{x}\| \notin -\mathbb{R}^l_{++}, \ \forall x \in \mathcal{F}.$$

Hence, $\bar{x}$ is a quasi-weak ε-efficient solution of the problem (NRMFP). □

5. Conclusions

We have established a necessary condition for robust approximate quasi-weak efficient solutions of a problem (NUMFP) based on the properties of the Gerstewitz's function. We have also introduced two kinds of generalized convex function pairs for the problem

(NUMFP), and under their assumptions we have presented sufficient conditions and saddle point theorems for robust approximate quasi-weak efficient solutions.

It would be meaningful to further investigate the proper efficient solutions, duality theorems and some special applications for the problem (NUMFP), such as multiobjective optimization problems and minimax optimization problems. Indeed, ref. [4] has discussed duality theorems and special applications for a nonsmooth semi-infinite multiobjective optimization problem, respectively. Therefore, the further works seem feasible.

Author Contributions: Conceptualization, L.G. and G.Y.; methodology, L.G., G.Y. and W.H.; writing—original draft, L.G.; writing—review and editing, L.G., G.Y. and W.H. All authors have read and agreed to the published version of the manuscript.

Funding: This work was supported in part by the Fundamental Research Funds for the Central Universities (No. 2021KYQD23, No. 2022XYZSX03), in part by the Natural Science Foundation of Ningxia Provincial of China (No. 2022AAC03260), in part by the Key Research and Development Program of Ningxia (Introduction of Talents Project) (No. 2022BSB03046), in part by the Natural Science Foundation of China under Grant No. 11861002 and the Key Project of North Minzu University under Grant No. ZDZX201804, Postgraduate Innovation Project of North Minzu University (YCX23081).

Data Availability Statement: Not applicable.

Conflicts of Interest: The authors declare no conflict of interest.

References

1. Khantree, C.; Wangkeeree, R. On quasi approximate solutions for nonsmooth robust semi-infinite optimization problems. *Carpathian J. Math.* **2019**, *35*, 417–426. [CrossRef]
2. Kanzi, N.; Nobakhtian, S. Nonsmooth semi-infinite programming problems with mixed constraints. *J. Math. Anal. Appl.* **2009**, *351*, 170–181. [CrossRef]
3. Sun, X.K.; Teo, K.L.; Zeng, J. Robust approximate optimal solutions for nonlinear semi-infinite programming with uncertainty. *Optimization* **2020**, *69*, 2109–2129. [CrossRef]
4. Pham, T.H. On Isolated/Properly Efficient Solutions in Nonsmooth Robust Semi-infinite Multiobjective Optimization. *Bull. Malays. Math. Sci. Soc.* **2023**, *46*, 73. [CrossRef]
5. Chuong, T.D. Nondifferentiable fractional semi-infinite multiobjective optimization problems. *Oper. Res.* **2016**, *44*, 260–266. [CrossRef]
6. Mishra, S.K.; Jaiswal, M. Optimality and duality for nonsmooth multiobjective fractional semi-infinite programming problem. *Adv. Nonlinear Var. Inequalities* **2013**, *16*, 69–83.
7. Antczak, T. Sufficient optimality conditions for semi-infinite multiobjective fractional programming under (Φ,ρ)-V-invexity and generalized (Φ,ρ)-V-invexity. *Filomat* **2017**, *30*, 3649–3665. [CrossRef]
8. Pan, X.; Yu, G.L.; Gong, T.T. Optimality conditions for generalized convex nonsmooth uncertain multi-objective fractional programming. *J. Oper. Res. Soc.* **2022**, *1*, 1–18. [CrossRef]
9. Dem'yanov, V.F.; Vasil'ev, L.V. Nondifferentiable Optimization. In *Optimization Software*; Inc. Publications Division: New York, NY, USA, 1985.
10. Han, W.Y.; Yu, G.L.; Gong, T.T. Optimality conditions for a nonsmooth uncertain multiobjective programming problem. *Complexity* **2020**, *2020*, 1–8. [CrossRef]
11. Long, X.J.; Huang, N.J.; Liu, Z.B. Optimality conditions, duality and saddle points for nondifferentiable multiobjective fractional programs. *J. Ind. Manag. Optim.* **2017**, *4*, 287–298. [CrossRef]
12. Kuroiwa, D.; Lee, G.M. On robust multiobjective optimization. *J. Nonlinear Convex. Anal.* **2012**, *40*, 305–317.
13. Ben-Tal, A.; Ghaoui, L.E.; Nemirovski, A. *Robust Optimization*; Princeton University Press: Princeton, NJ, USA, 2009; pp. 16–64.
14. Caristi, G.; Ferrara, M. Necessary conditions for nonsmooth multiobjective semi-infinite problems using Michel-Penot subdifferential. *Decis. Econ. Financ.* **2017**, *40*, 103–113. [CrossRef]
15. Kabgani, A.; Soleimani-damaneh, M. Characterization of (weakly/properly/robust) efficient solutions in nonsmooth semi-infinite multiobjective optimization using convexificators. *Optimization* **2018**, *67*, 217–235. [CrossRef]
16. Clarke, F.H. *Optimization and Nonsmooth Analysis*; Wiley: New York, NY, USA, 1983; pp. 46–78.
17. Fakhar, M.; Mahyarinia, M.R.; Zafarani, J. On nonsmooth robust multiobjective optimization under generalized convexity with applications to portfolio optimization. *Eur. J. Oper. Res.* **2018**, *265*, 39–48. [CrossRef]
18. Lee, G.M.; Kim, G.S.; Dinh, N. Optimality Conditions for Approximate Solutions of Convex Semi-Infinite Vector Optimization Problems. *Recent Dev. Vector Optim.* **2012**, *1*, 275–295.
19. Chen, J.W.; Köbis, E.; Yao, J.C. Optimality Conditions and Duality for Robust Nonsmooth Multiobjective Optimization Problems with Constraints. *J. Optim. Theory Appl.* **2019**, *265*, 411–436. [CrossRef]

20. Gerth, C.; Weidner, P. Nonconvex separation theorems and some applications in vector optimization. *J. Optim. Theory Appl.* **1990**, *67*, 297–320. [CrossRef]
21. Han, Y. Connectedness of the approximate solution sets for set optimization problems. *Optimization* **2022**, *71*, 4819–4834. [CrossRef]
22. Rockafellar, R.T. *Convex Analysis*; Princeton University Press: Princeton, NJ, USA, 1997; pp. 10–32.
23. Tung, N.M.; Van Duy, M. Constraint qualifications and optimality conditions for robust nonsmooth semi-infinite multiobjective optimization problems. *4OR* **2022**, *21*, 151–176. [CrossRef]

axioms

MDPI

Article

Fixed Point Results in Generalized Menger Probabilistic Metric Spaces with Applications to Decomposable Measures

Huaping Huang [1,*], Tatjana Došenović [2], Dušan Rakić [2] and Stojan Radenović [3]

1 School of Mathematics and Statistics, Chongqing Three Gorges University, Chongqing 404020, China
2 Faculty of Technology Novi Sad, University of Novi Sad, Bulevar cara Lazara 1, 21000 Novi Sad, Serbia; tatjanad@tf.uns.ac.rs (T.D.); dusan.rakic@uns.ac.rs (D.R.)
3 Faculty of Mechanical Engineering, University of Belgrade, Kraljice Marije 16, 11120 Belgrade, Serbia; sradenovic@mas.bg.ac.rs
* Correspondence: huaping@sanxiau.edu.cn

Abstract: The aim of this paper is to give some fixed point results in generalized Menger probabilistic metric spaces. Moreover, some nontrivial examples are presented to illustrate the superiority of the obtained results. In addition, several interesting applications are given to show that our results are meaningful and valuable.

Keywords: fixed point; probabilistic metric space; probabilistic Banach q-contraction; triangular norm; decomposable measure

MSC: 47H10; 54E25

1. Introduction and Preliminaries

Fixed point theory is a vital branch of nonlinear analysis. It has also been used extensively in the study of all kinds of scientific problems, such as fractional differential equations, stochastic operator theory, engineering mathematics, dynamical systems, physics, computer science, models in economy and related areas (see [1,2]). One of the most important results in fixed point theory is the Banach contraction principle [3], which is used in metric spaces. Nowadays, with the indefatigable efforts of several generations, it has been generalized to many other spaces, such as fuzzy metric space, Menger space, b-metric space, probabilistic metric space and so on (see [2,4–12]). It is worth mentioning that a generalization of this principle in the context of probabilistic metric spaces was performed by Ćirić [13], where quasi-contractive mappings were introduced and the triangle norm τ_m was used. In recent years, the pioneering fixed point theorem of Sehgal and Bharucha-Reid [14,15] is a strong incentive and motivation for the further development of the principle on probabilistic metric spaces. There are plenty of papers (see [12,16–21]) motivated by the above results. On the other hand, the theory of probabilistic metric spaces is the first area where the triangular norm plays a significant role. Therein, the concept of triangle norm was first introduced by Menger in [22] by initiating it from the basic triangle inequality. The original set of axioms is the content and core known today as triangle conorms, and it is necessary to make some changes. Schweeizer and Sklar [23] gave the final definition of triangular norms. In modern society, triangular norms have been affirmed to be an important operation in several fields as well, such as fuzzy logic theory, general measure theory, differential equation theory and so on.

Generally speaking, fixed point theorems in the framework of probabilistic metric spaces are interesting for two reasons: how much we can "relax" the contractive condition without "narrowing" the class of triangular norms too much, and vice versa. It is well-known that when using the minimum triangular norm, the contractive condition is the most "relaxed". However, because the minimum triangular norm is the strongest, fixed point theorem with such a strong condition on the triangular norm is the least interesting. In addition, most fixed point theorems that have been proven in metric spaces can be "translated" to probabilistic metric spaces if the triangular norm minimum is used. That is why it is a huge challenge for finding the "optimal relationship" between the contractive condition and the choice of the triangular norm with a potential additional condition on the probabilistic distribution function itself.

Based on the above statements, in this paper, we propose an additional condition both on the metric itself and on the triangular norm in probabilistic metric spaces. Many corollaries, examples and applications are also shown.

First of all, for the sake of readers, in what follows we recall some notions and known results.

Definition 1 ([24]). *The mapping $\tau : [0, 1]^2 \to [0, 1]$ is a triangular norm if, for all $a, b, c, d \in [0, 1]$, the following conditions are satisfied:*

(τ_1) $\tau(a, 1) = a$;
(τ_2) $\tau(a, b) = \tau(b, a)$;
(τ_3) $a \geq c, b \geq d \Rightarrow \tau(a, b) \geq \tau(c, d)$.

Basic examples of triangular norms are as follows:

$$\tau_m(a, b) = \min\{a, b\},\ \tau_p(a, b) = a \cdot b,\ \tau_l(a, b) = \max\{a + b - 1, 0\}.$$

In 1983, Schweizer and Sklar introduced the concept of triangular conorm as dual operations to the triangular norm.

Definition 2 ([23]). *The mapping $\zeta : [0, 1]^2 \to [0, 1]$ is a triangular conorm if, for all $a, b, c \in [0, 1]$, the following conditions are satisfied:*

(ζ_1) $\zeta(a, b) = \zeta(b, a)$;
(ζ_2) $\zeta(a, \zeta(b, c)) = \zeta(\zeta(a, b), c)$;
(ζ_3) $\zeta(a, b) \leq \zeta(a, c)$ *for* $b \leq c$.

The connection between triangular norm and triangular conorm is given by the following result.

Proposition 1 ([24]). *The function $\zeta : [0, 1]^2 \to [0, 1]$ is a triangular conorm if and only if there is a triangular norm τ such that for each $(a, b) \in [0, 1]^2$, $\zeta(a, b) = 1 - \tau(1 - a, 1 - b)$.*

The opposite statement is also true. Basic examples of triangular conorms are the following ones:

$$\zeta_m(a, b) = \max\{a, b\},\ \zeta_p(a, b) = a + b - ab,\ \zeta_l(a, b) = \min\{a + b, 1\}.$$

Triangular norms of h-type (see [5]) represent a very important class, especially in the theory of fixed point.

Definition 3. *Let τ be a triangular norm and $\tau_n : [0, 1] \to [0, 1]$ a mapping defined in the following way:*

$$\tau_1(a) = \tau(a, a),\ \tau_{n+1}(a) = \tau(\tau_n(a), a),\ n \in \mathbb{N},\ a \in [0, 1].$$

A triangular norm τ is h-type if the family $\{\tau_n(a)\}_{n \in \mathbb{N}}$ is equi-continuous at the point $a = 1$, that is, if for every $\theta \in (0, 1)$ there exists $\rho(\theta) \in (0, 1)$ such that $a > 1 - \rho(\theta)$ implies $\tau_n(a) > 1 - \theta$ for every $n \in \mathbb{N}$.

Using Definition 3, for every $(a_1, a_2, \ldots, a_n) \in [0, 1]^n$, we have

$$\tau_{i=1}^{1} a_i = a_1,\ \tau_{i=1}^{n} a_i = \tau(\tau_{i=1}^{n-1} a_i, a_n) = \tau(a_1, \ldots, a_n).$$

Because the sequence $\{\tau_{i=1}^{n} a_i\}_{n\in\mathbb{N}}$ is non-decreasing and bounded from below, we obtain

$$\tau_{i=1}^{\infty} a_i = \lim_{n\to\infty} \tau_{i=1}^{n} a_i$$

for every $\{a_i\}_{i\in\mathbb{N}} \in [0, 1]$. The analogous case could be applied to triangular conorms.

Proposition 2 ([11]). *Let $\{a_n\}_{n\in\mathbb{N}}$ be a sequence in $[0, 1]$ such that $\lim_{n\to\infty} a_n = 1$ and let the triangular norm τ be h-type. Then,*

$$\lim_{n\to\infty} \tau_{i=n}^{\infty} a_i = \lim_{n\to\infty} \tau_{i=1}^{\infty} a_{n+i} = 1.$$

For some families of triangular norms τ, there exists a sequence $\{a_n\}_{n\in\mathbb{N}}$ such that $\lim_{n\to\infty} a_n = 1$ and $\lim_{n\to\infty} \tau_{i=n}^{\infty} a_i = 1$.

Definition 4 ([11]). *The triangular norm τ is called geometrically convergent if for some $a_0 \in (0, 1)$, it satisfies*

$$\lim_{n\to\infty} \tau_{i=n}^{\infty}(1 - a_0^i) = 1. \tag{1}$$

It is proved from [2] that (1) implies $\lim_{n\to\infty} \tau_{i=n}^{\infty}(1 - a^i) = 1$ for every $a \in (0, 1)$.

Proposition 3 ([11]). *Let τ be a triangular norm and $\psi : (0, 1] \to [0, \infty)$ a mapping. If, for some $\delta \in (0, 1)$ and all $a \in [0, 1]$, $b \in [1 - \delta, 1]$, the following is satisfied,*

$$|\tau(a, b) - \tau(a, 1)| \leq \psi(b),$$

then for every sequence $\{a_n\}_{n\in\mathbb{N}}$ in $[0, 1]$ such that $\lim_{n\to\infty} a_n = 1$, the following implication is valid:

$$\sum_{n=1}^{\infty} \psi(a_n) < \infty \Rightarrow \lim_{n\to\infty} \tau_{i=n}^{\infty}(a_i - a_n) = 0.$$

Definition 5 ([11]). *The triangular norm τ is strict if it is continuous and strictly monotone, i.e., if $\tau(a,b) < \tau(a,c)$ whenever $a, b, c \in (0,1)$ and $b < c$.*

A simple example of a strict triangle norm is $\tau = \tau_p$.

Example 1. *The Dombi, Aczél–Alsina and Sugeno–Weber families of triangular norms are defined as follows:*

$$(i)\ \tau_\lambda^D(a, b) = \begin{cases} \tau_d(a, b), & \lambda = 0; \\ \tau_m(a, b), & \lambda = \infty; \\ \dfrac{1}{1+\left(\left(\frac{1-a}{a}\right)^\lambda + \left(\frac{1-b}{b}\right)^\lambda\right)^{1/\lambda}}, & \lambda \in (0, \infty). \end{cases}$$

$$(ii)\ \tau_\lambda^{AA}(a, b) = \begin{cases} \tau_d(a, b), & \lambda = 0; \\ \tau_m(a, b), & \lambda = \infty; \\ e^{-((-\log a)^\lambda + (-\log b)^\lambda)^{1/\lambda}}, & \lambda \in (0, \infty). \end{cases}$$

$$(iii)\ \tau_\lambda^{SW}(a, b) = \begin{cases} \tau_d(a, b), & \lambda = -1; \\ \tau_p(a, b), & \lambda = \infty; \\ \max(0, \frac{a+b-1+\lambda ab}{1+\lambda}), & \lambda \in (-1, \infty). \end{cases}$$

where $\tau_d(a, b) = \tau_m(a, b)$ if $\max(a, b) = 1$ and $\tau_d(a, b) = 0$, otherwise.

The following proposition is given in [11].

Proposition 4. *Let $(\tau_\lambda^{D})_{\lambda\in(0,\infty)}$, $(\tau_\lambda^{AA})_{\lambda\in(0,\infty)}$ and $(\tau_\lambda^{SW})_{\lambda\in(-1,\infty]}$ be Dombi, Aczél–Alsina and Sugeno–Weber families of triangular norms, respectively, and $\{a_n\}_{n\in\mathbb{N}}$ a sequence in $(0,1]$ such that $\lim_{n\to\infty} a_n = 1$. Then, the following equivalences hold:*

(a) $\sum_{i=1}^{\infty}(1-a_i)^{\lambda} < \infty \Longleftrightarrow \lim_{n\to\infty}(\tau_\lambda^{\star})_{i=n}^{\infty}a_i = 1$, *where* $\star \in \{D, AA\}$;

(b) $\sum_{i=1}^{\infty}(1-a_i) < \infty \Longleftrightarrow \lim_{n\to\infty}(\tau_\lambda^{SW})_{i=n}^{\infty}a_i = 1$.

Definition 6 ([5]). *The continuous triangular norm $\tau : [0,1]^2 \to [0,1]$ is said to be an Archimedean triangle norm if $\tau(a,a) < a$, for every $a \in (0,1)$.*

Theorem 1 ([11]). *(a) The function $\tau : [0,1]^2 \to [0,1]$ is a continuous Archimedean triangular norm if and only if there exists a continuous and strictly decreasing function $\mathbf{a} : [0,1] \to [0,\infty)$ called an additive generator of τ with $\mathbf{a}(1) = 0$ and $\tau(a,b) = \mathbf{a}^{-1}(\min\{\mathbf{a}(a)+\mathbf{a}(b), \mathbf{a}(0)\})$, for any $a, b \in [0,1]$.*

(b) The function $\tau : [0,1]^2 \to [0,1]$ is a continuous Archimedean triangular norm if and only if there exists a continuous and strictly increasing function $\mathbf{m} : [0,1] \to [0,1]$ called a multiplicative generator of τ with $\mathbf{m}(1) = 1$ and $\tau(a,b) = \mathbf{m}^{-1}(\max\{\mathbf{m}(a)\cdot\mathbf{m}(b), \mathbf{m}(0)\})$, for any $a, b \in [0,1]$.

Remark 1. *Triangular norm τ is strict if and only if $\mathbf{m}(0) = 0$.*

Proposition 5 ([11]). *Let τ be a strict triangular norm with an additive generator $\mathbf{a}$ and the corresponding multiplicative generator θ. Let $\{a_n\}_{n\in\mathbb{N}}$ be a sequence in $(0,1)$ such that $\lim_{n\to\infty} a_n = 1$. Then,*

(a) $\lim_{n\to\infty}\sum_{i=n}^{\infty}\mathbf{a}(a_i) = 0$,

(b) $\lim_{n\to\infty}\prod_{i=n}^{\infty}\mathbf{m}(a_i) = 1$

hold if and only if $\lim_{n\to\infty}\tau_{i=n}^{\infty}a_i = 1$.

Definition 7 ([23]). *Let Ω be a nonempty set and Δ^+ be the set of all distribution functions. Suppose that $\mathcal{F}_{pm} : \Omega\times\Omega \to \Delta^+$ is a mapping and $\mathcal{F}_{pm}(p,q) = f_{p,q}$ for each $(p,q) \in \Omega\times\Omega$. The ordered pair $(\Omega, \mathcal{F}_{pm})$ is called a probabilistic metric space if the following conditions are satisfied:*

(pm_0) $f_{p,q}(0) = 0$, *for all* $p, q \in \Omega$;
(pm_1) $f_{p,q}(t) = f_{q,p}(t)$, *for all* $p, q \in \Omega$, $t > 0$;
(pm_2) $f_{p,q}(t) = 1$ *if and only if* $p = q$ *for all* $p, q \in \Omega$, $t > 0$;
(pm_3) $f_{p,q}(t) = 1$ *and* $f_{q,r}(s) = 1$ *imply* $f_{p,r}(t+s) = 1$, *for all* $p, q, r \in \Omega$ *and all* $t, s > 0$.

Definition 8. *Let $(\Omega, \mathcal{F}_{pm})$ be a probabilistic metric space. The sequence $\{p_n\}_{n\in\mathbb{N}}$ from Ω is called a Cauchy sequence if for every $t > 0$ and $\omega \in (0,1)$, there exists $n_0(t,\omega) \in \mathbb{N}$ such that $f_{p_{n+m},p_n}(t) > 1-\omega$, for each $n \geq n_0(t,\omega)$ and each $m \in \mathbb{N}$.*

If the probabilistic metric space $(\Omega, \mathcal{F}_{pm})$ is such that every Cauchy sequence in Ω converges to Ω, then $(\Omega, \mathcal{F}_{pm})$ is called a complete space.

Definition 9. *Let $(\Omega, \mathcal{F}_{pm})$ be a probabilistic metric space and τ a triangular norm. The ordered triple $(\Omega, \mathcal{F}_{pm}, \tau)$ is called a generalized Menger probabilistic metric space if the following inequality is satisfied:*

(pm_4) $f_{p,r}(t+s) \geq \tau(f_{p,q}(t), f_{q,r}(s))$ *for all* $p, q, r \in \Omega$ *and all* $t, s > 0$.

Definition 10. *If $(\Omega, \mathcal{F}_{pm}, \tau)$ is a complete Menger probabilistic metric space with a continuous triangular norm τ, then Ω is called a Hausdorff topological space with topology induced by the family (ε, λ)-environment*

$$\mathcal{O} = \{O_p(\varepsilon, \lambda) : p \in \Omega, \varepsilon > 0, \lambda \in (0, 1)\},$$

wherein

$$O_p(\varepsilon, \lambda) = \{x \in S : f_{x,p}(\varepsilon) > 1 - \lambda\}.$$

Remark 2. *If $\sup_{a<1} \tau(a, a) = 1$, then the family $\{\mathcal{O}\}$ defined on Ω is a metrizable topology.*

One of the most important generalizations of probabilistic metric spaces is represented by fuzzy metric space which was introduced by Kramosil and Michalek [25]. They defined the notion of fuzzy metric space using the notion of a fuzzy number and gave a connection between probabilistic metric spaces and fuzzy metric spaces.

The fuzzy number u is the mapping of $u : \mathbb{R} \to [0, 1]$. We say that the fuzzy number u is normal if there exists $t_0 \in \mathbb{R}$ such that $u(t_0) = 1$, and it is convex if for each $t_1, t_2 \in \mathbb{R}$ and for each $\mu \in [0, 1]$ the following is satisfied:

$$u(\mu t_1 + (1 - \mu)t_2) \geq \min(u(t_1), u(t_2)).$$

By $\mathcal{E}$, we denote all fuzzy numbers that satisfy the condition that they are semi-continuous, normal and convex from above, where

$$\mathcal{E}^+ = \{u : u \in \mathcal{E}, u(t) = 0, \text{ for all } t < 0\}.$$

For the fuzzy number u, the α-cutting level is defined as follows, $[u]_\alpha = \{t : t \in \mathbb{R}, u(t) \geq \alpha\}$ $(\alpha \in (0, 1])$, where $[a^\alpha, b^\alpha]$ is a nonempty closed interval if $a^\alpha, b^\alpha \in \mathbb{R}$ and semi-open interval $(-\infty, b^\alpha]$, $[a^\alpha, \infty)$ if $a^\alpha = -\infty$ or $b^\alpha = +\infty$.

Let $L, R : [0, 1] \times [0, 1] \to [0, 1]$ be symmetric, non-decreasing in both argument functions, satisfying $L(0, 0) = 0$ and $R(1, 1) = 1$. Let Ω be a nonempty set, $d : \Omega^2 \to \mathcal{E}^+$ a mapping satisfying for each $\alpha \in (0, 1]$, and for $(k, i) \in \Omega^2$, one has

$$[d(k, i)]_\alpha = [\lambda_\alpha(k, i), \rho_\alpha(k, i)], \alpha \in (0, 1].$$

Fuzzy metric space is defined as an ordered quadruple (Ω, d, L, R) where d is the fuzzy metric if the following conditions are satisfied:

(f_1) $d(k, i) = I_{\{0\}} \iff k = i,$ for each $k, i \in \Omega$;

(f_2) $d(k, i) = d(i, k),$ for each $k, i \in \Omega$;

(f_{2a}) $d(k, z)(s + t) \geq L(d(k, i)(s), d(i, z)(t))$, whenever $s \leq \lambda_1(k, i)$, $t \leq \lambda_1(i, z)$ and $s + t \leq \lambda_1(k, ,z)$, for each $k, i, z \in \Omega$;

(f_{2b}) $d(k, z)(s + t) \leq R(d(k, i)(s), d(i, z)(t))$, whenever $s \geq \lambda_1(k, i)$, $t \geq \lambda_1(i, z)$ and $s + t \geq \lambda_1(k, z)$, for each $k, i, z \in \Omega$.

Every general Menger space $(\Omega, \mathcal{F}_{pm}, \tau)$ is also a fuzzy metric space (Ω, d, L, R) if

$$d(k, i)(u) = \begin{cases} 0, & u < \sup\{s : F_{k,i}(s) = 0\} = u_{k,i}, \\ 1 - F_{k,i}(u), & u \geq u_{k,i}. \end{cases}$$

The functions R and L are defined as follows:

$$L \equiv 0, \quad R(a, b) = 1 - \tau(1 - a, 1 - b)\ (a, b \in [0, 1]).$$

If

$$\lim_{u \to \infty} d(k, i)(u) = 0 \text{ for every } k, i \in \Omega,$$

then $(\Omega, \mathcal{F}_{pm}, \tau)$ is a Menger space, where $\tau(a, b) = 1 - R(1 - a, 1 - b)$, for each $a, b \in [0, 1]$, and the mapping $\mathcal{F}_{pm}$ is defined by

$$f_{k,i}(s) = \begin{cases} 0, & s < \lambda_1(k, i), \\ 1 - d(k, i)(s), & s \geq \lambda_1(k, i), \end{cases}$$

where $k, i \in \Omega$, $s \in \mathbb{R}$.

The following lemma from [10] gives the connection between fuzzy metric spaces and probabilistic metric spaces.

Lemma 1. *Let (Ω, d, L, R) be a fuzzy metric space, $\nu : [0, 1] \to [0, 1]$ a continuous, monotonically decreasing function such that $\nu(1) = 0$ and $\nu(0) = 1$ and d and R satisfy the following conditions:*

(a) $\lim_{s\to\infty} d(k, i)(s) = 0$, *for each $k, i \in \Omega$;*
(b) $R(a, 1) = 1, R(a, 0) = a$, *for each $a \in [0, 1]$;*
(c) *R is associative.*

Then, $(\Omega, \mathcal{F}_{pm}, \tau)$ is a generalized Menger space, where $\mathcal{F}_{pm}$ and τ are defined as follows:

$$f(k, i)(s) = \begin{cases} 0, & \text{if } s < \lambda_1(k, i), \\ \nu^{-1}[d(k, i)(s)], & \text{if } s \geq \lambda_1(k, i), \end{cases}$$

$$\tau(a, b) = \nu^{-1}[R(f(a), f(b))], \quad (a, b \in [0, 1]).$$

As we know, one of the most important results from fixed point theory is Banach's contraction principle in metric spaces:

Each Banach q-contraction $\xi : \mathcal{M} \to \mathcal{M}$ in the complete metric space $(\mathcal{M}, d_m)$ has a unique fixed point.

Sehgal and Bharucha-Reid generalized the concept of the Banach q-contraction in the framework of probabilistic metric spaces.

Definition 11 ([15]). *Let $(\Omega, \mathcal{F}_{pm})$ be a probabilistic metric space. The mapping $\xi : \Omega \to \Omega$ is said to be a probabilistic Banach q-contraction if there exists $q \in (0, 1)$ such that*

$$f_{\xi p, \xi q}(t) \geq f_{p,q}\left(\frac{t}{q}\right) \tag{2}$$

for each $p, q \in \Omega$ and $t > 0$.

2. Main Results

Once more, we emphasize the fixed point theorem of Sehgal and Bharucha-Reid [15] and its importance for fixed point investigations in the framework of probabilistic metric spaces. In the rest of this paper, it is not necessary to suppose that a triangle norm is Archimedean. It is a big challenge even today to find a weaker condition for the triangular norm than the triangular norm minimum, so that the Banach q-contraction, as well as its generalizations, are valid. In the following theorems, we give an additional condition that enables this statement.

Theorem 2. *Let $(\Omega, \mathcal{F}_{pm}, \tau)$ be a complete generalized Menger probabilistic metric space such that $\sup_{a<1} \tau(a, a) = 1$ and $\xi : \Omega \to \Omega$ be a probabilistic Banach q-contraction such that for some $p_0 \in \Omega$ and some $k > 0$, it satisfies*

$$\psi \circ f_{p_0, \xi p_0}(t) = O\left(\frac{1}{t^k}\right), \; t > 1, \tag{3}$$

where $\psi : [0, 1] \to [0, s]$ is a continuous, decreasing function such that $\psi(1) = 0$. If the triangular norm τ satisfies the condition

$$\lim_{n\to\infty} \tau_{i=n}^{\infty} \psi^{-1}((\varsigma^i)^k) = 1, \tag{4}$$

where $\varsigma \in (0, 1)$, then there is a unique fixed point z such that $z = \lim_{n\to\infty} \xi^n p_0$.

Proof. Let $p_0 \in \Omega$ satisfy condition (3) and define a sequence $p_{n+1} = \xi p_n$, $n \in \mathbb{N}_0$. Then, by (2), we have

$$f_{p_{n+1}, p_n}(t) \geq f_{p_n, p_{n-1}}\left(\frac{t}{q}\right) \geq \cdots \geq f_{\xi p_0, p_0}\left(\frac{t}{q^n}\right), \; t > 0, \; n \in \mathbb{N}.$$

Next, it is necessary to prove that $\{\xi^n p_0\}_{n\in\mathbb{N}}$ is a Cauchy sequence. Let $\delta \in (q,1)$. Because the series $\sum\limits_{i=1}^{\infty} \delta^i$ is convergent, it follows that there exists $n_1(\varepsilon) \in \mathbb{N}$ such that $\sum\limits_{i=n_1}^{\infty} \delta^i \leq \varepsilon$. Then, for each $n \geq n_1$ and $m \in \mathbb{N}$, one has

$$\begin{aligned}
f_{\xi^n p_0,\xi^{n+m} p_0}(\varepsilon) &\geq f_{\xi^n p_0,\xi^{n+m} p_0}\Big(\sum_{i=n}^{\infty} \delta^i\Big) \\
&\geq f_{\xi^n p_0,\xi^{n+m} p_0}\Big(\sum_{i=n}^{n+m-1} \delta^i\Big) \\
&\geq \underbrace{\tau(\tau(\ldots\tau}_{(m-1)-times}\,(f_{\xi^n p_0,\xi^{n+1} p_0}(\delta^n),\ldots,f_{\xi^{n+m-1} p_0,\xi^{n+m} p_0}(\delta^{n+m-1})) \\
&\geq \underbrace{\tau\Big(\tau\Big(\ldots\tau}_{(m-1)-times}\Big(f_{p_0,\xi p_0}\Big(\frac{\delta^n}{q^n}\Big),\ldots,f_{p_0,\xi p_0}\Big(\frac{\delta^{n+m-1}}{q^{n+m-1}}\Big)\Big).
\end{aligned}$$

Let $\varsigma = \frac{q}{\delta} \in (0,1)$, and then

$$f_{\xi^n p_0,\xi^{n+m} p_0}(\varepsilon) \geq \underbrace{\tau\Big(\tau\Big(\ldots\tau}_{(m-1)-times}\Big(f_{p_0,\xi p_0}\Big(\frac{1}{\varsigma^n}\Big),\ldots f_{p_0,\xi p_0}\Big(\frac{1}{\varsigma^{n+m-1}}\Big)\Big),\ n \geq n_1,\ m \in \mathbb{N}. \tag{5}$$

By (3), there is $G > 0$ and $k > 0$ such that $\psi(f_{p_0,\xi p_0}(t)) \leq G \cdot \frac{1}{t^k}$, $t > 1$, i.e., $f_{p_0,\xi p_0}(t) \geq \psi^{-1}(G \cdot \frac{1}{t^k})$, $t > 1$. Concretely, for $t = \frac{1}{\varsigma^n} > 1$, we have

$$f_{p_0,\xi p_0}\Big(\frac{1}{\varsigma^n}\Big) \geq \psi^{-1}(G(\varsigma^n)^k),\ n \in \mathbb{N}. \tag{6}$$

Choose $n_2 \in \mathbb{N}$ such that $G\varsigma^n \in [0, s)$, $n \geq n_2$. Using (5) and (6) for $n \geq \max\{n_1, n_2\}$ and $m \in \mathbb{N}$, it follows that

$$f_{\xi^n p_0,\xi^{n+m} p_0}(\varepsilon) \geq \underbrace{\tau(\tau(\ldots(\tau}_{(m-1)-times}\,(\psi^{-1}(G\varsigma^{kn}),\ \psi^{-1}(G\varsigma^{k(n+1)}),\ldots,\psi^{-1}(G\varsigma^{k(n+m-1)}))).$$

Let s_0 be a constant such that $G\varsigma^{k\cdot s_0} < \varsigma$. Then, using (5) for $n \geq \max\{n_1, n_2\}$ and $m \in \mathbb{N}$, we have

$$\begin{aligned}
f_{\xi^{n+s_0} p_0,\xi^{n+s_0+m} p_0}(\varepsilon) &\geq \underbrace{\tau(\tau(\ldots(\tau}_{(m-1)-times}\,(\psi^{-1}(G\,\varsigma^{k(n+s_0)})),\ (\psi^{-1}(G\,\varsigma^{k(n+s_0+1)})),\ldots,(\psi^{-1}(G\,\varsigma^{k(n+s_0+m-1)})) \\
&\geq \tau_{i=n+1}^{\infty}\psi^{-1}((\varsigma^i)^k).
\end{aligned}$$

Based on the condition (4), we conclude that $\{\xi^n p_0\}_{n\in\mathbb{N}}$ is a Cauchy sequence. Let $z = \lim\limits_{n\to\infty} \xi^n p_0$. We want to show that $z = \xi z$. Using (2), we have

$$f_{\xi p_n,\xi z}(t) \geq f_{p_n,z}\Big(\frac{t}{q}\Big).$$

Letting $n \to \infty$, we conclude that $f_{z,\xi z}(t) \geq f_{\xi z,z}(\frac{t}{q})$, and so $z = \xi z$.

Finally, we prove the uniqueness of fixed point. Indeed, suppose that there exists $v \neq z$ such that $v = \xi v$. Then, from (2), we have

$$f_{z,v}(t) = f_{\xi z, \xi v}(t) \geq f_{z,v}\Big(\frac{t}{q}\Big),$$

which follows that $z = v$. □

Remark 3. *In [26], the following statement was made: if condition (4) holds for some $\varsigma_0 \in (0,1)$, then it holds for every $\varsigma \in (0,1)$.*

Remark 4. *Theorem 2 follows via the following condition (which treats triangular norms and distribution functions mutually),*

$$\lim_{n\to\infty} \tau_{i=n}^{\infty} f_{p,r}(t_n) = 1,$$

for every s-increasing sequence $\{t_n\}$ and every $p, r \in \Omega$, instead of conditions (3) and (4). It seems that condition (4) is more appropriate to deal with different types of triangular norms which is one of the main goals of the current paper.

Let $\psi(x) = 1 - x$. It is easy to check that condition (3) holds for distribution functions of half-normally or exponentially distributed random variables.

Example 2. *Let $\Omega = [0,1]$, $\xi(p) = \dfrac{p}{a}$, $a > 1$, $f_{p,r}(t) = \dfrac{t}{t + |p - r|}$, $p, r \in \Omega$, $t > 0$, $\tau = \tau_p$ and $\psi(x) = 1 - x$. In view of*

$$f_{\xi p, \xi r}(t) = \frac{t}{t + \frac{1}{a}|p - r|} \geq \frac{t}{t + q|p - r|} = f_{p,r}\Big(\frac{t}{q}\Big),\ p, r \in \Omega,\ t > 0,$$

it follows that ξ is a probabilistic Banach q-contraction with $q \in [\frac{1}{a}, 1)$.

Condition (3) is fulfilled because of

$$\psi(f_{p, \xi p}(t)) = \frac{p}{\frac{a}{a-1} t^k + p} \leq \frac{1}{t^k},\ t > 1,\ k > 0.$$

Let $a_i = \psi^{-1}((\varsigma^i)^k) = 1 - (\varsigma^i)^k$. Then, $\sum\limits_{i=1}^{\infty}(1 - a_i) < \infty$, and because the following equivalence holds,

$$\prod_{i=1}^{\infty} a_i > 0 \Longleftrightarrow \lim_{n\to\infty} \prod_{i=n}^{\infty} a_i = 1 \Longleftrightarrow \sum_{i=1}^{\infty}(1 - a_i) < \infty,$$

we conclude that all conditions of the previous theorem are satisfied and hence $p = 0$ is the unique fixed point of ξ.

Corollary 1. *Let $(\Omega, \mathcal{F}_{pm}, \tau)$ be a complete generalized Menger probabilistic metric space such that $\sup_{a<1} \tau(a, a) = 1$. Let $\xi : \Omega \to \Omega$ be a probabilistic Banach q-contraction such that for some $p_0 \in \Omega$ and some $k > 0$, it satisfies*

$$\psi \circ f_{p_0, \xi p_0}(t) = O\Big(\frac{1}{t^k}\Big),\ t > 1,$$

where $\psi : [0, 1] \to [0, s]$ is a continuous, decreasing function such that $\psi(1) = 0$. If $\phi : (0, 1] \to [0, \infty)$ is a function such that for some $\delta \in (0, 1)$ the following is satisfied,

$$|\tau(a, b) - \tau(a, 1)| \leq \phi(b),\ a \in [0, 1],\ b \in [1 - \delta, 1],$$

and $\sum\limits_{n=1}^{\infty} \phi(\psi^{-1}((\varsigma^i)^k)) < \infty$*, for some* $\varsigma \in (0, 1)$*, then there is a unique fixed point* z *of mapping* ξ *and* $z = \lim\limits_{n\to\infty} \xi^n p_0$.

Proof. Based on Proposition 3, condition $\sum\limits_{n=1}^{\infty} \phi(\psi^{-1}((\varsigma^i)^k)) < \infty$ implies $\lim\limits_{n\to\infty} \tau_{i=n}^{\infty}\psi^{-1}((\varsigma^i)^k) = 1$, and hence all conditions of the previous theorem are satisfied. □

The following corollary is a fuzzy metric version of Theorem 2.

Corollary 2. *Let* (Ω, d, L, R) *be a complete fuzzy metric space such that* $\lim\limits_{t\to\infty} d(p, r)(t) = 0$, $p, r \in \Omega$, $R(a, 1) = 1$, $a \in [0, 1]$, $R(a, 0) = a$, $a \in [0, 1]$*, and* R *is continuous at* $(0, 0)$*. Let* $\xi : \Omega \to X$ *be a probabilistic Banach q-contraction such that for some* $p_0 \in \Omega$ *and some* $k > 0$*, it satisfies*

$$d(p_0, \xi p_0)(t) = O\Big(\frac{1}{t^k}\Big), \; t > 1.$$

If $\lim\limits_{n\to\infty} R_{i=n}^{\infty}((\varsigma^k)^i) = 0$ *for* $\varsigma \in (0, 1)$*, then there exists a unique fixed point* z *of* ξ *and* $z = \lim\limits_{n\to\infty} \xi^n p_0$.

Proof. If we choose $\psi(x) = 1 - x$, together with Lemma 1, then all conditions of Theorem 2 are satisfied. The proof is completed. □

As it is pointed out, we deal with triangular norms via condition (4) and, therefore, in the following corollaries it will be relaxed (or omitted). By Theorem 2 and Proposition 2, it follows the subsequent corollary where the triangular norms of h-type are used.

Corollary 3. *Let* $(\Omega, \mathcal{F}_{pm}, \tau)$ *be a complete generalized Menger probabilistic metric space such that* $\sup_{a<1} \tau(a, a) = 1$ *and* $\xi : \Omega \to \Omega$ *be a probabilistic Banach q-contraction such that for some* $p_0 \in \Omega$ *and some* $k > 0$*, it satisfies*

$$\psi \circ f_{p_0, \xi p_0}(t) = O\Big(\frac{1}{t^k}\Big), \; t > 1,$$

where $\psi : [0, 1] \to [0, s]$ *is a continuous, decreasing function such that* $\psi(1) = 0$*. If the triangular norm* τ *is of h-type, then there is a unique fixed point* z *of* ξ *and* $z = \lim\limits_{n\to\infty} \xi^n p_0$.

So, in the previous corollary we deal with a triangular norm of h-type, while in the next one τ is a strict triangular norm. Note that, for example, τ_m is not strict, while τ_p, τ_l and τ^{SW} are strict triangular norms.

Corollary 4. *Let* $(\Omega, \mathcal{F}_{pm}, \tau)$ *be a complete generalized Menger probabilistic metric space such that* $\sup_{a<1} \tau(a, a) = 1$ *and the triangular norm* τ *is strict with additive generator* $\mathbf{a}$ *(multiplicative generator* $\mathbf{m}$*). Let* $\xi : \Omega \to \Omega$ *be a probabilistic Banach q-contraction and* $\psi : [0, 1] \to [0, s]$ *be a continuous, decreasing function with* $\psi(1) = 0$ *such that for some* $p_0 \in \Omega$ *and some* $k > 0$*, it satisfies*

$$\psi \circ f_{p_0, \xi p_0}(t) = O\Big(\frac{1}{t^k}\Big), \; t > 1.$$

If there exits $\varsigma \in (0, 1)$ *such that*

$$\lim_{n\to\infty} \sum_{i=n}^{\infty} \mathbf{a}(\psi^{-1}((\varsigma^i)^k) = 0 \quad \Big(\lim_{n\to\infty} \prod_{i=n}^{\infty} \mathbf{m}(\psi^{-1}((\varsigma^i)^k)) = 1\Big),$$

then there is a unique fixed point z *of* ξ *and* $z = \lim\limits_{n\to\infty} \xi^n p_0$.

Proof. Using Proposition 5, we conclude that all conditions of Theorem 2 are satisfied. □

Further, different contractive conditions are suggested instead of the Banach q-contraction under the same class of triangular norms. The following conditions introduced in Theorem 2 are used, with the contractive condition in the spirit of one suggested in [27].

Theorem 3. *Let $(\Omega, \mathcal{F}_{pm}, \tau)$ be a complete generalized Menger probabilistic metric space such that $\sup_{a<1} \tau(a,a) = 1$ and the mapping $\xi : \Omega \to \Omega$ satisfy the following contractive condition*

$$f_{\xi p,\xi r}(t) \geq \min\left\{f_{p,r}\left(\frac{t}{q}\right), f_{\xi p,p}\left(\frac{t}{q}\right), f_{\xi r,r}\left(\frac{t}{q}\right)\right\},\ p,\ r \in \Omega,\ t > 0, \tag{7}$$

for some $q \in (0,1)$. Suppose that for some $p_0 \in \Omega$ and some $k > 0$, condition (3) is satisfied, where $\psi : [0, 1] \to [0, s]$ is a continuous, decreasing function such that $\psi(1) = 0$. If the triangular norm τ satisfies condition (4), then there is a unique fixed point z of mapping ξ and $z = \lim_{n\to\infty} \xi^n p_0$.

Proof. Take $p_0 \in \Omega$ determined in (3) and define a sequence $p_{n+1} = \xi p_n,\ n \in \mathbb{N}$. Then, by (7), we have

$$f_{p_{n+1},p_n}(t) \geq \min\left\{f_{p_n,p_{n-1}}\left(\frac{t}{q}\right), f_{p_{n+1},p_n}\left(\frac{t}{q}\right), f_{p_n,p_{n-1}}\left(\frac{t}{q}\right)\right\},\ n \in \mathbb{N},\ t > 0.$$

Since $f_{p_{n+1},p_n}(t) \geq f_{p_{n+1},p_n}(\frac{t}{q}) > f_{p_{n+1},p_n}(t)$ leads to a contradiction, then we conclude that

$$f_{p_{n+1},p_n}(t) \geq f_{p_n,p_{n-1}}\left(\frac{t}{q}\right) \geq \cdots \geq f_{p_0,\xi p_0}\left(\frac{t}{q^n}\right),\ n \in \mathbb{N},\ t > 0.$$

Further, the proof that $\{\xi^n p_0\}_{n\in\mathbb{N}}$ is a Cauchy sequence is analogous as in Theorem 2 due to the conditions (3) and (4).

Let $z = \lim_{n\to\infty} \xi^n p_0$. Suppose that $z \neq \xi z$. Using (7), we have

$$f_{\xi p_n,\xi z}(t) \geq \min\left\{f_{p_n,z}\left(\frac{t}{q}\right), f_{p_{n+1},p_n}\left(\frac{t}{q}\right), f_{\xi z,z}\left(\frac{t}{q}\right)\right\},\ n \in \mathbb{N},\ t > 0.$$

Letting $n \to \infty$, we obtain a contradiction on account of $f_{z,\xi z}(t) \geq f_{\xi z,z}(\frac{t}{q}) > f_{z,\xi z}(t)$ and so $z = \xi z$.

Finally, we prove the uniqueness of fixed point. To this end, suppose that there exists $v \neq z$ such that $v = \xi v$. Then, from (7), we have

$$f_{z,v}(t) = f_{\xi z,\xi v}(t) \geq \min\left\{f_{z,v}\left(\frac{t}{q}\right), f_{z,z}\left(\frac{t}{q}\right), f_{v,v}\left(\frac{t}{q}\right)\right\},\ t > 0,$$

i.e., $f_{z,v}(t) \geq f_{z,v}(\frac{t}{q})$ and so $z = v$. □

Example 3. *Let $\Omega = [0,1]$, $\xi(p) = \frac{p}{2}$, $f_{p,r}(t) = \mathrm{e}^{-\frac{|p-r|}{t}}$, $p,r \in \Omega$, $t > 0$, $\tau = \tau_p$ and $\psi(x) = 1 - x$. We need to check condition (7), i.e., the relation is written as*

$$\mathrm{e}^{-\frac{|p-r|}{2t}} \geq \min\left\{\mathrm{e}^{-\frac{q|p-r|}{t}}, \mathrm{e}^{-\frac{qp}{2t}}, \mathrm{e}^{-\frac{qr}{2t}}\right\},\ p,\ r \in \Omega,\ t > 0.$$

Due to the symmetric role of p and r without loss of generality, we suppose that $p > r$ and split the discussion into two cases, $p \geq 2r$ and $r < p < 2r$. If $p \geq 2r$, we have

$$\mathrm{e}^{-\frac{|p-r|}{2t}} \geq \mathrm{e}^{-\frac{q|p-r|}{t}},\ t > 0,$$

while for $r < p < 2r$, it follows that

$$\mathrm{e}^{-\frac{|p-r|}{2t}} \geq \mathrm{e}^{-\frac{qp}{2t}},\ t > 0,$$

and both inequalities are correct when $q \in [\frac{1}{2}, 1)$.

Condition (3) is fulfilled because for arbitrary $p_0 \in (0,1)$ and $k > 0$, one has

$$\psi(f_{p_0,\xi p_0}(t)) = 1 - \mathrm{e}^{-\frac{p_0}{2t^k}} \leq \frac{1}{t^k},\ t > 1.$$

Let $a_i = \psi^{-1}((\varsigma^i)^k) = 1-(\varsigma^i)^k$. *Then,* $\sum_{i=1}^{\infty}(1-a_i) < \infty$, *and because the following equivalence holds,*

$$\prod_{i=1}^{\infty} a_i > 0 \Longleftrightarrow \lim_{n\to\infty}\prod_{i=n}^{\infty} a_i = 1 \Longleftrightarrow \sum_{i=1}^{\infty}(1-a_i) < \infty,$$

we conclude that all conditions of Theorem 3 are satisfied and $p=0$ *is the unique fixed point of* ξ.

Remark 5. *Condition (7) could be extended with term* $f_{p,\xi r}(\frac{t}{q})$ *without changing the triangular norm, but if we want to add the symmetric term* $f_{\xi p,r}(\frac{t}{q})$ *too, then the class of triangular norm must be narrowed.*

Theorem 4. *Let* $(\Omega, \mathcal{F}_{pm}, \tau_m)$ *be a complete Menger probabilistic metric space such that* $\sup_{a<1}\tau(a,a)=1$ *and* $\xi:\Omega\to\Omega$ *be a mapping satisfying*

$$f_{\xi p,\xi r}(t) \geq \min\left\{f_{p,r}\left(\frac{t}{q}\right), f_{\xi p,p}\left(\frac{t}{q}\right), f_{\xi r,r}\left(\frac{t}{q}\right), f_{\xi p,r}\left(\frac{2t}{q}\right), f_{p,\xi r}\left(\frac{t}{q}\right)\right\}, \tag{8}$$

for some $q\in(0,1)$ *and every* $p,r\in\Omega$, $t>0$. *Suppose that for some* $p_0\in\Omega$ *and some* $k>0$ *condition (3) is satisfied, where* $\psi:[0,1]\to[0,s]$ *is a continuous, decreasing function such that* $\psi(1)=0$. *Then, there is a unique fixed point* z *of* ξ *and* $z=\lim_{n\to\infty}\xi^n p_0$.

Theorem 5. *Let* $(\Omega, \mathcal{F}_{pm}, \tau_p)$ *be a complete Menger probabilistic metric space such that* $\sup_{a<1}\tau(a,a)=1$ *and* $\xi:\Omega\to\Omega$ *be a mapping satisfying the following contractive condition,*

$$f_{\xi p,\xi r}(t) \geq \min\left\{f_{p,r}\left(\frac{t}{q}\right), f_{\xi p,p}\left(\frac{t}{q}\right), f_{\xi r,r}\left(\frac{t}{q}\right), f_{p,\xi r}\left(\frac{t}{q}\right), \sqrt{f_{r,\xi p}\left(\frac{2t}{q}\right)}\right\}, \tag{9}$$

for some $q\in(0,1)$ *and every* $p,r\in\Omega$, $t>0$. *Suppose that for some* $p_0\in\Omega$ *and some* $k>0$ *condition (3) is satisfied where* $\psi:[0,1]\to[0,s]$ *is a continuous, decreasing function such that* $\psi(1)=0$. *If the triangular norm* τ *satisfies*

$$\lim_{n\to\infty}\sum_{i=n}^{\infty}(1-\psi^{-1}((\varsigma^i)^k)) < \infty,$$

where $\varsigma\in(0,1)$, *then there is a unique fixed point* z *of* ξ *and* $z=\lim_{n\to\infty}\xi^n p_0$.

Theorem 6. *Let* $(\Omega, \mathcal{F}_{pm}, \tau)$ *be a complete Menger probabilistic metric space such that* $\sup_{a<1}\tau(a,a)=1$ *and* $\xi:\Omega\to\Omega$ *be a mapping satisfying*

$$f_{\xi p,\xi r}(t) \geq \min\left\{f_{p,r}\left(\frac{t}{q}\right), f_{\xi p,p}\left(\frac{t}{q}\right), f_{\xi r,r}\left(\frac{t}{q}\right), f_{p,\xi r}\left(\frac{t}{q}\right), \frac{1-f_{\xi p,r}(\frac{t}{q})+f_{p,\xi r}(\frac{t}{q})}{f_{\xi p,r}(\frac{t}{q})\cdot f_{p,\xi r}(\frac{t}{q})}\right\}, \tag{10}$$

for some $q\in(0,1)$ *and every* $p,r\in\Omega$, $t>0$. *Suppose that for some* $p_0\in\Omega$ *and some* $k>0$ *condition (3) is satisfied, where* $\psi:[0,1]\to[0,s]$ *is a continuous, decreasing function such that* $\psi(1)=0$. *If the triangular norm* τ *satisfies (4), then there is a unique fixed point* z *of* ξ *and* $z=\lim_{n\to\infty}\xi^n p_0$.

Proof. Let $p_0\in\Omega$ satisfy condition (3) and let $p_{n+1}=\xi p_n$, $n\in\mathbb{N}$. By (10), for $n\in\mathbb{N}$, $t>0$, we have

$$f_{p_{n+1},p_n}(t) \geq \min\left\{f_{p_n,p_{n-1}}\left(\frac{t}{q}\right), f_{p_{n+1},p_n}\left(\frac{t}{q}\right), f_{p_n,p_{n-1}}\left(\frac{t}{q}\right), f_{p_n,p_n}\left(\frac{t}{q}\right), \frac{2-f_{p_{n+1},p_{n-1}}(\frac{t}{q})}{f_{p_{n+1},p_{n-1}}(\frac{t}{q})}\right\},$$

which implies that

$$f_{p_{n+1},p_n}t \geq f_{p_n,p_{n-1}}\left(\frac{t}{q}\right) \geq \cdots \geq f_{p_0,\xi p_0}\left(\frac{t}{q^n}\right),\ n \in \mathbb{N},\ t > 0.$$

Using conditions (3) and (4) as in Theorem 2, one could prove that $\{\xi^n p_0\}_{n\in\mathbb{N}}$ is a Cauchy sequence.

Let $z = \lim_{n\to\infty} \xi^n p_0$ and suppose that $z \neq \xi z$. By (10), we arrive at

$$f_{\xi p_n,\xi z}(t) \geq \min\left\{f_{p_n,z}\left(\frac{t}{q}\right), f_{p_{n+1},p_n}\left(\frac{t}{q}\right), f_{\xi z,z}\left(\frac{t}{q}\right), f_{p_n,\xi z}\left(\frac{t}{q}\right), \frac{1 - f_{p_{n+1},z}\left(\frac{t}{q}\right) + f_{p_n,\xi z}\left(\frac{t}{q}\right)}{f_{p_{n+1},z}\left(\frac{t}{q}\right)\cdot f_{p_n,\xi z}\left(\frac{t}{q}\right)}\right\},$$

for every $n \in \mathbb{N}$ and $t > 0$. If we take $n \to \infty$ in the last inequality, it follows that

$$f_{z,\xi z}(t) \geq \min\left\{1, 1, f_{\xi z,z}\left(\frac{t}{q}\right), f_{z,\xi z}\left(\frac{t}{q}\right), 1\right\} = f_{\xi z,z}\left(\frac{t}{q}\right) > f_{z,\xi z}(t),$$

that is, $z = \xi z$.

Finally, we start to prove the uniqueness of fixed point. As a matter of fact, suppose that there exists $v \neq z$ such that $v = \xi v$. By (7), we obtain

$$f_{z,v}(t) = f_{\xi z,\xi v}(t) \geq \min\left\{f_{z,v}\left(\frac{t}{q}\right), f_{z,z}\left(\frac{t}{q}\right), f_{v,v}\left(\frac{t}{q}\right), f_{z,v}\left(\frac{t}{q}\right), \frac{1}{f^2_{z,v}\left(\frac{t}{q}\right)}\right\} = f_{z,v}\left(\frac{t}{q}\right),\ t > 0,$$

which means that $z = v$. □

Corollary 5. *Let $(\Omega, \mathcal{F}_{pm}, (\tau^\star_\lambda)_{\lambda\in(0,\infty)})$ be a complete Menger probabilistic metric space such that $\sup_{a<1} \tau^\star_\lambda(a,a) = 1$ and $\xi : \Omega \to \Omega$ be a probabilistic Banach q-contraction, where $\star \in \{D, AA\}$. Suppose that, for some $p_0 \in \Omega$ and some $k > 0$, condition (3) is satisfied, where $\psi : [0, 1] \to [0, s]$ is a continuous, decreasing function such that $\psi(1) = 0$. If $\sum_{i=1}^{\infty}(1 - \psi^{-1}((\varsigma^k)^i))^\lambda$ converges for $\varsigma \in (0,1)$, then there is a unique fixed point z of ξ such that $z = \lim_{n\to\infty} \xi^n p_0$.*

Proof. Let $\varsigma \in (0,1)$ and $\lambda \in (0, \infty)$. By Proposition 4, $\sum_{i=1}^{\infty}(1 - \psi^{-1}((\varsigma^k)^i))^\lambda < \infty$ and $\lim_{n\to\infty} (\tau^\star_\lambda)_{i=1}^{\infty}\psi^{-1}((\varsigma^k)^i) = 1$ are equivalent, and then the assertion holds by Theorem 2. □

Remark 6. *If $\psi(x) = \psi^{-1}(x) = 1 - x$, then the series $\sum_{i=1}^{\infty}(1 - \psi^{-1}(\varsigma^i))^\lambda = \sum_{i=1}^{\infty}(\varsigma^i)^\lambda$ converges to $\varsigma \in (0,1)$ and the condition could be omitted by Corollary 5.*

Theorem 7. *Let $(\Omega, \mathcal{F}_{pm}, \tau)$ be a complete Menger probabilistic metric space such that $\sup_{a<1} \tau(a,a) = 1$ and $\xi : \Omega \to \Omega$ be a probabilistic Banach q-contraction such that for some $p_0 \in \Omega$ and some $k > 0$, it satisfies*

$$\psi \circ f_{p_0,\xi p_0}(t) = O\left(\frac{1}{(g(t))^k}\right),\ t > 1, \tag{11}$$

where $\psi : [0, 1] \to [0, s]$ is a continuous, decreasing function such that $\psi(1) = 0$, and $g : (0,\infty) \to \mathbb{R}$ is a function such that $g(x) + g(y) = g(x \cdot y)$. If, for some $Q > 0$, the triangular norm τ satisfies

$$\lim_{n\to\infty} \tau_{i=n}^{\infty}\, \psi^{-1}\left(\frac{Q}{i^k}\right) = 1, \tag{12}$$

then there is a unique fixed point z of ξ such that $z = \lim_{n\to\infty} \xi^n p_0$.

Proof. Let $\mu \in (q, 1)$ and $\delta = \frac{q}{\mu}$. Then, $\delta \in (q, 1)$ and $\sum_{i=1}^{\infty} \delta^i < \infty$. So, for some $n_1 = n_1(\varepsilon) \in \mathbb{N}$, we obtain $\sum_{i=n_1}^{\infty} \delta^i \leq \varepsilon$.

Take $p_0 \in \Omega$ such that (11) is fulfilled and, similar as in the proof of Theorem 2, for $n \geq n_1,\ m \in \mathbb{N}$, one has

$$\begin{aligned} f_{\xi^n p_0, \xi^{n+m} p_0}(\varepsilon) &\geq f_{\xi^n p_0, \xi^{n+m} p_0}\left(\sum_{i=n}^{\infty} \delta^i\right) \\ &\geq f_{\xi^n p_0, \xi^{n+m} p_0}\left(\sum_{i=n}^{n+m-1} \delta^i\right) \\ &\geq \underbrace{\tau(\tau(\ldots\tau}_{(m-1)-times}\,(f_{\xi^n p_0, \xi^{n+1} p_0}(\delta^n), f_{\xi^{n+1} p_0, \xi^{n+2} p_0}(\delta^{n+1}), \ldots, f_{\xi^{n+m-1} p_0, f^{n+m} p_0}(\delta^{n+m-1})) \\ &\geq \underbrace{\tau\Big(\tau\Big(\ldots\tau}_{(m-1)-times}\left(f_{p_0, \xi p_0}\left(\frac{1}{\mu^n}\right), f_{p_0, \xi p_0}\left(\frac{1}{\mu^{n+1}}\right), \ldots f_{p_0, \xi p_0}\left(\frac{1}{\mu^{n+m-1}}\right)\Big)\Big). \end{aligned}$$

By (11), there exists $M > 0$ such that

$$f_{p_0, \xi p_0}(t) \geq \psi^{-1}\Big(\frac{M}{(g(t))^k}\Big),\ t > 1,$$

Let $t = \dfrac{1}{\mu^n} > 1$. Because $g(t^n) = ng(t),\ n \in \mathbb{N}$, for $Q = \dfrac{M}{(g(\frac{1}{\mu}))^k} > 0$, we have that

$$f_{p_0, \xi p_0}\Big(\frac{1}{\mu^n}\Big) \geq \psi^{-1}\Big(\frac{M}{n^k (g(\frac{1}{\mu}))^k}\Big) = \psi^{-1}\Big(\frac{Q}{n^k}\Big),\ n \in \mathbb{N}.$$

Now,

$$\begin{aligned} f_{\xi^n p_0, \xi^{n+m} p_0}(\varepsilon) &\geq \underbrace{\tau\Big(\tau\Big(\ldots\Big(\tau}_{(m-1)-times}\left(\psi^{-1}\Big(\frac{Q}{n^k}\Big), \psi^{-1}\Big(\frac{Q}{(n+1)^k}\Big), \cdots, \psi^{-1}\Big(\frac{Q}{(n+m-1)^k}\Big)\right)\Big) \\ &\geq \tau_{i=n}^{\infty}\Big(\psi^{-1}\Big(\frac{Q}{i^k}\Big)\Big) \\ &> 1 - \lambda, \end{aligned}$$

for $n \geq n_0(\varepsilon, \lambda)$. So, $\{\xi^n p_0\}_{n \in \mathbb{N}}$ is a Cauchy sequence.

Because ξ is a probabilistic Banach q-contraction (and consequently it is a continuous mapping), analogous as in the proof of Theorem 2, it follows that ξ exists a unique fixed point $z = \lim\limits_{n \to \infty} \xi^n p_0$. $\square$

Remark 7. *If we take that $g(x) = \ln x$, then by Theorem 7 we obtain Theorem 3 from [26].*

Corollary 6. *Let $(\Omega, \mathcal{F}_{pm}, (T_\lambda^{SW})_{\lambda \in (-1, \infty]})$ be a complete Menger probabilistic metric space such that $\sup_{a<1} \tau_\lambda^{\star}(a, a) = 1$ and $\xi : \Omega \to \Omega$ be a probabilistic Banach q-contraction such that, for some $p_0 \in \Omega$ and some $k > 0$, it satisfies*

$$\psi(f_{p_0, \xi p_0}(t)) = O\Big(\frac{1}{(\log_a t)^k}\Big),\ a > 1,\ t > 1,$$

where $\psi : [0, 1] \to [0, s]$ is a continuous, decreasing function such that $\psi(1) = 0$. If $\sum\limits_{i=1}^{\infty}(1 - \psi^{-1}(\frac{Q}{i^k}))$ converges for some $Q > 0$, then there is a unique fixed point z of ξ such that $z = \lim\limits_{n \to \infty} \xi^n p_0$.

Proof. Let $T = T_{\lambda}^{SW}$. By Proposition 4, $\sum_{i=1}^{\infty}(1-\psi^{-1}(\frac{Q}{i^k}))$ is equivalent to $\lim_{n\to\infty}(T_{\lambda}^{SW})_{i=n}^{\infty}(\psi^{-1}(\frac{Q}{i^k})) = 1$, and hence the assertion follows by Theorem 7. □

Remark 8. *If $\psi(x) = 1-x$, then the series $\sum_{i=1}^{\infty}(1-\psi^{-1}(\frac{Q}{i^k})) = \sum_{i=1}^{\infty}\frac{Q}{i^k}$ converges when $k>1$, so it is unnecessary to impose the condition in the previous corollary.*

3. Applications to Decomposable Measures

The following definitions are given in [11]. Let $\mathcal{A}$ be the σ-algebra of subsets of the given set Ω. The classical measure is a set function $m : \mathcal{A} \to [0,+\infty]$ such that $m(\emptyset) = 0$ and

$$m\left(\bigcup_{i=1}^{\infty} A_i\right) = \sum_{i=1}^{\infty} m(A_i),$$

for each sequence $\{A_i\}_{i\in\mathbb{N}}$ of mutually disjoint sets from $\mathcal{A}$. In the special case when $m : \mathcal{A} \to [0,1]$ and $m(\Omega) = 1$, m is a probability measure and is marked with P.

Definition 12. *Let ζ be a triangular conorm. We say that the ζ-decomposable measure m is a set function $m : \mathcal{A} \to [0,1]$ such that $m(\emptyset) = 0$ and $m(A \cup B) = \zeta(m(A), m(B))$, where $A, B \in \mathcal{A}$ and $A \cap B = \emptyset$.*

Definition 13. *Let ζ be a left continuous triangular conorm. The collective function $m : \mathcal{A} \to [0,1]$ is a ζ-decomposable measure if $m(\emptyset) = 0$ and*

$$m\left(\bigcup_{i=1}^{\infty} A_i\right) = \zeta_{i=1}^{\infty} m(A_i),$$

for each sequence$\{A_i\}_{i\in\mathbb{N}}$ from $\mathcal{A}$ whose elements are mutually disjoint gatherings.

The set function from the previous example is a σ-ζ_l-decomposable measure. We say that a ζ-decomposable measure m is monotone if for $A, B \in \mathcal{A}$, $A \subseteq B$ implies $m(A) < m(B)$. A measure m is an (NSA)-type if and only if $s \circ m$ is a finite additive measure, where s is an additive generator for the triangular conorm ζ, which is continuous, not strict, Archimedean and in relation to which m is decomposable ($s(l) = 1$).

Proposition 6 ([11]). *Let $(\Omega, \mathcal{A}, m)$ be a measurable space, where m is a continuous, ζ-decomposable measure (NSA)-type with a monotonically increasing generator s. Then, $(\zeta, \mathcal{F}_{pm}, \tau)$ is a Menger space, where $\mathcal{F}_{pm}$ and the triangular norm τ are defined as follows:*

$$(\mathcal{F}_{pm}(\widehat{X},\widehat{Y}) = f_{\widehat{X},\widehat{Y}} : f_{\widehat{X},\widehat{Y}}(u) = m\{\omega,\, \omega\in\Omega,\, d(X(\omega),Y(\omega)) < u\},\ \widehat{X},\widehat{Y}\in\zeta,\ u\in\mathbb{R},$$

and $\tau(a,b) = s^{-1}(\max(0, s(a)+s(b)-1))$, $a, b \in [0,1]$.

The following is a straightforward application of Theorem 2 to a decomposable measure.

Corollary 7. *Let $(\Omega,\, \mathcal{A},\, m)$ be a measurable space, where m is a continuous, s-decomposable measure (NSA)-type with monotone increasing additive generator s. Let $(\mathcal{M},\, d)$ be a complete, separable metric space and $\xi : \Omega\times\mathcal{M} \to \mathcal{M}$ be a continuous random operator such that for some $q \in (0,\,1)$, it satisfies*

$$m(\{\omega\,|\,\omega\in\Omega,\, d(\hat{f}\,\hat{X}(\omega),\, \hat{f}\,\hat{Y}(\omega)) < u\}) \geq m(\{\omega\,|\,\omega\in\Omega,\, d(X(\omega),\, Y(\omega)) < \frac{u}{q}\})$$

for all measurable mappings $X, Y : \Omega \to \mathcal{M}$ *and each* $u > 0$. *If there is a measurable mapping* $U : \Omega \to \mathcal{M}$ *such that for some* $k > 0$, *it satisfies*

$$\psi(m(d(\hat{U}, \xi\hat{U}) < t)) = O\Big(\frac{1}{t^k}\Big),\ t > 1,$$

where $\psi : [0, 1] \to [0, b]$ $(b > 0)$ *is a continuous, decreasing function such that* $\psi(1) = 0$ *and the triangular norm* τ *defined by*

$$\tau(u, v) = s^{-1}(\max(0, s(u) + s(v) - 1)),\ \ u, v \in [0, 1]$$

satisfies the condition $\lim_{n\to\infty} \tau_{i=n}^{\infty} \psi^{-1}((\varsigma^k)^i) = 1$, $\varsigma \in (0, 1)$, *then there is a random fixed point for the operator* ξ.

Remark 9. *Let* $(\Omega, \mathcal{A}, m)$, $(\mathcal{M}, d)$ *and* ξ *be the same as in Corollary 7 for some t-conorm* σ_λ^{SW}, $\lambda \in (-1, \infty)$, *where* σ_λ^{SW} *is a Sugeno–Weber family of t-conorms as follows:*

$$\sigma_\lambda^{SW}(a, b) = \sigma_m(a, b),\ \text{if } \lambda = \infty \text{ and } \sigma_\lambda^{SW}(a, b) = \min(1, a + b + \lambda ab),\ \text{if } \lambda \in (-1, \infty).$$

Put $\xi(x) = 1 - x$. *Because the triangular norm* τ_λ^{SW}, $\lambda \in (-1, \infty)$ *is geometrically convergent, it implies the existence of the random fixed point of the random operator* $\xi : \Omega \times \mathcal{M} \to \mathcal{M}$.

4. Conclusions

For more than a century, fixed point theory has widespread and significant applications in many fields at the core of many branches of pure and applied mathematics, including convex analysis, variational analysis, nonlinear ordinary and partial differential equations, critical point theory, nonlinear optimization, fractional calculus and so on. It is known that plenty of problems caused by the real world are often due to seeking to find a fixed point and then using different mathematical techniques. In this work, a technique is furnished, based on nontrivial results in generalized Menger probabilistic metric spaces. We establish several fixed point theorems with illustrative examples in the framework of such spaces. We make a conclusion that our results in this paper generalize and improve many known results in the existing literature. Additionally, we apply our results to cope with the decomposable measures. We make sure that the idea of further elaborating our method, which is presented throughout this paper, is quite important and can be applied to probability theory and nonlinear fractional differential equations in the upcoming future.

Author Contributions: H.H. designed the research and supported funding acquisition. T.D. offered draft preparation and wrote the paper. D.R. co-wrote and made revisions to the paper. S.R. gave the methodology and checked the final version before submission. All authors have read and agreed to the published version of the manuscript.

Funding: The first author acknowledges the financial support from the Natural Science Foundation of Chongqing of China (No. cstc2020jcyj-msxmX0762) and the Initial Funding of Scientific Research for High-level Talents of Chongqing Three Gorges University of China (No. 2104/09926601). The second and third authors acknowledge the Ministry of Education, Science and Technological Development of the Republic of Serbia (No. 451-03-47/2023-01/200134).

Institutional Review Board Statement: Not applicable.

Informed Consent Statement: Not applicable.

Data Availability Statement: The data presented in this study are available upon request from the corresponding author.

Acknowledgments: The authors thank the editor and the referees for their valuable comments and suggestions which greatly improved the quality of this paper.

Conflicts of Interest: The authors declare no conflict of interest.

References

1. Nazam, M.; Park, C.; Acar, O.; Arshad, M. On solution of a system of differential equations via fixed point theorem. *J. Comput. Anal. Appl.* **2018**, *27*, 417–426.
2. Hadžić, O.; Pap, E.; Budinčević, M. Countable extension of triangular norms and their applications to the fixed point theory in probabilistic metric spaces. *Kybernetika* **2002**, *38*, 363–382.
3. Banach, S. Sur les opérations dans les ensembles abstraits et leur application aux éuations intégrales. *Fund. Math.* **1922**, *3*, 133–181. [CrossRef]
4. Grabiec, M. Fixed points in fuzzy metric spaces. *Fuzzy Sets Syst.* **1988**, *27*, 385–389. [CrossRef]
5. Hadžić, O. A fixed point theorem in Menger spaces. *Publ. Inst. Math.* **1979**, *20*, 107–112.
6. Czerwik, S. Contraction mappings in *b*-metric spaces. *Acta Math. Inform. Univ. Ostrav.* **1993**, *1*, 5–11.
7. Karapınar, E. A short survey on the recent fixed point results on *b*-metric spaces. *Constr. Math. Anal.* **2018**, *1*, 15–44. [CrossRef]
8. Babu, A.S.; Došenović, T.; Mustaq Ali, M.D.; Radenović, S.; Rao K.P.R. Some Prešić type results in *b*-dislocated metric spaces. *Constr. Math. Anal.* **2019**, *2*, 40–48. [CrossRef]
9. Kadelburg, Z.; Radenović, S. Notes on some recent papers concerning *F*-contractions in *b*-metric spaces. *Constr. Math. Anal.* **2018**, *1*, 108–112. [CrossRef]
10. Hadžić, O. Fixed point theorems for multivalued mappings in probabilistic metric spaces. *Fuzzy Sets Syst.* **1997**, *88*, 219–226. [CrossRef]
11. Hadžić, O.; Pap, E. Fixed point theory in probabilistic metric spaces. In *Theory in Probabilistic Metric Spaces;* Kluwer Academic Publishers: Dordrecht, The Netherlands, 2001.
12. Jung, J.S.; Chang, S.S.; Lee, B.S.; Cho, Y.J.; Kang, S.M. On the generalizations of Siegel's fixed point theorem. *Mathware Soft Comput.* **2001**, *8*, 5–20.
13. Ćirić, L.B. A generalization of Banach's contraction principle. *Proc. Am. Math. Soc.* **1974**, *45*, 267–273. [CrossRef]
14. Bharucha-Reid, A.T. Fixed point theorems in probabilistic analysis. *Bull. Amer. Math. Soc.* **1976**, *82*, 641–657. [CrossRef]
15. Sehgal, V.M.; Baharucha-Reid, A.T. Fixed points of contraction mappings on probabilistic metric spaces. *Math. Syst. Theory* **1972**, *6*, 97–102. [CrossRef]
16. Amini-Harandi, A.; Mihet, D. Quasi-contractive mappings in fuzzy metric spaces. *J. Fuzzy Syst.* **2015**, *12*, 147–153.
17. Kumam, P.; Dung, N.V.; Sitytithakerngkiet, K. A generalization of Ćirić fixed point theorems. *Filomat* **2015**, *29*, 1549–1556. [CrossRef]
18. Liu, Y.; Li, Z. Coincidence point theorems in probabilistic and fuzzy metric spaces. *Fuzzy Sets Syst.* **2007**, *158*, 58–70. [CrossRef]
19. Mihet, D. On the existence and the uniqueness of fixed points of Sehgal contractions. *Fuzzy Sets Syst.* **2005**, *156*, 135–141. [CrossRef]
20. Rakić, D.; Došenović, T.; Mitrović, Z.D.; De la Sen, M.; Radenović, S. Some fixed point theorems of Ćirić type in fuzzy metric spaces. *Mathematics* **2020**, *8*, 297. [CrossRef]
21. Wairojjana, N.; Došenović, T.; Rakić, D.; Gopal, D.; Kumam, P. An altering distance function in fuzzy metric fixed point theorems. *Fixed Point Theory Appl.* **2015**, *2015*, 69. [CrossRef]
22. Menger, K. Statistical metric. *Proc. Nat. Acad. Sci. USA* **1942**, *28*, 535–537. [CrossRef] [PubMed]
23. Schweizer, B.; Sklar, A. *Probabilistic Metric Spaces;* Elsevier: New York, NY, USA, 1983.
24. Klement, E.P.; Mesiar, R.; Pap, E. *Triangular Norms;* Trends in Logic; Kluwer Academic Publishers: Dordrecht, The Netherlads, 2000; Volume 8.
25. Kramosil, I.; Michalek, J. Fuzzy metric and statistical metric spaces. *Kybernetica* **1975**, *11*, 336–344.
26. Žikić, T. On fixed point theorems of Gregori and Sapena. *Fuzzy Sets Syst.* **2004**, *144*, 421–429. [CrossRef]
27. Došenović, T.; Rakić, D.; Brdar, M. Fixed point theorem in fuzzy metric spaces using altering distance. *Filomat* **2014**, *28*, 1517–1524. [CrossRef]

axiomos

MDPI

Article

Determinantal Expressions, Identities, Concavity, Maclaurin Power Series Expansions for van der Pol Numbers, Bernoulli Numbers, and Cotangent

Zhen-Ying Sun [1], Bai-Ni Guo [2,*] and Feng Qi [3,*]

1 School of Basic Sciences, Zhengzhou University of Technology, Zhengzhou 450044, China; 19861010@zzut.edu.cn
2 School of Mathematics and Informatics, Henan Polytechnic University, Jiaozuo 454010, China
3 Independent Researcher, Dallas, TX 75252-8024, USA
* Correspondence: bai.ni.guo@gmail.com (B.-N.G.); honest.john.china@gmail.com (F.Q.)

Abstract: In this paper, basing on the generating function for the van der Pol numbers, utilizing the Maclaurin power series expansion and two power series expressions of a function involving the cotangent function, and by virtue of the Wronski formula and a derivative formula for the ratio of two differentiable functions, the authors derive four determinantal expressions for the van der Pol numbers, discover two identities for the Bernoulli numbers and the van der Pol numbers, prove the increasing property and concavity of a function involving the cotangent function, and establish two alternative Maclaurin power series expansions of a function involving the cotangent function. The coefficients of the Maclaurin power series expansions are expressed in terms of specific Hessenberg determinants whose elements contain the Bernoulli numbers and binomial coefficients.

Keywords: determinantal expression; identity; concavity; van der Pol number; Bernoulli number; Maclaurin power series expansion; cotangent; Wronski's formula; derivative formula; Hessenberg determinant; binomial coefficient

MSC: 11B68; 11B83; 15A15; 26A06; 26A09; 26A24; 26A51; 33B10; 41A58

1. Motivations

In [1] (p. 235), see also Section 1 in [2], the sequence of rational numbers V_k for $k \geq 0$ was defined by means of

$$\begin{aligned}\frac{x^3}{6x(e^x+1)-12(e^x-1)} &= \sum_{k=0}^{\infty} V_k \frac{x^k}{k!} \\ &= 1 - \frac{x}{2} + \frac{x^2}{10} - \frac{x^3}{120} - \frac{x^4}{8400} + \frac{x^5}{16{,}800} + \frac{x^6}{756{,}000} - \frac{x^7}{1{,}512{,}000} - \frac{37x^8}{2{,}328{,}480{,}000} - \cdots. \end{aligned} \tag{1}$$

The first few values of V_k for $0 \leq k \leq 8$ are

$$\begin{aligned} &V_0 = 1, \quad V_1 = -\frac{1}{2}, \quad V_2 = \frac{1}{5}, \quad V_3 = -\frac{1}{20}, \quad V_4 = -\frac{1}{350}, \\ &V_5 = \frac{1}{140}, \quad V_6 = \frac{1}{1050}, \quad V_7 = -\frac{1}{300}, \quad V_8 = -\frac{37}{57{,}750}. \end{aligned} \tag{2}$$

Let $J_\nu(z)$ denote the Bessel function and

$$\sigma_{2k}(\nu) = \sum_{m=1}^{\infty} \frac{1}{j_{\nu,m}^{2k}}, \quad k \geq 1,$$

where $j_{\nu,m}$ are the zeros of $\frac{J_\nu(z)}{z^\nu}$. Then,

$$\sigma_{2k}\left(\frac{3}{2}\right) = (-1)^{k-1}\frac{3\times 2^{2k-1}}{(2k)!}V_{2k}, \quad k > 1.$$

The van der Pol numbers V_k are also related to the Bernoulli numbers B_k for $k \geq 0$ via the relation

$$\sigma_{2k}\left(\frac{1}{2}\right) = (-1)^{k-1}\frac{2^{2k-1}}{(2k)!}B_{2k}, \quad k \geq 1,$$

where the Bernoulli numbers B_k for $k \geq 0$ are generated by

$$\frac{z}{e^z - 1} = \sum_{k=0}^{\infty} B_k \frac{z^k}{k!} = 1 - \frac{z}{2} + \sum_{k=1}^{\infty} B_{2k}\frac{z^{2k}}{(2k)!}, \quad |z| < 2\pi.$$

The Rayleigh function $\sigma_k(\nu)$ for $k > 1$ has an alternative notation

$$\zeta_\nu(k) = \sum_{m=1}^{\infty} \frac{1}{j_{\nu,m}^k}, \quad k > 1.$$

This is also called the Bessel zeta function in [3] and was originally introduced and studied in papers [4–7]. In paper [8], the authors derived closed-form expressions of the Bessel zeta function $\zeta_\nu(2k)$ for $k \geq 1$ in terms of specific Hessenberg determinants.

At the site https://math.stackexchange.com/q/4447783 (accessed on 27 May 2023), a question was asked: is there an explicit formula for the Maclaurin expansion of the function $\frac{x^2}{1-x\cot x}$ around the origin $x = 0$? At the site https://math.stackexchange.com/a/4449466 (accessed on 5 June 2023), an answer to this question was given. We now quote this answer as follows.

Using Bessel functions, we find

$$\begin{aligned}
\frac{x^2}{1 - x\cot x} &= 3 - x\frac{J_{5/2}(x)}{J_{3/2}(x)} \\
&= \frac{3}{2} + x\frac{J'_{3/2}(x)}{J_{3/2}(x)} \\
&= 3 - 2x^2 \sum_{k=1}^{\infty} \frac{1}{1 - \left(x/j_{3/2,k}^2\right)^2} \\
&= 3 - 2x^2 \sum_{k=1}^{\infty}\sum_{n=0}^{\infty} \frac{1}{j_{3/2,k}^{2n}} x^{2n} \\
&= 3 - 2x^2 \sum_{n=0}^{\infty}\left(\sum_{k=1}^{\infty} \frac{1}{j_{3/2,k}^{2n}}\right) x^{2n} \\
&= 3 - 2x^2 \sum_{n=0}^{\infty} \sigma_{2n}\left(\frac{3}{2}\right) x^{2n},
\end{aligned}$$

where $j_{3/2,k}$ denotes the kth positive zero of $J_{3/2}$ and σ_n is the Rayleigh function of order n. If $n \geq 1$, we can write

$$\sigma_{2n}\left(\frac{3}{2}\right) = (-1)^{n-1} 3 \times 2^{2n-1}\frac{V_{2n}}{(2n)!},$$

where V_n is the nth van der Pol number. See paper [2] for the properties of these numbers, including recurrence relations. In particular, the generating function is Equation (d) in Section 1.

In [2] (Sections 1 and 6), we find the series expansion

$$\frac{z^2}{1-z\cot z}=3-\frac{z^2}{5}+3\sum_{k=2}^{\infty}(-1)^k 2^{2k} V_{2k}\frac{z^{2k}}{(2k)!} \tag{3}$$

by defining $\frac{z^2}{1-z\cot z}$ to be 3 at $z=0$. According to the discussion in [2] (Section 6), the Maclaurin power series expansion (3) has a finite positive radius of convergence, and this radius of convergence, denoted by R, is located between $\frac{4\pi}{3}$ and $\frac{3\pi}{2}$. In fact, the number R is the first positive zero of the equation $\tan x - x = 0$.

Let

$$G(x)=\begin{cases}\dfrac{x^2}{1-x\cot x}, & 0<|x|<R;\\ 3, & x=0.\end{cases} \tag{4}$$

It is clear that the function $G(x)$ is even on $(-R,R)$.

In [9] (p. 75, Entry 4.3.70), it was listed that

$$\cot z=\frac{1}{z}-\sum_{k=1}^{\infty}\frac{(-1)^{k-1}2^{2k}}{(2k)!}B_{2k}z^{2k-1}, \quad |z|<\pi.$$

Hence, we have

$$G(x)=\frac{1}{\sum_{k=0}^{\infty}\frac{2^{2k+2}}{(2k+2)!}|B_{2k+2}|x^{2k}}, \quad 0<|x|<R. \tag{5}$$

On the other hand,

$$G(x)=\frac{x^2\sin x}{\sin x - x\cos x}=\frac{1}{2}\frac{\sum_{k=0}^{\infty}\frac{(-1)^k}{(2k+1)!}x^{2k}}{\sum_{k=0}^{\infty}\frac{(-1)^k(k+1)}{(2k+3)!}x^{2k}}, \quad |x|<R. \tag{6}$$

In this paper, basing on the generating function (1) for the van der Pol numbers V_n, on the Maclaurin power series expansion (3) of the function $G(z)$, and on the expressions in (5) and (6) of the function $G(x)$, by virtue of Wronski's formula in [10] (p. 17, Theorem 1.3), and in view of a derivative formula for the ratio of two differentiable functions, we will derive four determinantal expressions for the van der Pol numbers V_n and V_{2k}, discover two identities for the Bernoulli numbers B_{2k} and the van der Pol numbers V_{2k}, prove the increasing property and concavity of the function $G(x)$, and establish two alternative Maclaurin power series expansions of the function $G(x)$, whose coefficients are expressed in terms of specific Hessenberg determinants in which the Bernoulli numbers B_{2k} and binomial coefficients are involved.

2. Lemmas

For smoothly solving the above two problems, we need the following lemmas.

Lemma 1 (Wronski's formula [10] (p. 17, Theorem 1.3)). *If $a_0 \neq 0$ and*

$$P(x)=a_0+a_1x+a_2x^2+\cdots$$

is a formal series, then the coefficients of the reciprocal series

$$\frac{1}{P(x)}=b_0+b_1x+b_2x^2+\cdots$$

are given by

$$b_r = \frac{(-1)^r}{a_0^{r+1}} \begin{vmatrix} a_1 & a_0 & 0 & 0 & \cdots & 0 & 0 & 0 \\ a_2 & a_1 & a_0 & 0 & \cdots & 0 & 0 & 0 \\ a_3 & a_2 & a_1 & a_0 & \cdots & 0 & 0 & 0 \\ \vdots & \vdots & \vdots & \vdots & \ddots & \vdots & \vdots & \vdots \\ a_{r-2} & a_{r-3} & a_{r-4} & a_{r-5} & \cdots & a_1 & a_0 & 0 \\ a_{r-1} & a_{r-2} & a_{r-3} & a_{r-4} & \cdots & a_2 & a_1 & a_0 \\ a_r & a_{r-1} & a_{r-2} & a_{r-3} & \cdots & a_3 & a_2 & a_1 \end{vmatrix}, \quad r \in \mathbb{N}. \tag{7}$$

Lemma 2 ([11] (p. 40, Exercise 5)). *Let $u(x)$ and $v(x) \neq 0$ be two n-time differentiable functions on an interval I for a given integer $n \geq 0$. Then, the nth derivative of the ratio $\frac{u(x)}{v(x)}$ is*

$$\frac{\mathrm{d}^n}{\mathrm{d}x^n}\left[\frac{u(x)}{v(x)}\right] = (-1)^n \frac{|W_{(n+1)\times(n+1)}(x)|}{v^{n+1}(x)}, \quad n \geq 0, \tag{8}$$

where the matrix

$$W_{(n+1)\times(n+1)}(x) = \left(U_{(n+1)\times 1}(x) \quad V_{(n+1)\times n}(x)\right)_{(n+1)\times(n+1)},$$

the matrix $U_{(n+1)\times 1}(x)$ is an $(n+1) \times 1$ matrix whose elements satisfy $u_{k,1}(x) = u^{(k-1)}(x)$ for $1 \leq k \leq n+1$, the matrix $V_{(n+1)\times n}(x)$ is an $(n+1) \times n$ matrix whose elements are

$$v_{\ell,j}(x) = \begin{cases} \binom{\ell-1}{j-1} v^{(\ell-j)}(x), & \ell - j \geq 0 \\ 0, & \ell - j < 0 \end{cases}$$

for $1 \leq \ell \leq n+1$ and $1 \leq j \leq n$, and the notation $|W_{(n+1)\times(n+1)}(x)|$ denotes the determinant of the $(n+1) \times (n+1)$ matrix $W_{(n+1)\times(n+1)}(x)$.

3. A Relation and Two Identities for van der Pol and Bernoulli Numbers

In this section, by comparing the power series expansion (3) and two expressions (5) and (6), we derive a relation and two identities for van der Pol numbers V_{2k} and the Bernoulli numbers B_{2k}.

Theorem 1. *For $k \geq 2$, we have*

$$V_{2k} = (2k)!\left(\frac{3}{4}\right)^k \begin{vmatrix} a_1 & a_0 & 0 & 0 & \cdots & 0 & 0 & 0 \\ a_2 & a_1 & a_0 & 0 & \cdots & 0 & 0 & 0 \\ a_3 & a_2 & a_1 & a_0 & \cdots & 0 & 0 & 0 \\ \vdots & \vdots & \vdots & \vdots & \ddots & \vdots & \vdots & \vdots \\ a_{k-2} & a_{k-3} & a_{k-4} & a_{k-5} & \cdots & a_1 & a_0 & 0 \\ a_{k-1} & a_{k-2} & a_{k-3} & a_{k-4} & \cdots & a_2 & a_1 & a_0 \\ a_k & a_{k-1} & a_{k-2} & a_{k-3} & \cdots & a_3 & a_2 & a_1 \end{vmatrix}, \tag{9}$$

where

$$a_k = \frac{2^{2k+2}}{(2k+2)!}|B_{2k+2}|, \qquad k \geq 0.$$

Proof. Comparing the series expansion (3) and Expression (5), we find that

$$\left[3 - \frac{1}{5}x^2 + 3\sum_{k=2}^{\infty}(-1)^k \frac{2^{2k}}{(2k)!} V_{2k} x^{2k}\right] \sum_{k=0}^{\infty} \frac{2^{2k+2}}{(2k+2)!}|B_{2k+2}| x^{2k} = 1.$$

Applying Formula (7) in Lemma 1 and rearranging yield Formula (9). □

Remark 1. *When $k = 4$, we have*

$$V_8 = 8!\left(\frac{3}{4}\right)^4 \begin{vmatrix} a_1 & a_0 & 0 & 0 \\ a_2 & a_1 & a_0 & 0 \\ a_3 & a_2 & a_1 & a_0 \\ a_4 & a_3 & a_2 & a_1 \end{vmatrix} = 8!\left(\frac{3}{4}\right)^4 \begin{vmatrix} \frac{1}{45} & \frac{1}{3} & 0 & 0 \\ \frac{2}{945} & \frac{1}{45} & \frac{1}{3} & 0 \\ \frac{1}{4725} & \frac{2}{945} & \frac{1}{45} & \frac{1}{3} \\ \frac{2}{93555} & \frac{1}{4725} & \frac{2}{945} & \frac{1}{45} \end{vmatrix} = -\frac{37}{57750}.$$

When $k = 3$, we have

$$V_6 = 6!\left(\frac{3}{4}\right)^3 \begin{vmatrix} a_1 & a_0 & 0 \\ a_2 & a_1 & a_0 \\ a_3 & a_2 & a_1 \end{vmatrix} = 6!\left(\frac{3}{4}\right)^3 \begin{vmatrix} \frac{1}{45} & \frac{1}{3} & 0 \\ \frac{2}{945} & \frac{1}{45} & \frac{1}{3} \\ \frac{1}{4725} & \frac{2}{945} & \frac{1}{45} \end{vmatrix} = \frac{1}{1050}.$$

When $k = 2$, we have

$$V_4 = 4!\left(\frac{3}{4}\right)^2 \begin{vmatrix} a_1 & a_0 \\ a_2 & a_1 \end{vmatrix} = 4!\left(\frac{3}{4}\right)^2 \begin{vmatrix} \frac{1}{45} & \frac{1}{3} \\ \frac{2}{945} & \frac{1}{45} \end{vmatrix} = -\frac{1}{350}.$$

These three values are congruent to the corresponding ones in (2).

Theorem 2. *For $k \ge 0$, we have*

$$\sum_{j=0}^{k} (-1)^j 2^{2j} \binom{2k+3}{2j+2} |B_{2j+2}| = \frac{k+1}{2}. \tag{10}$$

Proof. From Expressions (5) and (6), it follows that

$$\begin{aligned}\sum_{k=0}^{\infty} \frac{(-1)^k (k+1)}{(2k+3)!} x^{2k} &= \frac{1}{2} \sum_{k=0}^{\infty} \frac{(-1)^k}{(2k+1)!} x^{2k} \sum_{k=0}^{\infty} \frac{2^{2k+2}}{(2k+2)!} |B_{2k+2}| x^{2k} \\ &= \frac{1}{2} \sum_{k=0}^{\infty} \frac{(-1)^k}{(2k+3)!} \left[\sum_{j=0}^{k} (-1)^j \binom{2k+3}{2j+2} 2^{2j+2} |B_{2j+2}| \right] x^{2k}.\end{aligned}$$

Accordingly, we obtain

$$\frac{(-1)^k (k+1)}{(2k+3)!} = \frac{1}{2} \frac{(-1)^k}{(2k+3)!} \left[\sum_{j=0}^{k} (-1)^j \binom{2k+3}{2j+2} 2^{2j+2} |B_{2j+2}| \right], \quad k \ge 0,$$

which can be simplified as the identity (10). □

Theorem 3. *For $k \ge 2$, we have*

$$\sum_{j=2}^{k} (k-j+1) 2^{2j} \binom{2k+3}{2j} V_{2j} = -\frac{4}{15} k(k^2-1). \tag{11}$$

Proof. Considering the series expansion (3) and Expression (6), we arrive at

$$\begin{aligned}\sum_{k=0}^{\infty} \frac{(-1)^k}{(2k+1)!} x^{2k} &= 2\left[3 - \frac{1}{5}x^2 + 3\sum_{k=2}^{\infty} (-1)^k \frac{2^{2k}}{(2k)!} V_{2k} x^{2k}\right] \sum_{k=0}^{\infty} \frac{(-1)^k (k+1)}{(2k+3)!} x^{2k} \\ &= 2\sum_{k=0}^{\infty} (-1)^k \left[\frac{3(k+1)}{(2k+3)!} + \frac{1}{5} \frac{k}{(2k+1)!} + 3\sum_{j=2}^{k} \frac{k-j+1}{(2j)!(2k-2j+3)!} 2^{2j} V_{2j} \right] x^{2k}.\end{aligned}$$

This means that

$$\frac{1}{(2k+1)!} = 2\left[\frac{3(k+1)}{(2k+3)!} + \frac{1}{5}\frac{k}{(2k+1)!} + 3\sum_{j=2}^{k}\frac{k-j+1}{(2j)!(2k-2j+3)!}2^{2j}V_{2j}\right],$$

which can be rewritten as identity (11). The proof of Theorem 3 is complete. □

4. A Determinantal Expression of van der Pol Numbers

In [12] (Theorem 2.7), an explicit formula of the van der Pol numbers V_n for $n \ge 0$ was given by

$$\begin{aligned} V_n = &\sum_{k=0}^{n}\frac{k!}{(n+2k)!}\binom{n}{k}\sum_{q=0}^{n-k}\langle -3k\rangle_q (n-k-q)!\binom{n-k}{q}\binom{n+2k}{n-k-q} \\ &\times \sum_{\ell=0}^{k} 12^{\ell}\binom{k}{\ell}\sum_{p=0}^{n+2k}(n+2k-p)!\binom{n+2k}{p}\frac{S(p+\ell,\ell)}{\binom{p+\ell}{\ell}} \\ &\times \sum_{s=0}^{k-\ell}\binom{k-\ell}{s}\frac{(-6)^s}{(n-p+2\ell+2s)!}\sum_{\beta=1}^{s}\binom{s}{\beta}\beta^{n-p+2\ell+2s}, \end{aligned} \tag{12}$$

where $S(p,q)$ for $p \ge q \ge 0$ denotes the Stirling numbers of the second kind and

$$\langle z\rangle_n = \prod_{k=0}^{n-1}(z-k) = \begin{cases} z(z-1)\cdots(z-n+1), & n \in \mathbb{N} \\ 1, & n = 0 \end{cases}$$

is the nth falling factorial of $z \in \mathbb{C}$.

In this section, by virtue of Lemma 2, we deduce an alternative formula of the van der Pol numbers V_n in terms of specific Hessenberg determinants.

Theorem 4. *For $n \ge 1$, the van der Pol numbers V_n can be expressed by the determinant*

$$\begin{aligned} V_n &= (-1)^n \begin{vmatrix} \binom{1}{0}\frac{1}{2} & \binom{1}{1} & 0 & \cdots & 0 \\ \binom{2}{0}\frac{3}{10} & \binom{2}{1}\frac{1}{2} & \binom{2}{2} & \cdots & 0 \\ \binom{3}{0}\frac{1}{5} & \binom{3}{1}\frac{3}{10} & \binom{3}{2}\frac{1}{2} & \cdots & 0 \\ \binom{4}{0}\frac{1}{7} & \binom{4}{1}\frac{1}{5} & \binom{4}{2}\frac{3}{10} & \cdots & 0 \\ \vdots & \vdots & \vdots & \ddots & \vdots \\ \binom{n-2}{0}\frac{6}{n(n+1)} & \binom{n-2}{1}\frac{6}{(n-1)n} & \binom{n-2}{2}\frac{6}{(n-2)(n-1)} & \cdots & 0 \\ \binom{n-1}{0}\frac{6}{(n+1)(n+2)} & \binom{n-1}{1}\frac{6}{n(n+1)} & \binom{n-1}{2}\frac{6}{(n-1)n} & \cdots & \binom{n-1}{n-1} \\ \binom{n}{0}\frac{6}{(n+2)(n+3)} & \binom{n}{1}\frac{6}{(n+1)(n+2)} & \binom{n}{2}\frac{6}{n(n+1)} & \cdots & \binom{n}{n-1}\frac{1}{2} \end{vmatrix} \\ &= (-1)^n \left|v_{i,j}\right|_{n\times n}, \end{aligned} \tag{13}$$

where

$$v_{i,j} = \begin{cases} 0, & 3 \le i+2 \le j \le n; \\ \binom{i}{j-1}\dfrac{6}{(i-j+3)(i-j+4)}, & n \ge i+2 > j \ge 1. \end{cases}$$

Proof. The generating function in (1) of the van der Pol numbers V_k can be written as

$$\frac{x^3}{6x(e^x+1)-12(e^x-1)} = \frac{1}{6}\frac{1}{\sum_{k=0}^{\infty}\frac{k+1}{(k+3)!}x^k}.$$

Therefore, by virtue of the derivative Formula (8), we obtain

$$
\begin{aligned}
V_n &= \lim_{x\to 0}\left[\frac{x^3}{6x(\mathrm{e}^x+1)-12(\mathrm{e}^x-1)}\right]^{(n)} \\
&= \lim_{x\to 0}\left[\frac{1}{\sum_{k=0}^{\infty}\frac{6(k+1)}{(k+3)!}x^k}\right]^{(n)} \\
&= (-1)^n\begin{vmatrix}
1 & 1 & 0 & 0 & \cdots & 0\\
0 & \frac{1}{2} & \binom{1}{1} & 0 & \cdots & 0\\
0 & \frac{3}{10} & \binom{2}{1}\frac{1}{2} & \binom{2}{2} & \cdots & 0\\
0 & \frac{1}{5} & \binom{3}{1}\frac{3}{10} & \binom{3}{2}\frac{1}{2} & \cdots & 0\\
0 & \frac{1}{7} & \binom{4}{1}\frac{1}{5} & \binom{4}{2}\frac{3}{10} & \cdots & 0\\
\vdots & \vdots & \vdots & \vdots & \ddots & \vdots\\
0 & \frac{6}{(n+1)(n+2)} & \binom{n-1}{1}\frac{6}{n(n+1)} & \binom{n-1}{2}\frac{6}{(n-1)n} & \cdots & \binom{n-1}{n-1}\\
0 & \frac{6}{(n+2)(n+3)} & \binom{n}{1}\frac{6}{(n+1)(n+2)} & \binom{n}{2}\frac{6}{n(n+1)} & \cdots & \binom{n}{n-1}\frac{1}{2}
\end{vmatrix} \\
&= (-1)^n\begin{vmatrix}
\binom{1}{0}\frac{1}{2} & \binom{1}{1} & 0 & \cdots & 0\\
\binom{2}{0}\frac{3}{10} & \binom{2}{1}\frac{1}{2} & \binom{2}{2} & \cdots & 0\\
\binom{3}{0}\frac{1}{5} & \binom{3}{1}\frac{3}{10} & \binom{3}{2}\frac{1}{2} & \cdots & 0\\
\binom{4}{0}\frac{1}{7} & \binom{4}{1}\frac{1}{5} & \binom{4}{2}\frac{3}{10} & \cdots & 0\\
\vdots & \vdots & \vdots & \ddots & \vdots\\
\binom{n-2}{0}\frac{6}{n(n+1)} & \binom{n-2}{1}\frac{6}{(n-1)n} & \binom{n-2}{2}\frac{6}{(n-2)(n-1)} & \cdots & 0\\
\binom{n-1}{0}\frac{6}{(n+1)(n+2)} & \binom{n-1}{1}\frac{6}{n(n+1)} & \binom{n-1}{2}\frac{6}{(n-1)n} & \cdots & \binom{n-1}{n-1}\\
\binom{n}{0}\frac{6}{(n+2)(n+3)} & \binom{n}{1}\frac{6}{(n+1)(n+2)} & \binom{n}{2}\frac{6}{n(n+1)} & \cdots & \binom{n}{n-1}\frac{1}{2}
\end{vmatrix} \\
&= (-1)^n\left|v_{i,j}\right|_{n\times n}
\end{aligned}
$$

for $n \ge 1$. The proof of Theorem 4 is thus complete. □

Remark 2. *It is obvious that the determinantal expression* (13) *is more beautiful, symmetric, and computable than the explicit expression* (12) *of the van der Pol numbers* V_n.

Remark 3. *By the determinantal expression* (13), *we can compute*

$$
V_4 = (-1)^4\begin{vmatrix}
\binom{1}{0}\frac{1}{2} & \binom{1}{1} & 0 & 0\\
\binom{2}{0}\frac{3}{10} & \binom{2}{1}\frac{1}{2} & \binom{2}{2} & 0\\
\binom{3}{0}\frac{1}{5} & \binom{3}{1}\frac{3}{10} & \binom{3}{2}\frac{1}{2} & \binom{3}{3}\\
\binom{4}{0}\frac{1}{7} & \binom{4}{1}\frac{1}{5} & \binom{4}{2}\frac{3}{10} & \binom{4}{3}\frac{1}{2}
\end{vmatrix} = -\frac{1}{350},
$$

$$
V_3 = (-1)^3\begin{vmatrix}
\binom{1}{0}\frac{1}{2} & \binom{1}{1} & 0\\
\binom{2}{0}\frac{3}{10} & \binom{2}{1}\frac{1}{2} & \binom{2}{2}\\
\binom{3}{0}\frac{1}{5} & \binom{3}{1}\frac{3}{10} & \binom{3}{2}\frac{1}{2}
\end{vmatrix} = -\frac{1}{20},
$$

$$
V_2 = (-1)^2\begin{vmatrix}
\binom{1}{0}\frac{1}{2} & \binom{1}{1}\\
\binom{2}{0}\frac{3}{10} & \binom{2}{1}\frac{1}{2}
\end{vmatrix} = \frac{1}{5}, \quad V_1 = (-1)^1\left|\binom{1}{0}\frac{1}{2}\right| = -\frac{1}{2}.
$$

These values of V_k *for* $1 \le k \le 4$ *coincide with the corresponding ones in* (2).

5. Decreasing Property and Concavity

In this section, we discuss the decreasing property and concavity of the even function $G(x)$ defined by (4).

Theorem 5. *The even function* $G(x)$ *defined by* (4) *is decreasing on* $[0, R) \supset [0, \pi]$ *and is concave on* $[0, \pi] \subset [0, R)$.

Proof. From Expression (5), it is easy to see that the even function $G(x)$ is decreasing on $(0,R)$.

Considering the first equality in (6) and directly differentiating give

$$G'(x) = \left(\frac{x^2\sin x}{\sin x - x\cos x}\right)' = -\frac{x[x\sin(2x) + 2\cos(2x) + 2x^2 - 2]}{2(\sin x - x\cos x)^2}$$

and

$$G''(x) = -\frac{\sin(3x) - (4x^4 - 12x^2 + 3)\sin x - 8x^3\cos x}{2(\sin x - x\cos x)^3}.$$

Let

$$h(x) = \sin(3x) - (4x^4 - 12x^2 + 3)\sin x - 8x^3\cos x. \tag{14}$$

The function $h(x)$ can be expanded to

$$h(x) = x^9\sum_{j=0}^{\infty}(-1)^j\frac{3^{2j+9} - (64j^4 + 896j^3 + 4640j^2 + 10{,}552j + 8931)}{(2j+9)!}x^{2j}.$$

Let

$$T_j = \frac{3^{2j+9} - (64j^4 + 896j^3 + 4640j^2 + 10{,}552j + 8931)}{(2j+9)!}, \quad j \ge 0.$$

Then

$$h(x) = x^9\sum_{j=0}^{\infty}(T_{2j} - T_{2j+1}x^2)x^{4j} = x^9\sum_{j=0}^{\infty}T_{2j+1}\left(\frac{T_{2j}}{T_{2j+1}} - x^2\right)x^{4j}.$$

By induction, we can verify that

$$3^{2j+9} > 64j^4 + 896j^3 + 4640j^2 + 10{,}552j + 8931, \quad j \ge 0.$$

This means that $T_j > 0$ for $j \ge 0$.

In order to prove that the inequality

$$\frac{T_{2j}}{T_{2j+1}} > \left(\frac{3\pi}{2}\right)^2 = 22.2\ldots > \pi^2 = 9.8\cdots \tag{15}$$

holds for $j \ge 0$, it suffices to show $T_{2j} > 25T_{2j+1}$ for $j \ge 0$, which is equivalent to

$$\begin{aligned}3^{4j+9}(16j^2 + 84j - 115) > 16{,}384j^6 + 200{,}704j^5 + 986{,}112j^4 \\ + 2{,}454{,}784j^3 + 3{,}186{,}032j^2 + 1{,}932{,}844j + 355{,}335, \quad j \ge 0.\end{aligned}$$

For $j \ge 2$, it is sufficient to prove that

$$3^{4j+9} > \frac{16{,}384j^6 + 200{,}704j^5 + 9{,}861{,}12j^4 + 2{,}454{,}784j^3 + 3{,}186{,}032j^2 + 1{,}932{,}844j + 355{,}335}{16j^2 + 84j - 115},$$

which can be verified by induction on $j \ge 2$. In short, Inequality (15) holds for $j \ge 2$.

Let

$$\begin{aligned}Y(y) = \sum_{j=0}^{1}T_{2j+1}\left(\frac{T_{2j}}{T_{2j+1}} - y\right)y^{2j} = \sum_{j=0}^{3}(-1)^jT_jy^j \\ = -\frac{713y^3}{65{,}488{,}500} + \frac{y^2}{4050} - \frac{2y}{525} + \frac{4}{135}, \quad 0 \le y \le \pi^2.\end{aligned}$$

Differentiating gives

$$Y'(y) = -\frac{713y^2}{21{,}829{,}500} + \frac{y}{2025} - \frac{2}{525} \quad \text{and} \quad Y''(y) = \frac{1}{2025} - \frac{713y}{10{,}914{,}750}.$$

The second derivative $Y''(y)$ is decreasing and has a zero $\frac{10{,}914{,}750}{713\times 2025} = \frac{5390}{713}$. The first derivative $Y'(y)$ has a maximum

$$Y'\left(\frac{5390}{713}\right) = -\frac{19{,}637}{10{,}106{,}775}.$$

Thus, the first derivative $Y'(y)$ is negative and the function $Y(y)$ is decreasing. Since

$$Y(\pi^2) = \frac{4}{135} - \frac{2\pi^2}{525} + \frac{\pi^4}{4050} - \frac{713\pi^6}{65{,}488{,}500} = 0.0056\ldots,$$

the function $Y(y)$ is positive on $[0, \pi^2]$.

Combining the above arguments, we conclude that the function $h(x)$ is positive on $(0, \pi]$. Then, the second derivative $G''(x)$ is negative on $(0, \pi)$. Hence, the function $G(x)$ is concave on $[0, \pi]$. □

Remark 4. *We guess that the function $h(x)$ defined in* (14) *is positive, and even increasing, on the interval $(0, \frac{3\pi}{2}] \supset (0, R]$. If this guess were true, then the even function $G(x)$ would be concave on $[0, R) \subset (0, \frac{3\pi}{2})$.*

Remark 5. *We note that a concave function must be a logarithmically concave function, but not conversely. However, a logarithmically convex function must be a convex function, but not conversely.*

6. Power Series Expansions

In this section, basing on (5) and (6) and utilizing the derivative Formula (8) in Lemma 2, we derive two Maclaurin power series expansions of the function $G(x)$ defined by (4) in terms of specific Hessenberg determinants. These two Maclaurin power series expansions are different from (3) in form.

Theorem 6. *For $m \ge 0$, let*

$$E_m = \frac{2^{2m+1}}{2m+1} \frac{|B_{2m+2}|}{m+1}$$

and

$$D_{2m} = \begin{vmatrix} 0 & \binom{1}{1}\frac{1}{3} & 0 & 0 & \cdots & 0 \\ \frac{2}{45} & 0 & \binom{2}{2}\frac{1}{3} & 0 & \cdots & 0 \\ 0 & \binom{3}{1}\frac{2}{45} & 0 & \binom{3}{3}\frac{1}{3} & \cdots & 0 \\ \frac{16}{315} & 0 & \binom{4}{2}\frac{2}{45} & 0 & \cdots & 0 \\ \vdots & \vdots & \vdots & \vdots & \ddots & \vdots \\ E_{m-1} & 0 & \binom{2m-2}{2}E_{m-2} & 0 & \cdots & 0 \\ 0 & \binom{2m-1}{1}E_{m-1} & 0 & \binom{2m-1}{3}E_{m-2} & \cdots & \binom{2m-1}{2m-1}\frac{1}{3} \\ E_m & 0 & \binom{2m}{2}E_{m-1} & 0 & \cdots & 0 \end{vmatrix}$$

$$= \left|e_{i,j}\right|_{(2m)\times(2m)}$$

with the convention $D_0 = 1$, where

$$e_{i,j} = \begin{cases} 0, & 2m \geq j > i+1 \geq 2; \\ 0, & 2m-2 \geq i-j = 2k \geq 0; \\ \binom{i}{j-1} E_{(i-j+1)/2}, & 2m-1 \geq i-j = 2k-1 \geq -1. \end{cases}$$

Then the function $G(x)$ defined in (4) *can be expanded to*

$$G(x) = \sum_{m=0}^{\infty} 3^{2m+1} D_{2m} \frac{x^{2m}}{(2m)!} = 3 - \frac{x^2}{5} - \frac{x^4}{175} - \frac{2x^6}{7875} - \frac{37x^8}{3{,}031{,}875} - \cdots. \tag{16}$$

Proof. Since the function $G(x)$ is even, its odd order derivative $G^{(2m+1)}(0) = 0$ for $m \geq 0$. Let $u(x) = 1$ and

$$v(x) = \sum_{k=0}^{\infty} \frac{2^{2k+2}}{(2k+2)!} |B_{2k+2}| x^{2k},$$

which are both even functions. Then

$$v^{(n)}(0) = \lim_{x \to 0} \sum_{k=0}^{m} \frac{2^{2k+2}}{(2k+2)!} |B_{2k+2}| \langle 2k \rangle_n x^{2k-n} = \begin{cases} 0, & n = 2m+1 \\ \frac{2^{2m+1}}{2m+1} \frac{|B_{2m+2}|}{m+1}, & n = 2m \end{cases}$$

for $m \geq 0$. Applying the derivative Formula (8) to Expression (5) leads to

$$G^{(2m)}(0) = \lim_{x \to 0} \left[\frac{1}{\sum_{k=0}^{\infty} \frac{2^{2k+2}}{(2k+2)!} |B_{2k+2}| x^{2k}} \right]^{(2m)}$$

$$= \frac{1}{E_0^{2m+1}} \begin{vmatrix} 1 & \binom{0}{0}E_0 & 0 & 0 & \cdots & 0 \\ 0 & 0 & \binom{1}{1}E_0 & 0 & \cdots & 0 \\ 0 & \binom{2}{0}E_1 & 0 & \binom{2}{2}E_0 & \cdots & 0 \\ 0 & 0 & \binom{3}{1}E_1 & 0 & \cdots & 0 \\ 0 & \binom{4}{0}E_2 & 0 & \binom{4}{2}E_1 & \cdots & 0 \\ \vdots & \vdots & \vdots & \vdots & \ddots & \vdots \\ 0 & \binom{2m-2}{0}E_{m-1} & 0 & \binom{2m-2}{2}E_{m-2} & \cdots & 0 \\ 0 & 0 & \binom{2m-1}{1}E_{m-1} & 0 & \cdots & \binom{2m-1}{2m-1}E_0 \\ 0 & \binom{2m}{0}E_m & 0 & \binom{2m}{2}E_{m-1} & \cdots & 0 \end{vmatrix}$$

$$= 3^{2m+1} \begin{vmatrix} 0 & \binom{1}{1}\frac{1}{3} & 0 & 0 & \cdots & 0 \\ \frac{2}{45} & 0 & \binom{2}{2}\frac{1}{3} & 0 & \cdots & 0 \\ 0 & \binom{3}{1}\frac{2}{45} & 0 & \binom{3}{3}\frac{1}{3} & \cdots & 0 \\ \frac{16}{315} & 0 & \binom{4}{2}\frac{2}{45} & 0 & \cdots & 0 \\ \vdots & \vdots & \vdots & \vdots & \ddots & \vdots \\ E_{m-1} & 0 & \binom{2m-2}{2}E_{m-2} & 0 & \cdots & 0 \\ 0 & \binom{2m-1}{1}E_{m-1} & 0 & \binom{2m-1}{3}E_{m-2} & \cdots & \binom{2m-1}{2m-1}\frac{1}{3} \\ E_m & 0 & \binom{2m}{2}E_{m-1} & 0 & \cdots & 0 \end{vmatrix}$$

$$= 3^{2m+1} D_{2m}.$$

Consequently, the Maclaurin power series expansion is

$$G(x) = \sum_{n=0}^{\infty} G^{(n)}(0) \frac{x^n}{n!} = \sum_{m=0}^{\infty} G^{(2m)}(0) \frac{x^{2m}}{(2m)!} = \sum_{m=0}^{\infty} 3^{2m+1} D_{2m} \frac{x^{2m}}{(2m)!}.$$

The proof of Theorem 6 is complete. □

Remark 6. *When $m = 2$ and $m = 1$, we obtain*

$$D_4 = \begin{vmatrix} 0 & \binom{1}{1}E_0 & 0 & 0 \\ \binom{2}{0}E_1 & 0 & \binom{2}{2}E_0 & 0 \\ 0 & \binom{3}{1}E_1 & 0 & \binom{3}{3}E_0 \\ \binom{4}{0}E_2 & 0 & \binom{4}{2}E_1 & 0 \end{vmatrix} = \begin{vmatrix} 0 & \binom{1}{1}\frac{1}{3} & 0 & 0 \\ \binom{2}{0}\frac{2}{45} & 0 & \binom{2}{2}\frac{1}{3} & 0 \\ 0 & \binom{3}{1}\frac{2}{45} & 0 & \binom{3}{3}\frac{1}{3} \\ \binom{4}{0}\frac{16}{315} & 0 & \binom{4}{2}\frac{2}{45} & 0 \end{vmatrix} = -\frac{8}{14{,}175}$$

and

$$D_2 = \begin{vmatrix} 0 & \binom{1}{1}E_0 \\ \binom{2}{0}E_1 & 0 \end{vmatrix} = \begin{vmatrix} 0 & \binom{1}{1}\frac{1}{3} \\ \binom{2}{0}\frac{2}{45} & 0 \end{vmatrix} = -\frac{2}{135}.$$

Accordingly, we have

$$\begin{aligned} G(x) &= 3D_0 + 3^3 D_2 \frac{x^2}{2!} + 3^5 D_4 \frac{x^4}{4!} + \sum_{m=3}^{\infty} 3^{2m+1} D_{2m} \frac{x^{2m}}{(2m)!} \\ &= 3 - \frac{x^2}{5} - \frac{x^4}{175} + \sum_{m=3}^{\infty} 3^{2m+1} D_{2m} \frac{x^{2m}}{(2m)!}, \end{aligned}$$

which coincides with the first three terms in the series expansions (3) *and* (16).

Remark 7. *Comparing the series expansions* (3) *and* (16) *reveals*

$$3\sum_{k=2}^{\infty}(-1)^k 2^{2k} V_{2k} \frac{x^{2k}}{(2k)!} = \sum_{m=2}^{\infty} 3^{2m+1} D_{2m} \frac{x^{2m}}{(2m)!}.$$

As a result, we deduce the relation

$$V_{2k} = (-1)^k \left(\frac{3}{2}\right)^{2k} D_{2k}, \quad k \ge 2, \tag{17}$$

which is different to the determinantal expression (9).

Theorem 7. *The function $G(x)$ defined in* (4) *can be expanded into*

$$G(x) = \sum_{m=0}^{\infty} 3^{2m+1} \mathcal{D}_{2m+1} \frac{x^{2m}}{(2m)!} = 3 - \frac{x^2}{5} - \frac{x^4}{175} - \frac{2x^6}{7875} - \frac{37x^8}{3{,}031{,}875} - \cdots, \tag{18}$$

where the determinants

$$\mathcal{D}_{2m+1} = |d_{i,j}|_{(2m+1)\times(2m+1)}$$

and the elements of the determinants $\mathcal{D}_{2m+1}$ are

$$d_{i,j} = \begin{cases} \dfrac{(-1)^{(i-1)/2}[1+(-1)^{i-1}]}{2i}, & 1 \le i \le 2m+1, j = 1; \\ \dbinom{i-1}{j-2} \dfrac{(-1)^{(i-j+1)/2}[1+(-1)^{i-j+1}]}{2(i-j+2)(i-j+4)}, & 1 \le i \le 2m+1, 2 \le j \le 2m+1. \end{cases}$$

Proof. Let

$$u(x) = \sum_{k=0}^{\infty} \frac{(-1)^k}{(2k+1)!} x^{2k} \quad \text{and} \quad v(x) = 2\sum_{k=0}^{\infty} \frac{(-1)^k (k+1)}{(2k+3)!} x^{2k}.$$

Differentiating results in

$$
\begin{aligned}
u^{(2m)}(0) &= \lim_{x\to 0}\sum_{k=0}^{\infty}\frac{(-1)^k}{(2k+1)!}\langle 2k\rangle_{2m}x^{2k-2m} = \frac{(-1)^m}{(2m+1)!}\langle 2m\rangle_{2m} = \frac{(-1)^m}{2m+1}, \\
v^{(2m)}(0) &= 2\lim_{x\to 0}\sum_{k=0}^{\infty}\frac{(-1)^k(k+1)}{(2k+3)!}\langle 2k\rangle_{2m}x^{2k-2m} = \frac{(-1)^m}{(2m+1)(2m+3)}, \\
& u^{(2m+1)}(0) = 0, \quad v^{2m+1}(0) = 0
\end{aligned}
$$

for $m \ge 0$. Applying the derivative Formula (8) to Expression (6) leads to

$$
\frac{G^{(2m)}(0)}{3^{2m+1}} = \left|\begin{array}{cccc}
1 & \frac{1}{1\cdot 3} & 0 & 0 \\
0 & 0 & \binom{1}{1}\frac{1}{1\cdot 3} & 0 \\
\frac{-1}{3} & \frac{-1}{3\cdot 5} & 0 & \binom{2}{2}\frac{1}{1\cdot 3} \\
0 & 0 & \binom{3}{1}\frac{-1}{3\cdot 5} & 0 \\
\frac{1}{5} & \frac{1}{5\cdot 7} & 0 & \binom{4}{2}\frac{-1}{3\cdot 5} \\
\vdots & \vdots & \vdots & \vdots \\
0 & 0 & \binom{2m-1}{1}\frac{(-1)^{m-1}}{(2m-1)(2m+1)} & 0 \\
\frac{(-1)^m}{2m+1} & \frac{(-1)^m}{(2m+1)(2m+3)} & 0 & \binom{2m}{2}\frac{(-1)^{m-1}}{(2m-1)(2m+1)}
\end{array}\right.
$$

$$
\left.\begin{array}{cccccc}
\cdots & 0 & 0 & 0 & 0 & 0 \\
\cdots & 0 & 0 & 0 & 0 & 0 \\
\cdots & 0 & 0 & 0 & 0 & 0 \\
\cdots & 0 & 0 & 0 & 0 & 0 \\
\cdots & 0 & 0 & 0 & 0 & 0 \\
\ddots & \vdots & \vdots & \vdots & \vdots & \\
\cdots & \binom{2m-1}{2m-5}\frac{1}{5\cdot 7} & 0 & \binom{2m-1}{2m-3}\frac{1}{3\cdot 5} & 0 & \binom{2m-1}{2m-1}\frac{1}{1\cdot 3} \\
\cdots & 0 & \binom{2m}{2m-4}\frac{1}{5\cdot 7} & 0 & \binom{2m}{2m-2}\frac{1}{3\cdot 5} & 0
\end{array}\right|
$$

$$
= \mathcal{D}_{2m+1}
$$

for $m \ge 0$. Consequently, we have the series expansion

$$
G(x) = \sum_{m=0}^{\infty} G^{(2m)}\frac{x^{2m}}{(2m)!} = \sum_{m=0}^{\infty} 3^{2m+1}\mathcal{D}_{2m+1}\frac{x^{2m}}{(2m)!}.
$$

The proof of Theorem 7 is complete. □

Remark 8. *Comparing the series expansions (16) and (18), we acquire the relation*

$$
D_{2m} = \mathcal{D}_{2m+1}, \quad m \ge 0. \tag{19}
$$

We note that the elements of D_{2m} contain products of the Bernoulli numbers B_{2k} and binomial coefficients, while the elements of $\mathcal{D}_{2m+1}$ just contain products of common fractions and binomial coefficients.

Can one verify relation (19) by a linear algebraic operation?

Remark 9. *The determinants D_{2m} and $\mathcal{D}_{2m+1}$ are both connected with the van der Pol numbers V_{2k} via the relation (17) and*

$$
V_{2k} = (-1)^k\left(\frac{3}{2}\right)^{2k}\mathcal{D}_{2k+1}, \quad k \ge 2. \tag{20}
$$

Remark 10. *When $m = 2$ and $m = 1$, we acquire*

$$\mathcal{D}_5 = \begin{vmatrix} 1 & \frac{1}{1\cdot3} & 0 & 0 & 0 \\ 0 & 0 & \binom{1}{1}\frac{1}{1\cdot3} & 0 & 0 \\ \frac{-1}{3} & \frac{-1}{3\cdot5} & 0 & \binom{2}{2}\frac{1}{1\cdot3} & 0 \\ 0 & 0 & \binom{3}{1}\frac{-1}{3\cdot5} & 0 & \binom{2}{2}\frac{1}{1\cdot3} \\ \frac{1}{5} & \frac{1}{5\cdot7} & 0 & \binom{4}{2}\frac{-1}{3\cdot5} & 0 \end{vmatrix} = -\frac{8}{14{,}175}$$

and

$$\mathcal{D}_3 = \begin{vmatrix} 1 & \frac{1}{1\cdot3} & 0 \\ 0 & 0 & \binom{1}{1}\frac{1}{1\cdot3} \\ \frac{-1}{3} & \frac{-1}{3\cdot5} & 0 \end{vmatrix} = -\frac{2}{135}.$$

Therefore, the relation (19) is confirmed for $m = 1, 2$.

7. Conclusions

In this paper, we established the following results.

1. Three determinantal expressions (9), (17), and (20) for the van der Pol numbers V_{2k} with $k \ge 2$ were derived in Theorem 1 and Remarks 7 and 9.
2. An identity (10) for the Bernoulli numbers B_{2k} with $k \ge 1$ was deduced in Theorem 2.
3. An identity (11) for the van der Pol numbers V_{2k} with $k \ge 1$ was acquired in Theorem 3.
4. A determinantal expression (13) for the van der Pol numbers V_n with $n \ge 1$ was presented in Theorem 4.
5. The even function $G(x)$ defined by (4) was proven in Theorem 5 to be decreasing in $[0, R) \supset [0, \pi]$ and to be concave in $[0, \pi] \subset [0, R)$.
6. Two Maclaurin power series expansions ((16) and (18)) of the function $G(x)$, whose coefficients are expressed in terms of specific Hessenberg determinants with elements containing the Bernoulli numbers B_{2k}, were discovered in Theorems 6 and 7.

Author Contributions: Writing—original draft, Z.-Y.S., B.-N.G. and F.Q. All authors contributed equally to the manuscript. All authors have read and agreed to the published version of the manuscript.

Funding: This research received no external funding.

Institutional Review Board Statement: Not applicable.

Informed Consent Statement: Not applicable.

Data Availability Statement: Not applicable.

Acknowledgments: The authors are grateful to three anonymous reviewers for their positive recommendation and high assessment of the original version of this paper.

Conflicts of Interest: The authors declare no conflict of interest.

References

1. van der Pol, B. Smoothing and "unsmoothing". In *Probability and Related Topics in Physical Sciences*; Kac, M., Ed.; Amer Mathematical Society: New York, NY, USA, 1957; pp. 223–235.
2. Howard, F.T. Properties of the van der Pol numbers and polynomials. *J. Reine Angew. Math.* **1973**, *260*, 35–46. [CrossRef]
3. Moll, V.H.; Vignat, C. On polynomials connected to powers of Bessel functions. *Int. J. Number Theory* **2014**, *10*, 1245–1257. [CrossRef]
4. Kishore, N. A structure of the Rayleigh polynomial. *Duke Math. J.* **1964**, *31*, 513–518. [CrossRef]
5. Kishore, N. Binary property of the Rayleigh polynomial. *Duke Math. J.* **1965**, *32*, 429–435. [CrossRef]
6. Kishore, N. Congruence properties of the Rayleigh functions and polynomials. *Duke Math. J.* **1968**, *35*, 557–562. [CrossRef]
7. Kishore, N. The Rayleigh polynomial. *Proc. Amer. Math. Soc.* **1964**, *15*, 911–917. [CrossRef]

8. Hong, Y.; Guo, B.-N.; Qi, F. Determinantal expressions and recursive relations for the Bessel zeta function and for a sequence originating from a series expansion of the power of modified Bessel function of the first kind. *CMES Comput. Model. Eng. Sci.* **2021**, *129*, 409–423. [CrossRef]
9. Abramowitz, M.; Stegun, I.A. (Eds.) *Handbook of Mathematical Functions with Formulas, Graphs, and Mathematical Tables*; National Bureau of Standards, Applied Mathematics Series 55, Reprint of the 1972 edition; Dover Publications, Inc.: New York, NY, USA, 1992.
10. Henrici, P. *Applied and Computational Complex Analysis*; Volume 1, Pure and Applied Mathematics; Wiley-Interscience [John Wiley & Sons]: New York, NY, USA; London, UK; Sydney, Australia, 1974.
11. Bourbaki, N. *Elements of Mathematics: Functions of a Real Variable: Elementary Theory*; Translated from the 1976 French original by Philip Spain; Elements of Mathematics (Berlin); Springer: Berlin/Heidelberg, Germany, 2004. [CrossRef]
12. Qi, F.; Niu, D.-W.; Lim, D.; Yao, Y.-H. Special values of the Bell polynomials of the second kind for some sequences and functions. *J. Math. Anal. Appl.* **2020**, *491*, 124382. [CrossRef]

axioms

MDPI

Article

Pricing of Credit Risk Derivatives with Stochastic Interest Rate

Wujun Lv and Linlin Tian *

College of Science, Donghua University, Shanghai 201620, China; lvwujun@dhu.edu.cn
* Correspondence: linlin.tian@dhu.edu.cn

Abstract: This paper deals with a credit derivative pricing problem using the martingale approach. We generalize the conventional reduced-form credit risk model for a credit default swap market, assuming that the firms' default intensities depend on the default states of counterparty firms and that the stochastic interest rate follows a jump-diffusion Cox–Ingersoll–Ross process. First, we derive the joint Laplace transform of the distribution of the vector process (r_t, R_t) by applying piecewise deterministic Markov process theory and martingale theory. Then, using the joint Laplace transform, we obtain the explicit pricing of defaultable bonds and a credit default swap. Lastly, numerical examples are presented to illustrate the dynamic relationships between defaultable securities (defaultable bonds, credit default swap) and the maturity date.

Keywords: reduced-form model; jump-diffusion CIR (JCIR) model; piecewise deterministic Markov process theory; martingale theory; defaultable bonds; credit default swap (CDS)

MSC: 91G30; 91G40

1. Introduction

Efficient tools for the management of credit risk in portfolios are always in high demand in financial institutions. This leads to a specialized market for credit derivatives. Due to the initiation of the credit derivatives market in the early 1990s, credit derivatives have maintained robust growth in the past decades. Being an enormous market that already surpasses the debt one, it has been attracting increasing research interest. For the modeling of credit risk in credit-risky securities markets, depending on the formulation, there are two well-established fundamental models available at present, i.e. the so-called reduced-form model [1–3] and the structural model [4,5]. In the reduced-form model, the influences on the default are assumed to be dominated by exogenous factors, for example, policies from the government; meanwhile, structural models mainly focus on endogenous factors—more specifically, the asset allocation of firms. Compared with the structural one, the reduced-form model is believed to be easier for constructing a tractable formula explaining the price of credit-risky securities in terms of economic covariates, which facilitates the estimation. In this work, we mainly focus on the reduced-form model.

There is a long history of insights into credit risk in the credit derivatives market with the reduced-form model, going back to the 1990s. When describing dependency default risks, bottom-up models as well as top-down models are commonly used. Bottom-up models focus on modeling default intensities of individual reference entities to characterize a portfolio default intensity. For more developments of bottom-up models, references [6–8] are highly recommended. The top-down models mainly focus on modeling default at the portfolio level; in other words, the default intensity of the entire investment portfolio is modeled without reference to the constituent names. Some works on top-down models are included in [9–11]. In our paper, we focus on bottom-up models.

In bottom-up models, the default intensity is generally assumed to be a stochastic process, while the relevant randomness is built up from state variables. Moreover, a further consideration of credit contagion is then pioneered by [12] (the so-called DL model) to incorporate the concentration risk in credit portfolios. In the meantime, the emergence of certain special phenomena—for instance, the banking crisis—reveals one of the defects of the conventional reduced-form models, which did not possess a full consideration of credit risk sources. Accordingly, a model with the concept of counterparty risk was brought forward by [7]. In recent years many scholars have considered this factor, for example in [13–18]. In conjunction with the credit contagion, this model emphasizes the so-called primary–secondary framework, which simplifies the payoff structure. The default intensity in such a framework is assumed to be mainly decided by the default state of the counterparty and the economy-wide state variables that follow the Vasicek process (see e.g., [19]). In addition, [13,15,16,20,21] also involved the effects of various other factors (such as the settlement risk, the replacement cost, credit rating, Markov Regime-Switching) in the pricing of CDSs. However, further effects are still desired for improving these models to better characterize the credit derivatives market.

One of the essential aspects of a fine modeling of credit risk is the proper addressing of the dynamic changes of economy-wide state variables. Among all economy-wide state variables, we only consider the risk-free interest rate in this work. As the mean reversion may come from the underlying macro-economic currents, or the corrections on account of bond market overreaction, the Cox–Ingersoll–Ross (CIR) process (for more details, see [22]) is applied to characterize the interest rate fluctuation [23–27]. This process covers the defect of the Vasicek model that makes it possible to get negative interest rates. In the CIR process, the volatility term $\theta\sqrt{r(t)}$ will approach zero when the interest rate gets close to zero, which cancels the effects of the randomness. Thus, the interest rate in such a case remains positive. Meanwhile, the volatility takes high value when the interest rate is high, which is a desired property for modeling. Moreover, in practice, when a primary event takes place, e.g., a change in monetary policies, there will be a positive jump in the interest rate process. Such a jump will be suppressed by the government over time. Then, the process continues until it is taken over by another jump caused by a new event. Therefore, to depict such a phenomenon, we consider a jump-diffusion Cox–Ingersoll–Ross (JCIR) process.

In this paper, we propose a revised reduced-form model [28]. It incorporates the assumption that the firms' default intensities are related to the default states of counterparty firms and the stochastic interest rate driven by the jump-diffusion Cox–Ingersoll–Ross (JCIR) process. This model, to some extent, is more in accordance with the actual CDS market than that of classical work [7]. The primary intention of this article is to derive an explicit expression for the joint Laplace transform of the distribution of the risk-free interest rate-related vector process (r_t, R_t) by applying the piecewise deterministic Markov process theory. The piecewise deterministic Markov process theory was developed by [29] and has been proven to be a very powerful mathematical tool in the field of non-diffusion models. Using the joint Laplace transform, we obtain the explicit pricing of defaultable bonds and default swap rates. Finally, according to this explicit expression, we present the dynamic relations between defaultable securities and the maturity date.

The rest of this paper is organized as follows. In Section 2, we present the setup of the counterparty structure. In Section 3, we derive the joint Laplace transform of the distribution of the vector process (r_t, R_t), and the pricing formulae for defaultable bonds are derived. Meanwhile, with several examples, we also explore the impact of counterparty risk and spot interest rate on bond pricing. In Section 4, we extend our model to the pricing of credit default swaps and the importance of default correlation and spot interest rate models in pricing a default swap. In Section 5, conclusive remarks and further academic challenges are presented.

2. Reduced-Form Model

In this section, to construct the model, a collection of doubly stochastic Poisson processes are assumed to represent the default. Then, the primary–secondary framework is applied to further simplify the subsequent exposition.

2.1. Model Setup

To set up the model, the filtered probability space $(\Omega, \mathscr{F}, \{\mathscr{F}\}_{t=0}^{T^*}, \mathbb{P})$ is used for the uncertainty in the economy, while X_t, an $\mathbb{R}^d$-valued process, and point processes N^i ($i = 1, \cdots, I$) are assumed to indicate the d economy-wide state variables and the default processes of firm i, respectively. N^i is 0 initially and changes to 1 once the default takes place. Denoting τ_i as the relevant default time, the default process of firm i could be presented as $N_t^i = 1_{\{\tau^i \le t\}}$. Then, the filtration could be generated according to X_t and N_t^i as

$$\mathscr{F}_t = \mathscr{F}_t^X \vee \mathscr{F}_t^1 \vee \cdots \vee \mathscr{F}_t^I,$$

with

$$\mathscr{F}_t^X = \sigma(X_s, 0 \le s \le t) \quad \text{and} \quad \mathscr{F}_t^i = \sigma(N_s^i, 0 \le s \le t)$$

being the filtrations obtained from X_t and N_t^i, respectively.

In addition, we indicate the filtration generated by the default process of all firms but the ith one as

$$\mathscr{F}_t^{-i} = \mathscr{F}_t^1 \vee \cdots \vee \mathscr{F}_t^{i-1} \vee \mathscr{F}_t^{i+1} \vee \cdots \vee \mathscr{F}_t^I.$$

Thus, $\mathscr{F}_{T^*}^X \vee \mathscr{F}_{T^*}^{-i}$ embraces the full information up to time T^* on the state variables and the default processes of all firms other than that of the ith. We could also choose an intensity process λ_t^i, for $t \in [0, T^*]$, being non-negative and $\mathscr{F}_{T^*}^X \vee \mathscr{F}_{T^*}^{-i}$-measurable, with

$$\int_0^t \lambda_s^i ds < \infty, \mathbb{P} - a.s.,$$

so that a Poisson process N^i can be defined.

2.2. Primary–Secondary Framework

As a typical case, in this work, we discuss the default probability of a commercial bank. We assume that bank A owns a large amount of debt from firm B. However, it is normally not vice versa, and thus not possible to affect B's default probability. Thus, we implement the constraints as follows. All I firms considered could be separated into two incompatible types, i.e., S_1 primary firms and the rest $I - S_1$ secondary firms. The default processes of the primary firms only depend on state variables, while those of secondary firms depend on both the state variables and the default status of the primary firms.

To start with, under probability measure $\mathbb{P}$, for the S_1 primary firms, there is a sequence of independent unit exponential random variables, $\{e^i, 1 \le i \le S_1\}$, being also independent of X_t. Thus, the relevant default times can be defined as

$$\tau^i = \inf\{t : \int_0^t \lambda_s^i ds \ge e^i\}, \quad 1 \le i \le S_1, \tag{1}$$

with λ_t^i adapted to $\mathscr{F}_t^X$, while the conditional and unconditional survival probability distributions of primary firm i are given by

$$\mathbb{P}(\tau^i > t | \mathscr{F}_{T^*}^X) = \exp(-\textstyle\int_0^t \lambda_s^i ds), \;\; t \in [0, T^*], \tag{2}$$

$$\mathbb{P}(\tau^i > t) = \mathbb{E}[\exp(-\textstyle\int_0^t \lambda_s^i ds)], \;\; t \in [0, T^*]. \tag{3}$$

Since the primary firms' default processes only depend on X_t, we denote their default intensities by

$$\lambda_t^i = a_{0,t}^i, \quad 1 \le i \le S_1. \tag{4}$$

Then, we proceed to the secondary default processes. Similarly, for the $I - S_1$ secondary firms, there is also a sequence of relevant independent variables, $\{e^j, S_1+1 \leq j \leq I\}$, being independent of X_t and $\{\tau^i, 1 \leq i \leq S_1\}$ as well. Hence, the default times can be defined as

$$\tau^j = \inf\{t : \int_0^t \lambda_s^j ds \geq e^j\}, \quad S_1+1 \leq j \leq I, \tag{5}$$

with λ_t^j adapted to $\mathscr{F}_t^X \vee \mathscr{F}_t^1 \vee \cdots \vee \mathscr{F}_t^{S_1}$, while the conditional and unconditional survival probability distributions of secondary firm j are expressed as

$$\mathbb{P}(\tau^j > t | \mathscr{F}_{T^*}^X \vee \mathscr{F}_{T^*}^1 \vee \cdots \vee \mathscr{F}_{T^*}^{S_1}) = \exp(-\textstyle\int_0^t \lambda_s^j ds), \ \ t \in [0, T^*], \tag{6}$$

$$\mathbb{P}(\tau^j > t) = \mathbb{E}[\exp(-\textstyle\int_0^t \lambda_s^j ds)], \ \ t \in [0, T^*]. \tag{7}$$

Since the default processes of secondary firms depend on X_t and the default processes of primary firms, we denote the default intensities by

$$\lambda_t^j = a_{0,t}^j + \sum_{k=1}^{S_1} a_{k,t}^j 1_{\{\tau^k \leq t\}}, \quad S_1+1 \leq j \leq I, \tag{8}$$

with $a_{k,t}^j$ adapted to $\mathscr{F}_t^X$. The default of firm k, according to the sign of $a_{k,t}^j$, can either increase ($a_{k,t}^j > 0$) or decrease ($a_{k,t}^j < 0$) the default probability of firm j. In addition, a more general default intensity can be achieved by involving the interactions of the indicator functions.

According to the assumptions above, we now derive the explicit pricing formulae of defaultable bonds and default swap rates in Sections 3 and 4, respectively.

3. Defaultable Bonds

In this section, we derive the pricing formulae for defaultable bonds. First, we present the general formulae for bonds in the primary–secondary framework that fulfills the assumptions in the previous sections. Under the equivalent martingale measure $\mathbb{P}$, the prices of the default-free and defaultable bonds are, respectively, given by

$$p(t,T) = \mathbb{E}[\exp(-\int_t^T r_s ds) | \mathscr{F}_t], \tag{9}$$

$$V^i(t,T) = \beta^i p(t,T) + 1_{\{\tau^i > t\}}(1-\beta^i)\mathbb{E}[\exp(-\int_t^T (r_s + \lambda_s^i) ds) | \mathscr{F}_t], \tag{10}$$

where β^i is the recovery rate of defaultable bond i, and $t \leq T < T^*$. Here, to reduce derivation complexity, we assume the recovery rate to be a constant for obtaining a simple martingale pricing formula. Obviously, due to (10), the prices of risky bonds consist of two parts, i.e., the recovery rate β^i and the rest factor $1 - \beta^i$, both discounted to t. The first part could be calculated explicitly, while the second one could be obtained in the absence of default. Moreover, the second part, being discounted at the adjusted spot rate, presents the default risk in the model. Therefore, the pricing under $\mathbb{P}$ depends on the expectation in (10).

Then, in the following, we assume firm A and B to be the primary and secondary firm, respectively. The default of firm A is independent of the default risk of others, while that of firm B depends on the default risk of firm A. Both firm A and B's default risk depends on the interest rate, which could be owing to the firms' big cash demands for debt repayments. In this work, we only consider the simple case, with the default intensities following the linear relations:

$$\lambda_t^A = b_0^A + b_1^A r_t, \tag{11}$$

$$\lambda_t^B \quad = \quad b_0^B + b_1^B r_t + b 1_{\{\tau^A \le t\}}, \tag{12}$$

where $b_0^A, b_1^A, b_0^B, b_1^B$, and b are positive constants. The only economy-wide state variable we account for here is the risk-free interest rate, which, more specifically, follows an extended CIR process with positive jumps:

$$dr_t = \alpha(\eta - r_t)dt + \theta\sqrt{r_t}dW_t + dJ_t, \tag{13}$$

where we assume that $\alpha, \eta, \theta \ge 0$, $J_t = \sum_{i=1}^{M_t} Y_i$. M_t is a Poisson process with frequency ρ, which indicates the total number of jumps up to time t. $\{Y_i, i \ge 1\}$ are the sizes of the jumps and are assumed to be independent and identically distributed random variables following a distribution function $F(x)(x > 0)$. When the value of the CIR process approaches 0, the behavior of such a process relies on its parameters. There are several conditions that assure that the jump-CIR process (13) remains strictly positive. We list those conditions as follows:

1. $\theta^2 \le 2\alpha\eta$. This condition is needed to guarantee $r_t > 0$ with probability 1 if $r_0 > 0$, 0 is not accessible, and the process never blows up to ∞. Since r_t follows a classical CIR process, the Feller condition $\theta^2 \le 2\alpha\eta$ assures that $r_t > 0$. Specifically, the probability of no jumps on a given time interval is positive, which also strengthens the importance of $\theta^2 \le 2\alpha\eta$. If $\theta^2 > 2\alpha\eta$, the process r_t will repeatedly cross zero and reflect at zero.
2. $F(Y_i) \in \mathcal{F}_{t-}$ $F(Y_i)$ is the distribution of Y_i, which ensures the Markov property of the r_t. That is, if one can predict the exact jump timing and jump-size at an instant before a jump occurs, one can make an arbitrarily large profit with certainty.
3. $EY_i \in [0, \infty)$, $-r_{t-} < Y_i < \infty$ at $M_t = 1$, which preserves non-negative jump intensity and a positive instantaneous volatility. For a more specific description about the conditions where the jump-CIR process remains strictly positive, one can refer to [30].

Comparing with the Vasicek model, the CIR process possesses the properties of mean-reverting and non-negativity, which is of better modeling for interest rates. When $\eta = \theta = 0$, then JCIR processes reduce to shot noise processes, which are widely used in various fields, e.g., actuarial science, mathematical finance and electronics. Accordingly, investigating JCIR processes has important academic value and application value.

In the following, a critical lemma is brought out to price credit securities. We can refer to [31] for specific proof methods via martingale theory as well as piecewise deterministic Markov process theory.

Lemma 1. *Assume that $\mu \ge 0$, $k \ge 0$, then the joint Laplace transform of the distribution of (r_t, R_t) (let $R_t = \int_0^t r_u du$) is*

$$\begin{aligned} g(\mu, k, t, T) &= \mathbb{E}\{e^{-\mu r_T} e^{-k(R_T - R_t)} | \mathscr{F}_t^r\} \\ &= \exp(-B_{\mu,k}(t,T) r_t) \exp\left(\frac{\alpha^2 \eta (T-t)}{\theta^2}\right) (C_{\mu,k}(t,T))^{-\frac{2\alpha\eta}{\theta^2}} \\ &\quad \times \exp(-\rho \int_0^{T-t} [1 - h(B_{\mu,k}(0,u))] du), \end{aligned} \tag{14}$$

where

$$h(B_{\mu,k}(0,u)) = \int_0^\infty e^{-B_{\mu,k}(0,u)x} dF(x), \tag{15}$$

$$B_{\mu,k}(t,T) = \frac{(2k - \alpha\mu) + \mu\sqrt{\alpha^2 + 2k\theta^2} coth(\sqrt{\alpha^2 + 2k\theta^2}(T-t)/2)}{(\theta^2\mu + \alpha) + \sqrt{\alpha^2 + 2k\theta^2} coth(\sqrt{\alpha^2 + 2k\theta^2}(T-t)/2)}, \tag{16}$$

$$C_{\mu,k}(t,T) \quad = \quad cosh(\sqrt{\alpha^2 + 2k\theta^2}(T-t)/2)$$

$$+(\theta^2\mu+\alpha)(\alpha^2+2k\theta^2)^{-\frac{1}{2}}sinh(\sqrt{\alpha^2+2k\theta^2}(T-t)/2). \quad (17)$$

Proof. 1. (Construct a martingale) Setting the infinitesimal generator operator $\mathscr{A}$ to 0, we construct a martingale. Let $f(R,r,t) = \exp\{-G(t)r - kR + H(t)\}$. By [32], letting $\mathscr{A}f(R,r,t) = 0$, we have

$$-G^{'}(t)r + H^{'}(t) - kr - \alpha(\eta - r)G(t) + \frac{1}{2}\theta^2 rG^2(t) + \rho[y(G(t)) - 1] = 0. \quad (18)$$

Solving Equation (18), we get

$$\begin{cases} -G^{'}(t) - k + \alpha G(t) + \frac{1}{2}\theta^2 G^2(t) = 0, \\ H^{'}(t) - \alpha\eta G(t) + \rho[y(G(t)) - 1] = 0. \end{cases} \quad (19)$$

By solving the above coupled equations, we can get the explicit expression of $G(t)$ and $H(t)$. Then for $l > 0$ and $k \geq 0$, when $0 \leq t < \frac{l}{\sqrt{\alpha^2+2k\theta^2}}$, $\exp\{-G(t)r_t - kR_t + \rho\int_0^t[1 - y(G(u))]du + \alpha\eta\int_0^t G(u)du\}$ is a martingale, where

$$y(\phi) = \int_0^\infty e^{-\phi x}dF(x), \quad (20)$$

and

$$G(t) = -\frac{\alpha}{\theta^2} - \frac{\sqrt{\alpha^2 + +2k\theta^2}}{\theta^2}\coth\left(\frac{\sqrt{\alpha^2+2k\theta^2}t - l}{2}\right). \quad (21)$$

2. (Laplace transforms of the distributions of r_t and R_t) For an arbitrary fixed time $t(0 \leq s \leq t < \frac{l}{\sqrt{\alpha^2+2k\theta^2}})$, by the properties of martingale, we have

$$\begin{aligned} &\mathbb{E}\{\exp\{-G(t)r_t - kR_t + \rho\int_0^t[1 - y(G(u))]du + \alpha\eta\int_0^t G(u)du\}|\mathscr{F}_s^r\} \\ &= \exp\{-G(s)r_s - kR_s + \rho\int_0^s[1 - y(G(u))]du + \alpha\eta\int_0^s G(u)du\}. \end{aligned} \quad (22)$$

Then,

$$\begin{aligned} &\mathbb{E}\{\exp\{-G(t)r_t - k(R_t - R_s)\}|\mathscr{F}_s^r\} \\ &= \exp\{-G(s)r_s\}\exp\{-\rho\int_s^t[1 - y(G(u))]du\}\exp\{-\alpha\eta\int_s^t G(u)du\}. \end{aligned} \quad (23)$$

Set $G(t) = \mu \geq 0$. By (21), we have

$$l = \sqrt{\alpha^2+2k\theta^2}t - \ln\frac{\mu\theta^2 + \alpha - \sqrt{\alpha^2+2k\theta^2}}{\mu\theta^2 + \alpha + \sqrt{\alpha^2+2k\theta^2}}. \quad (24)$$

From (24), we easily get that $l > \sqrt{\alpha^2+2k\theta^2}t$, i.e., $t < \frac{l}{\sqrt{\alpha^2+2k\theta^2}}$. Substituting (24) in to $G(s)$, we get

$$\begin{aligned} G(s) &= B_{\mu,k}(s,t) \\ &= \frac{(2k - \alpha\mu) + \mu\sqrt{\alpha^2+2k\theta^2}coth(\sqrt{\alpha^2+2k\theta^2}(t-s)/2)}{(\theta^2\mu + \alpha) + \sqrt{\alpha^2+2k\theta^2}coth(\sqrt{\alpha^2+2k\theta^2}(t-s)/2)}, \end{aligned} \quad (25)$$

then, we have

$$\begin{aligned} &\mathbb{E}\{\exp\{-G(t)r_t - k(R_t - R_s)\}|\mathscr{F}_s^r\} \\ &= \exp\{-B_{\mu,k}(s,t)r_s\}\exp\{-\rho\int_s^t[1 - y(B_{\mu,k}(u,t))]du\}\exp\{-\alpha\eta\int_s^t B_{\mu,k}(u,t)du\}. \end{aligned} \quad (26)$$

For the right side of (26), letting $v = t - u$ and by integral calculation, we get the results of Lemma 1. □

Until now, the closed-form solution of the Laplace transforms of r_t and R_t are derived. Setting $\mu = 0$ and $k = 0$ in (14) gives the following corollaries.

Corollary 1. *Assume that $\mu \geq 0$, $k \geq 0$; then, the Laplace transforms of the distributions of r_t and R_t are, respectively,*

$$\begin{aligned} &\mathbb{E}\{e^{-\mu r_T}|\mathscr{F}_t^r\} \\ =\ &\exp(-B_{\mu,0}(t,T)r_t)\exp\left(\frac{\alpha^2\eta(T-t)}{\theta^2}\right)(C_{\mu,0}(t,T))^{-\frac{2\alpha\eta}{\theta^2}} \\ &\times\exp(-\rho\int_0^{T-t}[1-h(B_{\mu,0}(0,u))]du), \end{aligned} \tag{27}$$

and

$$\begin{aligned} &\mathbb{E}\{e^{-k(R_T-R_t)}|\mathscr{F}_t^r\} \\ =\ &\exp(-B_{0,k}(t,T)r_t)\exp\left(\frac{\alpha^2\eta(T-t)}{\theta^2}\right)(C_{0,k}(t,T))^{-\frac{2\alpha\eta}{\theta^2}} \\ &\times\exp(-\rho\int_0^{T-t}[1-h(B_{0,k}(0,u))]du). \end{aligned} \tag{28}$$

For mathematical simplicity, the jump size $\{Y_i, i \geq 1\}$ is assumed to be exponentially distributed; in other words,

$$F(x) = 1 - e^{-\omega x}(\omega > 0, x > 0).$$

As a special case of Corollary 1, the following corollary is presented.

Corollary 2. *Assume that $\mu \geq 0$, $k \geq 0$, and the distribution of jump sizes is $F(x) = 1 - e^{-\omega x}(\omega > 0, x > 0)$; then, the Laplace transforms of the distributions of r_t and R_t are*

$$\begin{aligned} &\mathbb{E}\{e^{-\mu r_T}|\mathscr{F}_t^r\} \\ =\ &\exp(-B_{\mu,0}(t,T)r_t)\exp\left(\frac{\alpha^2\eta(T-t)}{\theta^2}\right)(C_{\mu,0}(t,T))^{-\frac{2\alpha\eta}{\theta^2}} \\ &\times\left(\frac{2\alpha(\omega+\mu)\exp(\alpha(T-t))}{\omega(\theta^2\mu+2\alpha)\exp(\alpha(T-t))+(2\alpha\mu-\omega\theta^2\mu)}\right)^{-\frac{2\rho}{2\alpha-\omega\theta^2}}, \end{aligned} \tag{29}$$

and

$$\begin{aligned} &\mathbb{E}\{e^{-k(R_T-R_t)}|\mathscr{F}_t^r\} \\ =\ &\exp(-B_{0,k}(t,T)r_t)\exp\{H_1(k)(T-t)+H_2(k)\ln D_k(t,T)-H_3\ln C_{0,k}(t,T)\}. \end{aligned} \tag{30}$$

where

$$D_k(t,T) = \cosh(\sqrt{\alpha^2+2k\theta^2}(T-t)/2) + \frac{\omega\alpha+2k}{\alpha\sqrt{\alpha^2+2k\theta^2}}\sinh(\alpha^2+2k\theta^2(T-t)/2),$$

$$H_1(k) = \frac{\alpha^2\eta(T-t)}{\theta^2} - \frac{2k\rho}{\omega(\sqrt{\alpha^2+2k\theta^2}+\alpha)+2k} - \frac{\omega\rho\sqrt{\alpha^2+2k\theta^2}}{2k+2\omega\alpha-\omega^2\theta^2},$$

$$H_2(k) = \frac{2\omega\rho}{2k+2\omega\alpha-\omega^2\theta^2},$$

$$H_3 = \frac{2\alpha\eta}{\theta^2}.$$

Thus, from (10) and Lemma 1, we can derive the pricing formulae of defaultable bonds. The time-t prices of the A- and B-bond with maturity date T will be shown in the following theorem.

Theorem 1. *In the primary–secondary framework, assume that firm A and firm B have the same maturity date with 0-valued recovery rate ($\beta^A = 0, \beta^B = 0$). Suppose that intensity process λ_t^A satisfies* (11) *and process λ_t^B satisfies* (12)*; then, the time-t prices of the bonds issued by primary firm A and secondary firm B, respectively, are*

$$V^A(t,T) = \mathbb{E}[e^{-(1+b_1^A)(R_T-R_t)}|\mathscr{F}_t^r]e^{-b_0^A(T-t)} = g(0, 1+b_1^A, t, T)e^{-b_0^A(T-t)}, \tag{31}$$

and

$$\begin{aligned} V^B(t,T) &= e^{-(b_0^B+b)(T-t)}g(0,1+b_1^B,t,T) + be^{-(b_0^B+b)T+(b_0^B+b_0^A)t} \\ &\quad \times \int_t^T e^{-(b_0^A-b)s}\cdot \exp\left(\frac{\alpha^2\eta(T-s)}{\theta^2}\right)(C_{0,1+b_1^B}(s,T))^{-\frac{2\alpha\eta}{\theta^2}} \\ &\quad \times \exp(-\rho\int_0^{T-s}[1-h(B_{0,1+b_1^B}(0,u))]du) \\ &\quad \times g(B_{0,1+b_1^B}(s,T), 1+b_1^B+b_1^A, t, s)ds. \end{aligned} \tag{32}$$

Proof. Firstly, from (11) and Lemma 1, we can easily illustrate that (31) holds. Secondly, according to (10), (12), and the property of conditional expectation, we obtain the time-t price of the bond with maturity date T issued by firm B

$$\begin{aligned} V^B(t,T) &= \mathbb{E}[\exp(-\int_t^T (r_s+\lambda_s^B)ds)|\mathscr{F}_t] \\ &= \mathbb{E}[\exp(-b_0^B(T-t)-(1+b_1^B)(R_T-R_t)-b(T-\tau^A)1_{\{\tau^A\le T\}})|\mathscr{F}_t] \\ &= \mathbb{E}[\exp(-b_0^B(T-t)-(1+b_1^B)(R_T-R_t)) \\ &\quad \times \mathbb{E}[\exp(-b(T-\tau^A)1_{\{\tau^A\le T\}})|\mathscr{F}_t\vee\mathscr{F}_{T^*}^r]|\mathscr{F}_t]. \end{aligned} \tag{33}$$

To calculate the time-t price of the B-bond with maturity T, we need to evaluate the conditional expectation embedded in (33). According to (2) and the law of integration by parts, we obtain that

$$\begin{aligned} &\mathbb{E}[\exp(-b(T-\tau^A)1_{\{\tau^A\le T\}})|\mathscr{F}_t\vee\mathscr{F}_{T^*}^r] \\ =\ & (\int_t^T + \int_T^\infty)e^{-b(T-s)1_{\{s\le T\}}}d(1-e^{-b_0^A(s-t)-b_1^A(R_s-R_t)}) \\ =\ & e^{-b(T-t)}(1+b\int_t^T e^{-(b_0^A-b)(s-t)-b_1^A(R_s-R_t)}ds). \end{aligned} \tag{34}$$

Hence, according to the expectation obtained, we get

$$\begin{aligned} V^B(t,T) &= e^{-(b_0^B+b)(T-t)}\mathbb{E}[e^{-(1+b_1^B)(R_T-R_t)}|\mathscr{F}_t] + be^{-(b_0^B+b)T+(b_0^B+b_0^A)t} \\ &\quad \times \int_t^T e^{-(b_0^A-b)s}\mathbb{E}[e^{-(1+b_1^B+b_1^A)(R_s-R_t)-(1+b_1^B)(R_T-R_s)}|\mathscr{F}_t]ds. \end{aligned} \tag{35}$$

For the first expectation term, we easily obtain

$$\mathbb{E}[e^{-(1+b_1^B)(R_T-R_t)}|\mathscr{F}_t] = g(0,1+b_1^B,t,T). \tag{36}$$

Furthermore, using the properties of iterated conditional expectation, we get

$$\begin{aligned}
& \mathbb{E}[e^{-(1+b_1^B+b_1^A)(R_s-R_t)-(1+b_1^B)(R_T-R_s)}|\mathscr{F}_t] \\
= & \mathbb{E}[e^{-(1+b_1^B+b_1^A)(R_s-R_t)} \cdot \mathbb{E}[e^{-(1+b_1^B)(R_T-R_s)}|\mathscr{F}_s]|\mathscr{F}_t] \\
= & \exp\left(\frac{\alpha^2\eta(T-s)}{\theta^2}\right)(C_{0,1+b_1^B}(s,T))^{-\frac{2\alpha\eta}{\theta^2}} \\
& \times \exp(-\rho\int_0^{T-s}[1-h(B_{0,1+b_1^B}(0,u))]du)g(B_{0,1+b_1^B}(s,T),1+b_1^B+b_1^A,t,s). \quad (37)
\end{aligned}$$

Now, substituting (36) and (37) into (35), (32) holds. The proof of Theorem 1 is complete. Next, we will present the numerical results of the yield spread. □

Until now, within the primary–secondary framework, we obtain the explicit pricing of defaultable bonds. Now, we pay attention to the yield spread, which is a function of maturity to explore the effect of counterparty risk on firm B's bond price. In continuous-time modeling, we define the yield spread ψ between defaultable bond v and default-free bond p as

$$\psi(t,T) = -\frac{1}{T-t}\ln\frac{v(t,T)}{p(t,T)}. \quad (38)$$

In the following, we present an example to discuss the term structure of yield spreads between primary firm A and secondary firm B.

Example 1. *Assume that $\beta^A = \beta^B = 0$, then the yield spread of firm B's bond is the corresponding martingale default probability averaged over $T-t$. In the economy, if we ignore the counterparty risk and the short-term interest rate, mathematically speaking, $b = 0$ and $b_1^B = 0$; then, the yield spread will be the constant b_0^B. When $b > 0$ ($b_1^B = 0$), firm B's default is "accelerated" by firm A's default with an increasing pattern in the yield spread. In contrast, a "deceleration" holds when $b < 0$ ($b_1^B = 0$), with the yield spread being a decreasing function of maturity. These effects are illustrated in Figure 1 with some given parameters.*

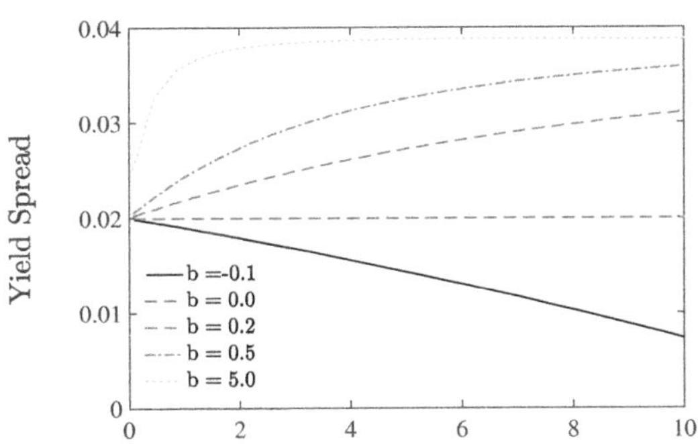

Figure 1. Secondary firm B: term structure of yield spreads with $b_0^B = 0.02, b_1^B = 0, b_0^A = 0.02, b_1^A = 0$. This figure characterizes the term structure of firm B's yield spread under different parameters b = −0.1, 0, 0.2, 0.5, 5.

In contrast with the Markov model based on the ratings of Jarrow et al. [33], in our model, we ignore the interaction between market risk and credit risk. Usually investment-grade issuers' credit spread curves are upward-sloping, while those of speculative-level issuers are tilted downward. However, when the possibility of default is affected by economy-wide risk factors, there will be additional aspects to this problem, as illustrated in Figure 1. Except for Panel (a), obviously, the *shape of the default-free term structure and the coefficient b_1^A jointly determine the term structure of the credit spread.*

When $b_1^B \neq 0$, r_t follows (13)*; here, we assume that the jump's sizes follow an exponential distribution with parameter $\omega > 0$. Since jump process is involved in our model, Equation (32) is far more complex for computing the yield spread compared to that of Figure 1. Futhermore, the shape of a contemporaneous default-free term structure also affects the yield spread. However, we expect the patterns exhibited in Figure 1 to persist. Namely, the yield spread will widen (narrow) over time with the default risk from the long (short) position.*

In Figure 2, this results come from both economy-wide state variables and counterparty risk. We find that jump diffusion risk and counterparty risk have caused significant changes in the effects of different b_1^B on yield spread, while the CIR process dilutes the effect of b_1^B on yield spread, so the impact of b_1^B on yield spread is minimal. Besides these conjectures, in Figure 3, we could also get a way to extract information on the counterparty risk with empirical evidence. The effect of counterparty risk has caused the distortion of the term structure of the primary firms' credit spreads (see Panel (d), (f) of Figure 4), which is basically the re-adjusted default-free term structure. In fact, during estimation, counterparty risk causes the derivation between the credit spread curve and the shape of the default-free term structure. This mainly comes from the simple one-factor term structure model as well as the default process, which only depends on the contemporaneous level of the spot rate. It is easy to extend our model to a multi-factor environment where other macro-economic factors can also affect default.

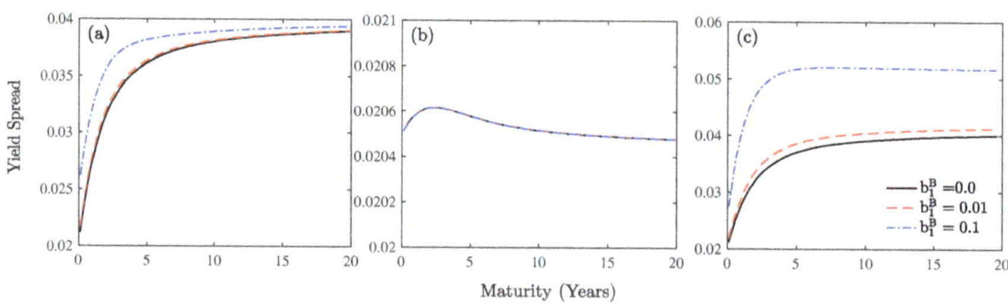

Figure 2. Secondary firm B: term structure of yield spreads with $b_0^A = 0.02, b_1^A = 0.01, b_0^B = 0.02$, $b = 1$ and different $b_1^B = 0.01, 0, -0.01$. Panel (**a**) exhibits a flat default-free term structure. Panel (**b**) assumes the risk-free interest rate follows the CIR process in which the parameters of the CIR model are taken from Wu [31] and Jarrow and Yu [7] with $\alpha = 0.05, \eta = 0.5, \theta = 0.4$. In Panel (**c**), its difference with Panel (**b**) is that interest rate is driven by a jump process, while the parameters are the same, except that $\omega = 2.0, \rho = 0.5$.

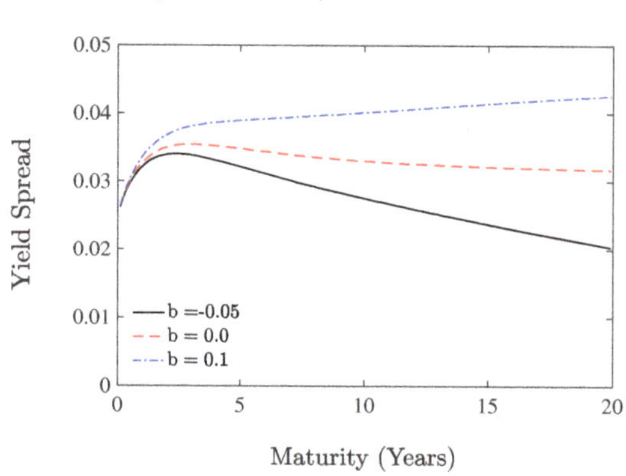

Figure 3. Secondary firm B: term structure of yield spreads $b_0^A = 0.02, b_1^A = 0, b_0^B = 0.02, b_1^B = 0.1$ with different value of $b = -0.05, 0, 0.1$. The risk-free interest rate is assumed to follow the JCIR process in which parameters are chosen from [7,31] with $\alpha = 0.05, \eta = 0.5, \theta = 0.4, \omega = 2.0, \rho = 0.5$.

In Figure 5, we also get the way to extract information on the economy-wide risk with empirical evidence. The secondary firms' possibility of default is affected by economy-wide risk factors, as is illustrated in Figure 4. Compared with Figure 4, interest rate is driven by the jump-diffusion Cox–Ingersoll–Ross (JCIR) process simultaneously in Figure 5. In addition, the default intensity is also correlated to the default states of counterparty firms. From Figure 5, we find that the larger the b_1^B*, the larger the short-term yield spread;* b_1^B *is very sensitive to yield spread, and this phenomenon is completely in line with the facts.*

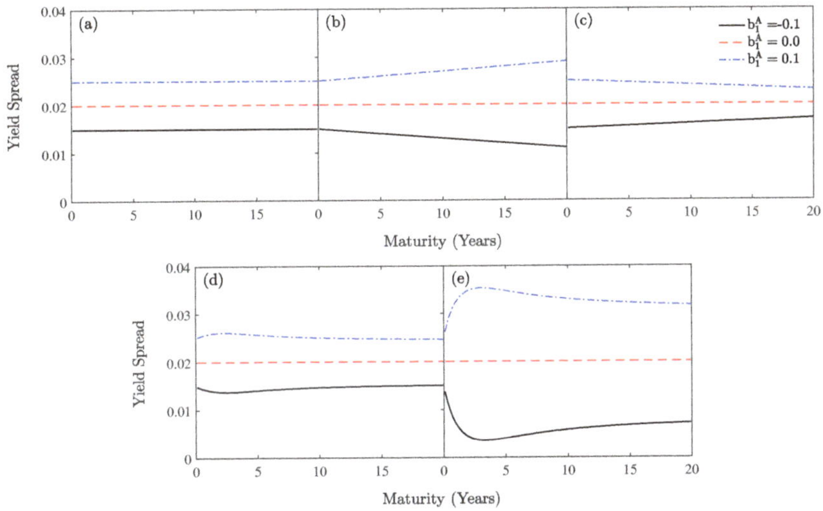

Figure 4. Primary firm A: term structure of yield spreads with initial interest rate $r_0 = 0.05$**,** $b_0^A = 0.02$ **and five different shapes of** r_t**.** The default intensity of firm A is presented in (11), where b_1^A is chosen to be different values $\{0.1, 0, -0.1\}$. Panel (**a**) exhibits a flat default-free term structure. In Panel (**b**), the interest rate is assumed to be a deterministic function of t with slope 0.2%. In Panel (**c**), the interest rate is assumed to be a deterministic function of t with slope -0.1%. Panel (**d**) assumes that the risk-free interest rate follows the CIR process in which the parameters of the CIR model are taken from Wu [31] and Jarrow and Yu [7] with $\alpha = 0.05, \eta = 0.5, \theta = 0.4$. In Panel (**e**), its difference with Panel (**d**) is that interest rate is driven by a jump process, while the parameters are same, except that $\omega = 2.0, \rho = 0.5$.

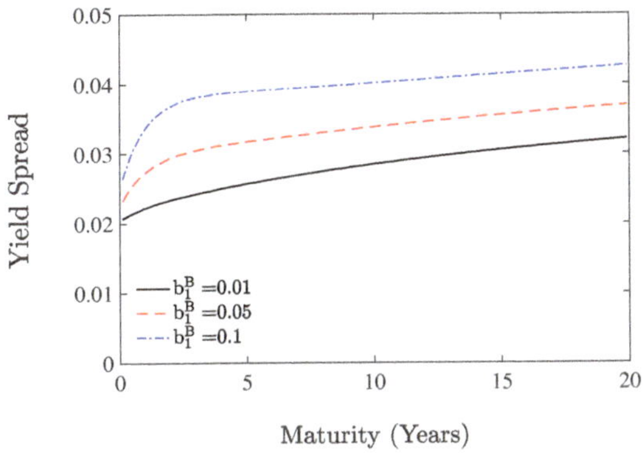

Figure 5. Secondary firm B: term structure of yield spreads with $b_0^A = 0.02, b_1^A = 0, b_0^B = 0.02, b = 0.1$ **and a different value of** $b_1^B = 0.01, 0.05, 0.1$**.** The risk-free interest rate is assumed to follow the JCIR process in which the parameters for the JCIR model are chosen from [7,31] with $\alpha = 0.05, \eta = 0.5, \theta = 0.4, \omega = 2.0, \rho = 0.5$.

4. Default Swap Rates

In this section, based on the results in Section 3, we derive the swap rate in the reduced-form model. We assume that firm C holds bonds from reference firm A, and in the meantime, is a CDS buyer from firm B for a compensation of the possible loss induced by firm A's default. The maturity dates of the bond and the CDS are assumed to be T_1 and T_2 ($T_2 \leq T_1$), respectively. Here, we only consider firm A and B as being the primary and secondary party, respectively. The recovery rate of the bond issued by firm A is assumed to be zero, with its face value being 1 dollar. The swap rate could be obtained by the following theorem.

Theorem 2. *Assume that r_t follows the stochastic differential Equation* (13)*, while λ^A and λ^B satisfy* (11) *and* (12)*, respectively. Then, the swap rate*

$$c = \frac{V^B(0,T_2) - e^{-(b_0^B+b_0^A)T_2}g(0,1+b_1^B+b_1^A,0,T_2)}{\int_0^{T_2} V^C(0,s)ds}, \tag{39}$$

where $g(\mu,k,t,T)$ and $V^B(0,T_2)$, $V^C(0,s)$ are given by Lemma 1 and Theorem 1, respectively.

Proof. First, the time 0 market value of buyer C's payment to B is

$$\mathbb{E}[\int_0^{T_2} \exp(-\int_0^s r_u du)c1_{\{\tau^C>s\}}ds] = c\int_0^{T_2} V^C(0,s)ds, \tag{40}$$

while that of B's promised compensation in the case of A's default is

$$\mathbb{E}[1_{\{\tau^A\leq T_2\}}\exp(-\int_0^{T_2} r_u du)1_{\{\tau^B>T_2\}}]. \tag{41}$$

Thus, using the principle of no-arbitrage, we obtain

$$c = \frac{\mathbb{E}[\exp(-\int_0^{T_2}(r_u+\lambda_u^B)du)] - \mathbb{E}[1_{\{\tau^A>T_2\}}\exp(-\int_0^{T_2}(r_u+\lambda_u^B)du)]}{\int_0^{T_2} V^C(0,s)ds}. \tag{42}$$

A brief inspection of the expression in (42) confirms two intuitions. First, c is equal to zero when the reference asset A is default-free. Second, the swap rate increases with the default probabilities of A and C, and decreases with that of B. For more details, one can refer to Appendix F of [7]. Note that $\int_0^{T_2} V^C(0,s)ds$ and the first term of the numerator of (42), which is equal to $V^B(0,T_2)$, can be derived by (31) and (32), respectively. Substituting (12) into the expectation term above, we obtain

$$\begin{aligned}
&\mathbb{E}[1_{\{\tau^A>T_2\}}\exp(-\int_0^{T_2}(r_u+\lambda_u^B)du)] \\
=\ &\mathbb{E}[1_{\{\tau^A>T_2\}}\exp(-\int_0^{T_2}(b_0^B+(1+b_1^B)r_u+b1_{\{\tau^A\leq u\}})du)] \\
=\ &\mathbb{E}[\mathbb{E}[1_{\{\tau^A>T_2\}}|\mathscr{F}_{T^*}]\exp(-b_0^B T_2-(1+b_1^B)R_{T_2})] \\
=\ &\mathbb{E}[\exp(-b_0^B T_2-(1+b_1^B)R_{T_2}-\int_0^{T_2}\lambda_u^A du)],
\end{aligned} \tag{43}$$

where the second equality involves the property of conditional expectation, the last one follows (2). Substituting (11) into (43), we obtain

$$\begin{aligned}
&\mathbb{E}[\exp(-b_0^B T_2-(1+b_1^B)R_{T_2}-\int_0^{T_2}\lambda_u^A du)] \\
=\ &\exp(-(b_0^B+b_0^A)T_2)g(0,1+b_1^A+b_1^B,0,T_2).
\end{aligned} \tag{44}$$

Now, substituting (44) into (42), (39) holds. The proof of Theorem 2 is complete. □

In conjunction with the pricing results of defaultable bonds, we obtain the explicit formula of default swap rates, which is an important indicator in the risk management market. With given parameters, we can obtain the relevant prices of defaultable bonds and swap rates. However, the method for evaluating the parameters is beyond the scope of our article and is left for future discussion. For an insight into the improvement of the results in our model, the numerical illustrations for swap rate are provided.

Example 2. *We assume that the jump's sizes follow an exponential distribution with parameter $\omega > 0$, and firm C is not defaulted in the past with $V^C(0,s) = E[e^{-R_s}] = g(0,1,0,s)$. We analyze the dynamic relations between the default swap rate c and the maturity date T (T_2 in Theorem 2) for different forms of risk-free interest rate, different mean positive jumps ω, and different counterparty risk levels b. The swap rate decreases with the maturity increasing by intuition.*

Firstly, in panel (a) of Figure 6, in terms of the influence of risk-free interest rate forms chosen, although the swap rate decreases with the same trends, consistent with the intuition, there is a clear difference between the results of our model and the others. The swap rate, compared with applying the JCIR process, is overestimated in the other cases. These results clarify the essential modification of the swap rate when applying JCIR process for the risk-free interest rate.

Secondly, in panel (b) of Figure 6, we find that the default swap rate is notably affected by ω. For larger ω, generally, there will be a higher jump probability in the interest rate process, leading to a more unstable interest rate, which increases the firms' default probability. Meanwhile, the swap rate increases with the default probabilities of firm A, but decreases with that of firm B. Moreover, firm B's default intensities, empirically, play a decisive role in pricing the swap rate. Consequently, as a function of the maturity date, the larger the ω, the slower c decreases, which agrees with the trend obtained in panel (b). This emphasizes the necessity of considering the jump factor in the stochastic interest rate process.

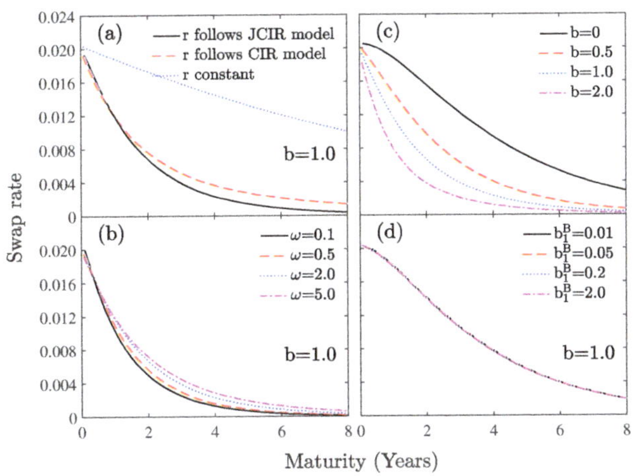

Figure 6. Credit default swap is correlated with the spot interest rate and counterparty risk. For the default swap rate as a function of the maturity date, see the text for detailed parameters. Panel (**a**): results of the models with three forms of risk-free interest rates as indicated in the panel at counterparty risk b=1.0. Panel (**b**): results of our model with different means of positive jumps ω at b=1.0. Panel (**c**): results of our model at different levels of counterparty risk. Panel (**d**): results of our model with different b_1^B. The basic parameters we used are $\alpha = 0.05, \eta = 0.5, \theta = 0.4, \omega = 2.0, \rho = 0.5, r_0 = 0.05, b_0^A = b_0^B = 0.02, b_1^A = b_1^B = 0.01, b = 1.0$, which follow [7,31]; ω, b, b_1^B are chosen to be different values in (**b**–**d**).

Thirdly, according to the results of different b in panel (c) of Figure 6, we find that the default swap rate is significantly overpriced when ignoring the default correlation ($b = 0$). Therefore, it is vital to consider the contagion. A successively higher b indicates an increasing default correlation between the swap seller, B, and the reference asset A. As b becomes very large, we expect the fair swap rate to drop to zero since the default swap is ineffective.

Finally, according to the results of different b_1^B in panel (d) of Figure 6, we discover that when the risk-free interest rate follows the same JCIR process, the default swap rate is affected by b_1^B to a very small extent. From a numerical perspective, in a short period of time, the larger the b_1^B value, the greater the rate of decline of the default swap rate.

5. Conclusions

In this paper, we derive the joint Laplace transform for the distribution of the vector process (r_t, R_t), and using the joint Laplace transform, we obtain explicit pricing formulae of defaultable securities in the primary–secondary framework, where the counterparty relationship among these firms and economy-wide state variables (risk-free interest rate) follow the JCIR process, being able to influence their default probabilities. Such configuration is found to be vital for a better approach to the CDS market. We show that the interaction of market-wide risk factors with company-specific counterparty risks lead to various shapes of term structure for credit spreads. Within such a framework, the pricing of the CDS is shown. In the end, numerical graphics vividly illustrate the effect of exponential distributed jump sizes on the yield spread and CDS.

In addition, it is also of interest and is challenging to further explore other heavy-tailed distributions of the jump sizes, for instance, the Pareto distribution, the Gumbel distribution, and the Féchet distribution. However, the expression of the joint Laplace transform might be implicit.

Author Contributions: Methodology, W.L.; computation, L.T. All authors have read and agreed to the published version of the manuscript.

Funding: The work was sponsored by the Fundamental Research Funds for the Central Universities NO. 2232021D-29, NO. 2232021D-31 and NO. 2232023D-22.

Institutional Review Board Statement: Not applicable.

Informed Consent Statement: Not applicable.

Data Availability Statement: The data presented in this study are available upon request from the corresponding author.

Acknowledgments: The authors thank the editor and the referees for their valuable comments and suggestions, which greatly improved the quality of this paper.

Conflicts of Interest: The authors declare no conflict of interest.

References

1. Jarrow, R.A.; Turnbull, S.M. Pricing options on derivative securities subject to credit risk. *J. Finance* **1995**, *50*, 53–86. [CrossRef]
2. Duffie, D.; Kenneth, S. Modeling term structures of defaultable bonds. *Rev. Financ. Stud.* **1999**, *12*, 687–720. [CrossRef]
3. Hull, J.C.; White, A. Valuing credit default swaps I: No counterparty default risk. *J. Deriv.* **2000**, *8*, 29–40. [CrossRef]
4. Merton, R.C. On the pricing of corporate debt: The risk structure of interest rates. *J. Finance* **1974**, *29*, 449–470.
5. Black, F.; Cox, J. Valuing corporate securities: Some effects of bond indentyre. *J. Finance* **1976**, *31*, 351–367. [CrossRef]
6. Duffie, D.; Gârleanu, N. Risk and valuation of collateralized debt obligations. *Financ. Anal. J.* **2001**, *57*, 41–59. [CrossRef]
7. Jarrow, R. A.; Yu, F. Counterparty risk and the pricing of defaultable securities. *J. Finance* **2001**, *56*, 1765–1799. [CrossRef]
8. Giesecke, K.; Goldberg, L. Sequential defaults and incomplete information. *J. Risk* **2004**, *7*, 1–26. [CrossRef]
9. Brigo, D.; Pallavicini, A.; Torresetti, R. Calibration of CDO tranches with the dynamical generalized Poission loss model. *Risk* **2007**, *20*, 70–75.
10. Giesecke, K.; Goldberg, L.; Ding, X. A top down approach to multi-name credit. *Oper. Res.* **2011**, *59*, 283–300. [CrossRef]
11. Ding, X.W.; Giesecke, K.; Tomecek, P.I. Time-changed birth processes and multiname credit derivatives. *Oper. Res.* **2009**, *57*, 990–1005. [CrossRef]
12. Davis, M.; Lo, V. Infectious defaults. *Quant. Financ.* **2001**, *1*, 382–387. [CrossRef]

13. Dong, Y.; Yuen, K.C.; Wang, G.; Wu, C. A reduced-form model for correlated defaults with regime-switching shot noise intensities. *Methodol. Comput. Appl. Probab.* **2016**, *18*, 459–486. [CrossRef]
14. Chen, Y.; Xing, Y. Credit default swap pricing with counterparty risk in a reduced form model with a common jump process. *Probab. Eng. Inf. Sci.* **2022**, *37*, 275–293. [CrossRef]
15. Dong, Y.; Yuen, K.C.; Wang, G. Valuation of CDS counterparty risk under a reduced-form model with regime-switching shot noise default intensities. *Front. Math. China* **2017**, *12*, 1085–1112. [CrossRef]
16. Guo, J.; Wang, G. A reduced-form model with default intensities containing contagion and regime-switching Vasicek processes. *Front. Math. China* **2018**, *13*, 535–554. [CrossRef]
17. Zhi, K.; Qian, X.; Xie, A. Valuation of *k*th-to-default credit-linked notes with counterparty risk in a reduced-form model. *Commun. Stat.-Theory Methods* **2021**, *4*, 1–24. [CrossRef]
18. Liu, Y.; Hao, R.; Wang, Z. Pricing loan CDS with Vasicek interest rate under the contagious model. *J. Math. Econ.* **2016**, 3, 416–430. [CrossRef]
19. Vasicek, O. An equilibrium characterization of the term structure. *J. Financ. Econ.* **1977**, *5*, 177–188. [CrossRef]
20. Leung, S.Y.; Kwork, Y.K. Credit default swap valuation with counterparty risk. *Kyoto Econ. Rev.* **2005**, *74*, 25–45.
21. Li, W.; Guo, H.; Liang, J.; Brahim, A.B. The valuation of multi-counterparties CDS with credit rating migration. *Appl. Math. Ser. B* **2020**, *35*, 379–391. [CrossRef]
22. Cox, J.; Ingersoll, J.; Ross, S. A theory of term structure of interest rates. *Econometrica* **1985**, *53*, 385–407. [CrossRef]
23. Heston, S.L. A closed form solution for options with stochastic volatility with applications to bond and currency options. *Rev. Financ. Stud.* **1993**, *6*, 327–343. [CrossRef]
24. Trutnau, G. Pathwise uniqueness of the squared Bessel and CIR processes with skew reflection on a deterministic time dependent curve. *Stoch. Proc. Appl.* **2011**, *121*, 1845–1863. [CrossRef]
25. Bao, J.H.; Yuan, C.G. Long-term behavior of stochastic interest rate models with jumps and memory. *Insur. Math. Econ.* **2013**, *53*, 266–272. [CrossRef]
26. Grasselli. M. The 4/2 stochastic volatility model: A unified approach for the heston and the 3/2 model. *Math. Financ.* **2017**, *27*, 1013–1034. [CrossRef]
27. Ballestra, L.V.; Pacelli, G.; Radi, D. Modeling CDS spreads: A comparison of some hybrid approaches. *J. Empir. Financ.* **2020**, *57*, 107–124. [CrossRef]
28. Artzner, P.; Delbaen, F. Default risk insurance and incomplete markets. *Math. Financ.* **1995**, *5*, 187–195. [CrossRef]
29. Davis, M.H. Piecewise-deterministic Markov processes: A general class of non-difiusion stochastic models. *J. R. Statist. Soc. Ser. B* **1984**, *46*, 353–388. [CrossRef]
30. Zhou, H. Jump-diffusion term structure and Itô conditional moment generator. *SSRN Electron. J.* **2001**, 36. [CrossRef]
31. Wu, Y.F. Jump-diffusion CIR model and its applications in credit risk. *Hacet. Bull. Nat. Sci. Eng. Ser. B* **2014**, *43*, 1095–1106. [CrossRef]
32. Jacobsen, M. *Point Process Theory and Applications: Marked Point and Piecewise Deterministic Processes*; Springer Birkhäuser: Boston, MA, USA, 2006.
33. Jarrow, R.A.; Lando, D.; Turnbull, S.M. A Markov model for the term structure of credit risk spreads. *Rev. Financ. Stud.* **1997**, *10*, 481–523. [CrossRef]

axioms

MDPI

Article

On the Study of Pseudo $\mathcal{S}$-Asymptotically Periodic Mild Solutions for a Class of Neutral Fractional Delayed Evolution Equations

Naceur Chegloufa [1,2], Belkacem Chaouchi [3], Marko Kostić [4] and Wei-Shih Du [5,*]

1 Department of Mathematics, Faculty of Sciences, Saad Dahlab University, Blida 09000, Algeria; chegloufa.naceur@etu.univ-blida.dz
2 Lab. LPTHIRM, Faculty of Sciences, Saad Dahlab University, Blida 09000, Algeria
3 Department of Mathematics, Faculty of Science and Technology, UDBKM University, Khemis Miliana 44225, Algeria; chaouchicukm@gmail.com
4 Faculty of Technical Sciences, University of Novi Sad, Trg D. Obradovića 6, 21125 Novi Sad, Serbia; marco.s@verat.net
5 Department of Mathematics, National Kaohsiung Normal University, Kaohsiung 82444, Taiwan
* Correspondence: wsdu@mail.nknu.edu.tw

Abstract: The goal of this paper is to investigate the existence and uniqueness of pseudo $\mathcal{S}$-asymptotically periodic mild solutions for a class of neutral fractional evolution equations with finite delay. We essentially use the fractional powers of closed linear operators, the semigroup theory and some classical fixed point theorems. Furthermore, we provide an example to illustrate the applications of our abstract results.

Keywords: pseudo $\mathcal{S}$-asymptotically periodic function; neutral fractional evolution equation; mild solution; fractional power

MSC: 26D15; 26A33; 60E15

1. Introduction

In this research article, we analyze the existence and uniqueness of pseudo-$\mathcal{S}$-asymptotically periodic mild solutions for the following abstract fractional Cauchy problem

$$\begin{cases} {}^{c}D_t^q(u(t) - G(t,u_t)) + Au(t) = F(t,u_t), & t \geq 0, \\ u(t) = \varphi(t), & -r \leq t \leq 0, \end{cases} \tag{1}$$

where the fractional derivative ${}^{c}D_t^q$, $q \in (0,1)$ is taken in the sense of Caputo approach and $(A, D(A))$ is a closed linear operator in a Banach space $(X, \|\cdot\|)$. We assume that $-A$ generates an exponentially stable analytic semigroup $(T(t))_{t\geq 0}$. Here,

$$F, G : \mathbb{R}^+ \times E \to X,\ r > 0,$$

are two continuous functions, where $\mathbb{R}^+ = [0, \infty)$ and $E = C([-r, 0], X)$. By u_t, we denote the classical history function defined by

$$u_t(s) := u(t+s) \quad \text{ for } -r \leq s \leq 0,$$

while the data $u(\cdot)$ belongs to the space E. Let us recall that a bounded continuous function $f : \mathbb{R}^+ \to X$ is said to be pseudo $\mathcal{S}$-asymptotically periodic if there exists $\omega > 0$ such that

$$\lim_{h\to+\infty} \frac{1}{h} \int_0^h \|f(t+\omega) - f(t)\| \, dt = 0. \tag{2}$$

The class of pseudo $\mathcal{S}$-asymptotically periodic functions was introduced in [1]. In that paper, the authors have considered the classical version of (1) with $q = 1$ and established several interesting results concerning the existence and uniqueness of pseudo $\mathcal{S}$-asymptotically periodic mild solutions for such problems. The class of pseudo $\mathcal{S}$-asymptotically periodic functions is a natural generalization of the class of $\mathcal{S}$-asymptotically periodic functions; see [2]. Consequently, our study can be viewed as an extension and continuation of the research study in [3], where the solvability of problem (1) was discussed and optimal results about the existence and uniqueness of $\mathcal{S}$-asymptotically periodic mild solutions were successfully established. The investigation of existence and uniqueness of pseudo $\mathcal{S}$-asymptotically periodic mild solutions for various classes of the abstract fractional Cauchy problems is an attractive field and was the principal subject of many works. For example, in [4] the authors have examined the existence and uniqueness of pseudo $\mathcal{S}$-asymptotically periodic solutions of the second-order abstract Cauchy problems. Another interesting class of the abstract fractional equations was analyzed in [5], where the authors have considered the following fractional integro-differential neutral equations

$$\begin{cases} \dfrac{d}{dt}D(t,u_t) = \int_0^t g_{\alpha-1}(t-s)AD(s,u_s)\,ds + f(t,u_t),\ t \geq 0, \\ u_0 = \varphi, \end{cases}$$

with $1 < \alpha < 2$, $(A, D(A))$ being a sectorial densely defined operator in the sense of [6] and

$$D(t,\varphi) = \varphi(0) + g(t,\varphi),$$

with f, g and φ being suitable vector-valued functions. Here,

$$g_\alpha(t) := t^{\alpha-1}/\Gamma(\alpha),$$

$\alpha > 0, t > 0$, where $\Gamma(\alpha)$ is the Euler Gamma function. For more details, we refer the reader to the recent research monographs [7,8] and the references cited therein. We would like to point out that this work is the first phase of another project, the aim of which is to study our main problem (1) set on non-regular domains. This study is motivated by the fact that these types of domains are often encountered in several concrete situations. Thus, the theory of such problems is interesting in itself. Moreover, the knowledge of the structure of solutions is useful in numerical analysis; see [9–12]. The organization of this paper can be briefly described as follows. In the Section 2, we collect some necessary definitions and results needed to justify our main results. In the Section 3, we furnish some sufficient conditions for the existence of a pseudo $\mathcal{S}$-asymptotically periodic mild solution for the problem (1). In the Section 5, we provide an example to demonstrate the abstract results obtained in this work.

2. Preliminaries

We use the standard notation throughout this paper. Unless stated otherwise, we will always assume that X denotes a complex Banach space equipped with the norm $\|\cdot\|$, and A is a closed linear operator with $0 \in \rho(A)$, where $\rho(A)$ denotes the resolvent set of A. In this work, we need to use the notion of fractional power of closed linear operators. Then, we know that, for every $\alpha > 0$, the operator $A^{-\alpha}$ is well defined and has the following explicit representation:

$$A^{-\alpha} := \frac{1}{\Gamma(\alpha)} \int_0^{\infty} t^{\alpha-1} T(t)\, dt,$$

for more details about fractional powers of closed linear operators, we refer the reader to the research monograph [6]. For $\alpha \in (0,1)$, we set

$$X_\alpha := D(A^\alpha).$$

In the particular situation $\alpha = 0$, we consider that $A^0 := I$ and $X_0 := X$. The fractional power space X_α is a Banach space when it is endowed with its natural norm

$$\|\cdot\|_\alpha = \|A^\alpha \cdot\|.$$

Furthermore, for $0 \le \alpha \le \beta \le 1$, one has

$$X_\beta \hookrightarrow X_\alpha,$$

and the embedding $X_\beta \hookrightarrow X_\alpha$ is compact whenever the resolvent operator of A is compact. In the sequel, we consider the Banach space

$$B_\alpha := C([-r,0], X_\alpha),$$

of all continuous vector-valued functions from $[-r,0]$ into X_α, equipped with the norm

$$\|\varphi\|_{B_\alpha} := \max_{s\in[-r,0]} \|\varphi(s)\|_\alpha.$$

Among the effective tools used in our work we cite the well known semigroup's theory. For the the reader's convenience, we refer him or her to the research monograph [13]. In this work, our basic assumption is that $-A$ generates an exponentially stable analytic semigroup in X. We need also to recall the following results (see, e.g., [13]):

Theorem 1. *Assume that $-A$ is the infinitesimal generator of an analytic semigroup $(T(t))_{t\ge 0}$ and let $\|T(t)\| \le Me^{-\delta t}$, $t \ge 0$ for some $\delta > 0$. If $0 \in \rho(A)$, then one has*

(i) $A^{-\alpha}$ *is a bounded linear operator for* $0 \le \alpha \le 1$.
(ii) $T(t) : X \to D(A^\alpha)$ *for every* $t > 0$ *and* $\alpha \ge 0$.
(iii) *For every* $t \ge 0$ *and* $x \in D(A^\alpha)$, *we have*

$$T(t)A^\alpha x = A^\alpha T(t)x.$$

(vi) *For every* $t > 0$, *the operator* $A^\alpha T(t)$ *is bounded and*

$$||A^\alpha T(t)|| \le M_\alpha t^{-\alpha} e^{-\delta t}. \tag{3}$$

(v) *If* $0 < \alpha < 1$ *and* $x \in D(A^\alpha)$, *then*

$$||T(t)x - x|| \le C_\alpha t^\alpha ||A^\alpha x||.$$

Now, let us define

$$U(t) := \int_0^{\infty} \xi_q(\tau) T(t^q \tau)\, d\tau \text{ and } V(t) := q \int_0^{\infty} \tau \xi_q(\tau) T(t^q \tau)\, d\tau,\ t \ge 0, \tag{4}$$

where

$$\xi_q(\tau) := \frac{1}{\pi q} \sum_{n\ge 1} (-\tau)^{n-1} \frac{\Gamma(nq-1)}{n!} \sin(n\pi q), \quad \tau \in \mathbb{R}^+ - \{0\},$$

is a probability density function defined on $\mathbb{R}^+ - \{0\}$. Let us recall that (see, e.g., [14])

$$\xi_q(\tau) \geq 0, \ \tau > 0 \text{ and } \int_0^\infty \tau^\alpha \xi_q(\tau)\, d\tau = 1$$

and

$$\int_0^\infty \tau^v \xi_q(\tau)\, d\tau = \frac{\Gamma(1+v)}{\Gamma(1+qv)}, \quad 0 \leq v \leq 1. \tag{5}$$

The main properties of these families are summarized in the following lemma (see [14]):

Lemma 1. *Let $(T(t))_{t\geq 0}$ be a C_0-semigroup. Then, the operator families $(U(t))_{t\geq 0}$ and $(V(t))_{t\geq 0}$ defined by (4) have the following properties:*

(i) $(U(t))_{t\geq 0}$ *and* $(V(t))_{t\geq 0}$ *are strongly continuous.*
(ii) *If $(T(t))_{t\geq 0}$ is uniformly bounded, then $U(t)$ and $V(t)$ are linear bounded operators for any fixed $t \geq 0$.*
(iii) *If $(T(t))_{t\geq 0}$ is compact, then $U(t)$ and $V(t)$ are compact operators for any $t \geq 0$.*
(vi) *If $x \in X$, α, $\beta \in (0,1)$ and $t > 0$, then*

$$AV(t)x = A^{1-\beta}V(t)A^\beta x$$

and

$$\|A^\alpha V(t)\| \leq \frac{M_\alpha}{t^{q\alpha}} \frac{q\Gamma(1-\alpha)}{\Gamma(q(1-\alpha))}. \tag{6}$$

(v) *If $t \geq 0$ and $x \in X_\alpha$, then*

$$\|U(t)x\|_\alpha \leq M\|x\|_\alpha$$

and

$$\|V(t)x\|_\alpha \leq M\frac{q}{\Gamma(1+q)}\|x\|_\alpha.$$

For $I \subseteq \mathbb{R}$, we denote by $C_b(I,X)$ the Banach space consisting of all bounded and continuous functions from I into X, equipped with the norm

$$\|u\|_{C_b(I,X)} := \sup_{t\in I}\|u(t)\|.$$

In order to develop our results, we need to introduce the following spaces $PSAP_\omega(X)$ and $PSAP_{\omega,p}(X)$. The space $PSAP_\omega(X)$ consists of all bounded and continuous functions from $\mathbb{R}^+$ to X satisfying (2), while the space $PSAP_{\omega,p}(X)$ is defined as follows:

Definition 1. *Let $p > 0$ and $u \in PSAP_\omega(X)$. Then, we say that $u(\cdot)$ is pseudo-$\mathcal{S}$-asymptotically ω-periodic of class p ($u \in PSAP_{\omega,p}(X)$, equivalently) if*

$$\lim_{h\to+\infty} \frac{1}{h} \int_p^h \sup_{t\in[\xi-p,\xi]} \|f(t+\omega) - f(t)\|\, d\xi = 0.$$

More information about this class of functions can be founded in [1,5,15], from which we find the following:

Proposition 1. *Let $p \geq 0$. Then,*

(i) $PSAP_{\omega,p}(X) \subseteq PSAP_\omega(X)$.
(ii) *$PSAP_{\omega,p}(X)$ is a closed subspace of $C_b(\mathbb{R}^+,X)$.*
(iii) *Assume that $f \in C_b(\mathbb{R}^+,X)$. Then, $f \in PSAP_{\omega,p}(X)$ if and only if, for every $\varepsilon > 0$, we have*

$$\lim_{h\to+\infty}\frac{1}{h}\mu(M_{h,\varepsilon}(f))=0,$$

where $\mu(\cdot)$ denotes the classical Lebesgue measure and

$$M_{h,\varepsilon}(f)=\left\{t\in[p,h]:\ \sup_{t\in[\xi-p,\xi]}\|f(t+\omega)-f(t)\|\geq\varepsilon\right\}.$$

At this level, for Banach space $(Z,\|\cdot\|_Z)$ and $(W,\|\cdot\|_W)$ we define another functional framework which will be used henceforth.

Definition 2. *We say that a function $f\in C_b(\mathbb{R}^+\times Z,W)$ is uniformly (Z,W) pseudo-$\mathcal{S}$-asymptotically ω-periodic of class p if*

$$\lim_{h\to\infty}\frac{1}{h}\int_p^h\left(\sup_{t\in[\xi-p,\xi]}\left(\sup_{\|x\|_Z\leq L}\|f(t+\omega,x)-f(t,x)\|_W\right)\right)d\xi=0,$$

for any $L>0$.

The notation $PSAP_{\omega,p}(\mathbb{R}^+\times Z,W)$ is adopted to denote the set formed by functions of this type. From the previous cited references, we also know the following:

Lemma 2. *Let $u\in C_b([-r,\infty),X)$ and*

$$u|_{\mathbb{R}^+}\in PSAP_{\omega,p}(X).$$

Then, the function $t\mapsto u_t$ belongs to $PSAP_{\omega,p}(E)$.

Lemma 3. *Let $f\in PSAP_{\omega,p}(\mathbb{R}^+\times E,X)$ and*

(1) *there exists $L_f\in C_b([0;\infty);\mathbb{R}^+)$ such that for all $(t,\phi_i)\in[0;\infty)\times E$:*

$$||f(t,\phi_1)-f(t,\phi_2)||\leq L_f(t)||\phi_1-\phi_2||_{C_b([-r,0],X)},$$

(2) $u\in C_b([-r,\infty),X)$,

(3) $u|_{\mathbb{R}^+}\in PSAP_{\omega,p}(X)$.

Then, the function $t\mapsto f(t,u_t)$ belongs to $PSAP_{\omega,p}(X)$.

The following result can be regarded as a generalization of Lemma 3.

Lemma 4. *Let $\alpha,\beta\in[0,1]$ and $f\in PSAP_{\omega,p}(\mathbb{R}^+\times B_\alpha,X_\beta)$. We assume that*

(1) *there exists $L_f\in C_b([0;\infty);\mathbb{R}^+)$ such that for all $(t,\phi_i)\in[0;\infty)\times B_\alpha$:*

$$||f(t,\phi_1)-f(t,\phi_2)||_\beta\leq L_f(t)||\phi_1-\phi_2||_{B_\alpha},$$

(2) $u\in C_b([-r,\infty),X_\alpha)$,

(3) $u|_{\mathbb{R}^+}\in PSAP_{\omega,p}(X_\alpha)$.

Then, the function $t\mapsto f(t,u_t)$ belongs to $PSAP_{\omega,p}(X_\beta)$.

Proof. First, according to Lemma 2, we can see that $t\mapsto u_t\in PSAP_{\omega,p}(B_\alpha)$. Now, for $h>0$, one has

$$\int_p^h \left(\sup_{t\in[\xi-p,\xi]} \|f(t+\omega,u_{t+\omega})-f(t,u_t)\|_\beta \right) d\xi$$
$$\leq \int_p^h \left(\sup_{t\in[\xi-p,\xi]} \|f(t+\omega,u_{t+\omega})-f(t,u_{t+\omega})\|_\beta \right) d\xi + \int_p^h \left(\sup_{t\in[\xi-p,\xi]} \|f(t,u_{t+\omega})-f(t,u_t)\|_\beta \right) d\xi,$$

which implies that

$$\begin{aligned}
&\int_p^h \left(\sup_{t\in[\xi-p,\xi]} \|f(t+\omega,u_{t+\omega})-f(t,u_t)\|_\beta \right) d\xi \\
\leq\ & \int_p^h \left(\sup_{t\in[\xi-p,\xi]} \left(\sup_{\|\phi\|_{B_\alpha}\leq L} \|f(t+\omega,\phi)-f(t,\phi)\|_\beta \right) \right) d\xi \\
&+ \left\|L_f\right\|_{C_b(\mathbb{R}^+,\mathbb{R}^+)} \int_p^h \left(\sup_{t\in[\xi-p,\xi]} \|u_{t+\omega}-u_t\|_{B_\alpha} \right) d\xi.
\end{aligned}$$

As a result, we obtain

$$\lim_{h\to+\infty} \frac{1}{h} \int_p^h \left(\sup_{t\in[\xi-p,\xi]} \|f(t+\omega,u_{t+\omega})-f(t,u_t)\|_\beta \right) d\xi = 0.$$

The proof is complete. □

In our study, we will use the following types of solutions:

Definition 3. *A function $u \in C([-r,+\infty),X_\alpha)$ is said to be an α-mild solution for problem* (1) *if u satisfies problem* (1) *and*

$$u(t) = \varphi(t),$$

for $\varphi \in B_\alpha$ and $t \in [-r,0]$. In this case, u is defined explicitly as follows:

$$\begin{aligned}
u(t) &= U(t)(\varphi(0) - G(0,\varphi) + G(t,u_t) \\
&\quad - \int_0^t \left((t-s)^{q-1} AV(t-s)G(s,u_s) \right) ds \\
&\quad + \int_0^t \left((t-s)^{q-1} V(t-s)F(s,u_s) \right) ds, \quad t \geq 0.
\end{aligned}$$

Moreover, if $u|_{\mathbb{R}_+} \in PSAP_{\omega,p}(X_\alpha)$, then $u(\cdot)$ is called pseudo $\mathcal{S}$-asymptotically ω-periodic α-mild solution of class p for problem (1).

In this study, our strategy is based on the use of two versions of the well known fixed point theorems; that is,

Theorem 2. ***(Banach Contraction Principle).*** *Let (E,d) be a complete metric space and $f : E \to E$ be contractive. Then, f has a unique fixed point u, and $f^n(y) \to u$ for each $y \in E$.*

Theorem 3. ***(Krasnoselskii's Fixed Point Theorem).*** *Let Ω be a closed convex nonempty subset of a Banach space $(X, \|\cdot\|)$. Suppose that $\mathcal{A}_1$ and $\mathcal{A}_2$ map Ω into X such that*

- $\mathcal{A}_1 x + \mathcal{A}_2 y \in \Omega$ *for every pair* $x, y \in \Omega$;
- $\mathcal{A}_1$ *is continuous and* $\mathcal{A}_1(\Omega)$ *is contained in a compact set;*
- $\mathcal{A}_2$ *is a contraction.*

Then, there exists $y \in \Omega$ *with* $\mathcal{A}_1 y + \mathcal{A}_2 y = y$.

For more details, we refer the reader to [16,17].

3. Main Results

In this section, we discuss some questions related to the existence and uniqueness of pseudo $\mathcal{S}$-asymptotically ω-periodic α-mild solutions of class p to problem (1). Our standing hypotheses are

(A1) $F \in PSAP_{\omega,p}(\mathbb{R}^+ \times B_\alpha, X)$ and $G \in PSAP_{\omega,p}(\mathbb{R}^+ \times B_\alpha, X_1)$.
(A2) There exists a function $L_G(\cdot) \in C_b(\mathbb{R}^+, \mathbb{R}^+)$ such that

$$\|AG(t,\phi_1) - AG(t,\phi_2)\| \leq L_G(t)\|\phi_1 - \phi_2\|_{B_\alpha},$$

for all $(t, \phi_i) \in \mathbb{R}^+ \times B_\alpha$.
(A3) There exists a function $L_F(\cdot) \in C_b(\mathbb{R}^+, \mathbb{R}^+)$ such that

$$\|F(t,\phi_1) - F(t,\phi_1)\| \leq L_F(t)\|\phi_1 - \phi_2\|_{B_\alpha},$$

for all $(t, \phi_i) \in \mathbb{R}^+ \times B_\alpha$.
(A4) Setting $L_G = \sup_{t \in \mathbb{R}^+} L_G(t)$ and $L_F = \sup_{t \in \mathbb{R}^+} L_F(t)$, we assume also that

$$\left(C_{\alpha-1} L_G + (L_G + L_F) \frac{M_\alpha \Gamma(1-\alpha)}{|v_0|^{1-\alpha}} \right) < 1,$$

with

$$C_{\alpha-1} = ||A^{\alpha-1}||.$$

Theorem 4. *Let* (A1)–(A4) *hold and let* $-A$ *be the generator of an exponentially stable analytic semigroup* $T(t)_{(t \geq 0)}$. *For* $\alpha \in [0,1)$, *we assume that* $\varphi \in B_\alpha$, $F : \mathbb{R}^+ \times B_\alpha \to X$ *and* $G : \mathbb{R}^+ \times B_\alpha \to X_1$ *are continuous functions. Then, problem (1) has a unique pseudo* $\mathcal{S}$*-asymptotic* ω*-periodic* α*-mild solution of class* p.

Proof. We consider the Banach space

$$C_{b,0}(X_\alpha) := \left\{ x : [-r, +\infty) \to X_\alpha : x|_{[-r,0]} = 0 \text{ and } x|_{\mathbb{R}^+} \in C_b(\mathbb{R}^+, X_\alpha) \right\},$$

endowed with the norm

$$\|x\|_{C_{b,0}} = \|x_0\|_{B_\alpha} + \sup_{t \geq 0} \|x(t)\|_\alpha = \sup_{t \geq 0} \|x(t)\|_\alpha.$$

According to Proposition 1, we define the closed subspace of $C_{b,0}(X_\alpha)$ as follows:

$$PSAP_{\omega,p,0}(X_\alpha) := \left\{ x : [-r, +\infty) \to X_\alpha : x|_{[-r,0]} = 0 \text{ and } x|_{\mathbb{R}^+} \in PSAP_{\omega,p}(X_\alpha) \right\}.$$

Throughout the proof, y denotes the function defined by

$$y(t) := \begin{cases} 0, & t \geq 0, \\ \varphi(t), & t \in [-r, 0]. \end{cases}$$

Let $x \in PSAP_{\omega,p,0}(X_\alpha)$. Due to the continuity of $F : \mathbb{R}^+ \times B_\alpha \to X$ and $G : \mathbb{R}^+ \times B_\alpha \to X_1$ and by taking into account assumptions (A1)–(A3) and Lemma 4, we can conclude that

$$\lim_{h \to +\infty} \frac{1}{h} \int_p^h \left(\sup_{t \in [\xi - p, \xi]} \|AG(t+\omega, x_{t+\omega} + y_{t+\omega}) - AG(t, x_t + y_t)\| \right) d\xi = 0 \tag{7}$$

and

$$\lim_{h \to +\infty} \frac{1}{h} \int_p^h \left(\sup_{t \in [\xi - p, \xi]} \|F(t+\omega, x_{t+\omega} + y_{t+\omega}) - F(t, x_t + y_t)\| \right) d\xi = 0,$$

which means that $F \in PSAP_{\omega,p}(X)$ and $G \in PSAP_{\omega,p}(X_1)$. Further, there exist $M_F > 0$ and $M_G > 0$ such that

$$||F(t, x_t + y_t)|| \le M_F \text{ and } ||AG(t, x_t + y_t)|| \le M_G \text{ for all } t \ge 0. \tag{8}$$

Now, we need to introduce the following operator

$$\begin{array}{rccc} \mathcal{N}: & PSAP_{\omega,p,0}(X_\alpha) & \longrightarrow & PSAP_{\omega,p,0}(X_\alpha) \\ & x & \mapsto & \mathcal{N}x \end{array},$$

where

$$\begin{aligned} \mathcal{N}x(t) \; := \; & U(t)(\varphi(0) - G(0, \varphi)) + G(t, x_t + y_t) \\ & - \int_0^t \Big((t-s)^{q-1} AV(t-s) G(s, x_s + y_s) \Big) ds \\ & + \int_0^t \Big((t-s)^{q-1} V(t-s) F(s, x_s + y_s) \Big) ds, \end{aligned}$$

with $t \in \mathbb{R}^+$. In what follows, we show that the operator $\mathcal{N}$ has a unique fixed point in $PSAP_{w,p,0}(X_\alpha)$. Firstly, we check that $\mathcal{N}$ is well defined. From Fubini's theorem and the definition of the operator V given by (4), it follows from (3), (5) and (8) that

$$\begin{aligned} & \int_0^t \Big((t-s)^{q-1} \|A^\alpha V(t-s)\| \|F(s, x_s + y_s)\| \Big) ds \\ \le \; & q M_F M_\alpha \int_0^t \left((t-s)^{q(1-\alpha)-1} \int_0^\infty \Big(\tau^{1-\alpha} \xi_q(\tau) e^{-|\nu_0|(t-s)^q \tau} \Big) d\tau \right) ds \\ \le \; & \frac{M_F M_\alpha \Gamma(1-\alpha)}{|\nu_0|^{1-\alpha}} \\ < \; & +\infty. \end{aligned}$$

Similarly,

$$\begin{aligned} & \int_0^t \Big((t-s)^{q-1} \|A^\alpha V(t-s)\| \|AG(s, x_s + y_s)\| \Big) ds \\ \le \; & q M_G M_\alpha \int_0^t \left((t-s)^{q(1-\alpha)-1} \int_0^\infty \Big(\tau^{1-\alpha} \xi_q(\tau) e^{-|\nu_0|(t-s)^q \tau} \Big) d\tau \right) ds \end{aligned}$$

$$\begin{aligned} &\leq \frac{M_G M_\alpha \Gamma(1-\alpha)}{|\nu_0|^{1-\alpha}} \\ &< +\infty, \end{aligned}$$

for every $x \in PSAP_{\omega,p,0}(X_\alpha)$. Consequently, we can see that $t \mapsto \mathcal{N}x(t)$ is a bounded function. Then, it remains to show that

$$\lim_{h\to+\infty} \frac{1}{h} \int_p^h \left(\sup_{t\in[\xi-p,\xi]} \|\mathcal{N}x(t+\omega) - \mathcal{N}x(t)\|_\alpha \right) d\xi = 0.$$

A direct computation allows us to obtain

$$\mathcal{N}x(t+\omega) - \mathcal{N}x(t) = \sum_{i=1}^{6} J_i(t),$$

where

$$J_1(t) = (U(t+\omega) - U(t))(\varphi(0) - G(0,\varphi)),$$

$$J_2(t) = G(t+\omega, x_{t+\omega} + y_{t+\omega}) - G(t, x_t + y_t),$$

$$J_3(t) = \int_0^\omega \Big((t+\omega-s)^{q-1} V(t+\omega-s) AG(s, x_s + y_s) \Big) ds,$$

$$J_4(t) = \int_0^t \Big((t-s)^{q-1} V(t-s) (AG(s+\omega, x_{s+\omega} + y_{s+\omega}) - AG(s, x_s + y_s)) \Big) ds,$$

$$J_5(t) = \int_0^\omega \Big((t+\omega-s)^{q-1} V(t+\omega-s) F(s, x_s + y_s) \Big) ds,$$

$$J_6(t) = \int_0^t \Big((t-s)^{q-1} V(t-s) (F(s+\omega, x_{s+\omega} + y_{s+\omega}) - F(s, x_s + y_s)) \Big) ds.$$

This implies that

$$\int_p^h \left(\sup_{t\in[\xi-p,\xi]} \|\mathcal{N}x(t+\omega) - \mathcal{N}x(t)\|_\alpha \right) d\xi \leq \sum_{i=1}^{6} \left(\int_p^h \sup_{t\in[\xi-p,\xi]} \|J_i(t)\|_\alpha \, d\xi \right).$$

Keeping in mind the exponential stability of semigroup $(T(t))_{t\geq 0}$ and the definition of the operator U given by (4), we deduce that for all $\varepsilon > 0$, there exists $t_\varepsilon > 0$, such that

$$\|U(t)\| \leq \frac{\varepsilon}{2}, \text{ for all } t \geq t_\varepsilon.$$

First, let us start with the estimation of the quantity J_1. We have

$$\|J_1(t)\|_\alpha \leq (\|U(t+\omega)\| + \|U(t)\|) \|\varphi(0) - G(0,\varphi)\|_\alpha,$$

so

$$\frac{1}{h} \int_p^h \left(\sup_{t\in[\xi-p,\xi]} \|J_1(t)\|_\alpha \right) d\xi$$

$$\leq \frac{1}{h}\int_p^h \left(\sup_{t\in[\xi-p,\xi]} (\|U(t+\omega)\| + \|U(t)\|)\|\varphi(0) - G(0,\varphi)\|_\alpha \right) d\xi$$
$$\leq \|\varphi(0) - G(0,\varphi)\|_\alpha \left(\frac{2Mt_\varepsilon}{h} + \varepsilon\left(1 - \frac{(p+t_\varepsilon)}{h}\right)\right),$$

which implies that

$$\lim_{h\to+\infty} \frac{1}{h}\int_p^h \left(\sup_{t\in[\xi-p,\xi]} \|J_1(t)\|_\alpha \right) d\xi = 0.$$

From (7) and taking into account that $X_1 \hookrightarrow X_\alpha$, we obtain

$$\frac{1}{h}\int_p^h \left(\sup_{t\in[\xi-p,\xi]} \|G(t+\omega, x_{t+\omega} + y_{t+\omega}) - G(t, x_t + y_t)\|_\alpha \right) d\xi$$
$$\leq \frac{C_{\alpha-1}}{h}\int_p^h \left(\sup_{t\in[\xi-p,\xi]} \|AG(t+\omega, x_{t+\omega} + y_{t+\omega}) - AG(t, x_t + y_t)\| \right) d\xi;$$

hence,

$$\lim_{h\to+\infty} \frac{1}{h}\int_p^h \left(\sup_{t\in[\xi-p,\xi]} \|G(t+\omega, x_{t+\omega} + y_{t+\omega}) - G(t, x_t + y_t)\|_\alpha \right) d\xi = 0$$

and

$$t \mapsto G(t, x_t + y_t) \in PSAP_{w,p}(X_\alpha).$$

At this level, let us show that

$$\lim_{h\to+\infty} \frac{1}{h}\int_p^h \left(\sup_{t\in[\xi-p,\xi]} \|J_i(t)\|_\alpha \right) d\xi = 0,\ i = 3,4,5,6.$$

Taking into account that

$$t+\omega-s \geq \frac{t+\omega}{\omega}(\omega - s)$$

and the estimates (6) and (8), we deduce that

$$\frac{1}{h}\int_p^h \left(\sup_{t\in[\xi-p,\xi]} \|J_3(t)\|_\alpha \right) d\xi$$
$$\leq M_G M_\alpha \frac{\omega\Gamma(1-\alpha)}{\Gamma(q(1-\alpha)+1)} \left(\frac{1}{h}\int_p^h \left(\sup_{t\in[\xi-p,\xi]} (t+\omega)^{q(1-\alpha)-1} \right) d\xi \right)$$
$$\leq M_G M_\alpha \frac{\omega\Gamma(1-\alpha)}{\Gamma(q(1-\alpha)+1)} \left(\frac{1}{h}\int_p^h (\xi - p + \omega)^{q(1-\alpha)-1}\, d\xi \right),$$

which implies that

$$\lim_{h\to+\infty} \frac{1}{h}\int_p^h \left(\sup_{t\in[\xi-p,\xi]} \|J_3(t)\|_\alpha \right) d\xi = 0,$$

and

$$\lim_{h\to+\infty}\frac{1}{h}\int_p^h\left(\sup_{t\in[\xi-p,\xi]}\|J_5(t)\|_\alpha\right)d\xi=0.$$

In fact, it suffices to see that

$$\begin{aligned}
&\frac{1}{h}\int_p^h\left(\sup_{t\in[\xi-p,\xi]}\|J_5(t)\|_\alpha\right)d\xi\\
\leq\;& M_F M_\alpha\frac{\omega\Gamma(1-\alpha)}{\Gamma(q(1-\alpha)+1)}\left(\frac{1}{h}\int_p^h\left(\sup_{t\in[\xi-p,\xi]}(t+\omega)^{q(1-\alpha)-1}\right)d\xi\right)\\
\leq\;& M_F M_\alpha\frac{\omega\Gamma(1-\alpha)}{\Gamma(q(1-\alpha)+1)}\left(\frac{1}{h}\int_p^h(\xi-p+\omega)^{q(1-\alpha)-1}d\xi\right).
\end{aligned}$$

It remains to show that

$$\lim_{h\to+\infty}\frac{1}{h}\int_p^h\left(\sup_{t\in[\xi-p,\xi]}\|J_i(t)\|_\alpha\right)d\xi=0,\; i=4,6.$$

We examine the term I_4. To make the notation less cluttered, we define the function $\mathcal{Q}_G$ as follows

$$\mathcal{Q}_G(t)=AG(t+\omega,x_{t+\omega}+y_{t+\omega})-AG(t,x_t+y_t),\; t\geq 0.$$

Thanks to (7), we can deduce that, for every $\varepsilon>0$, there exists $h_\varepsilon>0$ such that

$$\frac{1}{h}\int_p^h\sup_{t\in[\xi-p,\xi]}\|\mathcal{Q}_G(t)\|\,d\xi\leq\varepsilon,\text{ for all }h\geq h_\varepsilon. \tag{9}$$

Consequently,

$$\begin{aligned}
&\int_p^h\left(\sup_{t\in[\xi-p,\xi]}\|J_4(t)\|_\alpha\right)d\xi\\
\leq\;&\int_p^h\left(\sup_{t\in[\xi-p,\xi]}\int_0^{\xi-p}\Big((t-s)^{q-1}\|A^\alpha V(t-s)\|\|\mathcal{Q}_G(s)\|\Big)ds\right)d\xi\\
&+\int_p^h\left(\sup_{t\in[\xi-p,\xi]}\int_{\xi-p}^{t}\Big((t-s)^{q-1}\|A^\alpha V(t-s)\|\|\mathcal{Q}_G(s)\|\Big)ds\right)d\xi\\
:=\;&\sum_{i=1}^{2}J_4^i(t).
\end{aligned}$$

Taking into account the definition of the operator V given in (4) and the estimates (3), we obtain

$$\begin{aligned}
&J_4^1(t)\\
\leq\;& qM_\alpha\int_p^h\sup_{t\in[\xi-p,\xi]}\int_0^{\xi-p}(t-s)^{q(1-\alpha)-1}\left(\int_0^\infty\tau^{1-\alpha}\xi_q(\tau)e^{-|\nu_0|(t-s)^q\tau}d\tau\right)\|\mathcal{Q}_G(s)\|\,ds\,d\xi
\end{aligned}$$

$$\leq qM_\alpha \int_p^h \int_0^{-p} (\xi - p - s)^{q(1-\alpha)-1} \left(\int_0^\infty \tau^{1-\alpha} \xi_q(\tau) e^{-|\nu_0|(\xi-p-s)^q \tau} d\tau \right) \| \mathcal{Q}_G(s) \| \, ds \, d\xi$$

$$= qM_\alpha \int_p^h \int_p^\xi (\xi - s)^{q(1-\alpha)-1} \left(\int_0^\infty \tau^{1-\alpha} \xi_q(\tau) e^{-|\nu_0|(\xi-s)^q \tau} d\tau \right) \| \mathcal{Q}_G(s-p) \| ds \, d\xi.$$

Using the classical Fubini's theorem, we obtain

$$\begin{aligned} & J_4^1(t) \\ \leq \; & qM_\alpha \int_p^h \| \mathcal{Q}_G(s-p) \| \left(\int_s^h (\xi - s)^{q(1-\alpha)-1} \left(\int_0^\infty \tau^{1-\alpha} \xi_q(\tau) e^{-|\nu_0|(\xi-s)^q \tau} d\tau \right) d\xi \right) ds \\ \leq \; & qM_\alpha \int_p^h \| \mathcal{Q}_G(s-p) \| \left(\int_0^{h-s} (\xi)^{q(1-\alpha)-1} \left(\int_0^\infty \tau^{1-\alpha} \xi_q(\tau) e^{-|\nu_0|(\xi)^q \tau} d\tau \right) d\xi \right) ds. \end{aligned}$$

Similarly, as before, we obtain

$$J_4^1(t) \leq M_\alpha \frac{\Gamma(1-\alpha)}{|\nu_0|^{1-\alpha}} \int_p^h \| \mathcal{Q}_G(s-p) \| \, ds;$$

it follows from (9) and Proposition 1 that

$$\lim_{h \to +\infty} \frac{1}{h} J_4^1(t) = 0.$$

Assume that $h \geq 2p$; then, we obtain

$$\begin{aligned} J_4^2(t) &= \int_p^{2p} \left(\sup_{t \in [\xi-p, \xi]} \int_{\xi-p}^t \left((t-s)^{q-1} \| A^\alpha V(t-s) \| \| \mathcal{Q}_G(s) \| \right) ds \right) d\xi \\ &\quad + \int_{2p}^h \left(\sup_{t \in [\xi-p, \xi]} \int_{\xi-p}^t \left((t-s)^{q-1} \| A^\alpha V(t-s) \| \| \mathcal{Q}_G(s) \| \right) ds \right) d\xi \\ &:= \sum_{i=1}^2 J_4^{2,i}(t). \end{aligned}$$

Thanks to (8) and the estimate (6), we obtain

$$\begin{aligned} J_4^{2,1}(t) &\leq 2M_G M_\alpha \frac{\Gamma(1-\alpha)}{\Gamma(q(1-\alpha))} \int_p^{2p} \left(\sup_{t \in [\xi-p, \xi]} \int_{\xi-p}^t \left((t-s)^{q(1-\alpha)-1} \right) ds \right) d\xi \\ &= 2M_G M_\alpha \frac{\Gamma(1-\alpha)}{\Gamma(1+q(1-\alpha))} \int_p^{2p} \left(\sup_{t \in [\xi-p, \xi]} (t - \xi + p)^{q(1-\alpha)} \right) d\xi \\ &\leq 2M_G M_\alpha \frac{\Gamma(1-\alpha)}{\Gamma(1+q(1-\alpha))} \int_p^{2p} p^{q(1-\alpha)} \, d\xi, \end{aligned}$$

and hence,

$$\lim_{h \to +\infty} \frac{1}{h} J_4^{2,1}(t) = 0.$$

Concerning the term $J_4^{2,2}(t)$, we have

$$\begin{aligned}
J_4^{2,2}(t) &\leq M_\alpha \frac{q\Gamma(1-\alpha)}{\Gamma(q(1-\alpha))} \int_{2p}^{h} \left(\sup_{t\in[\xi-p,\xi]} \int_{\xi-p}^{t} (t-s)^{q(1-\alpha)-1} \|\mathcal{Q}_G(s)\| \, ds \right) d\xi \\
&\leq M_\alpha \frac{q\Gamma(1-\alpha)}{\Gamma(q(1-\alpha))} \int_{2p}^{h} \left(\int_{0}^{p} (s)^{q(1-\alpha)-1} \sup_{t\in[\xi-p,\xi]} \|\mathcal{Q}_G(t-s)\| \, ds \right) d\xi,
\end{aligned}$$

for $h \geq h_\varepsilon$, and the use of Fubini theorem implies

$$\begin{aligned}
& \frac{1}{h} J_4^{2,2}(t) \\
\leq\ & M_\alpha \frac{\Gamma(1-\alpha)}{\Gamma(q(1-\alpha))} \int_{0}^{p} (s)^{q(1-\alpha)-1} \left(\frac{1}{h} \int_{2p}^{h} \sup_{t\in[\xi-p,\xi]} \|\mathcal{Q}_G(t-s)\| \, d\xi \right) ds \\
\leq\ & M_\alpha \frac{\Gamma(1-\alpha)}{\Gamma(q(1-\alpha))} \int_{0}^{p} (s)^{q(1-\alpha)-1} \left(\frac{1}{h} \int_{p}^{h} \sup_{t\in[\xi-p,\xi]} \|\mathcal{Q}_G(t)\| \, d\xi \right) ds \\
\leq\ & \varepsilon M_\alpha \frac{\Gamma(1-\alpha)}{\Gamma(q(1-\alpha))} \int_{0}^{p} s^{q(1-\alpha)-1} \, ds \\
\to\ & 0, \text{ as } \varepsilon \to 0.
\end{aligned}$$

Combining all the previous estimates, we conclude that

$$\lim_{h\to+\infty} \frac{1}{h} \int_{p}^{h} \left(\sup_{t\in[\xi-p,\xi]} \|J_4(t)\|_\alpha \right) d\xi = 0.$$

Similarly,

$$\lim_{h\to+\infty} \frac{1}{h} \int_{p}^{h} \left(\sup_{t\in[\xi-p,\xi]} \|J_6(t)\|_\alpha \right) d\xi = 0.$$

Summing up, one can deduce that

$$\mathcal{N}(PSAP_{\omega,p,0}(X_\alpha)) \subseteq PSAP_{\omega,p,0}(X_\alpha). \tag{10}$$

Next, we will show that $\mathcal{N}$ is a contraction mapping. Let $x, z \in PSAP_{\omega,p,0}(X_\alpha)$; taking into account the assumptions (A2) and (A3), we obtain

$$\begin{aligned}
& \|\mathcal{N}x(t) - \mathcal{N}z(t)\|_\alpha \\
\leq\ & C_{\alpha-1} \|AG(t, x_t + y_t) - AG(t, z_t + y_t)\|_\alpha \\
& + \int_0^t \Big((t-s)^{q-1} \|A^\alpha V(t-s)\| \|AG(s, x_s + y_s) - AG(s, z_s + y_s)\| \Big) ds, \\
& + \int_0^t \Big((t-s)^{q-1} \|A^\alpha V(t-s)\| \|F(s, x_s + y_s) - F(s, z_s + y_s)\| \Big) ds \\
\leq\ & C_{\alpha-1} L_G \|x_t - z_t\|_{B_\alpha} \\
& + (L_G + L_F) \int_0^t \Big((t-s)^{q-1} \|A^\alpha V(t-s)\| \|x_s - z_s\|_{B_\alpha} \Big) ds
\end{aligned}$$

$$\leq \left(C_{\alpha-1}L_G + (L_G + L_F)\frac{M_\alpha \Gamma(1-\alpha)}{|v_0|^{1-\alpha}}\right)||x - z||_{C_{b,0}}.$$

As a result, we confirm that

$$||\mathcal{N}x - \mathcal{N}z||_{C_{b,0}} \leq \left(C_{\alpha-1}L_G + (L_G + L_F)\frac{M_\alpha \Gamma(1-\alpha)}{|v_0|^{1-\alpha}}\right)||x - z||_{C_{b,0}}.$$

Hence, taking into account assumption (A4), we conclude that the mapping

$$\mathcal{N} : PSAP_{w,p,0}(X_\alpha) \to PSAP_{w,p,0}(X_\alpha)$$

is a contraction. Then, it follows from the Banach contraction principle that $\mathcal{N}$ has a unique fixed point $x \in PSAP_{w,p,0}(X_\alpha)$. Set $u(t) = x(t) + y(t)$ for $t \in [-r, +\infty)$; we can confirm that u is a unique pseudo $\mathcal{S}$-asymptotic ω-periodic α-mild solution of class p of the problem (1). □

In the remainder of this section, we prove the existence of the pseudo $\mathcal{S}$-asymptotic ω-periodic α-mild solution of class p for problem (1) without assuming the Lipschitz property of the function F. Our strategy is based on the use of the Krasnoselskii's fixed point theorem. In order to accomplish that, we will need the following conditions:

(A5) Let $\psi_i : \mathbb{R}^+ \to \mathbb{R}^+$, $i = 1,2$ be non-negative functions that satisfy the following estimate:

$$\lim_{h\to+\infty} \frac{1}{h} \int_p^h \left(\sup_{t\in[\xi-p,\xi]} \psi_i(t) \right) d\xi = 0, \quad i = 1,2.$$

and assume that, for every $t \in \mathbb{R}^+$ and $\phi \in B_\alpha$, there exists $\omega > 0$ such that

$$||F(t+\omega,\phi) - F(t,\phi)|| \leq \psi_1(t), \text{ and } ||AG(t+\omega,\phi) - AG(t,\phi)|| \leq \psi_2(t).$$

(A6) There exists a function $k : \mathbb{R}^+ \to \mathbb{R}^+$ and a constant $\delta > 0$ such that for all $\phi \in B_\alpha$,

$$||F(t,\phi)|| \leq k(t), \text{ for all } t \geq 0, \tag{11}$$

and k satisfies the following estimate:

$$\lim_{h\to+\infty} \frac{1}{h} \int_\delta^h \left((\xi - p)^{q(1-\alpha)} \sup_{s\in[0,\xi]} k(s) \right) d\xi = 0. \tag{12}$$

(A7) There exists a positive constant L_G such that

$$||AG(t,\phi_1) - AG(t,\phi_2)|| \leq L_G||\phi_1 - \phi_2||_{B_\alpha},$$

for all $(t,\phi_i) \in \mathbb{R}^+ \times B_\alpha$.

(A8) Assume that

$$\left(C_{\alpha-1}L_G + L_G\frac{M_\alpha \Gamma(1-\alpha)}{|\nu_0|^{1-\alpha}}\right) < 1.$$

and one has the following interesting result:

Theorem 5. *Assume that* (A5)–(A8) *hold and* $-A$ *generates a compact, exponentially stable analytic semigroup* $(T(t))_{t\geq0}$ *on X. For* $\alpha \in [0,1)$*, we assume that* $\varphi \in B_\alpha$*,* $F : \mathbb{R}^+ \times B_\alpha \to X_\alpha$ *is a bounded continuous function and* $G : \mathbb{R}^+ \times B_\alpha \to X_1$ *is a continuous function that satisfies* $G(t,0) = 0$ *for* $t \geq 0$*. Then, the problem* (1) *has at least one pseudo* $\mathcal{S}$*-asymptotic* ω*-periodic* α*-mild solution of class* p*.*

Proof. For the sake of convenience, we will conserve the notation adopted in the proof of the Theorem 4. In the sequel, our aim is to show that

$$\mathcal{N}(PSAP_{w,p,0}(X_\alpha)) \subseteq PSAP_{w,p,0}(X_\alpha),$$

which means that for any $x \in PSAP_{w,p,0}(X_\alpha)$,

$$\begin{aligned} \mathcal{N}x \quad : \quad & t \mapsto U(t)(\varphi(0) - G(0,\varphi) + G(t, x_t + y_t) \\ & - \int_0^t \Big((t-s)^{q-1} AV(t-s) G(s, x_s + y_s)\Big) ds \\ & + \int_0^t \Big((t-s)^{q-1} V(t-s) F(s, x_s + y_s)\Big) ds, \quad t \in \mathbb{R}^+, \end{aligned}$$

belongs to the space $PSAP_{\omega,p}(X_\alpha)$. Since the function F is bounded and G is continuous and satisfies the conditions (A5) and (A7), then by the embedding $X_\alpha \hookrightarrow X$ and Lemma (4), there exist two positive constants M'_F and M'_G such that

$$||F(t, x_t + y_t)|| \leq M'_F \text{ and } ||AG(t, x_t + y_t)|| \leq M'_G \text{ for all } t > 0. \tag{13}$$

for any $x \in PSAP_{\omega,p,0}(X_\alpha)$. Furthermore, one has

$$t \mapsto G(t, x_t + y_t) \in PSAP_{w,p}(X_1). \tag{14}$$

Note that (13) guarantees the boundedness of the function $\mathcal{N}x$. Now, we look to prove that

$$\lim_{h \to +\infty} \frac{1}{h} \int_p^h \left(\sup_{t \in [\xi - p, \xi]} ||\mathcal{N}x(t+\omega) - \mathcal{N}x(t)||_\alpha \right) d\xi = 0,$$

i.e.,

$$\lim_{h \to +\infty} \frac{1}{h} \int_p^h \left(\sup_{t \in [\xi - p, \xi]} ||J_i(t)||_\alpha \right) d\xi = 0, \ i = \{1, 2, ..., 6\}.$$

From Theorem 4, it is immediate that

$$\lim_{h \to +\infty} \frac{1}{h} \int_p^h \left(\sup_{t \in [\xi - p, \xi]} ||J_1(t)||_\alpha \right) d\xi = 0.$$

Exploiting (14) and the fact that $X_1 \hookrightarrow X_\alpha$, we obtain

$$\lim_{h \to +\infty} \frac{1}{h} \int_p^h \left(\sup_{t \in [\xi - p, \xi]} ||J_2(t)||_\alpha \right) d\xi = 0. \tag{15}$$

Taking into account (13) and Theorem 4, we confirm that

$$\lim_{h \to \infty} \frac{1}{h} \int_p^h \left(\sup_{t \in [\xi - p, \xi]} ||J_i(t)||_\alpha \right) d\xi = 0, \quad i = 3, 5.$$

Our objective now is to show that

$$\lim_{h\to\infty}\frac{1}{h}\int_{p}^{h}\left(\sup_{t\in[\xi-p,\xi]}\|J_i(t)\|_\alpha\right)d\xi = 0, \quad i = 4,6.$$

First of all, for $t \geq 0$, we set

$$\mathcal{Q}_F(t) = F(t+\omega, x_{t+\omega}+y_{t+\omega}) - F(t, x_{t+\omega}+y_{t+\omega}).$$

According to (A5), it is evident to say that the function $\mathcal{Q}_F$ satisfies the following estimate:

$$\lim_{h\to+\infty}\frac{1}{h}\int_{p}^{h}\sup_{t\in[\xi-p,\xi]}\|\mathcal{Q}_F(t)\|\,d\xi = 0. \tag{16}$$

On other side, we observe that

$$\int_{p}^{h}\left(\sup_{t\in[\xi-p,\xi]}\|J_6(t)\|_\alpha\right)d\xi \leq \sum_{i=1}^{2}\int_{p}^{h}\left(\sup_{t\in[\xi-p,\xi]}\left\|J_6^i(t)\right\|_\alpha\right)d\xi,$$

where

$$J_6^1(t) = \int_0^t\Big((t-s)^{q-1}V(t-s)\mathcal{Q}_F(t)\Big)ds,$$

and

$$J_6^2(t) = \int_0^t\Big((t-s)^{q-1}V(t-s)(F(s, x_{s+\omega}+y_{s+\omega}) - F(s, x_s+y_s))\Big)ds.$$

Due to (13), (15) and (16) with Theorem 4,

$$\lim_{h\to+\infty}\frac{1}{h}\int_{p}^{h}\left(\sup_{t\in[\xi-p,\xi]}\|J_4(t)\|_\alpha\right)d\xi = 0,$$

$$\lim_{h\to+\infty}\frac{1}{h}\int_{p}^{h}\left(\sup_{t\in[\xi-p,\xi]}\left\|J_6^1(t)\right\|_\alpha\right)d\xi = 0.$$

It remains to show that

$$\lim_{h\to+\infty}\frac{1}{h}\int_{p}^{h}\left(\sup_{t\in[\xi-p,\xi]}\left\|J_6^2(t)\right\|_\alpha\right)d\xi = 0.$$

Taking into account the exponential stability of the semigroup $(T(t))_{t\geq 0}$ and the definition of the operator V as presented in (4), we can deduce that for every $\varepsilon > 0$, there exists

$$t'_\varepsilon = \left(qC_{-\beta}\frac{M_\beta\Gamma(1-\beta)}{\Gamma(q(1-\beta))\varepsilon}\right)^{\frac{1}{\beta q}} > 0,$$

such that $\|V(t)\| \leq \varepsilon$, for all $t \geq t'_\varepsilon$ and $\beta \in (0,1)$. In actual fact, it suffices to take into account the estimate (6) which allows us to write

$$\|V(t)x\| \leq \left\|A^{-\beta}\right\|\left\|A^{\beta}V(t)x\right\| \leq qC_{-\beta}\frac{M_\beta\Gamma(1-\beta)}{t^{q\beta}\Gamma(q(1-\beta))}\|x\|,$$

for any $\beta \in (0,1)$ and $x \in X$. Then, we can write

$$\begin{aligned}
&\int_p^h \sup_{t\in[\xi-p,\xi]} J_6^2(t)\, d\xi \\
=& \int_p^{t'_\varepsilon+p} \sup_{t\in[\xi-p,\xi]} \int_0^t \Big((t-s)^{q-1}V(t-s)(F(s,x_{s+\omega}+y_{s+\omega})-F(s,x_s+y_s))\Big)dsd\xi \\
&+\int_{t'_\varepsilon+p}^{h} \sup_{t\in[\xi-p,\xi]} \int_0^t \Big((t-s)^{q-1}V(t-s)(F(s,x_{s+\omega}+y_{s+\omega})-F(s,x_s+y_s))\Big)dsd\xi.
\end{aligned}$$

Thanks to (13) and the estimate (6), we conclude that

$$\begin{aligned}
&\frac{1}{h}\int_p^{t'_\varepsilon+p}\left(\sup_{t\in[\xi-p,\xi]}\int_0^t \Big((t-s)^{q-1}\|A^\alpha V(t-s)\|\|(F(s,x_{s+\omega}+y_{s+\omega})-F(s,x_s+y_s))\|\Big)ds\right)d\xi \\
\leq\;& \frac{2M'_F M_\alpha \Gamma(1-\alpha)}{\Gamma(q(1-\alpha))}\left(\frac{1}{h}\int_p^{t'_\varepsilon+p}\xi^{q(1-\alpha)}d\xi\right) \to 0, \quad \text{as } h\to+\infty.
\end{aligned}$$

Keeping in mind that the function

$$s \mapsto g(s) = (s+(\xi-p))^q - s^q,$$

is decreasing for $s \geq 0$, we obtain $g(0) \geq g(p)$ *i. e.*, $\xi^q - (\xi-p)^q \leq p^q$. Hence,

$$\begin{aligned}
&\frac{1}{h}\int_{t'_\varepsilon+p}^{h}\left(\sup_{t\in[\xi-p,\xi]}\int_0^{t-(\xi-p)}\Big((t-s)^{q-1}\|V(t-s)\|\|A^\alpha F(s,x_{s+\omega}+y_{s+\omega})-A^\alpha F(s,x_s+y_s)\|\Big)ds\right)d\xi \\
\leq\;& \frac{2M'_F\varepsilon}{qC_{-\alpha}}\left(\frac{1}{h}\int_{t'_\varepsilon+p}^{h}(\xi^q-(\xi-p)^q)d\xi\right) \leq \frac{2M'_F\varepsilon}{qC_{-\alpha}}p^q \to 0, \quad \text{as } \varepsilon\to 0.
\end{aligned}$$

At this level, the use of (11) justify the fact that

$$||F(t,x_s+y_s)|| \leq k(t).$$

Therefore, by (12), one can find

$$\begin{aligned}
&\frac{1}{h}\int_{t'_\varepsilon+p}^{h}\sup_{t\in[\xi-p,\xi]}\int_{t-(\xi-p)}^{t}\Big((t-s)^{q-1}\|A^\alpha V(t-s)\|\|F(s,x_{s+\omega}+y_{s+\omega})-F(s,x_s+y_s)\|\Big)dsd\xi \\
\leq\;& \frac{2M_\alpha\Gamma(1-\alpha)}{\Gamma(q(1-\alpha))}\left(\frac{1}{h}\int_{t'_\varepsilon+p}^{h}\left(\sup_{t\in[\xi-p,\xi]}\int_{t-(\xi-p)}^{t}\Big((t-s)^{q(1-\alpha)-1}k(s)\Big)ds\right)d\xi\right) \\
\leq\;& \frac{2M_\alpha\Gamma(1-\alpha)}{\Gamma(q(1-\alpha))}\left(\frac{1}{h}\int_{t'_\varepsilon+p}^{h}\left((\xi-p)^{q(1-\alpha)}\sup_{s\in[0,\xi]}k(s)\right)d\xi\right),
\end{aligned}$$

then

$$\lim_{h\to+\infty}\left(\frac{1}{h}\int_{t'_\varepsilon+p}^{h}\sup_{t\in[\xi-p,\xi]}\int_{t-(\xi-p)}^{t}\Big((t-s)^{q-1}\|A^\alpha V(t-s)\|\|F(s,x_{s+\omega}+y_{s+\omega})-F(s,x_s+y_s)\|\Big)dsd\xi\right)$$
$$=0.$$

Thus,

$$\lim_{h\to\infty}\frac{1}{h}\int_{p}^{h}\left(\sup_{t\in[\xi-p,\xi]}\|J_6(t)\|_\alpha\right)d\xi=0.$$

Summing up, the above results for J_i, $i\in\{1,2,\dots,6\}$, we conclude that

$$\mathcal{N}x\in PSAP_{\omega,p}(X_\alpha);$$

which justifies the following inclusion, that is,

$$\mathcal{N}(PSAP_{\omega,p,0}(X_\alpha))\subseteq PSAP_{\omega,p,0}(X_\alpha).$$

We are now in a position to show that the operator $\mathcal{N}$ has at least one fixed point $x\in PSAP_{\omega,p,0}(X_\alpha)$. For $R>0$, we define the closed ball of $PSAP_{\omega,p,0}(X_\alpha)$ with center 0 and radius R by

$$\Omega_R=\Big\{x\in PSAP_{\omega,p,0}(X_\alpha):\|x\|_{C_{b,0}}\le R\Big\}.$$

Set $\mathcal{N}=\mathcal{N}_1+\mathcal{N}_2$ with

$$\mathcal{N}_1x(t):=U(t)\varphi(0)+\int_0^t((t-s)^{q-1}V(t-s)F(s,x_s+y_s))ds,$$
$$\mathcal{N}_2x(t):=U(t)(G(0,\varphi))+G(t,x_t+y_t)-\int_0^t((t-s)^{q-1}AV(t-s)G(s,x_s+y_s))ds.$$

We first prove that there exists a positive constant R_0 such that $\mathcal{N}_1x+\mathcal{N}_2z\in\Omega_{R_0}$, for every pair $x,z\in\Omega_{R_0}$. For this purpose, we assume that for any $R>0$, there exist $x,z\in\Omega_R$ and $t\ge0$ such that

$$\begin{aligned}R&\le\|\mathcal{N}_1x(t)+\mathcal{N}_2z(t)\|_\alpha\\&\le\|U(t)\|\|\varphi(0)\|_\alpha+\int_0^t\Big((t-s)^{q-1}\|A^\alpha V(t-s)\|\|F(s,x_s+y_s)\|\Big)ds\\&\quad+\|U(t)\|\|G(0,\varphi)\|_\alpha+\|G(t,z_s+y_s)\|_\alpha+\int_0^t\Big((t-s)^{q-1}\|A^\alpha V(t-s)\|\|AG(s,z_s+y_s)\|\Big)ds.\end{aligned}$$

Hence, we have

$$\begin{aligned}R&\le M\|\varphi\|_{B_\alpha}+M'_F\int_0^t\Big((t-s)^{q-1}\|A^\alpha V(t-s)\|\Big)ds\\&\quad+MC_{-\alpha}L_G\|\varphi\|_{B_\alpha}+C_{\alpha-1}L_G\|z_s+y_s\|_{B_\alpha}+L_G\|z_s+y_s\|_{B_\alpha}\int_0^t\Big((t-s)^{q-1}\|A^\alpha V(t-s)\|\Big)ds,\end{aligned}$$

which implies

$$\begin{aligned} R \quad &\leq \quad M\|\varphi\|_{B_\alpha} + M'_F M_\alpha \frac{\Gamma(1-\alpha)}{|\nu_0|^{1-\alpha}} \\ &\quad + MC_{-\alpha} L_G \|\varphi\|_{B_\alpha} + C_{\alpha-1} L_G \Big(R + \|\varphi\|_{B_\alpha}\Big) + L_G \Big(R + \|\varphi\|_{B_\alpha}\Big) \frac{M_\alpha \Gamma(1-\alpha)}{|\nu_0|^{1-\alpha}}. \end{aligned}$$

Dividing both sides by R and taking the limit as R approaches infinity, we obtain

$$1 \leq C_{\alpha-1} L_G + L_G \frac{M_\alpha \Gamma(1-\alpha)}{|\nu_0|^{1-\alpha}}.$$

Combining all the above arguments, we can deduce that there exists a positive constant R_0, such that for any pair of $x, z \in \Omega_{R_0}$, one has $\mathcal{N}_1 x + \mathcal{N}_2 z \in \Omega_{R_0}$.

Now, let us show that the function $\mathcal{N}_1$ is compact and the function $\mathcal{N}_2$ is contraction. To accomplish that, we should perform several steps as follows:

Step 1. We show that the function $\mathcal{N}_1$ is continuous on Ω_{R_0}. In fact, due the continuity of the function F, for any sequence $(x^n) \in \Omega_{R_0}$ such that $x^n \to x$ on Ω_{R_0}, one can see

$$\|F(s, x_s^n + y_s) - F(s, x_s + y_s)\| \to 0, \text{ as } n \to +\infty.$$

Then, by the dominate convergence theorem, we can conclude that

$$\begin{aligned} \|\mathcal{N}_1 x^n(t) - \mathcal{N}_1 x(t)\|_\alpha \quad &\leq \quad \int_0^t \Big((t-s)^{q-1} \|A^\alpha V(t-s)\| \|F(s, x_s^n + y_s) - F(s, x_s + y_s)\|\Big) ds \\ &\to \quad 0, \text{ as } n \to +\infty. \end{aligned}$$

Step 2. Following [3], for $t \geq 0$, we define

$$\mathcal{N}_1^{\varepsilon,\delta} x(t) := U(t)\varphi(0) + q \int_0^t \left((t-s)^{q-1} \int_\delta^\infty (\tau \xi_q(\tau) T(t^q \tau) F(s, x_s + y_s)) d\tau \right) ds.$$

The compactness of the operator $T(t)$ and Lemma 1 implies that the set $\mathcal{N}_1^{\varepsilon,\delta}(\Omega_{R_0})(t)$ is relatively compact in X_α. Moreover, it follows from (3) and (13) that

$$\begin{aligned} &\Big\| \mathcal{N}_1 x(t) - \mathcal{N}_1^{\varepsilon,\delta} x(t) \Big\|_\alpha \\ \leq \quad & q \int_0^t \left((t-s)^{q-1} \int_0^\delta (\tau \xi_q(\tau) \|A^\alpha T(t^q \tau)\| \|F(s, x_s + y_s)\|) d\tau \right) ds \\ & + q \int_{t-\varepsilon}^t \left((t-s)^{q-1} \int_\delta^\infty (\tau \xi_q(\tau) \|A^\alpha T(t^q \tau)\| \|F(s, x_s + y_s)\|) d\tau \right) ds \\ \leq \quad & q M_\alpha M'_F \left[\int_0^\delta \left(\tau^{1-\alpha} \xi_q(\tau) \int_0^t \Big((t-s)^{q(1-\alpha)-1} e^{-|\nu_0|(t-s)^q \tau} \Big) ds \right) d\tau \right. \\ & \left. + \int_{t-\varepsilon}^t \Big((t-s)^{q(1-\alpha)-1} \Big) ds \int_0^\infty \Big(\tau^{1-\alpha} \xi_q(\tau) \Big) d\tau \right] \\ \leq \quad & M_\alpha M'_F \frac{\Gamma(1-\alpha)}{|\nu_0|^{1-\alpha}} \left[\int_0^\delta \xi_q(\tau) d\tau + \frac{1}{q(1-\alpha)} \varepsilon^{q(1-\alpha)} \right], \end{aligned}$$

in other words,

$$\lim_{\varepsilon,\delta\to 0}\left\|\mathcal{N}_1x(t)-\mathcal{N}_1^{\varepsilon,\delta}x(t)\right\|_\alpha=0.$$

Consequently, the set $\mathcal{N}_1(\Omega_{R_0})(t)$ is relatively compact in X_α.

Step 3. Let $t_1>t_2\geq 0$ and $x\in\Omega_{R_0}$. Observe that, from Lemma 2.9 in [14], we deduce that

$$\|A^\alpha V(t_1-s)-A^\alpha V(t_2-s)\|\to 0,\ \text{as}\ t_1\to t_2$$

and

$$\|U(t_1)-U(t_2)\|\to 0,\ \text{as}\ t_1\to t_2.$$

On other side, one has

$$\begin{aligned}
&\int_0^{t_2}\left(\frac{(t_2-s)^{q-1}-(t_1-s)^{q-1}}{(t_2-s)^{\alpha q}}\right)ds\\
=&\int_0^{t_2}\left((t_2-s)^{q(1-\alpha)-1}-(t_1-s)^{q(1-\alpha)-1}\left(\frac{t_1-s}{t_2-s}\right)^{\alpha q}\right)ds\\
\leq&\int_0^{t_2}\left((t_2-s)^{q(1-\alpha)-1}-(t_1-s)^{q(1-\alpha)-1}\right)ds\\
\to&\ 0,\ \text{as}\ t_1\to t_2.
\end{aligned}$$

This gives

$$\begin{aligned}
&\|\mathcal{N}_1x(t_1)-\mathcal{N}_1x(t_2)\|_\alpha\\
\leq&\ \|U(t_1)-U(t_2)\|\|A^\alpha\varphi(0)-A^\alpha G(0,\varphi)\|\\
&+\int_0^{t_2}\left((t_1-s)^{q-1}\|A^\alpha V(t_1-s)-A^\alpha V(t_2-s)\|\|F(s,x_s+y_s)\|\right)ds\\
&+\int_0^{t_2}\left(\left[(t_2-s)^{q-1}-(t_1-s)^{q-1}\right]\|A^\alpha V(t_2-s)\|\|F(s,x_s+y_s)\|\right)ds\\
&+\int_{t_2}^{t_1}\left((t_1-s)^{q-1}\|A^\alpha V(t_1-s)\|\|F(s,x_s+y_s)\|\right)ds\\
\leq&\ \|U(t_1)-U(t_2)\|(\|A^\alpha\varphi(0)\|+C_{\alpha-1}\|AG(0,\varphi)\|)\\
&+M_F'\left[\int_0^{t_2}\left((t_1-s)^{q-1}\|A^\alpha V(t_1-s)-A^\alpha V(t_2-s)\|\right)ds\right.\\
&\left.+M_\alpha\int_0^{t_2}\left(\frac{(t_2-s)^{q-1}-(t_1-s)^{q-1}}{(t_2-s)^{\alpha q}}\right)ds+M_\alpha\int_{t_2}^{t_1}\left((t_1-s)^{q(1-\alpha)-1}\right)ds\right]
\end{aligned}$$

Then,

$$\lim_{t_1\to t_2}\|\mathcal{N}_1x(t_1)-\mathcal{N}_1x(t_2)\|_\alpha=0,$$

which means that $\mathcal{N}_1(\Omega_{R_0})$ is equicontinuous. Combining the above steps, the Arzela-Ascoli theorem guarantees that $\mathcal{N}_1$ is a compact operator on Ω_{R_0}.

Step 4. What is left is to show that $\mathcal{N}_2$ is a contraction. Let $x,z\in\Omega_{R_0}$, for $t\geq 0$; one has

$$\|\mathcal{N}_2x(t)-\mathcal{N}_2z(t)\|_\alpha$$

$$\leq \|G(t,x_t+y_t)-G(t,z_t+y_t)\|_\alpha$$
$$+\int_0^t \Big((t-s)^{q-1}\|A^\alpha V(t-s)\|\|AG(s,x_s+y_s)-AG(s,z_s+y_s)\|\Big)ds,$$

then

$$\|\mathcal{N}_2x(t)-\mathcal{N}_2z(t)\|_\alpha \leq \left(C_{\alpha-1}L_G+L_G\frac{M_\alpha\Gamma(1-\alpha)}{|\nu_0|^{1-\alpha}}\right)\|x-z\|_{C_{b,0}},$$

it follows from (A8) that $\mathcal{N}_2$ is contraction. Finally, by applying Theorem 3, we conclude that the operator $\mathcal{N}$ has at least one fixed point $x \in \Omega_{R_0} \subset PSAP_{\omega,p,0}(X_\alpha)$. Hence, we can affirm that $u = x + y$ is the pseudo $\mathcal{S}$-asymptotically ω-periodic α-mild solution of class p for problem (1). □

4. Applications

In this section, we present a concrete example to apply of our abstract theoretical results. Of concern is the following delayed partial differential: equation

$$\begin{cases} \dfrac{\partial^{\frac{1}{2}}}{\partial t^{\frac{1}{2}}}\left(u(t,\xi)-k_2(t)\int\limits_{t-r}^{t}\left(\int_a^\xi b_2(s-t)u(s,\eta)\,d\eta\right)ds\right)-\dfrac{\partial^2}{\partial\xi^2}u(t,\xi) \\ \qquad = k_1(t)\int_{t-r}^t b_1(s-t)u(s,\xi)\,ds,\ \xi\in[0,\pi],\ t\in\mathbb{R}^+, \\ u(t,0)=u(t,\pi)=0,\ \ t\in\mathbb{R}^+, \\ u(\tau,\xi)=\varphi(\tau)(\xi),\ \ \tau\in[-r,0],\xi\in[0,\pi], \end{cases} \tag{17}$$

where $\partial^{\frac{1}{2}}/\partial t^{\frac{1}{2}}$ is a Caputo fractional partial derivative of order $1/2$, $r > 0$ is a constant, $\varphi \in C([-r,0],L^2([0,\pi]))$ and $b_1(\cdot),b_2(\cdot) \in C([-r,0],\mathbb{R})$ and $k_1(.),k_2(.)$ are suitable functions. Let $X := L^2([0,\pi])$ and $A : D(A) \subseteq X \to X$ is the operator defined by

$$\begin{cases} Au := -u'', \\ D(A) = \{u \in X | -u'' \in X,\ u(0)=u(\pi)=0\}. \end{cases}$$

Remark 1. *Most of the useful spectral properties of this operator can be founded in Section 5 in [18] and Example 5.1 in [19]. For the reader's convenience, we recall that*

- *A has a discrete spectrum with eigenvalues n^2, $n \in \mathbb{N}$. Furthermore,*
- *A generates an exponentially stable analytic semigroup $(T(t))_{(t\geq 0)}$ defined by*

$$T(t)u := \sum_{n=1}^{\infty} e^{-n^2t}\langle u,e_n\rangle e_n \ \ and\ \ \|T(t)\|\leq e^{-t},$$

where $\{e_n \mid n \in \mathbb{N}\}$ is an orthonormal basis of X and $e_n(\xi) = (\frac{2}{\pi})^{\frac{1}{2}}\sin(n\xi)$ are the associated normalized eigenvectors .

- *The operator $A^{1/2}$ is well defined and can be characterized as follows*

$$\begin{cases} (A)^{\frac{1}{2}}u := \sum_{n=1}^{\infty} n\langle u,e_n\rangle e_n, \\ (A)^{-\frac{1}{2}}u := \sum_{n=1}^{\infty} \dfrac{1}{n}\langle u,e_n\rangle e_n, \\ D(A^{1/2}) := \{u \in X : \sum_{n=1}^{\infty} n\langle u,e_n\rangle e_n \in X\}. \end{cases}$$

- *For $u \in D(A^{1/2})$:$\|u\|_{\frac{1}{2}} = \|u'\|$.*

Let us introduce the following functions $F : \mathbb{R}^+ \times B_{\frac{1}{2}} \to X$ and $G : \mathbb{R}^+ \times B_{\frac{1}{2}} \to X_1$ as follows

$$\begin{cases} F(t,\phi)(\xi) = k_1(t) \int_{-r}^{0} b_1(s)\phi(s,\xi)\, ds, \\ \text{and} \\ G(t,\phi)(\xi) = k_2(t) \int_{-r}^{0} \int_{a}^{\xi} b_2(s)\phi(s,\eta)\, d\eta\, ds. \end{cases}$$

According to Theorem 4, we have the following result

Proposition 2. *Suppose that the functions k_1, k_2 belong to $PSAP_{w,p}(\mathbb{R})$ and*

$$(1+\pi)\left(\int_{-r}^{0}|b_1(s)|^2 ds\right)^{\frac{1}{2}}\|k_1\|_{C_b(\mathbb{R})} + \pi\left(\int_{-r}^{0}|b_2(s)|^2 ds\right)^{\frac{1}{2}}\|k_2\|_{C_b(\mathbb{R})} < r^{-\frac{1}{2}}. \tag{18}$$

Then, the problem (17) has a unique pseudo $\mathcal{S}$-asymptotic ω-periodic α-mild solution of class p.

Proof. Note that, for $t \geq 0$ and $\phi \in B_{\frac{1}{2}}$, one has

$$\begin{aligned} |F(t,\phi)(\xi)|^2 &\leq |k_1(t)|^2\left(\int_{-r}^{0}|b_1(s)||\phi(s,\xi)|ds\right)^2 \\ &\leq |k_1(t)|^2\int_{-r}^{0}|b_1(s)|^2 ds\int_{-r}^{0}|\phi(s,\xi)|^2 ds. \end{aligned}$$

Using the Fubini theorem, we have

$$\begin{aligned} \|F(t,\phi)\|^2 &\leq |k_1(t)|^2\int_{-r}^{0}|b_1(s)|^2 ds\int_{-r}^{0}\|\phi(s,\cdot)\|^2_{L^2([0,\pi])}ds \\ &\leq r|k_1(t)|^2\int_{-r}^{0}|b_1(s)|^2 ds \sup_{s\in[-r,0]}\|\phi(s,\cdot)\|^2_{L^2([0,\pi])}. \end{aligned}$$

Furthermore,

$$\|F(t,\phi)\| \leq r^{\frac{1}{2}}|k_1(t)|\left(\int_{-r}^{0}|b_1(s)|^2 ds\right)^{\frac{1}{2}}\|\phi\|_{B_{\frac{1}{2}}}$$

and

$$\begin{aligned} &\frac{1}{h}\int_{p}^{h}\sup_{t\in[\xi-p,\xi]}\sup_{\|\phi\|_{B_{\frac{1}{2}}}\leq L}\|F(t+\omega,\phi)-F(t,\phi)\|d\xi \\ \leq\ & Lr^{\frac{1}{2}}\left(\int_{-r}^{0}|b_1(s)|^2 ds\right)^{\frac{1}{2}}\left(\frac{1}{h}\int_{p}^{h}\sup_{t\in[\xi-p,\xi]}|k_1(t+\omega)-k_1(t)|d\xi\right), \end{aligned}$$

which implies that

$$\lim_{h\to+\infty}\frac{1}{h}\int_{p}^{h}\sup_{t\in[\xi-p,\xi]}\sup_{\|\phi\|_{B_{\frac{1}{2}}}\leq L}\|F(t+\omega,\phi)-F(t,\phi)\|d\xi = 0$$

and

$$F \in PSAP_{\omega,p}(\mathbb{R}^+ \times B_{\frac{1}{2}}, X). \tag{19}$$

Moreover, we can easily see that

$$\|F(t,\phi_1) - F(t,\phi_2)\| \leq r^{\frac{1}{2}} \|k_1\|_{C_b(\mathbb{R}^+,\mathbb{R}^+)} \left(\int_{-r}^{0} |b_1(s)|^2 ds \right)^{\frac{1}{2}} \|\phi_1 - \phi_2\|_{B_{\frac{1}{2}}}, \tag{20}$$

for any $\phi_1,\ \phi_2 \in B_{\frac{1}{2}}$. Similarly, one has

$$\begin{aligned} \left| \frac{\partial^2}{\partial \xi^2} G(t,\phi)(\xi) \right|^2 &= |k_2(t)|^2 \left| \int_{-r}^{0} b_2(s) \frac{\partial^2}{\partial \xi^2} \int_a^{\xi} \phi(s,\eta)\, d\eta\, ds \right|^2 \\ &\leq |k_2(t)|^2 \left| \int_{-r}^{0} b_2(s) \frac{\partial}{\partial \xi} \phi(s,\xi) ds \right|^2 \\ &\leq |k_2(t)|^2 \int_{-r}^{0} |b_2(s)|^2\, ds \int_{-r}^{0} \left| \frac{\partial}{\partial \xi} \phi(s,\xi) \right|^2 ds. \end{aligned}$$

This yields

$$\begin{aligned} \left\| \frac{\partial^2}{\partial \xi^2} G(t,\phi) \right\| &\leq r^{\frac{1}{2}} |k_2(t)| \left(\int_{-r}^{0} |b_2(s)|^2 ds \right)^{\frac{1}{2}} \sup_{s \in [-r,0]} \|\phi'(s,\cdot)\|_{L^2([0,\pi])} \\ &= r^{\frac{1}{2}} |k_2(t)| \left(\int_{-r}^{0} |b_2(s)|^2 ds \right)^{\frac{1}{2}} \|\phi\|_{B_{\frac{1}{2}}}. \end{aligned}$$

Therefore,

$$\begin{aligned} & \frac{1}{h} \int_p^h \sup_{t \in [\xi - p, \xi]} \sup_{\|\phi\|_{B_{\frac{1}{2}}} \leq L} \left\| \frac{\partial^2}{\partial \xi^2} G(t+\omega,\phi) - \frac{\partial^2}{\partial \xi^2} G(t,\phi) \right\| d\xi \\ \leq\ & L r^{\frac{1}{2}} \left(\int_{-r}^{0} |b_2(s)|^2 ds \right)^{\frac{1}{2}} \left(\frac{1}{h} \int_p^h \sup_{t \in [\xi - p, \xi]} |k_2(t+\omega) - k_2(t)| d\xi \right), \end{aligned}$$

which means that

$$\lim_{h \to +\infty} \frac{1}{h} \int_p^h \sup_{t \in [\xi - p, \xi]} \sup_{\|\phi\|_{B_{\frac{1}{2}}} \leq L} \left\| \frac{\partial^2}{\partial \xi^2} G(t+\omega,\phi) - \frac{\partial^2}{\partial \xi^2} G(t,\phi) \right\| d\xi = 0$$

and consequently,

$$G \in PSAP_{\omega,p}(\mathbb{R}^+ \times B_{\frac{1}{2}}, X_1). \tag{21}$$

On other side, we have

$$\begin{aligned} & \left\| \tfrac{\partial^2}{\partial \xi^2} G(t,\phi_1) - \tfrac{\partial^2}{\partial \xi^2} G(t,\phi_2) \right\| \\ \leq\ & r^{\frac{1}{2}} \|k_2\|_{C_b(\mathbb{R}^+,\mathbb{R}^+)} \left(\int_{-r}^{0} |b_2(s)|^2 ds \right)^{\frac{1}{2}} \|\phi_1 - \phi_2\|_{B_{\frac{1}{2}}}, \end{aligned} \tag{22}$$

for any $\phi_1,\ \phi_2 \in B_{\frac{1}{2}}$. Observe that, from (19)–(22), we can deduce that the condition (A1), (A2) and (A3) from Section 3 hold. It is immediate that (18) implies that the condition (A4) holds with $\|A^{-1/2}\| = 1$, $M_{\frac{1}{2}} = \Gamma(1/2) = \sqrt{\pi}$ and $\nu_0 = -1$. By Theorem 4, we conclude that the problem (17) has a unique pseudo $\mathcal{S}$-asymptotical ω-periodic α-mild solution of class p. □

5. Conclusions

In this paper, we furnish some sufficient conditions for the existence of pseudo $\mathcal{S}$-asymptotically periodic mild solutions for the following abstract fractional Cauchy problem:

$$\begin{cases} {}^cD_t^q(u(t) - G(t,u_t)) + Au(t) = F(t,u_t), & t \geq 0, \\ u(t) = \varphi(t), & -r \leq t \leq 0, \end{cases}$$

where the fractional derivative ${}^cD_t^q$, $q \in (0,1)$ is taken in the sense of Caputo approach and $(A, D(A))$ is a closed linear operator in a Banach space $(X, \|\cdot\|)$. An important example is given to demonstrate the abstract results obtained in our work. We hope that our new results will have important applications in nonlinear analysis, mathematical physics, mechanics, biology and related fields in the future.

Author Contributions: Writing–original draft, N.C., B.C., M.K. and W.-S.D.; writing–review and editing, N.C., B.C., M.K. and W.-S.D. All authors contributed equally to the manuscript. All authors have read and agreed to the published version of the manuscript.

Funding: Marko Kostić is partially supported by grant 451-03-68/2020/14/200156 of Ministry of Science and Technological Development, Republic of Serbia. Wei-Shih Du is partially supported by Grant No. NSTC 112-2115-M-017-002 of the National Science and Technology Council of the Republic of China.

Institutional Review Board Statement: Not applicable.

Informed Consent Statement: Not applicable.

Data Availability Statement: Not applicable.

Acknowledgments: The authors wish to express their hearty thanks to the anonymous referees for their valuable suggestions and comments.

Conflicts of Interest: The authors declare no conflict of interest.

References

1. Pierri, M.; Rolnik, V. On pseudo $\mathcal{S}$-asymptotically periodic functions. *Bull. Aust. Math. Soc.* **2013**, *87*, 238–254. [CrossRef]
2. Henriquez, H.; Pierri, M.; Taboas, P. On $\mathcal{S}$-asymptotically periodic functions on Banach spaces and applications. *J. Math. Anal. Appl.* **2008**, *343*, 1119–1130. [CrossRef]
3. Wei, M.; Li, Q. Existence and uniqueness of $\mathcal{S}$-asymptotically periodic α-mild solutions for neutral fractional delayed evolution equation. *Appl. Math. J. Chin. Univ.* **2022**, *37*, 228–245. [CrossRef]
4. Henriquez, H.R.; Pierri, M.; Rolnik, V. Pseudo $\mathcal{S}$-asymptotically periodic solutions of second-order abstract Cauchy problems. *Appl. Math. Comput.* **2016**, *274*, 590–603. [CrossRef]
5. Yang, M.; Wang, Q. Pseudo asymptotically periodic solutions for fractional integro-differential neutral equations. *Sci. China Math.* **2019**, *62*, 1705–1718. [CrossRef]
6. Haase, M. *The Functional Calculus for Sectorial Operators, Operator Theory: Advances and Applications 169*; Birkhäuser Verlag: Basel, Switzerland, 2006.
7. Kostić, M. *Almost Periodic and Almost Automorphic Type Solutions to Integro-Differential Equations*; W. de Gruyter: Berlin, Germany, 2019.
8. Kostić, M. *Selected Topics in Almost Periodicity*; W. de Gruyter: Berlin, Germany, 2022.
9. Chaouchi, B.; Labbas, R.; Sadallah, B.K. Laplace equation on a domain with a cuspidal point in little Hölder spaces. *Mediterr. J. Math.* **2012**, *10*, 157–175. [CrossRef]
10. Chaouchi, B.; Boutaous, F. An abstract approach for the study of an elliptic problem in a nonsmooth cylinder. *Arab. J. Math.* **2014**, *3*, 325–340. [CrossRef]
11. Chaouchi, B.; Kostić, M. An efficient abstract method for the study of an initial boundary value problem on singular domain. *Afr. Mat.* **2019**, *30*, 551–562. [CrossRef]
12. Chaouchi, B.; Kostić, M. An abstract approach for the study of the Dirichlet problem for an elliptic system on a conical domain. *Mat. Vesn.* **2021**, *73*, 131–140.
13. Pazy, A. *Semigroups of Linear Operators and Applications to Partial Differential Equations*; Springer: New York, NY, USA, 1993.
14. Wang, J.; Zhou, Y. A class of fractional evolution equations and optimal controls. *Nonlinear Anal. Real World Appl.* **2011**, *12*, 262–272. [CrossRef]
15. Xia, Z.N. Pseudo asymptotically periodic solutions of two-term time fractional differential equations with delay. *Kodai Math. J.* **2015**, *38*, 310–332. [CrossRef]
16. Burton, T.A. A fixed-point theorem of Krasnoselskii. *Appl. Math. Lett.* **1998**, *11*, 85–88. [CrossRef]

17. Granas, A.; Dugundji, J. *Fixed Point Theory*; Springer: New York, NY, USA, 2003.
18. Li, Q.; Wei, M. Existence and asymptotic stability of periodic solutions for neutral evolution equations with delay. *Evol. Equ. Control. Theory* **2020**, *9*, 753–772. [CrossRef]
19. Travis, C.; Webb, G. Existence, stability and compactness with α-norm for partial functional differential equations. *Trans. Amer. Math. Soc.* **1978**, *240*, 129–143.

axioms

MDPI

Article

Common Fixed Point of (ψ, β, L)-Generalized Contractive Mapping in Partially Ordered b-Metric Spaces

Binghua Jiang [1], Huaping Huang [2,*] and Stojan Radenović [3]

1 School of Mathematics and Statistics, Hubei Normal University, Huangshi 435002, China
2 School of Mathematics and Statistics, Chongqing Three Gorges University, Chongqing 404020, China
3 Faculty of Mechanical Engineering, University of Belgrade, Kraljice Marije 16, 11120 Beograd, Serbia
* Correspondence: huaping@sanxiau.edu.cn

Abstract: The purpose of this paper is to attain the existence of coincidences and common fixed points in four mappings satisfying (ψ, β, L)-generalized contractive conditions in the framework of partially ordered b-metric spaces. The main results presented in this paper generalize some recent results in the existing literature. Furthermore, a nontrivial example is presented to support the obtained results.

Keywords: coincidence point; partially ordered b-metric space; weakly compatible; partially weakly increasing

MSC: 54H25; 47H10; 54E50

1. Introduction

It is world-renowned that the Banach contraction principle (for short, BCP) (see [1]) occupies a significant role in different fields of basic mathematics, applied mathematics and other subjects, and it has been generalized and improved in many aspects. Numerous generalizations and improvements come forth by changing metric spaces into general abstract metric spaces (see [2,3]). In [4], Vulpe et al. introduced b-metric space (sometimes so-called metric-type space, see [5]) as a new generalization of usual metric space. He provided the generalized BCP in b-metric space. From then on, a large number of papers have considered fixed point theory and its applications or variational methods for single-valued and multi-valued operators in b-metric spaces (the reader may see [5–10] and the related references therein). The mappings satisfying certain contractive conditions can be utilized to establish the existence of solutions to all kinds of operator equations such as integral equations, differential equations and fractional differential equations. Beg and Abbas (see [11]) obtained common fixed point theorems by extending a weakly contractive condition into two mappings. Abbas et al. (see [12]) investigated common fixed points for four mappings satisfying generalized weakly contractive conditions in complete partially ordered metric spaces. Esmaicy et al. (see [13]) initiated coincidence point results for four mappings in partially ordered metric spaces and used their results to seek the common solution of two integral equations. Recently, Abbas et al. (see [14]) acquired coincidence and common fixed points for four mappings satisfying generalized (ψ, β)-contractive conditions in complete partially ordered metric spaces.

Based on the previous work, throughout this paper, we aim to established coincidence and common fixed points for four mappings under generalized (ψ, β, L)-contractive conditions in complete partially ordered b-metric spaces. Our results make great progress in extending, unifying and generalizing the corresponding results in [14–16].

2. Preliminaries

In this paper, unless there are special statements, we always denote $\mathbb{R}$, $\mathbb{R}^+$, $\mathbb{N}$ and $\mathbb{N}^*$ as the set of all real numbers, the set of all non-negative real numbers, the set of all non-negative integers and the set of all positive integers, respectively.

First, we give some basic definitions and results which will be needed in what follows.

Definition 1 ([17]). *Let X be a nonempty set and $d : X \times X \to \mathbb{R}^+$ a mapping satisfying*

(1) $d(\xi,\eta) = 0$ *if and only if* $\xi = \eta$;

(2) $d(\xi,\eta) = d(\eta,\xi)$ *for all* $\xi,\eta \in X$;

(3) $d(\xi,\eta) \leq s[d(\xi,\zeta) + d(\zeta,\eta)]$ *for all* $\xi,\eta,\zeta \in X$,
where $s \geq 1$ *is a given real number, d is then said to be a b-metric on X, and* (X,d) *is said to be a b-metric space. If* $(X,\preceq)$ *is still a partially ordered set, then* $(X,\preceq,d)$ *is said to be a partially ordered b-metric space.*

Otherwise, for more notions such as *b*-convergence, *b*-completeness, *b*-Cauchy sequence and *b*-continuity in *b*-metric spaces, the reader may refer to [1,4–11,13,15–28] and the references mentioned therein.

In general, *b*-metric is not continuous; kindly see the following examples.

Example 1 ([16]). *Let* $X = \mathbb{N}^* \cup \{\infty\}$; *define a mapping* $d : X \times X \to \mathbb{R}^+$ *using*

$$d(\xi,\eta) = \begin{cases} 0, & \text{when } \xi = \eta; \\ \left|\frac{1}{\xi} - \frac{1}{\eta}\right|, & \text{when one of } \xi,\eta \text{ is even and another is distinctly even or infinity;} \\ 5, & \text{when one of } \xi,\eta \text{ is odd and another is distinctly odd or infinity;} \\ 2, & \text{otherwise.} \end{cases}$$

It is easy to see that when

$$d(\xi,\zeta) \leq \frac{5}{2}[d(\xi,\eta) + d(\eta,\zeta)] \quad (\xi,\eta,\zeta \in X),$$

then (X,d) *is a b-metric space with coefficient* $s = \frac{5}{2}$. *Put* $\xi_n = 2n$ $(n \in \mathbb{N})$, *then*

$$d(\xi_n,\infty) = \frac{1}{2n} \to 0 \quad (n \to \infty),$$

so $\xi_n \to \infty$ $(n \to \infty)$, *but* $d(\xi_n,1) = 2 \nrightarrow 5 = d(\infty,1)$ $(n \to \infty)$. *That is to say, the b-metric is not continuous.*

Example 2 ([6]). *Let* $X = \mathbb{R}$ *and* $\alpha > 1$ *be a constant. Define a mapping* $d : X \times X \to \mathbb{R}^+$ *using*

$$d(\xi,\eta) = \begin{cases} |\xi - \eta|, & \xi\eta \neq 0, \\ \alpha|\xi - \eta|, & \xi\eta = 0, \end{cases} \quad \text{for all } \xi,\eta \in X.$$

Then, (X,d) *is a b-metric space with coefficient* $s = \alpha$, *but the b-metric d is not continuous.*

Definition 2 ([20,27,28]). *Let* $(X,\preceq,d)$ *be a partially ordered b-metric space and* f,g,h *be self-mappings on X such that* $f(X) \cup g(X) \subseteq h(X)$.

(1) *If* $\xi,\eta \in X$, $\xi \preceq \eta$ *or* $\eta \preceq \xi$ *holds, then the elements* ξ,η *are called comparable;*

(2) *If* $f\xi \preceq gf\xi$ *for all* $\xi \in X$, *then the pair* (f,g) *is called partially weakly increasing;*

(3) *If* $f\xi \preceq g\eta$ *for all* $\eta \in h^{-1}(f\xi)$, *then the pair* (f,g) *is called partially weakly increasing with respect to h;*

(4) *If* $\lim_{n\to\infty} d(fg\xi_n, gf\xi_n) = 0$, *whenever* $\{\xi_n\}$ *is a sequence in X such that* $\lim_{n\to\infty} f\xi_n = \lim_{n\to\infty} g\xi_n = t$ *for some* $t \in X$, *then the pair* (f,g) *is called compatible;*

(5) *If $w = f\xi = g\xi$ for some ξ in X, then ξ is called a coincidence point of f and g, and w is called a point of coincidence of f and g.*
(6) *If f and g commute at their coincidence points, i.e., $fg\xi = gf\xi$, where $f\xi = g\xi$, then the pair (f, g) is called weakly compatible;*
(7) *If $\xi \preceq f\xi$ for each $\xi \in X$, then f is called dominating. If $f\xi \preceq \xi$ for each $\xi \in X$, then f is called dominated.*

Example 3 ([14]). *Let $f : X \to X$ be a mapping defined by $f\xi = \xi^{\frac{1}{4}}$, where $X = [0, 1]$ is endowed with usual ordering. Clearly, $\xi \leq \xi^{\frac{1}{4}} = f\xi$ for all $\xi \in X$; thus, f is a dominating map.*

Example 4 ([14]). *Let $f : X \to X$ be a mapping defined by $f\xi = \frac{1}{\xi+1}$, where $X = [1, +\infty)$ is endowed with usual ordering. Clearly, $f\xi = \frac{1}{\xi+1} \leq \xi$ for all $\xi \in X$; hence, f is a dominated map.*

An assertion similar to the following lemma was used (and proved) in the course of proofs of several fixed point results in various articles.

Lemma 1 ([26]). *Every sequence $\{\xi_n\}_{n\in\mathbb{N}}$ from a b-metric space (X, d) with the property that there exists $\gamma \in [0, 1)$ such that*

$$d(\xi_n, \xi_{n+1}) \leq \gamma d(\xi_{n-1}, \xi_n)$$

for every $n \in \mathbb{N}$ is b-Cauchy.

Lemma 2. *Let (X, d) be a b-metric space with $s \geq 1$ and $\{\eta_n\}$ a sequence in X such that $\lim\limits_{n\to\infty} d(\eta_{n+1}, \eta_n) = 0$. If $\{\eta_{2n}\}$ or $\{\eta_{2n-1}\}$ is a b-Cauchy sequence, then $\{\eta_n\}$ is a b-Cauchy sequence in X.*

Proof. We only prove the case that $\{\eta_{2n}\}$ is a b-Cauchy sequence. The another case can be proved similarly.

In view of $\lim\limits_{n\to\infty} d(\eta_{n+1}, \eta_n) = 0$, then for every $\varepsilon > 0$, there is a natural number N_1 such that, for all $n \geq N_1$,

$$d(\eta_{n+1}, \eta_n) < \frac{\varepsilon}{3s^2}. \tag{1}$$

Since $\{\eta_{2n}\}$ is a b-Cauchy sequence, then for the above $\varepsilon > 0$ there is a natural number N_2 such that, for all $n \geq N_2$ and any $p \in \mathbb{N}$, one has

$$d(\eta_{2n}, \eta_{2n+2p}) < \frac{\varepsilon}{3s^2}. \tag{2}$$

Now, let $N = \max\{N_1, N_2\}$. We shall claim that, for all $n > N$, it satisfies $d(\eta_n, \eta_{n+p}) < \varepsilon$. We complete the proof with four cases.

(c1) If n and p are even numbers, then, by (2), it follows that

$$d(\eta_n, \eta_{n+p}) < \frac{\varepsilon}{3s^2} < \varepsilon.$$

(c2) If n is an odd number and $n + p$ is an even number, then, by (1) and (2), one has

$$d(\eta_n, \eta_{n+p}) \leq s[d(\eta_n, \eta_{n+1}) + d(\eta_{n+1}, \eta_{n+p})] < s\Big(\frac{\varepsilon}{3s^2} + \frac{\varepsilon}{3s^2}\Big) < \varepsilon.$$

(c3) If n is an even number and $n + p$ is an odd number, then, by (1) and (2), it is easy to see that

$$d(\eta_n, \eta_{n+p}) \leq s[d(\eta_n, \eta_{n+p+1}) + d(\eta_{n+p}, \eta_{n+p+1})] < s\Big(\frac{\varepsilon}{3s^2} + \frac{\varepsilon}{3s^2}\Big) < \varepsilon.$$

(c4) If n and $n+p$ all are odd numbers, then, by (1) and (2), we have

$$\begin{aligned} d(\eta_n, \eta_{n+p}) &\leq s[d(\eta_n, \eta_{n+1}) + d(\eta_{n+1}, \eta_{n+p})] \\ &\leq sd(\eta_n, \eta_{n+1}) + s^2[d(\eta_{n+1}, \eta_{n+p+1}) + d(\eta_{n+p}, \eta_{n+p+1})] \\ &\leq s \cdot \frac{\varepsilon}{3s^2} + s^2 \cdot \left(\frac{\varepsilon}{3s^2} + \frac{\varepsilon}{3s^2}\right) \\ &< \varepsilon. \end{aligned}$$

Hence, $\{\eta_n\}$ is a b-Cauchy sequence. □

3. Main Results

In this section, we improve and generalize some common fixed point theorems from several references in several sides.

Throughout this paper, let P be the family of all functions $\beta : [0, +\infty) \to [0, 1)$. Let Ψ be the family of all functions $\psi : \mathbb{R}^+ \to \mathbb{R}^+$ satisfying the condition that ψ is continuous, nondecreasing and $\psi(t) = 0$ if and only if $t = 0$. In this case, ψ is called altering distance function.

Let $(X, \preceq, d)$ be a partially ordered b-metric space with $s > 1$ and $f, g, S, T : X \to X$ be mappings. If there exist $\beta \in P$ and $\psi \in \Psi$ and a constant $L \geq 0$ such that for every two comparable elements $\xi, \eta \in X$, it satisfies

$$\psi(s^\varepsilon d(f\xi, g\eta)) \leq \beta(M(\xi, \eta))\psi(\max\{d(S\xi, T\eta), d(S\xi, f\xi), d(T\eta, g\eta)\}) + L\psi(N(\xi, \eta)), \tag{3}$$

where

$$M(\xi, \eta) = \psi\left(\max\left\{d(S\xi, T\eta), d(S\xi, f\xi), d(T\eta, g\eta), \frac{d(S\xi, g\eta) + d(T\eta, f\xi)}{2s}\right\}\right), \tag{4}$$

$$N(\xi, \eta) = \min\{d(S\xi, T\eta), d(S\xi, g\eta), d(T\eta, f\xi), d(g\eta, T\eta), d(\xi, g\eta)\}, \tag{5}$$

and $\varepsilon > 0$ is a constant, then (f, g) is said to be a (ψ, β, L)-ordered contractive pair with respect to S and T.

Theorem 1. *Let f, g, S and T be self-mappings on a partially ordered b-complete b-metric space $(X, \preceq, d)$ with $s > 1$. Let $fX \subseteq TX$ and $gX \subseteq SX$. Suppose that (f, g) of dominating maps is a (ψ, β, L)-ordered contractive pair with respect to dominated maps S and T. If $\{\xi_n\}$ is a nondecreasing sequence with $\xi_n \preceq \eta_n$ for all n and $\eta_n \to u$ implies $\xi_n \preceq u$ and either*

(i) f or S is b-continuous, (f, S) are compatible and (g, T) are weakly compatible;

(ii) g or T is b-continuous, (g, T) are compatible and (f, S) are weakly compatible, then the mappings f, g, S and T possess a common fixed point in X. Moreover, the set of common points of f, g, S and T is well ordered if f, g, S and T have a unique common fixed point.

Proof. Let ξ_0 be an arbitrary point of X. Similar to [14], we construct a sequence $\{\eta_n\}$ in X such that $\eta_{2n-1} = T\xi_{2n-1} = f\xi_{2n-2}$ and $\eta_{2n} = S\xi_{2n} = g\xi_{2n-1}$. Since f, g are dominating maps and S, T are dominated maps, it follows that $\xi_{2n-2} \preceq f\xi_{2n-2} = T\xi_{2n-1} \preceq \xi_{2n-1}$ and $\xi_{2n-1} \preceq g\xi_{2n-1} = S\xi_{2n} \preceq \xi_{2n}$. Thus, for all $n \geq 1$, we have $\xi_n \preceq \xi_{n+1}$.

Without loss of generality, we assume $d(\eta_{2n}, \eta_{2n+1}) > 0$ for every n. If not, then $\eta_{2n_0} = \eta_{2n_0+1}$ for some $n_0 \in \mathbb{N}$. From (3) to (5), we obtain

$$\begin{aligned} &\psi(s^\varepsilon d(\eta_{2n_0+1}, \eta_{2n_0+2})) = \psi(s^\varepsilon d(f\xi_{2n_0}, g\xi_{2n_0+1})) \\ &\leq \beta(M(\xi_{2n_0}, \xi_{2n_0+1})) \times \psi(\max\{d(S\xi_{2n_0}, T\xi_{2n_0+1}), d(S\xi_{2n_0}, f\xi_{2n_0}), d(T\xi_{2n_0+1}, g\xi_{2n_0+1})\}) \\ &\quad + L\psi(N(\xi_{2n_0}, \xi_{2n_0+1})) \\ &= \beta(M(\xi_{2n_0}, \xi_{2n_0+1})) \times \psi(\max\{d(\eta_{2n_0}, \eta_{2n_0+1}), d(\eta_{2n_0}, \eta_{2n_0+1}), d(\eta_{2n_0+1}, \eta_{2n_0+2})\}) \end{aligned}$$

$$
\begin{aligned}
&+ L\psi(N(\xi_{2n_0}, \xi_{2n_0+1})) \\
&= \beta(M(\xi_{2n_0}, \xi_{2n_0+1})) \times \psi(\max\{0, 0, d(\eta_{2n_0+1}, \eta_{2n_0+2})\}) \\
&= \beta(M(\xi_{2n_0}, \xi_{2n_0+1}))\psi(d(\eta_{2n_0+1}, \eta_{2n_0+2})) \\
&\leq \psi(d(\eta_{2n_0+1}, \eta_{2n_0+2})),
\end{aligned} \tag{6}
$$

where

$$
\begin{aligned}
&N(\xi_{2n_0}, \xi_{2n_0+1})) \\
&= \min\{d(S\xi_{2n_0}, T\xi_{2n_0+1}), d(S\xi_{2n_0}, g\xi_{2n_0+1}), d(T\xi_{2n_0+1}, f\xi_{2n_0}), d(g\xi_{2n_0+1}, T\xi_{2n_0+1}), d(\xi_{2n_0}, g\xi_{2n_0+1})\} \\
&= \min\{d(\eta_{2n_0}, \eta_{2n_0+1}), d(\eta_{2n_0}, \eta_{2n_0+2}), d(\eta_{2n_0+1}, \eta_{2n_0+1}), d(\eta_{2n_0+2}, \eta_{2n_0+1}), d(\xi_{2n_0}, \eta_{2n_0+2})\} \\
&= \min\{0, d(\eta_{2n_0}, \eta_{2n_0+2}), 0, d(\eta_{2n_0+2}, \eta_{2n_0+1}), d(\xi_{2n_0}, \eta_{2n_0+2})\} \\
&= 0,
\end{aligned}
$$

then

$$\psi(N(\xi_{2n_0}, \xi_{2n_0+1})) = 0.$$

Thus, by the monotonicity of function ψ, it is valid from (6) that

$$s^{\varepsilon} d(\eta_{2n_0+1}, \eta_{2n_0+2}) \leq d(\eta_{2n_0+1}, \eta_{2n_0+2}),$$

that is,

$$d(\eta_{2n_0+1}, \eta_{2n_0+2}) \leq \frac{1}{s^{\varepsilon}} d(\eta_{2n_0+1}, \eta_{2n_0+2}),$$

so $d(\eta_{2n_0+1}, \eta_{2n_0+2}) = 0$ (because $s^{\varepsilon} > 1$). Hence, $\eta_{2n_0+1} = \eta_{2n_0+2}$.

Following similar arguments, we obtain $\eta_{2n_0+2} = \eta_{2n_0+3}$. Thus, $\{\eta_n\}$ becomes a constant sequence, and η_{2n_0} is the common fixed point of f, g, S and T. In this case, the conclusion we need to prove is clear.

Now, we take $d(\eta_{2n}, \eta_{2n+1}) > 0$ for each n. As ξ_{2n} and ξ_{2n+1} are comparable, by inequality (3) we have

$$
\begin{aligned}
&\psi(s^{\varepsilon} d(\eta_{2n+1}, \eta_{2n+2})) = \psi(s^{\varepsilon} d(f\xi_{2n}, g\xi_{2n+1})) \\
&\leq \beta(M(\xi_{2n}, \xi_{2n+1})) \times \psi(\max\{d(S\xi_{2n}, T\xi_{2n+1}), d(S\xi_{2n}, f\xi_{2n}), d(T\xi_{2n+1}, g\xi_{2n+1})\}) \\
&\quad + L\psi(N(\xi_{2n}, \xi_{2n+1})) \\
&= \beta(M(\xi_{2n}, \xi_{2n+1})) \times \psi(\max\{d(\eta_{2n}, \eta_{2n+1}), d(\eta_{2n}, \eta_{2n+1}), d(\eta_{2n+1}, \eta_{2n+2})\}) \\
&\quad + L\psi(N(\xi_{2n}, \xi_{2n+1})) \\
&= \beta(M(\xi_{2n}, \xi_{2n+1})) \times \psi(\max\{d(\eta_{2n}, \eta_{2n+1}), d(\eta_{2n+1}, \eta_{2n+2})\}), \\
&< \psi(\max\{d(\eta_{2n}, \eta_{2n+1}), d(\eta_{2n+1}, \eta_{2n+2})\}),
\end{aligned}
$$

which follows immediately from the monotonicity of function ψ that

$$s^{\varepsilon} d(\eta_{2n+1}, \eta_{2n+2}) < \max\{d(\eta_{2n}, \eta_{2n+1}), d(\eta_{2n+1}, \eta_{2n+2})\}. \tag{7}$$

Now, if

$$d(\eta_{2n}, \eta_{2n+1}) \leq d(\eta_{2n+1}, \eta_{2n+2}),$$

then by using (7) we have

$$s^{\varepsilon} d(\eta_{2n+1}, \eta_{2n+2}) < d(\eta_{2n+1}, \eta_{2n+2}),$$

which leads to a contradiction because of $s^{\varepsilon} > 1$. Therefore, $d(\eta_{2n}, \eta_{2n+1}) > d(\eta_{2n+1}, \eta_{2n+2})$. In this case, we have

$$s^{\varepsilon} d(\eta_{2n+1}, \eta_{2n+2}) < d(\eta_{2n}, \eta_{2n+1}),$$

which implies that

$$d(\eta_{2n+1}, \eta_{2n+2}) < \frac{1}{s^{\varepsilon}} d(\eta_{2n}, \eta_{2n+1}). \tag{8}$$

Again, by inequality (3) we have

$$\begin{aligned}
&\psi(s^{\varepsilon} d(\eta_{2n+1}, \eta_{2n})) = \psi(s^{\varepsilon} d(f\xi_{2n}, g\xi_{2n-1})) \\
&\leq \beta(M(\xi_{2n}, \xi_{2n-1})) \times \psi(\max\{d(S\xi_{2n}, T\xi_{2n-1}), d(S\xi_{2n}, f\xi_{2n}), d(T\xi_{2n-1}, g\xi_{2n-1})\}) \\
&\quad + L\psi(N(\xi_{2n}, \xi_{2n-1})) \\
&= \beta(M(\xi_{2n}, \xi_{2n-1})) \times \psi(\max\{d(\eta_{2n}, \eta_{2n-1}), d(\eta_{2n}, \eta_{2n+1}), d(\eta_{2n-1}, \eta_{2n})\}) \\
&\quad + L\psi(N(\xi_{2n}, \xi_{2n-1})) \\
&= \beta(M(\xi_{2n}, \xi_{2n-1})) \times \psi(\max\{d(\eta_{2n}, \eta_{2n-1}), d(\eta_{2n}, \eta_{2n+1})\}) \\
&< \psi(\max\{d(\eta_{2n}, \eta_{2n-1}), d(\eta_{2n}, \eta_{2n+1})\}),
\end{aligned} \tag{9}$$

where

$$\begin{aligned}
&N(\xi_{2n}, \xi_{2n-1})) \\
&= \min\{d(S\xi_{2n}, T\xi_{2n-1}), d(S\xi_{2n}, g\xi_{2n-1}), d(T\xi_{2n-1}, f\xi_{2n}), d(g\xi_{2n-1}, T\xi_{2n-1}), d(\xi_{2n}, g\xi_{2n-1})\} \\
&= \min\{d(\eta_{2n}, \eta_{2n-1}), d(\eta_{2n}, \eta_{2n}), d(\eta_{2n-1}, \eta_{2n+1}), d(\eta_{2n}, \eta_{2n-1}), d(\xi_{2n}, \eta_{2n})\} \\
&= \min\{d(\eta_{2n}, \eta_{2n-1}), 0, d(\eta_{2n-1}, \eta_{2n+1}), d(\eta_{2n}, \eta_{2n-1}), d(\xi_{2n}, \eta_{2n})\} \\
&= 0.
\end{aligned}$$

By (9) and the monotonicity of function ψ, we have

$$s^{\varepsilon} d(\eta_{2n+1}, \eta_{2n}) < \max\{d(\eta_{2n}, \eta_{2n-1}), d(\eta_{2n}, \eta_{2n+1})\}. \tag{10}$$

Now, if

$$d(\eta_{2n}, \eta_{2n-1}) \leq d(\eta_{2n}, \eta_{2n+1}),$$

then by using (10) we have

$$s^{\varepsilon} d(\eta_{2n}, \eta_{2n+1}) < d(\eta_{2n}, \eta_{2n+1}),$$

which leads to a contradiction because of $s^{\varepsilon} > 1$. Therefore, $d(\eta_{2n}, \eta_{2n-1}) > d(\eta_{2n}, \eta_{2n+1})$. In this case, we have

$$s^{\varepsilon} d(\eta_{2n}, \eta_{2n+1}) < d(\eta_{2n-1}, \eta_{2n}),$$

which implies that

$$d(\eta_{2n}, \eta_{2n+1}) < \frac{1}{s^{\varepsilon}} d(\eta_{2n-1}, \eta_{2n}). \tag{11}$$

Making full use of (8) and (11), we have

$$d(\eta_n, \eta_{n+1}) < \frac{1}{s^{\varepsilon}} d(\eta_{n-1}, \eta_n).$$

Accordingly, by Lemma 1, we claim that $\{\eta_n\}$ is a b-Cauchy sequence. Since $(X, \preceq, d)$ is b-complete, then there exists a point ζ in X such that $\{\eta_n\}$ converges to ζ.

We first suppose that (i) holds. Assume that S is b-continuous. Because (f, S) are compatible, we have

$$\lim_{n\to\infty} d(fS\xi_{2n+2}, Sf\xi_{2n+2}) = 0,$$

that is,

$$\lim_{n\to\infty} d(f\eta_{2n+2}, S\eta_{2n+3}) = 0.$$

As a result, by the b-continuity of S, we speculate that

$$d(f\eta_{2n+2}, S\zeta) \le s[d(f\eta_{2n+2}, S\eta_{2n+3}) + d(S\eta_{2n+3}, S\zeta)] \to 0 \ \ (n \to \infty),$$

which implies that

$$\lim_{n\to\infty} d(f\eta_{2n+2}, S\zeta) = 0. \tag{12}$$

Now, we show that $\zeta = S\zeta$. If not, that is, $d(S\zeta, \zeta) > 0$. As $\xi_{2n+1} \preceq g\xi_{2n+1} = S\xi_{2n+2}$, from inequality (3), we have

$$\begin{aligned}
&\psi(s^{\varepsilon} d(f\eta_{2n+2}, \eta_{2n+2})) \\
&= \psi(s^{\varepsilon} d(fS\xi_{2n+2}, g\xi_{2n+1})) \\
&\le \beta(M(S\xi_{2n+2}, \xi_{2n+1})) \times \psi(\max\{d(SS\xi_{2n+2}, T\xi_{2n+1}), \\
&\quad d(SS\xi_{2n+2}, fS\xi_{2n+2}), d(T\xi_{2n+1}, g\xi_{2n+1})\} \\
&\quad + L\psi(N(S\xi_{2n+2}, \xi_{2n+1})) \\
&< \psi(\max\{d(SS\xi_{2n+2}, T\xi_{2n+1}), d(SS\xi_{2n+2}, fS\xi_{2n+2}), d(T\xi_{2n+1}, g\xi_{2n+1})\}) \\
&= \psi(\max\{d(S\eta_{2n+2}, \eta_{2n+1}), d(S\eta_{2n+2}, f\eta_{2n+2}), d(\eta_{2n+1}, \eta_{2n+2})\}),
\end{aligned} \tag{13}$$

where

$$\begin{aligned}
N(S\xi_{2n+2}, \xi_{2n+1})) &= \min\{d(SS\xi_{2n+2}, T\xi_{2n+1}), d(SS\xi_{2n+2}, g\xi_{2n+1}), d(T\xi_{2n+1}, fS\xi_{2n+2}), \\
&\quad d(g\xi_{2n+1}, T\xi_{2n+1}), d(S\xi_{2n+2}, g\xi_{2n+1})\} \\
&= \min\{d(S\eta_{2n+2}, \eta_{2n+1}), d(S\eta_{2n+2}, \eta_{2n+2}), d(\eta_{2n+1}, f\eta_{2n+2}), \\
&\quad d(\eta_{2n+2}, \eta_{2n+1}), d(\eta_{2n+2}, \eta_{2n+2})\} \\
&= 0.
\end{aligned}$$

By (13) and the monotonicity of function ψ, we have

$$s^{\varepsilon} d(f\eta_{2n+2}, \eta_{2n+2}) < \max\{d(S\eta_{2n+2}, \eta_{2n+1}), d(S\eta_{2n+2}, f\eta_{2n+2}), d(\eta_{2n+1}, \eta_{2n+2})\}. \tag{14}$$

Combing (12) and the b-continuity of function S, we obtain

$$d(S\eta_{2n+2}, f\eta_{2n+2}) \le s[d(S\eta_{2n+2}, S\zeta) + d(S\zeta, f\eta_{2n+2})] \to s(0+0) = 0 \ (n \to \infty),$$

which means that

$$\lim_{n\to\infty} d(S\eta_{2n+2}, f\eta_{2n+2}) = 0. \tag{15}$$

Moreover, since $\{\eta_n\}$ is a b-Cauchy sequence, we have

$$\lim_{n\to\infty} d(\eta_{2n+1}, \eta_{2n+2}) = 0. \tag{16}$$

By (15) and (16), there exists $N_1 \in \mathbb{N}$ such that, for all $n > N_1$, one has

$$d(S\eta_{2n+2}, \eta_{2n+1}) > d(S\eta_{2n+2}, f\eta_{2n+2}), \quad d(S\eta_{2n+2}, \eta_{2n+1}) > d(\eta_{2n+1}, \eta_{2n+2}). \tag{17}$$

Via (14) and (17), it is easy to see that

$$s^{\varepsilon} d(f\eta_{2n+2}, \eta_{2n+2}) < d(S\eta_{2n+2}, \eta_{2n+1}) \ \ (n > N_1). \tag{18}$$

Using the triangular inequality of the b-metric (12) and the b-continuity of function S, we obtain

$$
\begin{aligned}
&|d(f\eta_{2n+2},\eta_{2n+2}) - d(S\eta_{2n+2},\eta_{2n+1})| \\
&= \big|[d(f\eta_{2n+2},\eta_{2n+2}) - sd(\eta_{2n+2},S\zeta)] + [sd(\eta_{2n+2},S\zeta) - d(S\zeta,\zeta)] \\
&\quad + [d(S\zeta,\zeta) - sd(S\eta_{n+2},\zeta)] + [sd(S\eta_{n+2},\zeta) - d(S\eta_{n+2},\eta_{2n+1})]\big| \\
&\leq \big|d(f\eta_{2n+2},\eta_{2n+2}) - sd(\eta_{2n+2},S\zeta)\big| + \big|sd(\eta_{2n+2},S\zeta) - d(S\zeta,\zeta)\big| \\
&\quad + \big|d(S\zeta,\zeta) - sd(S\eta_{n+2},\zeta)\big| + \big|sd(S\eta_{n+2},\zeta) - d(S\eta_{n+2},\eta_{2n+1})\big| \\
&\leq sd(f\eta_{2n+2},S\zeta) + sd(\eta_{2n+2},\zeta) + sd(S\zeta,S\eta_{n+2}) + sd(\zeta,\eta_{2n+1}) \\
&\to 0 \ \ (n \to \infty),
\end{aligned}
$$

which establishes that

$$
\limsup_{n\to\infty} d(f\eta_{2n+2},\eta_{2n+2}) = \limsup_{n\to\infty} d(S\eta_{2n+2},\eta_{2n+1}). \tag{19}
$$

Consider (18) and (19), they lead to a contradiction because of $s^{\varepsilon} > 1$. Consequently, $S\zeta = \zeta$.

Now, by virtue of $\xi_{2n+1} \prec g\xi_{2n+1}$ and $g\xi_{2n+1} \to \zeta$ as $n \to \infty$, $\xi_{2n+1} \prec \zeta$. It suffices to prove $\zeta = f\zeta$. As a matter of fact, firstly, notice that

$$
\begin{aligned}
&|d(f\zeta,\eta_{n+2}) - d(\zeta,f\zeta)| \\
&= \big|[d(f\zeta,\eta_{n+2}) - sd(f\zeta,\eta_{n+1})] + [sd(f\zeta,\eta_{n+1}) - d(\zeta,f\zeta)]\big| \\
&\leq \big|d(f\zeta,\eta_{n+2}) - sd(f\zeta,\eta_{n+1})\big| + \big|sd(f\zeta,\eta_{n+1}) - d(\zeta,f\zeta)\big| \\
&\leq sd(\eta_{n+2},\eta_{n+1}) + sd(\eta_{n+1},\zeta) \to 0 \ \ (n \to \infty),
\end{aligned}
$$

which follows that

$$
\limsup_{n\to\infty} d(f\zeta,\eta_{n+2}) = d(\zeta,f\zeta). \tag{20}
$$

Secondly, by inequality (3), we have

$$
\begin{aligned}
&\psi(s^{\varepsilon} d(f\zeta,\eta_{2n+2})) \\
&= \psi(s^{\varepsilon} d(f\zeta,g\xi_{2n+1})) \\
&\leq \beta(M(\zeta,\xi_{2n+1})) \times \psi(\max\{d(S\zeta,T\xi_{2n+1}),d(S\zeta,f\zeta),d(T\xi_{2n+1},g\xi_{2n+1})\}) \\
&\quad + L\psi(N(\zeta,\xi_{2n+1})) \\
&= \beta(M(\zeta,\xi_{2n+1})) \times \psi(\max\{d(\zeta,T\xi_{2n+1}),d(\zeta,f\zeta),d(T\xi_{2n+1},g\xi_{2n+1})\}) \\
&\quad + L\psi(N(\zeta,\xi_{2n+1})) \\
&< \psi(\max\{d(\zeta,\eta_{2n+1}),d(\zeta,f\zeta),d(\eta_{2n+1},\eta_{2n+2})\}) \\
&\quad + L\psi(N(\zeta,\xi_{2n+1})),
\end{aligned} \tag{21}
$$

where

$$
\begin{aligned}
\psi(N(\zeta,\xi_{2n+1})) = \psi(\min\{&d(S\zeta,T\xi_{2n+1}),d(S\zeta,g\xi_{2n+1}),d(T\xi_{2n+1},f\zeta), \\
&d(g\xi_{2n+1},T\xi_{2n+1}),d(\zeta,g\xi_{2n+1})\})
\end{aligned}
$$

tends to

$$
\psi\left(\min\left\{\limsup_{n\to\infty} d(S\zeta,T\xi_{2n+1}),\limsup_{n\to\infty} d(S\zeta,g\xi_{2n+1}),\limsup_{n\to\infty} d(T\xi_{2n+1},f\zeta),0,0\right\}\right) = \psi(0) = 0
$$

as $n \to \infty$. By taking the upper limit as $n \to \infty$ from (21), we obtain

$$
s^{\varepsilon} \limsup_{n\to\infty} d(f\zeta,\eta_{2n+2}) \leq d(f\zeta,\zeta),
$$

which is a contradiction with $s^{\varepsilon} > 1$ and (20) unless $\limsup_{n\to\infty} d(f\zeta, \eta_{2n+2}) = 0$. As a result, by

$$\frac{1}{s}d(f\zeta,\zeta) \leq d(f\zeta,\eta_{2n+2}) + d(\eta_{2n+2},\zeta),$$

we have

$$\frac{1}{s}d(f\zeta,\zeta) \leq \limsup_{n\to\infty}[d(f\zeta,\eta_{2n+2}) + d(\eta_{2n+2},\zeta)] = 0,$$

which implies that $d(f\zeta,\zeta) = 0$. Hence, $f\zeta = \zeta$.

In view of $f(X) \subseteq T(X)$, then there exists a point $w \in X$ such that $\zeta = f\zeta = Tw$. Now, we show $d(Tw, gw) = 0$. If not, i.e., $d(Tw, gw) > 0$. Since $\zeta \preceq f\zeta = Tw \preceq w$ implies $\zeta \preceq w$, from inequality (3), we have

$$\begin{aligned}
&\psi(s^{\varepsilon}d(Tw,gw))\\
&= \psi(s^{\varepsilon}d(f\zeta,gw))\\
&\leq \beta(M(\zeta,w)) \times \psi(\max\{d(S\zeta,Tw),d(S\zeta,f\zeta),d(Tw,gw)\})\\
&\quad + L\psi(N(\zeta,w))\\
&= \beta(M(\zeta,w)) \times \psi(\max\{0,0,d(Tw,gw)\})\\
&\quad + L\psi(\min\{d(S\zeta,Tw),d(S\zeta,gw),d(Tw,f\zeta),d(gw,Tw),d(\zeta,gw)\}))\\
&= \beta(M(\zeta,w)) \times \psi(d(Tw,gw))\\
&\quad + L\psi(\min\{0,d(\zeta,gw),0,d(gw,\zeta),d(\zeta,gw)\}))\\
&= \beta(M(\zeta,w))\psi(d(Tw,gw))\\
&< \psi(d(Tw,gw)).
\end{aligned}$$

Hence, by the monotonicity of function ψ, we have

$$s^{\varepsilon}d(Tw,gw) < d(Tw,gw),$$

which leads to a contradiction with $s^{\varepsilon} > 1$. As a result, $Tw = gw$. On account of the fact that g and T are weakly compatible, we obtain

$$g\zeta = gf\zeta = gTw = Tgw = Tf\zeta = T\zeta.$$

Thus, ζ is a coincidence point of g and T. Next, we show that $\zeta = g\zeta$. As $\xi_{2n} \preceq f\xi_{2n}$ and $f\xi_{2n} \to \zeta$ $(n \to \infty)$ implies that $\xi_{2n} \preceq \zeta$, from (3) we have

$$\begin{aligned}
&\psi(s^{\varepsilon}d(\eta_{2n+1},g\zeta)) = \psi(s^{\varepsilon}d(f\xi_{2n},g\zeta))\\
&\leq \beta(M(\xi_{2n},\zeta)) \times \psi(\max\{d(S\xi_{2n},T\zeta),d(S\xi_{2n},f\xi_{2n}),d(T\zeta,g\zeta)\}) + L\psi(N(\xi_{2n},\zeta))\\
&< \psi(\max\{d(S\xi_{2n},T\zeta),d(S\xi_{2n},f\xi_{2n}),d(T\zeta,g\zeta)\})\\
&\quad + L\psi(\min\{d(S\xi_{2n},T\zeta),d(S\xi_{2n},g\zeta),d(T\zeta,f\xi_{2n}),d(g\zeta,T\zeta),d(\xi_{2n},g\zeta)\})\\
&= \psi(\max\{d(S\xi_{2n},T\zeta),d(S\xi_{2n},f\xi_{2n}),0\})\\
&\quad + L\psi(\min\{d(S\xi_{2n},T\zeta),d(S\xi_{2n},g\zeta),d(T\zeta,f\xi_{2n}),0,d(\xi_{2n},g\zeta)\})\\
&= \psi(\max\{d(S\xi_{2n},T\zeta),d(S\xi_{2n},f\xi_{2n})\}) + L\psi(0)\\
&= \psi(\max\{d(\eta_{2n},g\zeta),d(\eta_{2n},\eta_{2n+1})\}),
\end{aligned}$$

which follows immediately from the monotonicity of function ψ that

$$s^{\varepsilon}d(f\eta_{2n+1},g\zeta) < \max\{d(\eta_{2n},g\zeta),d(\eta_{2n},\eta_{2n+1})\}. \quad (22)$$

Since $\lim_{n\to\infty} d(\eta_{2n}, \eta_{2n+1}) = 0$, then there exists $N_2 \in \mathbb{N}$ such that, for all $n > N_2$, one has

$$d(\eta_{2n}, g\zeta) > d(\eta_{2n}, \eta_{2n+1}). \tag{23}$$

Considering (22) and (23), we acquire

$$s^{\varepsilon} d(\eta_{2n+1}, g\zeta) < d(\eta_{2n}, g\zeta) \ \ (n > N_2).$$

Thus, it implies

$$s^{\varepsilon} \limsup_{n\to\infty} d(\eta_{2n+1}, g\zeta) \le \limsup_{n\to\infty} d(\eta_{2n}, g\zeta). \tag{24}$$

By virtue of

$$\begin{aligned}
&|d(\eta_{2n+1}, g\zeta) - d(\eta_{2n}, g\zeta)| \\
&= |[d(\eta_{2n+1}, g\zeta) - sd(g\zeta, \eta_{2n-1})] + [sd(g\zeta, \eta_{2n-1}) - d(\eta_{2n}, g\zeta)]| \\
&\le |d(\eta_{2n+1}, g\zeta) - sd(g\zeta, \eta_{2n-1})| + |sd(g\zeta, \eta_{2n-1}) - d(\eta_{2n}, g\zeta)| \\
&\le sd(\eta_{2n+1}, \eta_{2n-1}) + sd(\eta_{2n-1}, \eta_{2n}) \to 0 \ \ (n \to \infty),
\end{aligned}$$

which follows that

$$\limsup_{n\to\infty} d(\eta_{2n+1}, g\zeta) = \limsup_{n\to\infty} d(\eta_{2n}, g\zeta).$$

Consequently, (24) is a contradiction with $s^{\varepsilon} > 1$ unless $\limsup_{n\to\infty} d(\eta_{2n+1}, g\zeta) = 0$. That is to say, $\limsup_{n\to\infty} d(\eta_{2n+1}, g\zeta) = 0$. Now, by

$$\frac{1}{s} d(g\zeta, \zeta) \le d(g\zeta, \eta_{2n+1}) + d(\eta_{2n+1}, \zeta),$$

we claim that

$$\frac{1}{s} d(g\zeta, \zeta) \le \limsup_{n\to\infty} d(g\zeta, \eta_{2n+1}) + \limsup_{n\to\infty} d(\eta_{2n+1}, \zeta) = 0,$$

which follows that $d(g\zeta, \zeta) = 0$. Thus, $g\zeta = \zeta$.

To sum up, $f\zeta = g\zeta = S\zeta = T\zeta = \zeta$. In other words, ζ is a common fixed point of f, g, S and T. The proof is similar when f is b-continuous.

Similarly, the result follows when (ii) holds. Now, suppose that the set of common fixed points of f, g, S and T is well ordered; we will show that the common fixed point of f, g, S and T is unique. Indeed, assume, on the contrary, that $fq = gq = Sq = Tq = q$ and $fr = gr = Sr = Tr = r$ but $d(q, r) > 0$. By the given assumption, we replace ξ with q and η with r in (3). Then,

$$\begin{aligned}
&\psi(s^{\varepsilon} d(q, r)) = \psi(s^{\varepsilon} d(fq, gr)) \\
&\le \beta(M(q, r)) \times \psi(\max\{d(Sq, Tr), d(Sq, fq), d(Tr, gr)\}) \\
&\quad + L\psi(N(q, r)) \\
&< \psi(d(q, r)).
\end{aligned}$$

Consequently, we claim that $s^{\varepsilon} d(q, r) < d(q, r)$, a contradiction. As a result, $q = r$ (because $s^{\varepsilon} > 1$). In reverse, if f, g, S and T are single, then it is well ordered. □

Remark 1. *Theorem 1 greatly generalizes Theorem 12 of [14] from several sides. On the one hand, Theorem 1 refers to the conclusion in the setting of b-metric spaces, whereas Theorem 12 of [14] considered the result in usual metric space. It is well-known that b-metric space is a sharp generalization of usual metric space since the given b-metric usually is not necessarily continuous,* *but the usual metric must be a continuous function. Therefore, Theorem 1 is more important than Theorem 12 of [14]. On the other hand, as compared with Theorem 12 of [14], function β from Theorem 1 satisfies the simpler condition. In addition, the proof of Theorem 1 is more straightforward than the one of Theorem 12 of [14].*

Remark 2. *We use Lemma 2 to prove that the constructed sequence is a b-Cauchy sequence instead of using Lemma 11 from [14] or Lemma 1 from [16]. This is a straightforward improvement because Lemma 2 is easily understood for most of our readers. Otherwise, by Lemma 2, we also can prove that the sequence is a b-Cauchy sequence but, due to the complicated process, we omit it in this paper. In addition, in order to overcome the discontinuity of b-metric, we use a new method to prove our theorem. This is a great innovation.*

Example 5. *Let $X = \{1,2,3,4\}$ be a partially ordered set defined as $\xi \preceq \eta$ if and only if $\xi \geq \eta$ and $d(\xi,\eta) = |\xi-\eta|^2$ for all $\xi,\eta \in X$. Then, (X,d) is a b-complete b-metric space with $s = \frac{9}{5}$. Define ordered self-mappings f, g, S, and T on X using*

$$f = \begin{pmatrix} 1 & 2 & 3 & 4 \\ 1 & 1 & 2 & 2 \end{pmatrix}, \quad g = \begin{pmatrix} 1 & 2 & 3 & 4 \\ 1 & 1 & 1 & 2 \end{pmatrix},$$

$$S = \begin{pmatrix} 1 & 2 & 3 & 4 \\ 1 & 3 & 4 & 4 \end{pmatrix}, \quad T = \begin{pmatrix} 1 & 2 & 3 & 4 \\ 1 & 4 & 3 & 4 \end{pmatrix}.$$

It is easy to verify that the mappings f and g are dominating and S and T are dominated. Take $\psi(\xi) = \ln(\xi+1)$ and $\beta = \frac{\psi(\xi)}{\xi}$; then, the mappings f, g, S and T satisfy all the conditions given in Theorem 1 with $\varepsilon = \frac{1}{4}$. Moreover, one is the unique common fixed point of f, g, S, and T.

Theorem 2. *Let f, g, S and T be self-mappings on a partially ordered b-complete b-metric space $(X, \preceq, d)$ with $s > 1$. Let $f(X) \subseteq T(X)$ and $g(X) \subseteq S(X)$. Suppose that the mappings f, g, S and T are b-continuous, the pairs (f,S) and (g,T) are compatible, and the pairs (f,g) and (g,f) are partially weakly increasing with respect to T and S, respectively. Assume that (f,g) is a (ψ,β,L)-ordered contractive pair with respect to S and T for each $\xi,\eta \in X$, for which $S\xi$ and $T\eta$ are comparable. Then, the pairs (f,S) and (g,T) have a coincidence point $\zeta \in X$. Moreover, ζ is a coincidence point of the mappings f, g, S and T provided that $S\zeta$ and $T\zeta$ are comparable.*

Proof. Choose $\xi_0 \in X$. Define a sequence $\{\eta_n\}$ in X that satisfies $\eta_{2n} = f\xi_{2n} = T\xi_{2n+1}$ and $\eta_{2n+1} = g\xi_{2n+1} = S\xi_{2n+2}$ for all $n \in \mathbb{N}$. By the hypothesis, it is easy to see that $\eta_n \preceq \eta_{n+1}$ for all $n \geq 1$. We start the proof with two steps.

Step 1. We prove that

$$d(\eta_{n+1},\eta_{n+2}) \leq \lambda d(\eta_n,\eta_{n+1}), \tag{25}$$

for each $n \in \mathbb{N}$, where $\lambda \in [0,1)$ is a constant.

Firstly, we assume $\eta_n \neq \eta_{n+1}$ for each $n \in \mathbb{N}$. Since $S\xi_{2n} = \eta_{2n-1} = g\xi_{2n-1}$ and $T\xi_{2n+1} = \eta_{2n} = f\xi_{2n}$ are comparable, then, via (3), it has

$$\begin{aligned}
&\psi(s^{\varepsilon} d(\eta_{2n},\eta_{2n+1})) \\
&= \psi(s^{\varepsilon} d(f\xi_{2n}, g\xi_{2n+1})) \\
&\leq \beta(M(\xi_{2n},\xi_{2n+1})) \times \psi(\max\{d(S\xi_{2n},T\xi_{2n+1}), d(S\xi_{2n},f\xi_{2n}), d(T\xi_{2n+1},g\xi_{2n+1})\}) \\
&\quad + L\psi(\min\{d(S\xi_{2n},T\xi_{2n+1}), d(S\xi_{2n},g\xi_{2n+1}), d(T\xi_{2n+1},f\xi_{2n}), d(g\xi_{2n+1},T\xi_{2n+1}), d(\xi_{2n},g\xi_{2n+1})\}) \\
&< \psi(\max\{d(\eta_{2n-1},\eta_{2n}), d(\eta_{2n-1},\eta_{2n}), d(\eta_{2n},\eta_{2n+1})\}) \\
&\quad + L\psi(\min\{d(\eta_{2n-1},\eta_{2n}), d(\eta_{2n-1},\eta_{2n+1}), d(\eta_{2n},\eta_{2n}), d(\eta_{2n+1},\eta_{2n}), d(\xi_{2n},\eta_{2n+1})\})) \\
&= \psi(\max\{d(\eta_{2n-1},\eta_{2n}), d(\eta_{2n},\eta_{2n+1})\}),
\end{aligned}$$

which follows from the monotonicity of function ψ that

$$s^{\varepsilon}d(\eta_{2n},\eta_{2n+1}) < \max\{d(\eta_{2n-1},\eta_{2n}), d(\eta_{2n},\eta_{2n+1})\}. \tag{26}$$

If $d(\eta_{2n-1},\eta_{2n}) \leq d(\eta_{2n},\eta_{2n+1})$, then by (26) it means that

$$s^{\varepsilon}d(\eta_{2n},\eta_{2n+1}) < d(\eta_{2n},\eta_{2n+1}),$$

which leads to a contradiction (because $s^{\varepsilon} > 1$). Then,

$$s^{\varepsilon}d(\eta_{2n},\eta_{2n+1}) < d(\eta_{2n-1},\eta_{2n}). \tag{27}$$

Again, since $S\xi_{2n+2} = \eta_{2n+1} = g\xi_{2n+1}$ and $T\xi_{2n+1} = \eta_{2n} = f\xi_{2n}$ are comparable, then, by (3), it implies that

$$\begin{aligned}
&\psi(s^{\varepsilon}d(\eta_{2n+1},\eta_{2n+2})) = \psi(s^{\varepsilon}d(f\xi_{2n+2}, g\xi_{2n+1}))\\
&\leq \beta(M(\xi_{2n+2},\xi_{2n+1})) \times \psi(\max\{d(S\xi_{2n+2},T\xi_{2n+1}), d(S\xi_{2n+2},f\xi_{2n+2}), d(T\xi_{2n+1},g\xi_{2n+1})\})\\
&\quad + L\psi(\min\{d(S\xi_{2n+2},T\xi_{2n+1}), d(S\xi_{2n+2},g\xi_{2n+1}), d(T\xi_{2n+1},f\xi_{2n+2}),\\
&\qquad d(g\xi_{2n+1},T\xi_{2n+1}), d(\xi_{2n+2},g\xi_{2n+1})\})\\
&< \psi(\max\{d(\eta_{2n+1},\eta_{2n}), d(\eta_{2n+1},\eta_{2n+2}), d(\eta_{2n},\eta_{2n+1})\})\\
&\quad + L\psi(\min\{d(\eta_{2n+1},\eta_{2n}), d(\eta_{2n+1},\eta_{2n+1}), d(\eta_{2n},\eta_{2n+2}), d(\eta_{2n+1},\eta_{2n}), d(\xi_{2n+2},\eta_{2n+1})\}))\\
&= \psi(\max\{d(\eta_{2n+1},\eta_{2n+2}), d(\eta_{2n},\eta_{2n+1})\}),
\end{aligned}$$

which follows from the monotonicity of function ψ that

$$s^{\varepsilon}d(\eta_{2n+1},\eta_{2n+2}) < \max\{d(\eta_{2n+1},\eta_{2n+2}), d(\eta_{2n},\eta_{2n+1})\}. \tag{28}$$

If $d(\eta_{2n},\eta_{2n+1}) \leq d(\eta_{2n+1},\eta_{2n+2})$, then, by means of (28), it establishes

$$s^{\varepsilon}d(\eta_{2n+1},\eta_{2n+2}) < d(\eta_{2n+1},\eta_{2n+2}),$$

which leads to a contradiction (because $s^{\varepsilon} > 1$). Thus,

$$s^{\varepsilon}d(\eta_{2n+1},\eta_{2n+2}) < d(\eta_{2n},\eta_{2n+1}). \tag{29}$$

Now, by using (27) and (29), we obtain (25), where $\lambda = \frac{1}{s^{\varepsilon}} \in [0,1)$.

We now assume $\eta_{n_0} = \eta_{n_0+1}$ for some $n_0 \in \mathbb{N}$. If $n_0 = 2k-1$, then $\eta_{2k-1} = \eta_{2k}$ implies $\eta_{2k} = \eta_{2k+1}$. As a matter of fact, if $\eta_{2k} \neq \eta_{2k+1}$, i.e., $d(\eta_{2k},\eta_{2k+1}) > 0$, then, by the fact that $\eta_{2k} = f\xi_{2k} = T\xi_{2k+1}$ and $\eta_{2k-1} = g\xi_{2k-1} = S\xi_{2k}$ are comparable, then, via (26), we speculate that

$$s^{\varepsilon}d(\eta_{2k},\eta_{2k+1}) < \max\{d(\eta_{2k-1},\eta_{2k}), d(\eta_{2k},\eta_{2k+1})\} = d(\eta_{2k},\eta_{2k+1}).$$

This is a contradiction (because $s^{\varepsilon} > 1$). Hence, $d(\eta_{2k},\eta_{2k+1}) = 0$, i.e., $\eta_{2k} = \eta_{2k+1}$. If $n_0 = 2k$, then $\eta_{2k} = \eta_{2k+1}$ leads to $\eta_{2k+1} = \eta_{2k+2}$. Actually, if $\eta_{2k+1} \neq \eta_{2k+2}$, then, i.e., $d(\eta_{2k+1},\eta_{2k+2}) > 0$. Since $\eta_{2k+1} = g\xi_{2k+1} = S\xi_{2k+2}$ and $\eta_{2k} = f\xi_{2k} = T\xi_{2k+1}$ are comparable, then, by (28), we claim that

$$s^{\varepsilon}d(\eta_{2k+1},\eta_{2k+2}) < \max\{d(\eta_{2k},\eta_{2k+1}), d(\eta_{2k+1},\eta_{2k+2})\} = d(\eta_{2k+1},\eta_{2k+2}).$$

This is a contradiction (because $s^{\varepsilon} > 1$). Thus, $d(\eta_{2k+1},\eta_{2k+2}) = 0$, i.e., $\eta_{2k+1} = \eta_{2k+2}$. Therefore, the sequence $\{\eta_n\}$ in both cases is equal to a constant for $n \geq n_0$ and so (25) holds.

Step 2. We prove that f, g, S and T have a coincidence point. Taking advantage of (25) and Lemma 1, we say that $\{\eta_n\}$ is a b-Cauchy sequence. Since (X,d) is b-complete, then there is a $\zeta \in X$ satisfying that $\lim_{n\to\infty} \eta_n = \zeta$. We obtain

$$\lim_{n\to\infty} d(S\xi_{2n},\zeta) = \lim_{n\to\infty} d(f\xi_{2n},\zeta) = \lim_{n\to\infty} d(S\xi_{2n+2},\zeta) = \lim_{n\to\infty} d(T\xi_{2n+1},\zeta) = \lim_{n\to\infty} d(g\xi_{2n+1},\zeta) = 0.$$

Since the pairs (f,S) and (g,T) are compatible, then

$$\lim_{n\to\infty} d(Sf\xi_{2n}, fS\xi_{2n}) = \lim_{n\to\infty} d(Tg\xi_{2n+1}, gT\xi_{2n+1}) = 0.$$

On the other hand, owing to the b-continuity of f, g, S and T, we obtain

$$\lim_{n\to\infty} d(Sf\xi_{2n}, S\zeta) = \lim_{n\to\infty} d(fS\xi_{2n}, f\zeta) = 0,$$

$$\lim_{n\to\infty} d(Tg\xi_{2n+1}, T\zeta) = \lim_{n\to\infty} d(gT\xi_{2n+1}, g\zeta) = 0.$$

We now acquire that

$$\begin{aligned}\frac{1}{s}d(S\zeta, f\zeta) &\leq d(S\zeta, Sf\xi_{2n}) + d(Sf\xi_{2n}, f\zeta)\\ &\leq d(S\zeta, Sf\xi_{2n}) + s[d(Sf\xi_{2n}, fS\xi_{2n}) + d(fS\xi_{2n}, f\zeta)],\end{aligned} \tag{30}$$

and

$$\begin{aligned}\frac{1}{s}d(T\zeta, g\zeta) &\leq d(T\zeta, Tg\xi_{2n+1}) + d(Tg\xi_{2n+1}, g\zeta)\\ &\leq d(T\zeta, Tg\xi_{2n+1}) + s[d(Tg\xi_{2n+1}, gT\xi_{2n+1}) + d(gT\xi_{2n+1}, g\zeta)].\end{aligned} \tag{31}$$

On taking the limit as $n \to \infty$ from both sides of (30) and (31), we obtain $\frac{1}{s}d(S\zeta, f\zeta) \leq 0$ and $\frac{1}{s}d(T\zeta, g\zeta) \leq 0$, that is, $f\zeta = S\zeta, g\zeta = T\zeta$.

Since $S\zeta$ and $T\zeta$ are comparable, we prove $f\zeta = g\zeta$. Suppose the contrary, then, by (3), it is valid that

$$\begin{aligned}&\psi(s^{\varepsilon}d(f\zeta, g\zeta)\\ &\leq \beta(M(\zeta,\zeta)) \times \psi(\max\{d(S\zeta, T\zeta), d(S\zeta, f\zeta), d(T\zeta, g\zeta)\}) + L\psi(N(\zeta,\zeta))\\ &< \psi(d(S\zeta, T\zeta)) = \psi(d(f\zeta, g\zeta)),\end{aligned}$$

that is to say,

$$s^{\varepsilon}d(f\zeta, g\zeta) < d(f\zeta, g\zeta).$$

This is a contradiction (because $s^{\varepsilon} > 1$). Accordingly, $f\zeta = g\zeta = S\zeta = T\zeta$. □

Remark 3. *According to the main results of [14,15], Theorem 2 makes a general generalization. That is to say, it generalizes Theorem 15 in [14] and Theorem 2.1 in [15]. Similar superiority is discussed in Remarks 1 and 2.*

The following result is a straightforward outcome of Theorem 2.

Corollary 1. *Let f and T be self-mappings on a partially ordered b-complete b-metric space $(X, \preceq, d)$ with $s > 1$. Assume that $f(X) \subseteq T(X)$ and the pair (f, T) is compatible, f and T are b-continuous, and f is partially weakly increasing with respect to T. Assume that f satisfies the following inequality*

$$\psi(s^{\varepsilon}d(f\xi, f\eta)) \leq \beta(M(\xi,\eta))\psi\big(\max\{d(T\xi, T\eta), d(T\xi, f\xi), d(T\eta, f\eta)\}\big) + L\psi(N(\xi,\eta)),$$

for every $\xi, \eta \in X$, for which $T\xi$ and $T\eta$ are comparable, where

$$M(\xi,\eta) = \psi\Big(\max\Big\{d(T\xi, T\eta), d(T\xi, f\xi), d(T\eta, f\eta), \frac{d(T\xi, f\eta) + d(T\eta, f\xi)}{2s}\Big\}\Big),$$

$$N(\xi,\eta) = \min\{d(T\xi,T\eta), d(T\xi,f\eta), d(T\eta,f\xi), d(f\eta,T\eta), d(\xi,f\eta)\},$$

and $\varepsilon > 0$ is a constant. Then, the pair (f,T) has a coincidence point $\zeta \in X$. Moreover, ζ is a coincidence point of f and T.

Author Contributions: B.J. offered the draft preparation and gave the support of funding acquisition. H.H. designed the research and made revisions to the paper. S.R. gave the methodology and checked the final version before submission. All authors have read and agreed to the published version of the manuscript.

Funding: The second author is partially supported by Grant No. NSTC 111-2115-M-017-002 of the National Science and Technology Council of the Republic of China.

Institutional Review Board Statement: Not applicable.

Informed Consent Statement: Not applicable.

Data Availability Statement: The data presented in this study are available upon request from the corresponding author.

Acknowledgments: The authors thank the Editor and the Referees for their valuable comments and suggestions, which improved greatly the quality of this paper.

Conflicts of Interest: The authors declare no conflict of interest.

References

1. Banach, S. Sur les opérations dans les ensembles abstraits et leur application auxéquations intégrales. *Fundam. Math.* **1922**, *3*, 133–181. [CrossRef]
2. Eshraghisamani, M.; Vaezpour, S.M.; Asadi, M. New fixed point results on Branciari metric spaces. *J. Math. Appl.* **2017**, *8*, 132–141.
3. Gabeleh, M. Best proximity points for weak proximal contractions. *Bull. Malays. Math. Sci. Soc.* **2015**, *38*, 143–154. [CrossRef]
4. Vulpe, I.M.; Ostrajkh, D.; Khojman, F. The topological structure of a quasi-metric space. In *Investigations in Functional Analysis and Differential Equations*; Math. Sci., Interuniv. Work Collect., Kishinev; 1981; pp. 14–19; Prosevechtchénié, St. Petersburg. (In Russian)
5. Jovanović, M.; Kadelburg, Z.; Radenović, S. Common fixed point results in metric-type spaces. *Fixed Point Theory Appl.* **2010**, *2010*, 978121. [CrossRef]
6. Lu, N.; He, F.; Du, W.-S. Fundamental questions and new counterexamples for *b*-metric spaces and Fatou property. *Mathematics* **2019**, *7*, 1107. [CrossRef]
7. Boriceanu, M.; Bota, M.; Petrusel, A. Mutivalued fractals in *b*-metric spaces. *Cent. Eur. J. Math.* **2010**, *8*, 367–377. [CrossRef]
8. Lu, N.; He, F.; Du, W.-S. On the best areas for Kannan system and Chatterjea system in *b*-metric spaces. *Optimization* **2021**, *70*, 973–986. [CrossRef]
9. Czerwik, S. Nonlinear set-valued contraction mappings in *b*-metric spaces. *Atti Semin. Mat. Fis. Univ. Modena* **1998**, *46*, 263–276.
10. Khamsi, M.A.; Hussain, N. KKM mappings in metric type spaces. *Nonlinear Anal.* **2010**, *73*, 3123–3129. [CrossRef]
11. Beg, I.; Abbas, M. Coincidence point and invariant approximation for mappings satisfying generalized weak contractive condition. *Fixed Point Theory Appl.* **2006**, *2006*, 978121. [CrossRef]
12. Abbas, M.; Nazir, T.; Radenović, S. Common fixed points of four maps in partially ordered metric spaces. *Appl. Math. Lett.* **2011**, *24*, 1520–1526. [CrossRef]
13. Esmaily, J.; Vaezpour, S.M.; Rhoades, B.E. Coincidence point theorem for generalized weakly contractions in ordered metric spaces. *Appl. Math. Comput.* **2012**, *219*, 1536–1548. [CrossRef]
14. Abbas, M.; Zulfaqar, I.; Radenović, S. Common fixed point of (ψ, β)-generalized contractive mappings in partially ordered metric spaces. *Chin. J. Math.* **2014**, *9*, 5497–5509. [CrossRef]
15. Huang, H.; Stojan, R.; Jelena, V. On some recent coincidence and immediate consequences in partially ordered *b*-metric spaces. *Fixed Point Theory Appl.* **2015**, *2015*, 63. [CrossRef]
16. Hussain, N.; Parvaneh, V.; Roshan, J.R.; Kadelburg, Z. Fixed points of cyclic weakly (ψ, φ, L, A, B)-contractive mappings in ordered *b*-metric spaces with applications. *Fixed Point Theory Appl.* **2013**, *2013*, 256. [CrossRef]
17. Czerwik, S. Contraction mappings in *b*-metric spaces. *Acta Math. Inform. Univ. Ostrav.* **1993**, *1*, 5–11.
18. Berinde, V.; Păcurar, M. The early developments in fixed point theory on *b*-metric spaces: A brief survey and some important related aspects. *Carpathian J. Math.* **2022**, *38*, 523–538. [CrossRef]
19. Aydi, H.; Bota, M.-F.; Karapınar, E.; Moradi, S. A common fixed point for weak φ-contractions on *b*-metric spaces. *Fixed Point Theory* **2012**, *13*, 337–346.
20. Berinde, V.; Borcut, M. Tripled fixed point theorems for contractive type mappings in partially ordered metric spaces. *Nonlinear Anal.* **2011**, *74*, 4889–4897. [CrossRef]

21. Bota, M.-F.; Karapınar, E. A note on " Some results on multi-valued weakly Jungck mappings in *b*-metric spaces". *Cent. Eur. J. Math.* **2013**, *11*, 1711–1712. [CrossRef]
22. Bota, M.-F.; Karapınar, E.; Mlesnite, O. Ulam-Hyers stability results for fixed point problems via (α, ψ)-contractive mappings in *b*-metric spaces. *Abstr. Appl. Anal.* **2013**, *2013*, 825293. [CrossRef]
23. Romaguera, S. On the correlation between Banach contraction principle and Caristi's fixed point theorem in *b*-metric spaces. *Mathematics* **2022**, *10*, 136. [CrossRef]
24. Kutbi, M.-A.; Karapınar, E.; Ahmad, J.; Azam, A. Some fixed point results for multi-valued mappings in *b*-metric spaces. *J. Inequal. Appl.* **2014**, *2014*, 126. [CrossRef]
25. Radenović, S.; Kadelburg, Z.; Jandrlic D.; Jandrlic, A. Some results on weakly contractive maps. *Bull. Iranian Math. Soc.* **2012**, *38*, 625–645.
26. Radu, M.; Alexandru, M. New fixed point theorems for set-valued contractions in *b*-metric spaces. *J. Fixed Point Theory Appl.* **2017**, *10*, 2153–2163.
27. Roshan, J.R.; Parvaneh, V.; Altun, I. Some coincidence point results in ordered *b*-metric spaces and applications in a system of integral equations. *Appl. Math. Comput.* **2014**, *226*, 725–737. [CrossRef]
28. Roshan, J.R.; Parvaneh, V.; Kadelburg, Z. Common fixed point theorems for weakly isotone increasing mappings in ordered *b*-metric spaces. *J. Nonlinear Sci. Appl.* **2014**, *7*, 229–245. [CrossRef]

axioms

MDPI

Article

On Local Unique Solvability for a Class of Nonlinear Identification Problems

Vladimir E. Fedorov *, Marina V. Plekhanova and Daria V. Melekhina

Mathematical Analysis Department, Chelyabinsk State University, 129, Kashirin Brothers St., Chelyabinsk 454001, Russia; mariner79@mail.ru (M.V.P.); melehina.d.v@csu.ru (D.V.M.)

* Correspondence: kar@csu.ru; Tel.: +7-351-799-7235

Abstract: Nonlinear identification problems for evolution differential equations, solved with respect to the highest-order Dzhrbashyan–Nersesyan fractional derivative, are studied. An equation of the considered class contains a linear unbounded operator, which generates analytic resolving families for the corresponding linear homogeneous equation, and a continuous nonlinear operator, which depends on lower-order Dzhrbashyan–Nersesyan derivatives and a depending on time unknown element. The identification problem consists of the equation, Dzhrbashyan–Nersesyan initial value conditions and an abstract overdetermination condition, which is defined by a linear continuous operator. Using the contraction mappings theorem, we prove the unique local solvability of the identification problem. The cases of mild and classical solutions are studied. The obtained abstract results are applied to an investigation of a nonlinear identification problem to a linearized phase field system with time dependent unknown coefficients at Dzhrbashyan–Nersesyan time-derivatives of lower orders.

Keywords: fractional differential equation; Dzhrbashyan–Nersesyan fractional derivative; coefficient inverse problem; identification problem; initial boundary value problem

MSC: 34G20; 35R30; 35R11; 34K29

1. Introduction

Works on fractional integro-differential calculus in contemporary mathematics are very diverse. They concern both various theoretical aspects (properties of fractional integration and differentiation operators, issues of solvability of new problems to equations with various fractional derivatives and integrals, and much more [1–5]) and applications of fractional calculus methods in various applied problems [6–9]. To the reader's attention, we present an article on the existence of a unique solution of a new class of coefficient inverse problems to equations containing fractional derivatives, also called forecast-control problems [10], or identification problems [11,12]. We are talking about a problem for an equation containing, in addition to an unknown solution function, also unknown functional parameters and overdetermination conditions of a corresponding nature.

Consider the equation

$$\mathcal{D}^{\sigma_n}z(t) = Az(t) + B(t, \mathcal{D}^{\sigma_0}z(t), \mathcal{D}^{\sigma_1}z(t), \dots, \mathcal{D}^{\sigma_{n-1}}z(t), u(t)), \tag{1}$$

endowed by the Dzhrbashyan–Nersesyan initial conditions [1]

$$\mathcal{D}^{\sigma_k}z(0) = z_k, \quad k = 0, 1, \dots, n-1, \tag{2}$$

and by the additional overdetermination condition

$$\Phi z(t) = \Psi(t), \quad t \in [0, T]. \tag{3}$$

Here, $\mathcal{D}^{\sigma_k}$, $k = 0, 1, \ldots, n \in \mathbb{N}$ are the Dzhrbashyan–Nersesyan differentiation operator, which corresponds to the set $\{\alpha_k\}$, $0 < \alpha_k \leq 1$, (see Formula (4) below), A is a linear closed operator with a domain D_A in a Banach space $\mathcal{Z}$, $\mathcal{U}$ is another Banach space, $B : [0, T] \times \mathcal{Z}^n \times \mathcal{U} \to \mathcal{Z}$ is a nonlinear mapping, $\Phi : \mathcal{Z} \to \mathcal{U}$ is a linear bounded operator; initial values $z_k \in D_A$, $k = 0, 1, \ldots, n$, and $\Psi : [0, T] \to \mathcal{U}$ are known. A solution of (1)–(3) is a pair of functions (z, u). The main aim of the work are theorems on the existence and the uniqueness of a mild and a classical local solution (z, u).

Various linear inverse problems for differential equations containing Riemann–Liouville or Gerasimov–Caputo fractional derivatives were studied in papers [12–16]. Unique solvability issues for a nonlinear identification problem of form (1)–(3) with Gerasimov–Caputo derivatives and with a closed operator A, which generates an analytic resolving family of operators for a respective linear homogeneous equation, were investigated in [17].

The notion of the Dzhrbashyan–Nersesyan derivative includes Riemann–Liouville and Gerasimov–Caputo fractional derivatives as particular cases; for a study of various problems with this general fractional derivative, see [1], its English translation [18], in works [19–24]. The unique solvability conditions and a form of a solution for linear inhomogeneous problem with the Dzhrbashyan–Nersesyan derivative (1), (2) ($B \equiv f(t)$) in a Banach space were obtained in work [25] in the case of a bounded operator A, and in paper [26] for a closed operator A from the class $\mathcal{A}_{\{\alpha_k\}}$ of generators of analytic resolving families for a linear Equation (1) ($B \equiv 0$). Problem (2) for quasilinear Equation (1) with known u and with a bounded operator A was researched in [27].

The results of [25] were used for obtaining a theorem on the existence of a unique solution of nonlinear inverse problem (1)–(3) with a linear continuous operator A in [28]. In the present work, we extend these results on the case of a nonlinear identification problem with Dzhrbashyan–Nersesyan derivatives and with $A \in \mathcal{A}_{\{\alpha_k\}}$. It is clear that such results on Problem (1)–(3) with a closed operator A provide much greater possibilities for their application to inverse problems to partial differential equations and systems of them than results on the abstract inverse problem with a bounded operator A.

In the second section, preliminary definitions and statements are given; in particular, a theorem on the existence of a unique solution of Dzhrbashyan–Nersesyan problem (2) to linear Equation (1) ($B \equiv f(t)$) with $A \in \mathcal{A}_{\{\alpha_k\}}$ is presented. The first subsection of the third section contains a proof of the theorem on the existence and the uniqueness of a local mild solution of identification problem (1)–(3). In the second subsection, for the case of continuous mapping B:$[0, T] \times \mathcal{Z}^n \times \mathcal{U} \to D_A$, the existence of a unique local classical solution is proven. A similar result is proven under the additional conditions of Hölder continuity in t of problem data. In the fourth section, obtained general results are used for the investigation of a nonlinear identification problem to modified phase field equations with depending on t unknown coefficients at Dzhrbashyan–Nersesyan time-fractional derivatives of lower orders.

2. Preliminaries

For $h : (0, T] \to \mathcal{Z}$,where $\mathcal{Z}$ is a Banach space, and for $\beta > 0$, we introduce the following notations:

$$D^{-\beta}h(t) := J^{\beta}h(t) := \int_0^t \frac{(t-s)^{\beta-1}}{\Gamma(\beta)} h(s)ds, \quad t \in (0, T]$$

for the Riemann–Liouville fractional integral of the order $\beta > 0$, and $D^{\beta} := D^m J^{m-\beta}$ for the Riemann–Liouville fractional derivative of the order $\beta \in (m-1, m]$, $m \in \mathbb{N}$. For sequence $\{\alpha_0, \alpha_1, \ldots, \alpha_n\}$, $\alpha_k \in (0, 1]$, $k = 0, 1, \ldots, n \in \mathbb{N}$, we define the Dzhrbashyan–Nersesyan fractional derivatives $\mathcal{D}^{\sigma_k}$, $k = 0, 1, \ldots, n$ by equalities [1]

$$\mathcal{D}^{\sigma_0}z(t) := D^{\alpha_0-1}z(t), \quad \mathcal{D}^{\sigma_k}z(t) := D^{\alpha_k-1}D^{\alpha_{k-1}}D^{\alpha_{k-2}}\ldots D^{\alpha_0}z(t), \quad k = 1, 2, \ldots, n. \quad (4)$$

They are natural general constructions of fractional derivatives (see, e.g., [1,19,20]), they generalize the Riemann–Liouville fractional derivatives ($\alpha_0 \in (0,1)$, $\alpha_k = 1$, $k = 1,2,\ldots,n$) and the Gerasimov–Caputo fractional derivatives ($\alpha_k = 1$, $k = 0,1,\ldots,n-1$, $\alpha_n \in (0,1)$). We also use notations

$$\sigma_k := \sum_{j=0}^{k} \alpha_j - 1, \quad k = 0,1,\ldots,n.$$

For $h:\mathbb{R}_+ \to \mathcal{Z}$, we denote by $\mathfrak{L}[h]$ the Laplace transform of this function. The following equalities are known [3,26]:

$$\mathfrak{L}[J^\alpha h](\lambda) = \lambda^{-\alpha}\mathfrak{L}[h](\lambda), \quad \mathfrak{L}[D^\alpha h](\lambda) = \lambda^\alpha \mathfrak{L}[h](\lambda) - \sum_{k=0}^{m-1} D^{\alpha-1-k}h(0)\lambda^k,$$

$$\mathfrak{L}[\mathcal{D}^{\sigma_n} h](\lambda) = \lambda^{\sigma_n}\mathfrak{L}[h](\lambda) - \sum_{k=0}^{n-1} \mathcal{D}^{\sigma_k}h(0)\lambda^{\sigma_n-1-\sigma_k}. \tag{5}$$

We let $\mathcal{L}(\mathcal{Z})$ be the Banach algebra of all linear bounded operators in the Banach space $\mathcal{Z}$ and $\mathcal{C}l(\mathcal{Z})$ be the set of all linear closed densely defined in $\mathcal{Z}$ operators. We consider the domain D_A of an operator $A \in \mathcal{C}l(\mathcal{Z})$ with the graph norm of A as a Banach space due to the closedness of A. We consider the linear inhomogeneous equation

$$\mathcal{D}^{\sigma_n} z(t) = Az(t) + f(t), \quad t \in (0,T] \tag{6}$$

endowed by the Dzhrbashyan–Nersesyan initial conditions [1]

$$\mathcal{D}^{\sigma_k} z(0) = z_k \in D_A, \quad k = 0,1,\ldots,n-1. \tag{7}$$

Here, $f \in C([0,T];\mathcal{Z})$.

A solution to Problem (6), (7) is function $z \in C((0,T];D_A)$, such that $\mathcal{D}^{\sigma_k} z \in C([0,T];\mathcal{Z})$, $k = 0,1,\ldots,n-1$, $\mathcal{D}^{\sigma_n} z \in C((0,T];\mathcal{Z})$. Equalities (6) for all $t \in (0,T]$ and (7) are fulfilled.

IWe itroduce notations $\rho(A) := \{\lambda \in \mathbb{C} : (\lambda I - A)^{-1} \in \mathcal{L}(\mathcal{Z})\}$, $R_\lambda(A) := (\lambda I - A)^{-1}$ for $\lambda \in \mathbb{C}$.

Definition 1. *We denote by $\mathcal{A}_{\{\alpha_k\}}(\theta_0, a_0)$ for some $\theta_0 \in (\pi/2, \pi]$, $a_0 \geq 0$, $\alpha_k \in (0,1]$, $k = 0,1,\ldots,n$, a class of operators $A \in \mathcal{C}l(\mathcal{Z})$, such that*

(i) $\lambda^{\sigma_n} \in \rho(A)$ for all $\lambda \in S_{\theta_0,a_0} := \{\mu \in \mathbb{C} : |\arg(\mu - a_0)| < \theta_0,\ \mu \neq a_0\}$;

(ii) for any $\theta \in (\pi/2, \theta_0)$, $a > a_0$, there exists such a constant $K(\theta, a) > 0$, that for all $\lambda \in S_{\theta,a}$

$$\|R_{\lambda^{\sigma_n}}(A)\|_{\mathcal{L}(\mathcal{Z})} \leq \frac{K(\theta,a)}{|\lambda - a|^{\alpha_0}|\lambda|^{\sigma_n - \alpha_0}}.$$

If $A \in \mathcal{A}_{\{\alpha_k\}}(\theta_0, a_0)$, then we define for $t > 0$ operators

$$Y_\beta(t) = \frac{1}{2\pi i}\int_\Gamma \lambda^\beta R_{\lambda^{\sigma_n}}(A) e^{\lambda t} d\lambda, \quad \beta \in \mathbb{R}.$$

Here, for some $\delta > 0$, $a > a_0$, $\theta \in (\pi/2, \theta_0)$ $\Gamma := \Gamma_+ \cup \Gamma_- \cup \Gamma_0$, $\Gamma_\pm := \{\lambda \in \mathbb{C} : \lambda = a + re^{\pm i\theta},\ r \in (\delta,\infty)\}$, $\Gamma_0 := \{\lambda \in \mathbb{C} : \lambda = a + \delta e^{i\varphi},\ \varphi \in (-\theta,\theta)\}$. For brevity, we use the notations of frequently used operators $Z_k(t) := Y_{\sigma_n - \sigma_k - 1}(t)$, $k = 0,1,\ldots,n-1$.

We denote also

$$\mathcal{A}_{\{\alpha_k\}} = \bigcup_{\substack{\theta_0 \in (\pi/2,\pi] \\ a_0 \geq 0}} \mathcal{A}_{\{\alpha_k\}}(\theta_0, a_0).$$

We let $C^\gamma([0,T];\mathcal{Z})$ be the set of all Hölder continuous functions from $[0,T]$ to $\mathcal{Z}$ with the power $\gamma \in (0,1]$.

Theorem 1 ([26]). *We let $\alpha_k \in (0,1]$, $k = 0,1,\dots,n$, $\alpha_0 + \alpha_n > 1$, $\theta_0 \in (\pi/2,\pi]$, $a_0 \geq 0$, $A \in \mathcal{A}_{\{\alpha_k\}}(\theta_0,a_0)$, $z_k \in D_A$, $k = 0,1,\dots,n-1$, $f \in C([0,T];D_A) \cup C^\gamma([0,T];\mathcal{Z})$, $\gamma \in (0,1]$. Then, Problem (6), (7) has a unique solution. It has the form*

$$z(t) = \sum_{k=0}^{n-1} Z_k(t)z_k + \int_0^t Y_0(t-s)f(s)ds.$$

Remark 1. *We note that $Z_k(t)z_k$ is a unique solution of the initial value problem $\mathcal{D}^{\sigma_k}z(0) = z_k$, $\mathcal{D}^{\sigma_l}z(0) = 0$, $l \in \{0,1,\dots,n-1\} \setminus \{k\}$ to equation $\mathcal{D}^{\sigma_n}z(t) = Az(t)$. In addition, the unique solution of Problem (6), (7) with zero initial conditions $\mathcal{D}^{\sigma_l}z(0) = 0$, $l \in \{0,1,\dots,n-1\}$, is*

$$\int_0^t Y_0(t-s)f(s)ds.$$

Remark 2. *In the proof of Lemma 1 in [26], it was shown that for some $C > 0$ and for all $t \in (0,T]$ $\|Y_\beta(t)\|_{\mathcal{L}(\mathcal{Z})} \leq Ct^{\sigma_n-1-\beta}$. Hence, for $j,k \in \{0,1,\dots,n-1\}$, $k > j$, $\|\mathcal{D}^{\sigma_j}Z_k(t)\|_{\mathcal{L}(\mathcal{Z})} = \|Y_{\sigma_n-\sigma_k-1+\sigma_j}(t)\|_{\mathcal{L}(\mathcal{Z})} \leq Ct^{\sigma_k-\sigma_j}$. In addition, for $j,k \in \{0,1,\dots,n-1\}$, $k < j$, $z_k \in D_A$, in the proof of Theorem 3 in [26], the following relations were proven:*

$$\mathfrak{L}[\mathcal{D}^{\sigma_j}Z_k(t)z_k] = \lambda^{\sigma_n-\sigma_k-1+\sigma_j}R_{\lambda^{\sigma_n}}(A)z_k - \lambda^{\sigma_j-\sigma_k-1}z_k = \lambda^{\sigma_j-\sigma_k-1}R_{\lambda^{\sigma_n}}(A)Az_k,$$

$$\|\lambda^{\sigma_j-\sigma_k-1}R_{\lambda^{\sigma_n}}(A)Az_k\|_{\mathcal{Z}} \leq \frac{K\|Az_k\|_{\mathcal{Z}}}{|\lambda|^{\sigma_n+1+\sigma_k-\sigma_j}} \leq \frac{K\|Az_k\|_{\mathcal{Z}}}{|\lambda|^{\alpha_0+\alpha_1+\dots+\alpha_{k-1}+\alpha_k+\alpha_{j+1}+\alpha_{j+2}+\dots+\alpha_{n-1}+\alpha_n}},$$

consequently, $\|\mathcal{D}^{\sigma}_j Z_k(t)z_k\|_{\mathcal{Z}} \leq C_1 t^{\alpha_0+\alpha_1+\dots+\alpha_{k-1}+\alpha_k+\alpha_{j+1}+\alpha_{j+2}+\dots+\alpha_{n-1}+\alpha_n-1} \leq Ct^{\alpha_0+\alpha_n-1}$,

$$\|\mathcal{D}^{\sigma_k}Z_k(t)z_k - z_k\|_{\mathcal{Z}} \leq \frac{1}{2\pi}\int_\Gamma \|\lambda^{-1}R_{\lambda^{\sigma_n}}(A)Az_k\|_{\mathcal{Z}}|d\lambda| \leq Ct^{\alpha_0+\alpha_n-1}, \quad t \in (0,T].$$

3. Local Solvability of Identification Problem

3.1. Mild Solution

We take Banach spaces $\mathcal{Z}$ and $\mathcal{U}$, an open set Z in $\mathbb{R} \times \mathcal{Z}^n$, a nonlinear mapping $B : Z \times \mathcal{U} \to \mathcal{Z}$, a linear operator $\Phi \in \mathcal{L}(\mathcal{Z};\mathcal{U})$ and a function $\Psi : [0,T] \to \mathcal{U}$. The purpose of Problem (1)–(3) is to find $z : [0,T] \to \mathcal{Z}$, $u : [0,T] \to \mathcal{U}$ from Relations (1)–(3).

We denote $\overline{y} = (y_0,y_1,\dots,y_{n-1})$ and formulate several conditions.

($\mathcal{A}$) The operator $B : Z \times \mathcal{U} \to \mathcal{Z}$ can be presented as

$$B(t,\overline{y},u) = B_1(t,\overline{y}) + B_2(t,\overline{y},u), \quad (t,\overline{y},u) \in Z \times \mathcal{U}.$$

For $\overline{a} = (a_0,a_1,\dots,a_{n-1}) \in \mathcal{Z}^n$, $R,T > 0$, we use the following notations:

$$S_{\mathcal{Z}^n}(\overline{a},R) = \{\overline{y} \in \mathcal{Z}^n : \|y_j - a_j\|_{\mathcal{Z}} < R, j = 0,1,\dots,n-1\},$$
$$S_{\mathcal{Z}^n}(\overline{a},R,T) = [0,T] \times S_{\mathcal{Z}^n}(\overline{a},R).$$

For sufficiently smooth Ψ, we define

$$v_0 := \mathcal{D}^{\sigma_n}\Psi(0) - \overline{\Phi A}z_0 - \Phi B_1(0,z_0,z_1,\dots,z_{n-1}). \quad (8)$$

Here, the line above ΦA means the closure of this operator.

We let the next conditions ($\mathcal{B}$)–($\mathcal{F}$) be satisfied:

($\mathcal{B}$) the equation $\Phi B_2(0,y_0,y_1,\dots,y_{n-1},u) = v_0$ with unknown u has a unique solution $u_0 \in \mathcal{U}$;

$(\mathcal{C})$ there is an operator $B_3 : [0,T] \times \mathcal{U}^{n+1} \to \mathcal{U}$, for which

$$\Phi B_2(t,\overline{y},u) = B_3(t,\Phi y_0,\Phi y_1,\ldots,\Phi y_{n-1},u), \quad (t,\overline{y},u) \in Z \times \mathcal{U};$$

$(\mathcal{D})$ there is such a constant, $R > 0$, that for every $t \in [0,T]$, the mapping $v = B_3(t, \mathcal{D}^{\sigma_0}\Psi(t), \mathcal{D}^{\sigma_1}\Psi(t),\ldots,\mathcal{D}^{\sigma_{n-1}}\Psi(t),u)$ with u in $S_{\mathcal{U}}(u_0,R)$ has an inverse mapping $u = F(t,v)$;

$(\mathcal{E})$ there is such a constant, $R > 0$, that operator F is continuous with respect to the totality of the variables (t,v) on the set $S_{\mathcal{U}}(u_0,R,T)$ and is Lipschitz continuous in v;

$(\mathcal{F})$ there is $R > 0$ such that mappings $B_1(t,\overline{y})$ and $B_2(t,\overline{y},u)$ are continuous with respect to the totality of the variables on set $S_{\mathcal{Z}^n\times\mathcal{U}}((z_0,z_1,\ldots,z_{n-1},u_0),R,T)$ and are Lipschitz continuous in $(\overline{y},u)$.

Using the form of a classical solution from Theorem 1, we can introduce the notion of a mild solution.

Definition 2. *Pair* $(z,u) \in C([0,T];\mathcal{Z}) \times C([0,T];\mathcal{U})$ *for which* $\mathcal{D}^{\sigma_j}z \in C([0,T];\mathcal{Z})$ *for* $j = 0,1,\ldots,n-1$, *the inclusion* $(\mathcal{D}^{\sigma_0}z(t),\mathcal{D}^{\sigma_1}z(t),\ldots,\mathcal{D}^{\sigma_{n-1}}z(t)) \in Z$ *and Condition* (3) *are valid for all* $t \in [0,T]$, *and equality*

$$z(t) = \sum_{k=0}^{n-1} Z_k(t)z_k + \int_0^t Y_0(t-s)B(s,\mathcal{D}^{\sigma_0}z(s),\ldots,\mathcal{D}^{\sigma_{n-1}}z(s),u(s))ds \tag{9}$$

is fulfilled for all $t \in (0,T]$. *It is called a mild solution of identification problem (1)–(3) on* $[0,T]$.

Lemma 1. *We let* $\alpha_k \in (0,1]$, $k = 0,1,\ldots,n$, $\alpha_0+\alpha_n > 1$, $\theta_0 \in (\pi/2,\pi]$, $a_0 \geq 0$, $A \in \mathcal{A}_{\{\alpha_k\}}(\theta_0,a_0)$, $\Phi,\overline{\Phi A} \in \mathcal{L}(\mathcal{Z};\mathcal{U})$, $z_k \in \mathcal{Z}$, $f_k(t) := \Phi Z_k(t)z_k$, $k = 0,1,\ldots,n-1$. *Then,* $\mathcal{D}^{\sigma_n}f_k(t) = \overline{\Phi A}Z_k(t)z_k \in C([0,T];\mathcal{U})$, $k = 0,1,\ldots,n-1$.

Proof. For some $\lambda \in \rho(A)$, we take $y_k = R_\lambda(A)z_k \in D_A$, $k = 0,1,\ldots,n-1$. Then, by Remark 1, $\mathcal{D}^{\sigma_n}Z_k(t)y_k = AZ_k(t)y_k$, $f_k(t) = \Phi Z_k(t)(\lambda I - A)y_k = \lambda\Phi Z_k(t)y_k - \Phi AZ_k(t)y_k$,

$$\mathcal{D}^{\sigma_n}f_k(t) = \lambda\Phi\mathcal{D}^{\sigma_n}Z_k(t)y_k - \overline{\Phi A}\mathcal{D}^{\sigma_n}Z_k(t)y_k =$$

$$= \lambda\overline{\Phi A}Z_k(t)y_k - \overline{\Phi A}Z_k(t)Ay_k = \overline{\Phi A}Z_k(t)z_k \in C([0,T];\mathcal{U}).$$

□

Lemma 2. *We let* $\alpha_k \in (0,1]$, $k = 0,1,\ldots,n$, $\alpha_0+\alpha_n > 1$, $\theta_0 \in (\pi/2,\pi]$, $a_0 \geq 0$, $A \in \mathcal{A}_{\{\alpha_k\}}(\theta_0,a_0)$, $g \in C([0,T];\mathcal{Z})$, $\Phi,\overline{\Phi A} \in \mathcal{L}(\mathcal{Z};\mathcal{U})$,

$$h(t) := \Phi\int_0^t Y_0(t-s)g(s)ds.$$

Then,

$$\mathcal{D}^{\sigma_n}h(t) = \overline{\Phi A}\int_0^t Y_0(t-s)g(s)ds + \Phi g(t) \in C([0,T];\mathcal{U}).$$

Proof. For $\lambda \in \rho(A)$, we put $f(t) = R_\lambda(A)g(t) \in D_A$, $t \in [0,T]$. Hence, $Af(t) = \lambda R_\lambda(A)g(t) - g(t) \in C([0,T];\mathcal{Z})$; consequently, $f \in C([0,T];D_A)$. Therefore,

$$h(t) = \Phi\int_0^t Y_0(t-s)(\lambda I - A)f(s)ds = (\lambda\Phi - \overline{\Phi A})\int_0^t Y_0(t-s)f(s)ds,$$

and, by Remark 1, we obtain

$$\mathcal{D}^{\sigma_n} h(t) = (\lambda\Phi - \overline{\Phi A})\mathcal{D}^{\sigma_n} \int_0^t Y_0(t-s)f(s)ds$$

$$= (\lambda\Phi - \overline{\Phi A})\left(A\int_0^t Y_0(t-s)f(s)ds + f(t)\right)$$

$$= \overline{\Phi A}\left(\lambda \int_0^t Y_0(t-s)f(s)ds - A\int_0^t Y_0(t-s)f(s)ds\right) + (\lambda\Phi - \overline{\Phi A})f(t)$$

$$= \overline{\Phi A}\int_0^t Y_0(t-s)g(s)ds + (\lambda\Phi - \Phi A)f(t) = \overline{\Phi A}\int_0^t Y_0(t-s)g(s)ds + \Phi g(t).$$

Here, $\overline{\Phi A}f(t) = \Phi A f(t)$, since $f(t) \in D_A$. □

Theorem 2. *We let* $\alpha_0 = 1$, $\alpha_k \in (0,1]$, $k = 1,2,\ldots,n$, $\theta_0 \in (\pi/2,\pi]$, $a_0 \geq 0$, $A \in \mathcal{A}_{\{\alpha_k\}}(\theta_0, a_0)$, $z_k \in D_A$, $k = 0,1,\ldots,n-1$, $(0, z_0, z_1, \ldots, z_{n-1}) \in Z$, $\Phi, \overline{\Phi A} \in \mathcal{L}(\mathcal{Z};\mathcal{U})$, $\mathcal{D}^{\sigma_k}\Psi \in C([0,T];\mathcal{U})$, $k = 0,1,\ldots,n$, $\Phi z_0 = \Psi(0)$, *and we let conditions* $(\mathcal{A})$–$(\mathcal{F})$ *be fulfilled. Then, for some* $T_1 \in (0,T]$, *inverse problem* (1)–(3) *has a unique mild solution* $(z,u) \in C([0,T_1];\mathcal{Z}) \times C([0,T_1];\mathcal{U})$ *on segment* $[0,T_1]$.

Proof. We take $z_k \in D_A$, $k = 0,1,\ldots,n-1$; then, we have $\mathcal{D}^{\sigma_j} Z_k(t)z_k = Y_{\sigma_n-\sigma_k-1+\sigma_j}(t)z_k \in C([0,T];\mathcal{L}(\mathcal{Z}))$ as it is shown in the proof of Theorem 3 [26]. Lemma 1 in [26] implies that

$$\mathcal{D}^{\sigma_j}\int_0^t Y_0(t-s)g(s)ds = \int_0^t Y_{\sigma_j}(t-s)g(s)ds, \quad j = 0,1,\ldots,n-1. \tag{10}$$

Therefore, due to Remark 2 and Equation (9), we have correlations for $j = 0,1,\ldots,n-1$

$$\mathcal{D}^{\sigma_j} z(t) = \sum_{k=0}^{m-1} Y_{\sigma_n-\sigma_k-1+\sigma_j}(t)z_k + \int_0^t Y_{\sigma_j}(t-s)B(s,\mathcal{D}^{\sigma_0}z(s),\ldots,\mathcal{D}^{\sigma_{n-1}}z(s),u(s))ds. \tag{11}$$

For a mild solution (z,u), Equality (9) is valid; then, Condition (3) implies that

$$\sum_{k=0}^{m-1}\Phi Z_k(t)z_k + \Phi\int_0^t Y_0(t-s)B(s,\mathcal{D}^{\sigma_0}z(s),\mathcal{D}^{\sigma_1}z(s),\ldots,\mathcal{D}^{\sigma_{n-1}}z(s),u(s))ds = \Psi(t).$$

Therefore, due to Lemmas 1 and 2, we have

$$\mathcal{D}^{\sigma_n}\sum_{k=0}^{m-1}\Phi Z_k(t)z_k + \mathcal{D}^{\sigma_n}\Phi\int_0^t Y_0(t-s)B(s,\mathcal{D}^{\sigma_0}z(s),\mathcal{D}^{\sigma_1}z(s),\ldots,\mathcal{D}^{\sigma_{n-1}}z(s),u(s))ds$$

$$= \overline{\Phi A}\sum_{k=0}^{m-1} Z_k(t)z_k + \overline{\Phi A}\int_0^t Y_0(t-s)B(s,\mathcal{D}^{\sigma_0}z(s),\mathcal{D}^{\sigma_1}z(s),\ldots,\mathcal{D}^{\sigma_{n-1}}z(s),u(s))ds$$

$$+\Phi B(t,\mathcal{D}^{\sigma_0}z(t),\mathcal{D}^{\sigma_1}z(t),\ldots,\mathcal{D}^{\sigma_{n-1}}z(t),u(t)) = \mathcal{D}^{\sigma_n}\Psi(t).$$

Due to condition $(\mathcal{A})$, we can write the last equality as

$$\begin{aligned} \Phi B_2(t, \mathcal{D}^{\sigma_0}z(t), \dots, \mathcal{D}^{\sigma_{n-1}}z(t), u(t)) = \mathcal{D}^{\sigma_n}\Psi(t) - \overline{\Phi A} \sum_{k=0}^{m-1} Z_k(t) z_k \\ -\overline{\Phi A} \int_0^t Y_0(t-s) B(s, \mathcal{D}^{\sigma_0}z(s), \mathcal{D}^{\sigma_1}z(s), \dots, \mathcal{D}^{\sigma_{n-1}}z(s), u(s)) ds \\ -\Phi B_1(t, \mathcal{D}^{\sigma_0}z(t), \mathcal{D}^{\sigma_1}z(t), \dots, \mathcal{D}^{\sigma_{n-1}}z(t)). \end{aligned} \tag{12}$$

Then, under assumptions $(\mathcal{C})$, $(\mathcal{D})$, Equation (12) implies equality

$$u(t) = F(t, v(t)), \tag{13}$$

where

$$\begin{aligned} v(t) = \mathcal{D}^{\sigma_n}\Psi(t) - \overline{\Phi A} \sum_{k=0}^{m-1} Z_k(t) z_k - \Phi B_1(t, \mathcal{D}^{\sigma_0}z(t), \mathcal{D}^{\sigma_1}z(t), \dots, \mathcal{D}^{\sigma_{n-1}}z(t)) \\ -\overline{\Phi A} \int_0^t Y_0(t-s) B(s, \mathcal{D}^{\sigma_0}z(s), \mathcal{D}^{\sigma_1}z(s), \dots, \mathcal{D}^{\sigma_{n-1}}z(s), u(s)) ds. \end{aligned} \tag{14}$$

Thus, we obtained a nonlinear system of equations (11) with $j = 0, 1, \dots, n-1$ and Equation (13) for unknown functions $y_0 := \mathcal{D}^{\sigma_0}z$, $y_1 := \mathcal{D}^{\sigma_1}z, \dots, y_{n-1} := \mathcal{D}^{\sigma_{n-1}}z$, u.

We consider set

$$\mathfrak{M}_T = \{(\overline{y}, u) \in C([0,T]; \mathcal{Z}^n \times \mathcal{U}) : \|y_j(t) - z_j\|_{\mathcal{Z}} \le R, j = 0, 1, \dots, n-1, \\ \|u(t) - u_0\|_{\mathcal{U}} \le R\}$$

with metrics $d((\overline{x}, u), (\overline{y}, w)) = \|(\overline{x}, u) - (\overline{y}, w)\|_{C([0,T];\mathcal{Z}^n \times \mathcal{U})}$ and mapping $H = (H^0, H^1, \dots, H^n)$, which is defined by equalities

$$H^j(y_0, y_1 \dots, y_{n-1}, u) = \sum_{k=0}^{n-1} Y_{\sigma_n - \sigma_k - 1 + \sigma_j}(t) z_k \\ + \int_0^t Y_{\sigma_j}(t-s) B(s, y_0(s), y_1(s), \dots, y_{n-1}(s), u(s)) ds, \quad j = 0, 1, \dots, n-1,$$

$$\begin{aligned} H^n(y_0, y_1, \dots, y_{n-1}, u) = F\Bigg(t, \mathcal{D}^{\sigma_n}\Psi(t) - \overline{\Phi A} \sum_{k=0}^{n-1} Z_k(t) z_k \\ -\Phi B_1(t, y_0(t), y_1(t), \dots, y_{n-1}(t)) \\ - \int_0^t \overline{\Phi A} Y_0(t-s) B(s, y_0(s), y_1(s), \dots, y_{n-1}(s), u(s)) ds \Bigg). \end{aligned}$$

Thus, Problem (1)–(3) are represented in the form of system

$$\begin{aligned} y_0(t) = H^0(y_0(t), y_1(t), \dots, y_{n-1}(t), u(t)), \\ y_1(t) = H^1(y_0(t), y_1(t), \dots, y_{n-1}(t), u(t)), \\ \dots, \\ y_{n-1}(t) = H^{n-1}(y_0(t), y_1(t), \dots, y_{n-1}(t), u(t)), \\ u(t) = H^n(y_0(t), y_1(t), \dots, y_{n-1}(t), u(t)). \end{aligned} \tag{15}$$

We take $t = 0$ in (15); then, we have $H^j(z_0, z_1, \dots, z_{n-1}, u_0) = z_j$ for $j = 0, 1, \dots, n-1$,

$$H^n(z_0, z_1, \dots, z_{n-1}, u_0) = F(0, v_0) = u_0.$$

Due to the assumptions of Theorem, if $(y_0, y_1, \dots, y_{n-1}, u) \in \mathfrak{M}_T$, then

$$H(y_0(t), y_1(t), \dots, y_{n-1}(t), u(t))$$

is continuous with respect to t on $[0,T]$. Taking into account Remark 2 and assumptions $(\mathcal{E})$, $(\mathcal{F})$, we have, for $t \in (0,T]$,

$$\|H^j(y_0(t), y_1(t), \dots, y_{n-1}(t), u(t)) - z_j\|_{\mathcal{Z}}$$

$$\leq \sum_{\substack{k=0\\k\neq j}}^{n-1} \|Y_{\sigma_n-\sigma_k-1+\sigma_j}(t)z_k\|_{\mathcal{Z}} + \|Y_{\sigma_n-1}(t)z_k - z_k\|_{\mathcal{Z}}$$

$$+\int_0^t \|Y_{\sigma_j}(t-s)\|_{\mathcal{L}(\mathcal{Z})}\|B(s, y_0(s), \dots, y_{n-1}(s), u(s)) - B(0, z_0, z_1, \dots, z_{n-1}, u_0)\|_{\mathcal{Z}} ds$$

$$+\int_0^t \|Y_{\sigma_j}(t-s)\|_{\mathcal{L}(\mathcal{Z})}\|B(0, z_0, z_1, \dots, z_{n-1}, u_0)\|_{\mathcal{Z}} ds$$

$$\leq nCt^{\alpha_0+\alpha_n-1} + C_1 t^{\sigma_n-\sigma_j}\left(\sum_{k=0}^{n-1} \|y_k(t) - z_k\|_{\mathcal{Z}} + \|u(t) - u_0\|_{\mathcal{U}}\right)$$

$$+C_1 t^{\sigma_n-\sigma_j}\|B(0, z_0, z_1, \dots, z_{n-1}, u_0)\|_{\mathcal{Z}} \leq C_2 t^{\alpha_n}(1 + (n+1)R + C_3), \ j = 0, 1, \dots, n-1,$$

$$\|H^n(y_0(t), y_1(t), \dots, y_{n-1}(t), u(t)) - u_0\|_{\mathcal{U}}$$

$$\leq \|F(t, v(t)) - F(t, v_0)\|_{\mathcal{U}} + \|F(t, v_0) - F(0, v_0)\|_{\mathcal{U}}$$

$$\leq l\|v(t) - v_0\|_{\mathcal{U}} + \|F(t, v_0) - F(0, v_0)\|_{\mathcal{U}} \leq \|F(t, v_0) - F(0, v_0)\|_{\mathcal{U}}$$

$$+l\|D^{\sigma_n}\Psi(t) - D^{\sigma_n}\Psi(0)\|_{\mathcal{U}} + l\|\overline{\Phi A}\|_{\mathcal{L}(\mathcal{Z};\mathcal{U})}\|Z_0(t)z_0 - z_0\|_{\mathcal{Z}} + l\left\|\overline{\Phi A}\sum_{k=1}^{n-1} Z_k(t)z_k\right\|_{\mathcal{U}}$$

$$+l\|\Phi B_1(t, y_0(t), \dots, y_{n-1}(t)) - \Phi B_1(0, z_0, \dots, z_{n-1})\|_{\mathcal{U}}$$

$$+l\int_0^t \|\overline{\Phi A}Y_0(t-s)B(0, z_0, z_1, \dots, z_{n-1}, u_0)\|_{\mathcal{U}} ds$$

$$+l\int_0^t \|\overline{\Phi A}Y_0(t-s)(B(s, y_0(s), y_1(s), \dots, y_{n-1}(s), u(s)) - B(0, z_0, z_1, \dots, z_{n-1}, u_0))\|_{\mathcal{U}} ds$$

$$\leq \|F(t, v_0) - F(0, v_0)\|_{\mathcal{U}} + l\|D^{\sigma_n}\Psi(t) - D^{\sigma_n}\Psi(0)\|_{\mathcal{U}}$$

$$+C_4(1 + t^{\alpha_n})\sum_{k=0}^{n-1} \|y_k(t) - z_k\|_{\mathcal{Z}} + C_4 t^{\alpha_n}$$

$$\leq \|F(t, v_0) - F(0, v_0)\|_{\mathcal{U}} + l\|D^{\sigma_n}\Psi(t) - D^{\sigma_n}\Psi(0)\|_{\mathcal{U}}$$

$$+t^{\alpha_n}(1 + t^{\alpha_n})nC_2C_4(1 + (n+1)R + C_3) + C_4 t^{\alpha_n} \leq C_5 t^{\alpha_n},$$

where l is a Lipschitz constant for F, and v_0 and $v(t)$ are defined by (8) and (14). Here and further, various constants the value of which is not important are denoted by symbols C_1, C_2, and so on. Thus, for a sufficiently small $T_1 \in (0,T]$, H acts from the set $\mathfrak{M}_{T_1}$ into itself.

We denote for $i = 1, 2$, $j = 0, 1, \dots, n-1$ $y_j^i(t) = H^j(y_0^i(t), y_1^i(t), \dots, y_{n-1}^i(t), u^i(t))$, $u^i(t) = H^n(y_0^i(t), y_1^i(t), \dots, y_{n-1}^i(t), u^i(t))$; then, for $k = 0, 1, \dots, n-1$, the Lipschitz condition for B implies that

$$\|y_k^1(t) - y_k^2(t)\|_{\mathcal{Z}} \leq C_1 T^{\alpha_n} \left(\sum_{j=0}^{n-1} \sup_{s \in [0,T]} \|y_j^1(s) - y_j^2(s)\|_{\mathcal{Z}} + \sup_{s \in [0,T]} \|u^1(s) - u^2(s)\|_{\mathcal{U}} \right),$$

$$\|u^1(t) - u^2(t)\|_{\mathcal{U}} \leq C_2 \sum_{j=0}^{n-1} \sup_{s \in [0,T]} \|y_j^1(s) - y_j^2(s)\|_{\mathcal{Z}}$$

$$+ C_2 T^{\alpha_n} \left(\sum_{j=0}^{n-1} \sup_{s \in [0,T]} \|y_j^1(s) - y_j^2(s)\|_{\mathcal{Z}} + \sup_{s \in [0,T]} \|u^1(s) - u^2(s)\|_{\mathcal{U}} \right)$$

$$\leq (nC_1 + 1) C_2 T^{\alpha_n} \left(\sum_{j=0}^{n-1} \sup_{s \in [0,T]} \|y_j^1(s) - y_j^2(s)\|_{\mathcal{Z}} + \sup_{s \in [0,T]} \|u^1(s) - u^2(s)\|_{\mathcal{U}} \right).$$

Hence, for a small enough $T_1 > 0$, H is a contraction operator on $\mathfrak{M}_{T_1}$ and has in the complete metric space $\mathfrak{M}_{T_1}$ a unique fixed point $(y_0^0, y_1^0, \dots, y_{n-1}^0, u^0)$.

Since $\alpha_0 = 1$, we have

$$y_0^0(t) = D^{\sigma_0} y_0^0(t) = \sum_{k=0}^{m-1} Z_k(t) z_k + \int_0^t Y_0(t-s) B(s, y_0^0(s), \dots, y_{n-1}^0(s), u^0(s)) ds.$$

Hence, pair $(y_0^0(t), u^0(t))$ is a mild solution of (1)–(3).

Each of the two mild solutions (z^0, u^0) and (z^1, u^1) corresponds to a fixed point $(z^0, D^{\sigma_1} z^0, \dots, D^{\sigma_{n-1}} z^0, u^0)$ and $(z^1, D^{\sigma_1} z^1, \dots, D^{\sigma_{n-1}} z^1, u^1)$ of the mapping H. The uniqueness of a fixed point for H in $\mathfrak{M}_{T_1}$ with a small enough $T_1 > 0$ implies that $z^0(t) = z^1(t)$, $u^0(t) = u^1(t)$ for $t \in [0, T_1]$. □

3.2. Classical Solution

Definition 3. *A classical solution of Problem* (1)–(3) *on* $[0,T]$ *is pair* $(z,u) \in C((0,T]; D_A) \times C([0,T]; \mathcal{U})$, *for which* $D^{\sigma_k} z \in C([0,T]; \mathcal{Z})$, $k = 0, 1, \dots, n-1$, $D^{\sigma_n} z \in C((0,T]; \mathcal{Z})$. *Inclusion* $(t, D^{\sigma_0} z(t), D^{\sigma_1} z(t), \dots, D^{\sigma_{n-1}} z(t)) \in Z$ *and Condition* (3) *for* $t \in [0,T]$, *Equality* (1) *for* $t \in (0,T]$ *and Condition* (2) *are fulfilled.*

To obtain the unique solvability theorem in the sense of classical solution for the identification problem, we first use an additional condition $B \in C(Z; D_A)$.

Theorem 3. *We let* $\alpha_0 = 1$, $\alpha_k \in (0,1]$, $k = 1, 2, \dots, n$, $\theta_0 \in (\pi/2, \pi]$, $a_0 \geq 0$, $A \in \mathcal{A}_{\{\alpha_k\}}(\theta_0, a_0)$, $z_k \in D_A$, $k = 0, 1, \dots, n-1$, $(0, z_0, z_1, \dots, z_{n-1}) \in Z$, $\Phi, \overline{\Phi A} \in \mathcal{L}(\mathcal{Z}; \mathcal{U})$, $D^{\sigma_k} \Psi \in C([0,T]; \mathcal{U})$, $k = 0, 1, \dots, n-1$, $\Phi z_0 = \Psi(0)$, *and conditions* $(\mathcal{A})$–$(\mathcal{F})$ *be satisfied,* $B \in C(Z; D_A)$. *Then, Problem* (1)–(3) *has a unique classical solution* (z,u) *on segment* $[0, T_1]$ *with some* $T_1 \in (0, T]$.

Proof. By Theorem 2, Problem (1)–(3) has a mild solution $(z(t), u^0(t))$ on a small enough segment $[0, T_1]$. Then, $f(t) := B(t, D^{\sigma_0} z(t), D^{\sigma_1} z(t), \dots, D^{\sigma_{n-1}} z(t))$ is contained in class $C([0,T]; D_A)$, and by Theorem 1, z is a classical solution of direct Problem (1), (2) with a given u^0. □

But condition $B \in C(Z; D_A)$ is not often met in applications, so we replace it with conditions for additional smoothness of B. For this aim, we replace assumptions $(\mathcal{E})$ and $(\mathcal{F})$ with stronger conditions:

$(\mathcal{E}_1)$ there is such a constant, $R > 0$, that F is continuous with respect to the totality of the variables (t, v) on the set $S_{\mathcal{U}}(u_0, R, T)$, which is Lipschitz continuous in v and is Hölder continuous with a power of $\gamma \in (0, 1]$ in t;

$(\mathcal{F}_1)$ there exists $R > 0$, such that mappings $B_1(t, \overline{y})$ and $B_2(t, \overline{y}, u)$ are continuous with respect to the totality of the variables on the set $S_{\mathcal{Z}^n \times \mathcal{U}}((z_0, z_1, \ldots, z_{n-1}, u_0), R, T)$, which is Lipschitz continuous in $(\overline{y}, u)$ and is Hölder continuous with a power of $\gamma \in (0, 1]$ in t.

Lemma 3. *We let $\alpha \in (0, 1)$, $h, D^\alpha h \in C([0, T]\mathcal{Z})$; then,*

$$\exists C > 0 \ \forall s, t \in [0, T] \ \ \|h(s) - h(t)\|_{\mathcal{Z}} \le C \|D^\alpha h\|_{C([0,T];\mathcal{Z})} |s - t|^\alpha.$$

Proof. We take $0 \le s < t \le T$; hence,

$$h(t) = D^1 J^1 h(t) = D^1 J^\alpha J^{1-\alpha} h(t) = J^\alpha D^1 J^{1-\alpha} h(t) = J^\alpha D^\alpha h(t),$$

since $J^{1-\alpha} h(0) = 0$. Then,

$$h(t) - h(s) = J^\alpha D^\alpha h(t) - J^\alpha D^\alpha h(s)$$

$$= \int_0^s \frac{(t-\tau)^{\alpha-1} - (s-\tau)^{\alpha-1}}{\Gamma(\alpha)} D^\alpha h(\tau) d\tau + \int_s^t \frac{(t-\tau)^{\alpha-1}}{\Gamma(\alpha)} D^\alpha h(\tau) d\tau,$$

$$\|h(t) - h(s)\|_{\mathcal{Z}} \le \|D^\alpha h\|_{C([0,T];\mathcal{Z})} \left(\frac{(t-s)^\alpha}{\Gamma(\alpha+1)} + \left| \int_0^s \int_s^t \frac{(r-\tau)^{\alpha-2}}{\Gamma(\alpha-1)} dr d\tau \right| \right)$$

$$= \frac{\|D^\alpha h\|_{C([0,T];\mathcal{Z})}}{\Gamma(\alpha+1)} \left((t-s)^\alpha + \alpha \left| \int_s^t (r^{\alpha-1} - (r-s)^{\alpha-1}) dr \right| \right)$$

$$\le \frac{\|D^\alpha h\|_{C([0,T];\mathcal{Z})}}{\Gamma(\alpha+1)} \left((t-s)^\alpha + \alpha \int_s^t (r-s)^{\alpha-1} dr \right) = \frac{2\|D^\alpha h\|_{C([0,T];\mathcal{Z})}}{\Gamma(\alpha+1)} (t-s)^\alpha.$$

□

Theorem 4. *We let $\alpha_0 = 1$, $\alpha_k \in (0, 1]$, $k = 1, 2, \ldots, n$, $\theta_0 \in (\pi/2, \pi]$, $a_0 \ge 0$, $A \in \mathcal{A}_{\{\alpha_k\}}(\theta_0, a_0)$, $z_k \in D_A$, $k = 0, 1, \ldots, n-1$, $(0, z_0, z_1, \ldots, z_{n-1}) \in Z$, $\Phi, \overline{\Phi A} \in \mathcal{L}(\mathcal{Z}; \mathcal{U})$, $\mathcal{D}^{\sigma_k} \Psi \in C([0, T]; \mathcal{U})$, $k = 0, 1, \ldots, n-1$, $\mathcal{D}^{\sigma_n} \Psi \in C^\gamma([0, T]; \mathcal{U})$, $\gamma \in (0, 1]$, $\Phi z_0 = \Psi(0)$, and conditions $(\mathcal{A})$–$(\mathcal{D})$, $(\mathcal{E}_1)$, $(\mathcal{F}_1)$ be satisfied. Then, Problem (1)–(3) has a unique classical solution (z, u) on segment $[0, T_1]$ with some $T_1 \in (0, T]$.*

Proof. As before, $(z(t), u^0(t))$ is a mild solution of (1)–(3) on some small enough segment $[0, T_1]$, which exists by Theorem 2. We take $\alpha \in (0, \min\{\alpha_k : k = 0, 1, \ldots, n\})$, $\alpha \le \gamma$. Then, due to Remark 2, for $k, j \in \{0, 1, \ldots, n-1\}$, $k > j$, we have $D^\alpha D^{\alpha_j} Z_k(t) = D^\alpha Y_{\sigma_n - \sigma_k - 1 + \sigma_j}(t) = Y_{\sigma_n - \sigma_k - 1 + \sigma_j + \alpha}(t)$ by Formula (5),

$$\|D^\alpha D^{\alpha_j} Z_k(t)\|_{\mathcal{L}(\mathcal{Z})} = \|Y_{\sigma_n - \sigma_k - 1 + \sigma_j + \alpha}(t)\|_{\mathcal{L}(\mathcal{Z})} \le C t^{\sigma_k - \sigma_j - \alpha}, \quad t \in [0, T],$$

$\sigma_k - \sigma_j - \alpha \ge \alpha_k - \alpha > 0$. If $k < j$, $z_k \in D_A$; then, we have, due to (5), $D^\alpha D^{\alpha_j} Z_k(t) z_k = D^\alpha Y_{\sigma_j - \sigma_k - 1}(t) A z_k = Y_{\sigma_j - \sigma_k - 1 + \alpha}(t) A z_k$,

$$\|D^\alpha D^{\alpha_j} Z_k(t) z_k\|_{\mathcal{Z}} = \|Y_{\sigma_j - \sigma_k - 1 + \alpha}(t) A z_k\|_{\mathcal{Z}} \le C t^{\sigma_n - \sigma_j + \sigma_k - \alpha} \|A z_k\|_{\mathcal{Z}},$$

$\sigma_n - \sigma_j + \sigma_k - \alpha \geq \alpha_n + \alpha_0 - 1 - \alpha = \alpha_n - \alpha > 0$. In addition, for $z_k \in D_A$,

$$\|D^\alpha(\mathcal{D}^{\sigma_k}Z_k(t)z_k - z_k)\|_{\mathcal{Z}} = \|D^\alpha Y_{-1}(t)Az_k\|_{\mathcal{Z}} = \|Y_{\alpha-1}(t)Az_k\|_{\mathcal{Z}} \leq Ct^{\sigma_n-\alpha}\|Az_k\|_{\mathcal{Z}},$$

$\sigma_n - \alpha = \alpha_1 + \alpha_2 + \ldots \alpha_n - \alpha > 0$. Thus, $D^\alpha \mathcal{D}^{\sigma_j}Z_k(\cdot)z_k, D^\alpha(\mathcal{D}^{\sigma_k}Z_k(t)z_k - z_k) \in C([0,T];\mathcal{Z})$ for $z_k \in D_A, k,j \in \{0,1,\ldots,n-1\}, k \neq j$; therefore, by Lemma 3, $\mathcal{D}^{\sigma_j}Z_k(\cdot)z_k \in C^\alpha([0,T];\mathcal{Z})$.

Moreover, Equality (10) implies that

$$D^\alpha D^{\alpha_j}\int_0^t Y_0(t-s)B(s,\mathcal{D}^{\sigma_0}z(s),\mathcal{D}^{\sigma_1}z(s),\ldots,\mathcal{D}^{\sigma_{n-1}}z(s),u(s))ds$$

$$= D^1\int_0^t Y_{\sigma_j-1+\alpha}(t-s)B(s,\mathcal{D}^{\sigma_0}z(s),\mathcal{D}^{\sigma_1}z(s),\ldots,\mathcal{D}^{\sigma_{n-1}}z(s),u(s))ds$$

$$= \int_0^t Y_{\sigma_j+\alpha}(t-s)B(s,\mathcal{D}^{\sigma_0}z(s),\mathcal{D}^{\sigma_1}z(s),\ldots,\mathcal{D}^{\sigma_{n-1}}z(s),u(s))ds,$$

$$\left\|D^\alpha D^{\alpha_j}\int_0^t Y_0(t-s)B(s,\mathcal{D}^{\sigma_0}z(s),\mathcal{D}^{\sigma_1}z(s),\ldots,\mathcal{D}^{\sigma_{n-1}}z(s),u(s))ds\right\|_{\mathcal{Z}}$$

$$\leq \frac{C}{\sigma_n - \sigma_j - \alpha}\max_{s\in[0,t]}\|B(s,\mathcal{D}^{\sigma_0}z(s),\mathcal{D}^{\sigma_1}z(s),\ldots,\mathcal{D}^{\sigma_{n-1}}z(s),u(s))\|_{\mathcal{Z}}t^{\sigma_n-\sigma_j-\alpha}.$$

Here, we use inequalities $\|Y_{\sigma_j-1+\alpha}(t)\|_{\mathcal{L}(\mathcal{Z})} \leq Ct^{\sigma_n-\sigma_j-\alpha}$, $\sigma_n - \sigma_j - \alpha \geq \alpha_n - \alpha > 0$. Hence,

$$D^{\alpha_j}\int_0^t Y_0(t-s)B(s,\mathcal{D}^{\sigma_0}z(s),\mathcal{D}^{\sigma_1}z(s),\ldots,\mathcal{D}^{\sigma_{n-1}}z(s),u(s))ds \in C^\alpha([0,T];\mathcal{Z})$$

and $D^{\alpha_j}z \in C^\alpha([0,T];\mathcal{Z}), j = 0,1,\ldots,n-1$.

We recall that $u^0(t) = F(t,v(t))$, where

$$v(t) = \mathcal{D}^{\sigma_n}\Psi(t) - \overline{\Phi A}\sum_{k=0}^{n-1}Z_k(t)z_k - \Phi B_1(t,\mathcal{D}^{\sigma_0}z(t),\mathcal{D}^{\sigma_1}z(t),\ldots,\mathcal{D}^{\sigma_{n-1}}z(t))$$

$$-\int_0^t \overline{\Phi A}Y_0(t-\tau)B(\tau,\mathcal{D}^{\sigma_0}z(\tau),\mathcal{D}^{\sigma_1}z(\tau),\ldots,\mathcal{D}^{\sigma_{n-1}}z(\tau),u(\tau))d\tau.$$

Consequently, under conditions $(\mathcal{E}_1)$, $(\mathcal{F}_1)$,

$$u^0(t) - u^0(s) = F(t,v(t)) - F(s,v(s)) = F(t,v(t)) - F(t,v(s)) + F(t,v(s)) - F(s,v(s)),$$

$$\|u^0(t) - u^0(s)\|_{\mathcal{U}} \leq C_1(|s-t|^\alpha + \|v(t) - v(s)\|_{\mathcal{U}}) \leq C_1|s-t|^\alpha +$$

$$+C_2\|B_1(t,\mathcal{D}^{\sigma_0}z(t),\mathcal{D}^{\sigma_1}z(t),\ldots,\mathcal{D}^{\sigma_{n-1}}z(t)) - B_1(t,\mathcal{D}^{\sigma_0}z(s),\mathcal{D}^{\sigma_1}z(s),\ldots,\mathcal{D}^{\sigma_{n-1}}z(s))\|_{\mathcal{Z}}$$

$$+C_2\|B_1(t,\mathcal{D}^{\sigma_0}z(s),\mathcal{D}^{\sigma_1}z(s),\ldots,\mathcal{D}^{\sigma_{n-1}}z(s)) - B_1(s,\mathcal{D}^{\sigma_0}z(s),\mathcal{D}^{\sigma_1}z(s),\ldots,\mathcal{D}^{\sigma_{n-1}}z(s))\|_{\mathcal{Z}}$$

$$\leq C_3|s-t|^\alpha + C_3\sum_{k=0}^{n-1}\|\mathcal{D}^{\sigma_k}z(s) - \mathcal{D}^{\sigma_k}z(s)\|_{\mathcal{Z}} \leq C_3|s-t|^\alpha.$$

Therefore, mapping $t \to B(t,\mathcal{D}^{\sigma_0}z(s),\mathcal{D}^{\sigma_1}z(s),\ldots,\mathcal{D}^{\sigma_{n-1}}z(s),u(t))$ satisfies the Hölder condition with power α due to condition $(\mathcal{F}_1)$. Thus, by Theorem 1, z is a solution of direct problem (1), (2) with a given u^0; therefore, (z,u^0) is a classical solution of identification problem (1)–(3). □

4. Time-Fractional Phase Field System of Equations

We let $\Omega \subset \mathbb{R}^d$ be a bounded domain with a smooth boundary $\partial\Omega$, $\delta, \nu, \kappa \in \mathbb{R}$, $\alpha_0 = 1$, $\alpha_1, \alpha_2, \dots, \alpha_n \in (0,1)$, $\sigma_k = \alpha_0 + \alpha_1 + \dots + \alpha_k - 1$, $k = 0,1,\dots,n$; $\Delta = \frac{\partial^2}{\partial^2 \xi_1} + \dots + \frac{\partial^2}{\partial^2 \xi_d}$ is the Laplace operator, $\langle \cdot, \cdot \rangle$ is the inner product in space $L_2(\Omega)$, $\eta_l \in H^2(\Omega)$, $l = 1,2,\dots,2n$. We consider problem

$$D_t^{\sigma_k} x(\xi, 0) = x_k(\xi), \quad D_t^{\sigma_k} y(\xi, 0) = y_k(\xi), \quad k = 0,1,\dots,n-1, \quad \xi \in \Omega, \tag{16}$$

$$(1-\delta)x(\xi,t) + \delta \frac{\partial x}{\partial n}(\xi,t) = 0, \ (1-\delta)y(\xi,t) + \delta \frac{\partial y}{\partial n}(\xi,t) = 0, \ (\xi,t) \in \partial\Omega \times [0,T], \tag{17}$$

$$\langle x(\cdot,t), \eta_l \rangle = \phi_l(t), \ \langle y(\cdot,t), \eta_l \rangle = \psi_l(t), \ l = 1,2,\dots,2n, \ t \in [0,T], \tag{18}$$

to the system of equations in $\Omega \times [0,T]$,

$$D_t^{\sigma_n} x(\xi,t) = \Delta x(\xi,t) - \Delta y(\xi,t) + \sum_{k=0}^{n-1} u_k^1(t) D_t^{\sigma_k} x(\xi,t) + \sum_{k=0}^{n-1} v_k^1(t) D_t^{\sigma_k} y(\xi,t) + f(\xi,t), \tag{19}$$

$$D_t^{\sigma_n} y(\xi,t) = \nu \Delta y(\xi,t) - \kappa y^3(\xi,t) + \sum_{k=0}^{n-1} u_k^2(t) D_t^{\sigma_k} x(\xi,t) + \sum_{k=0}^{n-1} v_k^2(t) D_t^{\sigma_k} y(\xi,t) + g(\xi,t) \tag{20}$$

with unknown functions x, y, u_k^i, v_k^i, $k = 0,1,\dots,n-1$, $i = 1,2$. At $n = 1$, $\alpha_1 = 1$, $u_k^1 = v_k^1 = 0$, $k = 0,1,\dots,n-1$, $u_k^2 = v_k^2 = 0$, $k = 1,2,\dots,n-1$, System (19), (20) up to linear replacement $x(\xi,t) = \tilde{x}(\xi,t) + \frac{l}{2}\tilde{y}(\xi,t)$, $y(\xi,t) = \frac{l}{2}\tilde{y}(\xi,t)$, $l \in \mathbb{R}$, and stretching over t coincide with the linearization of phase field equations [29,30].

We put $j \in \mathbb{N}$, $j > d/2$, $\mathcal{Z} = (H^j(\Omega))^2$,

$$A = \begin{pmatrix} \Delta & -\Delta \\ 0 & \nu\Delta \end{pmatrix}, \quad D_A = (H_\delta^{j+2}(\Omega))^2,$$

$$H_\delta^{j+2}(\Omega) := \left\{ h \in H^{j+2}(\Omega) : \left(\delta \frac{\partial}{\partial n} + 1 - \delta \right) h(\xi) = 0, \ \xi \in \partial\Omega \right\}.$$

Therefore, $A \in Cl(\mathcal{Z})$.

By $\{\varphi_k : k \in \mathbb{N}\}$, we denote orthonormal in the sense of the inner product $\langle \cdot, \cdot \rangle$ in $L_2(\Omega)$ eigenfunctions of the Laplace operator with domain $H_\delta^{j+2}(\Omega)$, which are numbered in the order of non-increasing eigenvalues $\{\lambda_k : k \in \mathbb{N}\}$ taking into account their multiplicities.

Theorem 5. *We let* $\alpha_0, \alpha_1, \dots, \alpha_n \in (0,1)$, $\alpha_0 + \alpha_n > 1$, $\sigma_n = 1$, $\nu > 0$, $\delta \in \mathbb{R}$, $j \in \mathbb{N}_0 := \mathbb{N} \cup \{0\}$, *then* $A \in \mathcal{A}_{\{\alpha_k\}}(\theta_0, a_0)$ *for some* $\theta_0 \in (\pi/2, \pi)$, $a_0 \geq 0$ *in this case* $\sigma(A) = \{\lambda_k, \nu\lambda_k : k \in \mathbb{N}\}$.

Proof. We take the basis $\{\varphi_k : k \in \mathbb{N}\}$ in $L_2(\Omega)$ and obtain for $\lambda \neq \lambda_k$, $\lambda \neq \nu\lambda_k$, $k \in \mathbb{N}$ operators

$$\lambda^{\sigma_n} I - A = \begin{pmatrix} \lambda I - \Delta & \Delta \\ 0 & \lambda^{\sigma_n} I - \nu\Delta \end{pmatrix},$$

$$(\lambda^{\sigma_n} I - A)^{-1} = \sum_{k=1}^{\infty} \begin{pmatrix} \frac{1}{\lambda - \lambda_k} & -\frac{\lambda_k}{(\lambda-\lambda_k)(\lambda-\nu\lambda_k)} \\ 0 & \frac{1}{\lambda-\nu\lambda_k} \end{pmatrix} \langle \cdot, \varphi_k \rangle \varphi_k.$$

We take arbitrary $\theta_0 \in (\pi/2, \pi)$, $a_0 > \max\{\lambda_k, \nu\lambda_k : k \in \mathbb{N}\}$; then, for any $a \geq a_0$, $\lambda \in S_{\theta_0, a_0}$,

$$\left| \frac{1}{\lambda - \lambda_k} \right| \leq \frac{-1}{|\lambda - a| \sin\theta_0}, \quad \left| \frac{1}{\lambda - \nu\lambda_k} \right| \leq \frac{-1}{|\lambda - a| \sin\theta_0},$$

$$\left|\frac{\lambda_k}{(\lambda-\lambda_k)(\lambda-\nu\lambda_k)}\right| = \left|\frac{1}{(1-\lambda/\lambda_k)(\lambda-\nu\lambda_k)}\right| \leq \frac{C_1}{|\lambda-a|\sin^2\theta_0}$$

for some $C_1 > 0$, since for all $\lambda \in S_{\theta_0,a_0}$, $k \in \mathbb{N}$,

$$\left|\frac{1}{1-\lambda/\lambda_k}\right| \leq C_1.$$

Therefore, for all $\lambda \in S_{\theta_0,a_0}$,

$$\|R_{\lambda^{\sigma_n}}(A)\|^2_{\mathcal{L}(\mathcal{Z})} \leq \frac{C_2}{|\lambda^{\sigma_n}-a|^{\alpha_0}|\lambda|^{\sigma_n-\alpha_0}}$$

and $A \in \mathcal{A}_{\{\alpha_k\}}(\theta_0,a_0)$. □

Theorem 6. *We let $\alpha_0 = 1$, $\alpha_1,\alpha_2,\ldots,\alpha_n \in (0,1)$, $\sigma_n = 1$, $\nu > 0$, $\delta,\kappa \in \mathbb{R}$, $j \in \mathbb{N}$, $j > d/2$, $g,h \in C([0,T];H^j(\Omega))$, $x_k,y_k \in H^{2+j}_\delta(\Omega)$, $k = 0,1,\ldots,n-1$, $\eta_l \in H^2(\Omega)$, $\mathcal{D}^{\sigma_k}\phi_l, \mathcal{D}^{\sigma_k}\psi_l \in C([0,T];\mathbb{R})$, $k = 0,1,\ldots,n$, $\langle x_0,\eta_l\rangle = \phi_l(0)$, $\langle y_0,\eta_l\rangle = \psi_l(0)$, $l = 1,2,\ldots,2n$,*

$$\det\begin{pmatrix} \mathcal{D}^{\sigma_0}\phi_1(t) & \mathcal{D}^{\sigma_0}\psi_1(t) & \ldots & \mathcal{D}^{\sigma_{n-1}}\phi_1(t) & \mathcal{D}^{\sigma_{n-1}}\psi_1(t) \\ \mathcal{D}^{\sigma_0}\phi_2(t) & \mathcal{D}^{\sigma_0}\psi_2(t) & \ldots & \mathcal{D}^{\sigma_{n-1}}\phi_2(t) & \mathcal{D}^{\sigma_{n-1}}\psi_2(t) \\ \ldots & \ldots & \ldots & \ldots & \\ \mathcal{D}^{\sigma_0}\phi_{2n}(t) & \mathcal{D}^{\sigma_0}\psi_{2n}(t) & \ldots & \mathcal{D}^{\sigma_{n-1}}\phi_{2n}(t) & \mathcal{D}^{\sigma_{n-1}}\psi_{2n}(t) \end{pmatrix} \neq 0 \qquad (21)$$

for all $t \in [0,T]$. Then, Problem (16)–(20) has a unique mild solution.

Proof. We take $\mathcal{U} = \mathbb{R}^{4n}$, $(b_k,c_k) \in \mathcal{Z}$, $k = 0,1,\ldots,n-1$, $u^i_k,v^i_k \in \mathbb{R}$, $k = 0,1,\ldots,n-1$, $i = 1,2$,

$$B(t,b_0,c_0,\ldots,b_{n-1},c_{n-1},u^1_0,v^1_0,\ldots,u^1_{n-1},v^1_{n-1},u^2_0,v^2_0,\ldots,u^2_{n-1},v^2_{n-1})$$

$$= \begin{pmatrix} \sum\limits_{k=0}^{n-1} u^1_k b_k + \sum\limits_{k=0}^{n-1} v^1_k c_k + f(\cdot,t) \\ \sum\limits_{k=0}^{n-1} u^2_k b_k + \sum\limits_{k=0}^{n-1} v^2_k c_k - \kappa c_0^3 + g(\cdot,t) \end{pmatrix}.$$

Hence, $B : \mathcal{Z}^n \times \mathcal{U} \to \mathcal{Z}$,

$$B_1(t,b_0,c_0,\ldots,b_{n-1},c_{n-1}) = \begin{pmatrix} f(\cdot,t) \\ -\kappa c_0^3 + g(\cdot,t) \end{pmatrix}.$$

We have $\Phi = (\Phi_1,\Phi_2,\ldots,\Phi_{2n})$, where for $h = (h_1,h_2)$ $\Phi_l h = (\langle h_1,\eta_l\rangle, \langle h_2,\eta_l\rangle)$, $l = 1,2,\ldots,2n$. Then,

$$\Phi_l A h = (\langle \Delta h_1 - \Delta h_2,\eta_l\rangle, \langle \nu\Delta h_2,\eta_l\rangle) = (\langle h_1 - h_2,\Delta\eta_l\rangle, \langle h_2,\nu\Delta\eta_l\rangle), \quad l = 1,2,\ldots,2n,$$

since $\eta_l \in H^2(\Omega)$, $l = 1,2,\ldots,2n$. Hence, $\overline{\Phi A} \in \mathcal{L}(\mathcal{Z};\mathcal{U})$.

Condition $(\mathcal{B})$ is satisfied due to Condition (21) at $t = 0$. In Condition $(\mathcal{C})$, we take for $u_{lk},v_{lk},u^i_k,v^i_k \in \mathbb{R}$, $k = 0,1,\ldots,n-1$, $l = 1,2,\ldots,2n$, $i = 1,2$, $B_3 : \mathbb{R}^{4n(n+1)} \to \mathbb{R}^{4n}$,

$$B_3(u_{10},v_{10},\ldots,u_{2n\,n-1},v_{2n\,n-1},u^1_0,v^1_0,\ldots,u^1_{n-1},v^1_{n-1},u^2_0,v^2_0,\ldots,u^2_{n-1},v^2_{n-1})$$

$$= \begin{pmatrix} u_{10}u^1_0 + v_{10}v^1_0 + \cdots + u_{1\,n-1}u^1_{n-1} + v_{1\,n-1}v^1_{n-1} \\ \ldots \\ u_{2n\,0}u^1_0 + v_{2n\,0}v^1_0 + \cdots + u_{2n\,n-1}u^1_{n-1} + v_{2n\,n-1}v^1_{n-1} \\ u_{10}u^2_0 + v_{10}v^2_0 + \cdots + u_{1\,n-1}u^2_{n-1} + v_{1\,n-1}v^2_{n-1} \\ \ldots \\ u_{2n\,0}u^2_0 + v_{2n\,0}v^2_0 + \cdots + u_{2n\,n-1}u^2_{n-1} + v_{2n\,n-1}v^2_{n-1} \end{pmatrix}.$$

By Inequality (21), Condition $(\mathcal{D})$ is valid.

Due to inequality $j > d/2$, by virtue of the Sobolev embedding theorem, $\mathcal{Z} \subset (C(\overline{\Omega}))^2$. In such a case, a nonlinear operator $N(b_0, c_0) = (0, -\kappa c_0^3)$ acts from $\mathcal{Z}$ into $\mathcal{Z}$ and satisfies the local Lipschitz condition. Therefore, Condition $(\mathcal{F})$ is satisfied by the construction of operators B_1 and $B_2 = B - B_1$. In addition, $F(t, v) = G(t)^{-1}v$, where matrix

$$G(t) = \begin{pmatrix} D^{\sigma_0}\phi_1(t) & D^{\sigma_0}\psi_1(t) & \dots & D^{\sigma_{n-1}}\phi_1(t) & D^{\sigma_{n-1}}\psi_1(t) \\ D^{\sigma_0}\phi_2(t) & D^{\sigma_0}\psi_2(t) & \dots & D^{\sigma_{n-1}}\phi_2(t) & D^{\sigma_{n-1}}\psi_2(t) \\ \dots & \dots & \dots & \dots & \dots \\ D^{\sigma_0}\phi_{2n}(t) & D^{\sigma_0}\psi_{2n}(t) & \dots & D^{\sigma_{n-1}}\phi_{2n}(t) & D^{\sigma_{n-1}}\psi_{2n}(t) \end{pmatrix} \in C([0,T]; \mathbb{R}^{2n\times 2n}),$$

hence, due to (21) $G^{-1} \in C([0,T]; \mathbb{R}^{2n\times 2n})$, Condition $(\mathcal{E})$ is fulfilled.

Reference to Theorems 2 and 5 completes the proof. □

By slightly increasing the smoothness of some data, we obtain a theorem on the classical solution of identification problem (16)–(20).

Theorem 7. *We let* $\alpha_0 = 1, \alpha_1, \alpha_2, \dots, \alpha_n \in (0,1)$, $\sigma_n = 1$, $\nu > 0$, $\delta, \kappa \in \mathbb{R}$, $j \in \mathbb{N}$, $j > d/2$, $g, h \in C^\gamma([0,T]; H^j(\Omega))$, $\gamma \in (0,1]$, $x_k, y_k \in H_\delta^{2+j}(\Omega)$, $k = 0,1,\dots,n-1$, $\eta_l \in H^2(\Omega)$, $D^{\sigma_k}\phi_l, D^{\sigma_k}\psi_l \in C([0,T]; \mathbb{R})$, $k = 0,1,\dots,n-1$, $D^{\sigma_n}\phi_l, D^{\sigma_n}\psi_l \in C^\gamma([0,T]; \mathbb{R})$, $\langle x_0, \eta_l\rangle = \phi_l(0)$, $\langle y_0, \eta_l\rangle = \psi_l(0)$, $l = 1,2,\dots,2n$, *Condition* (21) *be fulfilled for all* $t \in [0,T]$, $G^{-1} \in C^\gamma([0,T]; \mathbb{R}^{2n\times 2n})$. *Then, Problem* (16)–(20) *has a unique classical solution.*

Proof. Under the additional condition $g, h \in C^\gamma([0,T]; H^j(\Omega))$, assumption $(\mathcal{E}_1)$ is satisfied. Due to condition $G^{-1} \in C([0,T]; \mathbb{R}^{2n\times 2n})$, assumption $(\mathcal{F}_1)$ is valid. By Theorems 4 and 5, we obtain the required result. □

5. Conclusions

The obtained abstract results of the unique solvability in the sense of mild and classical solutions for a wide new class of identification problems can find their applications in the study of coefficient inverse problems for various evolutionary equations and systems of equations with the general fractional derivative. In particular, it can be useful for parabolic equations, for equations of hydrodynamics, the theory of visoelasticity, etc. Moreover, the unique solvability theorems can be used for the correct formulation of initial boundary value problems in applied research and for the development of numerical methods for solving these problems.

Author Contributions: Conceptualization, V.E.F.; methodology, V.E.F. and M.V.P.; software, D.V.M.; validation, M.V.P. and D.V.M.; formal analysis, D.V.M.; investigation, V.E.F. and M.V.P.; resources, D.V.M.; data curation, D.V.M.; writing—original draft preparation, V.E.F. and M.V.P.; writing—review and editing, V.E.F.; visualization, D.V.M.; supervision, V.E.F. and M.V.P.; project administration, V.E.F.; funding acquisition, M.V.P. All authors have read and agreed to the published version of the manuscript.

Funding: The work is supported by the grant of Russian Science Foundation and of the Government of the Chelyabinsk Region, project number 23-21-10015.

Data Availability Statement: Data sharing not applicable.

Conflicts of Interest: The authors declare no conflict of interest. The funders had no role in the design of the study; in the collection, analysis, or interpretation of data; in the writing of the manuscript; or in the decision to publish the results.

References

1. Dzhrbashyan, M.M.; Nersesyan, A.B. Fractional derivatives and Cauchy problem for differential equations of fractional order. *Izv. AN Arm. SSR. Mat.* **1968**, *3*, 3–28. (In Russian) [CrossRef]
2. Samko, S.G.; Kilbas, A.A.; Marichev, O.I. *Fractional Integrals and Derivatives. Theory and Applications*; Gordon and Breach Science Publishers: Philadelphia, PA, USA, 1993.
3. Podlubny, I. *Fractional Differential Equations*; Academic: Boston, MA, USA, 1999.
4. Pskhu, A.V. *Partial Differential Equations of Fractional Order*; Nauka: Moscow, Russia, 2005. (In Russian)
5. Kilbas, A.A.; Srivastava, H.M.; Trujillo, J.J. *Theory and Applications of Fractional Differential Equations*; Elsevier Science Publishing: Amsterdam, The Netherlands; Boston, MA, USA; Heidelberg, Germany, 2006.
6. Hilfer, R. *Applications of Fractional Calculus in Physics*; WSPC: Singapore, 2000.
7. Nakhushev, A.M. *Fractional Calculus ant Its Applications*; Fizmatlit: Moscow, Russia, 2003. (In Russian)
8. Tarasov, V.E. *Fractional Dynamics: Applications of Fractional Calculus to Dynamics of Particles*; Springer: New York, NY, USA, 2011.
9. Uchaykin, V.V. *Fractional Derivatives for Physicists and Engineers*; Higher Education Press: Beijing, China, 2012.
10. Prilepko, A.I.; Orlovsky, D.G.; Vasin, I.A. *Methods for Solving Inverse Problems in Mathematical Physics*; Marcel Dekker, Inc.: New York, NY, USA, 2000.
11. Favini, A.; Lorenzi, A. *Differential Equations. Inverse and Direct Problems*; Chapman and Hall/CRC: New York, NY, USA, 2006.
12. Fedorov, V.E.; Ivanova, N.D. Identification problem for degenerate evolution equations of fractional order. *Fract. Calc. Appl. Anal.* **2017**, *20*, 706–721. [CrossRef]
13. Orlovsky, D.G. Parameter determination in a differential equation of fractional order with Riemann–Liouville fractional derivative in a Hilbert space. *J. Sib. Fed. Univ. Math. Phys.* **2015**, *8*, 55–63. [CrossRef]
14. Orlovsky, D.G. Determination of the parameter of the differential equation of fractional order with the Caputo derivative in Hilbert space. *J. Phys. Conf. Ser.* **2019**, *1205*, 012042. [CrossRef]
15. Kostin, A.B.; Piskarev, S.I. Inverse source problem for the abstract fractional differential equation. *J. Inverse Ill-Posed Probl.* **2021**, *29*, 267–281. [CrossRef]
16. Orlovsky, D.; Piskarev, S. Inverse problem with final overdetermination for time-fractional differential equation in a Banach space. *J. Inverse Ill-Posed Probl.* **2022**, *30*, 221–237. [CrossRef]
17. Fedorov, V.E.; Ivanova, N.D.; Borel, L.V.; Avilovich, A.S. Nonlinear inverse problems for fractional differential equations with sectorial operators. *Lobachevskii J. Math.* **2022**, *43*, 3125–3141. [CrossRef]
18. Dzhrbashyan, M.M.; Nersesyan, A.B. Fractional derivatives and Cauchy problem for differential equations of fractional order. *Fract. Calc. Appl. Anal.* **2020**, *23*, 1810–1836. [CrossRef]
19. Pskhu, A.V. The fundamental solution of a diffusion-wave equation of fractional order. *Izv. Math.* **2009**, *73*, 351–392. [CrossRef]
20. Pskhu, A.V. Fractional diffusion equation with discretely distributed differentiation operator. *Sib. Electron. Math. Rep.* **2016**, *13*, 1078–1098.
21. Pskhu, A.V. Boundary value problem for a first-order partial differential equation with a fractional discretely distributed differentiation operator. *Differ. Equ.* **2016**, *52*, 1610–1623. [CrossRef]
22. Bogatyreva, F.T. Boundary value problems for first order partial differential equation with the Dzhrbashyan–Nersesyan operators. *Chelyabinsk Phys. Math. J.* **2021**, *6*, 403–416.
23. Mamchuev, M.O. Boundary value problem for a system of partial differential equations with the Dzhrbashyan–Nersesyan fractional differentiation operators. *Bull. Karaganda Univ. Math. Ser.* **2022**, *2*, 143–160. [CrossRef]
24. Ahmad, A.; Baleanu, D. On two backward problems with Dzherbashian–Nersesian operator. *AIMS Math.* **2023**, *8*, 887–904. [CrossRef]
25. Fedorov, V.E.; Plekhanova, M.V.; Izhberdeeva, E.M. Initial value problem for linear equations with the Dzhrbashyan–Nersesyan derivative in Banach spaces. *Symmetry* **2021**, *13*, 1058. [CrossRef]
26. Fedorov, V.E.; Plekhanova, M.V.; Izhberdeeva, E.M. Analytic resolving families for equations with the Dzhrbashyan–Nersesyan fractional derivative. *Fractal Fract.* **2022**, *6*, 541. [CrossRef]
27. Plekhanova, M.V.; Izhberdeeva, E.M. Local unique solvability of a quasilinear equation with the Dzhrbashyan–Nersesyan derivatives. *Lobachevskii J. Math.* **2022**, *43*, 1379–1388. [CrossRef]
28. Fedorov, V.E.; Plekhanova, M.V.; Melekhina, D.V. Nonlinear inverse problems for equations with Dzhrbashyan–Nersesyan derivatives. *Fractal Fract.* **2023**, *7*, 464. [CrossRef]
29. Caginalp, G. An analysis of a phase field model of a free boundary. *Arch. Ration. Mech. Anal.* **1986**, *92*, 205–245. [CrossRef]
30. Caginalp, G. Stefan and Hele–Shaw type models as asymptotic limits of the phase-field equations. *Phys. Rev. A* **1989**, *39*, 5887–5896. [CrossRef] [PubMed]

axiomas MDPI

Article

Finite-Time Stability of Impulsive Fractional Differential Equations with Pure Delays

Tingting Xie and Mengmeng Li *

Department of Mathematics and Statistics, Guizhou University, Guiyang 550025, China
* Correspondence: mmli@gzu.edu.cn

Abstract: This paper introduces a novel concept of the impulsive delayed Mittag–Leffler-type vector function, an extension of the Mittag–Leffler matrix function. It is essential to seek explicit formulas for the solutions to linear impulsive fractional differential delay equations. Based on explicit formulas of the solutions, the finite-time stability results of impulsive fractional differential delay equations are presented. Finally, we present four examples to illustrate the validity of our theoretical results.

Keywords: fractional delay differential equations; impulsive delayed Mittag–Leffler-type vector function; finite-time stability

MSC: 34A08; 34A37; 34D20

1. Introduction

In recent decades, researchers have found that fractional differential equations are appropriate for describing real-life problems with memory and genetic characteristics. Thus, the topic of fractional differential equations has received increasing attention. More details can be found in [1–3]. Impulsive fractional differential equations (IFDEs) are used to depict various practical dynamical systems, including the evolution of states that mutate into features at certain times, with the wide application of IFDE theory in the modeling of genetic phenomena and abrupt dynamical systems. The research on the existence, uniqueness and stability of IFDEs has attracted increasing attention [4–9].

At the same time, fractional delay differential equations (FDDEs) and impulsive fractional delay differential equations (IFDDEs) are often used to depict state changes that occurred in the time interval of the previous period. In [10], the authors presented the idea of a delayed matrix function and provided an explicit formula for FDDEs by the method of constant variation. In [11,12], the idea of an impulsive delayed solution vector function was developed. This notion aided the authors in finding the exact solutions of IFDDEs. In [13], the author obtained the exact solutions of higher-fractional-order nonhomogeneous delayed differential equations with Caputo-type derivatives by using the new generalized delay Mittag matrix function, Laplace transform and inductive construction.

The finite-time stability (FTS) of fractional differential equations has attracted much interest. After decades of research, FTS has contributed remarkable achievements in modern science and technology, chemical engineering, and other areas. Thus, we studied the FTS of a system, which is of great practical significance. Scholars have recently used the Lyapunov function, and Gronwall's integral inequality to research the FTS of integer and fractional differential equations. In [14–17], the authors investigated finite-time stability by means of the generalized Gronwall inequality. Other related research can be found in [18–21]. Once we obtain the exact solution of the system, we can find a suitable method to obtain the sufficient conditions for FTS. Motivated by [12], we seek to construct an impulsive delayed solution vector function to express the explicit solution and study the FTS of IFDDEs.

In [22], the authors gave a representation of the solution of linear FDDEs:

$$\begin{cases} ({}^{RL}\mathbb{D}^{\beta}_{-\varsigma^+}v)(\xi) = Bv(\xi-\varsigma) + g(\xi),\ \varsigma > 0,\ \xi \in (0,T], \\ v(\xi) = \varpi(\xi),\ -\varsigma \le \xi \le 0, \\ (\mathbb{I}^{1-\beta}_{-\varsigma^+}v)(-\varsigma^+) = \varpi(-\varsigma),\ \varpi(-\varsigma) \in \mathbb{R}^n, \end{cases} \tag{1}$$

where ${}^{RL}\mathbb{D}^{\beta}_{-\varsigma^+}(0 < \beta < 1)$ denotes the Riemann–Liouville derivative (see Definition 2), $\mathbb{I}^{1-\beta}_{-\varsigma^+}(0 < \beta < 1)$ denotes the fractional integral (see Definition 1), $B \in \mathbb{R}^{n\times n}$, $T = k^*\varsigma$, $k^* \in \mathbb{N} := \{0,1,2,\cdots\}$, $g \in C([-\varsigma,T],\mathbb{R}^n)$, ς is a fixed delay time and ${}^{RL}\mathbb{D}^{\beta}_{-\varsigma^+}\varpi$ exists. For any $\xi \in [-\varsigma,T]$, the solution $v \in C(\Omega,\mathbb{R}^n) \cap C([-\varsigma,T],\mathbb{R}^n)$ of (1) is given by

$$v(\xi) = e^{B\xi^{\beta}}_{-\varsigma,\beta}\varpi(-\varsigma) + \int_{-\varsigma}^{0} e^{B(\xi-\varsigma-s)^{\beta}}_{-\varsigma,\beta}({}^{RL}\mathbb{D}^{\beta}_{-\varsigma^+}\varpi)(s)ds + \int_{-\varsigma}^{\xi} e^{B(\xi-\varsigma-t)^{\beta}}_{-\varsigma,\beta}g(t)dt, \tag{2}$$

where either $\Omega = ((k-1)\varsigma, k\varsigma]$ for $0 < \beta < \frac{1}{k+1}$ or $\Omega = [(k-1)\varsigma, k\varsigma]$ for $\beta \ge \frac{1}{k+1}$.

In this paper, we deduce the general solution of linear IFDDEs:

$$\begin{cases} ({}^{RL}\mathbb{D}^{\beta}_{-\varsigma^+}v)(\xi) = Bv(\xi-\varsigma),\ \xi \ne \xi_\imath,\ \varsigma > 0,\ \xi \in (0,T], \\ v(\xi_\imath^+) = v(\xi_\imath^-) + C_\imath,\ \xi = \xi_\imath,\ \imath = 1,2,\cdots,p(T,0), \\ v(\xi) = \varpi(\xi),\ -\varsigma \le \xi \le 0, \\ (\mathbb{I}^{1-\beta}_{-\varsigma^+}v)(-\varsigma^+) = \varpi(-\varsigma),\ \varpi(-\varsigma) \in \mathbb{R}^n, \end{cases} \tag{3}$$

where $p(T,0)$ denotes the number of impulsive points belong to $(0,T)$ and the symbols $v(\xi_\imath^+) = \lim_{\epsilon\to 0^+} v(\xi_\imath+\epsilon)$ and $v(\xi_\imath^-) = \lim_{\epsilon\to 0^-} v(\xi_\imath+\epsilon)$ denote, respectively, the right and left limits of $v(\xi)$ at $\xi = \xi_\imath$.

After that, we will give some new sufficient conditions to ensure that (4) is finite-time stable.

$$\begin{cases} ({}^{RL}\mathbb{D}^{\beta}_{-\varsigma^+}v)(\xi) = Bv(\xi-\varsigma) + g(\xi),\ \xi \ne \xi_\imath,\ \xi \in (0,T], \\ v(\xi_\imath^+) = v(\xi_\imath^-) + C_\imath,\ \xi = \xi_\imath,\ \imath = 1,2,\cdots,p(T,0), \\ v(\xi) = \varpi(\xi),\ -\varsigma \le \xi \le 0, \\ (\mathbb{I}^{1-\beta}_{-\varsigma^+}v)(-\varsigma^+) = \varpi(-\varsigma),\ \varpi(-\varsigma) \in \mathbb{R}^n. \end{cases} \tag{4}$$

This paper mainly has the following three aspects of innovation:

(i) The mathematical model is novel, and the newly constructed impulsive delay vector function is of great significance for extending from time-delay systems to impulsive time-delay systems.

(ii) Using the relationship between the Riemann–Liouville fractional derivative and the Caputo fractional derivative, the two are skillfully transformed to prove that the impulsive delay vector function is the fundamental solution of (3), which provides more ideas for future research.

(iii) The position of the pulse point in this paper is arbitrary, which renders the research more universal.

The rest of this paper is constituted as follows. Firstly, we review the symbols and definitions. Secondly, we construct an impulsive delayed solution vector function and give the explicit solutions of (3) and (4). Then, we give four practical conditions to guarantee that (4) is finite-time stable. Finally, we give three numerical examples to illustrate our theoretical results.

2. Preliminaries

Let $C([-\varsigma,T],\mathbb{R}^n)$ be the space of a continuous function with $\|v\|_C=\max_{\xi\in[-\varsigma,T]}\|v(\xi)\|$, $PC([-\varsigma,T],\mathbb{R}^n)=\{v\in C((\xi_\imath,\xi_{\imath+1}],\mathbb{R}^n),\imath=1,2,\cdots,p(T,0)$. There exist $v(\xi_\imath^+)$ and $v(\xi_\imath^-)$ with $v(\xi_\imath^-)=v(\xi_\imath)\}$ with $\|v\|_{PC}=\sup_{\xi\in[-\varsigma,T]}\|v(\xi)\|$. For any $0<\gamma<1$, we denote $C_\gamma([a,b],\mathbb{R}^n)=\{v\in C((a,b],\mathbb{R}^n)|(\xi-a)^\gamma v(\xi)\in C([a,b],\mathbb{R}^n)\}$ with $\|v\|_{C_\gamma}=\max_{a<\xi<b}\|(\xi-a)^\gamma v(\xi)\|$. Let $\|v\|=\sum_{i=1}^n|v_i|$, $\|B\|=\max_{1\leq j\leq n}\sum_{i=1}^n|b_{ij}|$ and $\|\varpi\|_C=\max_{\xi\in[-\varsigma,0]}\|\varpi(\xi)\|$.

Definition 1 (see [2]). *Let $0<\beta<1$ and $y:[-\varsigma,+\infty)\to\mathbb{R}^n$. The fractional integral of y is defined by*

$$\mathbb{I}^\beta_{-\varsigma}y(\xi)=\frac{1}{\Gamma(\beta)}\int_{-\varsigma}^{\xi}\frac{y(t)}{(\xi-t)^{1-\beta}}dt,\ \xi>-\varsigma,$$

where $\Gamma(\cdot)$ is the Gamma function.

Definition 2 (see [2]). *Let $0<\beta<1$ and $y:[-\varsigma,+\infty)\to\mathbb{R}^n$. The Riemann–Liouville fractional derivative of y is defined by*

$$({}^{RL}\mathbb{D}^\beta_{-\varsigma^+}y)(\xi)=\frac{1}{\Gamma(1-\beta)}\frac{d}{d\xi}\int_{-\varsigma}^{\xi}\frac{y(t)}{(\xi-t)^{\beta}}dt,\ \xi>-\varsigma.$$

Definition 3 (see [2]). *Let $0<\beta<1$ and $y:[-\varsigma,+\infty)\to\mathbb{R}^n$. The Caputo fractional derivative of y is defined by*

$$({}^{C}\mathbb{D}^\beta_{-\varsigma^+}y)(\xi)=\frac{1}{\Gamma(1-\beta)}\int_{-\varsigma}^{\xi}(\xi-t)^{-\beta}y'(t)dt,\ \xi>-\varsigma.$$

Definition 4 (see [2]). *If $0<\beta<1$, y is a function for which the Caputo fractional derivative $({}^{C}\mathbb{D}^\beta_{-\varsigma^+}y)(\xi)$ exists together with the Riemann–Liouville fractional derivative $({}^{RL}\mathbb{D}^\beta_{-\varsigma^+}y)(\xi)$. Then,*

$$({}^{C}\mathbb{D}^\beta_{-\varsigma^+}y)(\xi)=({}^{RL}\mathbb{D}^\beta_{-\varsigma^+}y)(\xi)-\frac{y(-\varsigma)}{\Gamma(1-\beta)}(\xi+\varsigma)^{-\beta}. \tag{5}$$

In particular, when $y(-\varsigma)\equiv 0$, then $({}^{C}\mathbb{D}^\beta_{-\varsigma^+}y)(\xi)=({}^{RL}\mathbb{D}^\beta_{-\varsigma^+}y)(\xi)$.

Definition 5. *The delayed one-parameter Mittag–Leffler-type matrix function $\mathbb{E}^{B,\beta}_{-\varsigma}:\mathbb{R}\to\mathbb{R}^{n\times n}$ is defined by*

$$\mathbb{E}^{B\xi^\beta}_{-\varsigma}=\begin{cases}\Theta, & -\infty<\xi<-2\varsigma,\\ E, & -2\varsigma\leq\xi\leq-\varsigma,\\ E+B\dfrac{(\xi+\varsigma)^\beta}{\Gamma(\beta+1)}+B^2\dfrac{\xi^{2\beta}}{\Gamma(2\beta+1)}+\cdots+B^{k+1}\dfrac{(\xi-(k-1)\varsigma)^{(k+1)\beta}}{\Gamma((k+1)\beta+1)}, \\ (k-1)\varsigma<\xi\leq k\varsigma,\ k\in\mathbb{N},\end{cases} \tag{6}$$

where Θ is a zero matrix and E is an identity matrix.

Definition 6 (see [22]). *The delayed two-parameter Mittag–Leffler-type matrix function* $e^{B\cdot\beta}_{-\varsigma,\alpha}$: $\mathbb{R} \to \mathbb{R}^{n\times n}$ *is defined by*

$$e^{B\xi^{\beta}}_{-\varsigma,\alpha} = \begin{cases} \Theta, \ -\infty < \xi < -\varsigma, \\ E\dfrac{(\xi+\varsigma)^{\beta-1}}{\Gamma(\beta)}, \ -\varsigma \leq \xi \leq 0, \\ E\dfrac{(\xi+\varsigma)^{\beta-1}}{\Gamma(\beta)} + B\dfrac{\xi^{2\beta-1}}{\Gamma(\beta+\alpha)} + \cdots + B^{k}\dfrac{(\xi-(k-1)\varsigma)^{(k+1)\beta-1}}{\Gamma(k\beta+\alpha)}, \\ (k-1)\varsigma < \xi \leq k\varsigma, \ k \in \mathbb{N}. \end{cases} \tag{7}$$

Definition 7. *For any* $\xi \in ((k-1)\varsigma, k\varsigma]$ *and* $k = 1, 2, \cdots, k^*$, *the impulsive delayed Mittag–Leffler-type vector function* $Q_{-\varsigma,\beta}(\cdot) : \mathbb{R} \to \mathbb{R}^n$ *is defined by*

$$Q_{-\varsigma,\beta}(\xi) = \sum_{0<\xi_\iota<\xi} \mathbb{E}^{B(\xi-\xi_\iota-2\varsigma)^{\beta}}_{-\varsigma} C_\iota. \tag{8}$$

Definition 8. *System* (4) *is finite-time stable with regard to* $\{0, J, \varsigma, \delta, \eta\}$ *if and only if* $\|\omega\|_C < \delta$ *implies* $\|v\|_{C_\gamma} < \eta$ *and* $\delta < \eta$, *where* $J := ((k-1)\varsigma, k\varsigma]$ *and* $k = 1, 2, \cdots, k^*$.

Lemma 1 (see [12]). *For any* $\xi \in ((k-1)\varsigma, k\varsigma]$, $k = 1, 2, \cdots, k^*$ *and* $\xi_\iota \in (0, \xi)$, *we have*

$$\begin{aligned} &\int_{\xi_\iota+(k-1)\varsigma}^{\xi} (\xi-t)^{-\beta}(t-\xi_\iota-(k-1)\varsigma)^{(k-1)\beta-1}dt \\ &= (\xi-\xi_\iota-(k-1)\varsigma)^{(k-2)\beta}\mathbb{B}[(k-1)\beta, 1-\beta], \end{aligned}$$

where $\mathbb{B}[x, y] = \int_0^1 s^{x-1}(1-s)^{y-1}ds$.

Lemma 2 (see [18]). *For any* $\xi \in ((k-1)\varsigma, k\varsigma]$, $k = 1, 2, \cdots, k^*$ *and* $0 < \gamma < 1$, *we obtain that*

(i) For any $0 < \beta < \frac{1}{k+1}$, *one has*

$$\|(\xi-(k-1)\varsigma)^{\gamma} e^{B\xi^{\beta}}_{-\varsigma,\beta}\| \leq (\xi-(k-1)\varsigma)^{\beta+\gamma-1}E_{\beta,\beta}(\|B\|(\xi-(k-1)\varsigma)^{\beta}).$$

(ii) For any $\frac{1}{k+1} \leq \beta < \frac{1}{2}$, *one has*

$$\|(\xi-(k-1)\varsigma)^{\gamma} e^{B\xi^{\beta}}_{-\varsigma,\beta}\| \leq (\xi-(k-1)\varsigma)^{\gamma} \sum_{l=0}^{k} \|B\|^{l} \frac{(\xi-(l-1)\varsigma)^{(l+1)\beta-1}}{\Gamma(l\beta+\beta)}.$$

(iii) For any $\beta \geq \frac{1}{2}$, *one has*

$$\|(\xi-(k-1)\varsigma)^{\gamma} e^{B\xi^{\beta}}_{-\varsigma,\beta}\| \leq \xi^{\beta+\gamma-1}E_{\beta,\beta}(\|B\|\xi^{\beta}),$$

where $E_{\beta,\beta}(z) = \sum\limits_{k=0}^{\infty} \frac{z^k}{\Gamma(k\beta+\beta)}$, $z \in \mathbb{R}$.

Lemma 3 (see [18]). *For any* $\xi \in ((k-1)\varsigma, k\varsigma]$ *and* $k = 1, 2 \cdots k^*$, *we have*

$$\begin{aligned} &\int_{-\varsigma}^{0} \|e^{B(\xi-\varsigma-s)^{\beta}}_{-\varsigma,\beta}\|ds \\ \leq\ & \sum_{m=0}^{k} \frac{\|B\|^m}{\Gamma((m+1)\beta+1)}(\xi-(m-1)\varsigma)^{(m+1)\beta} - \sum_{m=1}^{k} \frac{\|B\|^{m-1}}{\Gamma(m\beta+1)}(\xi-(m-1)\varsigma)^{m\beta}. \end{aligned}$$

Lemma 4 (see [18]). *For any $\xi \in ((k-1)\varsigma, k\varsigma]$, $k = 1, 2 \cdots k^*$ and $\beta > 1 - \frac{1}{p}(p > 1)$, we have*

$$\begin{aligned}
&\int_{-\varsigma}^{0} \|e_{-\varsigma,\beta}^{B(\xi-\varsigma-s)^\beta}\| \|({}^{RL}\mathbb{D}_{-\varsigma^+}^{\beta}\varpi)(s)\| ds \\
\leq\ & \sum_{m=0}^{k} \left(\frac{\|B\|^m (\xi-(m-1)\varsigma)^{(m+1)\beta-1-\frac{1}{p}}}{\Gamma(m\beta+\beta)(p(m+1)\beta-p+1)^{\frac{1}{p}}} \right) \left(\int_{-\varsigma}^{0} \|({}^{RL}\mathbb{D}_{-\varsigma^+}^{\beta}\varpi)(s)\|^q ds \right)^{\frac{1}{q}}.
\end{aligned}$$

Lemma 5. *For any $\xi \in ((k-1)\varsigma, k\varsigma]$ and $k = 1, 2 \cdots k^*$, we have*

$$\int_{-\varsigma}^{\xi} \|e_{-\varsigma,\beta}^{B(\xi-\varsigma-s)^\beta}\| ds \leq \sum_{m=0}^{k} \frac{\|B\|^m}{\Gamma((m+1)\beta+1)} (\xi-(m-1)\beta)^{(m+1)\beta}.$$

Proof. By (7), one has

$$\begin{aligned}
&\int_{-\varsigma}^{\xi} \|e_{-\varsigma,\beta}^{B(\xi-\varsigma-s)^\beta}\| ds \\
\leq\ & \int_{-\varsigma}^{\xi-k\varsigma} \|e_{-\varsigma,\beta}^{B(\xi-\varsigma-s)^\beta}\| ds + \int_{\xi-k\varsigma}^{\xi-(k-1)\varsigma} \|e_{-\varsigma,\beta}^{B(\xi-\varsigma-s)^\beta}\| ds + \int_{\xi-\varsigma}^{\xi} \|e_{-\varsigma,\beta}^{B(\xi-\varsigma-s)^\beta}\| ds \\
\leq\ & \int_{-\varsigma}^{\xi-k\varsigma} \left(\frac{(\xi-s)^{\beta-1}}{\Gamma(\beta)} + \|B\| \frac{(\xi-\varsigma-s)^{2\beta-1}}{\Gamma(2\beta)} + \cdots + \|B\|^k \frac{(\xi-k\varsigma-s)^{(k+1)\beta-1}}{\Gamma((k+1)\beta)} \right) ds \\
&+ \int_{\xi-k\varsigma}^{\xi-(k-1)\varsigma} \left(\frac{(\xi-s)^{\beta-1}}{\Gamma(\beta)} + \|B\| \frac{(\xi-\varsigma-s)^{2\beta-1}}{\Gamma(2\beta)} \right. \\
&\left. + \cdots + \|B\|^{k-1} \frac{(\xi-(k-1)\varsigma-s)^{k\beta-1}}{\Gamma(k\beta)} \right) ds + \int_{\xi-\varsigma}^{\xi} \frac{(\xi-s)^{\beta-1}}{\Gamma(\beta)} ds \\
=\ & \sum_{m=0}^{k} \frac{\|B\|^m}{\Gamma((m+1)\beta)} \int_{-\varsigma}^{\xi-m\varsigma} (\xi-m\varsigma-s)^{(m+1)\beta-1} ds \\
=\ & \sum_{m=0}^{k} \frac{\|B\|^m}{\Gamma((m+1)\beta+1)} (\xi-(m-1)\beta)^{(m+1)\beta}.
\end{aligned}$$

The proof is finished. □

3. The Solution of System (4)

In this section, we will establish the general solution of (3) by using (6)–(8).

Theorem 1. *Let $\xi \in ((k-1)\varsigma, k\varsigma]$, and let $\xi_\imath \in (0, \xi)$ be a fixed impulsive point. Then, we have*

$$({}^{RL}\mathbb{D}_{-\varsigma^+}^{\beta} \mathbb{E}_{-\varsigma}^{B(t-\xi_\imath-2\varsigma)^\beta} C_\imath)(\xi) = B\mathbb{E}_{-\varsigma}^{B(\xi-\xi_\imath-3\varsigma)^\beta} C_\imath.$$

Proof. By Definition 4, we have

$$({}^{RL}\mathbb{D}_{-\varsigma^+}^{\beta} \mathbb{E}_{-\varsigma}^{B(t-\xi_\imath-2\varsigma)^\beta})(\xi) = ({}^{C}\mathbb{D}_{-\varsigma^+}^{\beta} \mathbb{E}_{-\varsigma}^{B(t-\xi_\imath-2\varsigma)^\beta})(\xi),$$

where we use the fact $\mathbb{E}_{-\varsigma}^{B(-\varsigma-\xi_\imath-2\varsigma)} = 0$. We will split down the entire proof into three steps.

(i) For $\xi_\imath \in (\xi-\varsigma, \xi]$, we have

$$\mathbb{E}_{-\varsigma}^{B(\xi-\xi_\imath-2\varsigma)^\beta} C_\imath = EC_\imath. \tag{9}$$

By Definition 3 and Equation (9), one has

$$\begin{aligned}({}^{RL}\mathbb{D}^{\beta}_{-\varsigma^+}\mathbb{E}^{B(t-\xi_\iota-2\varsigma)^\beta}_{-\varsigma}C_\iota)(\xi) &= ({}^{C}\mathbb{D}^{\beta}_{-\varsigma^+}\mathbb{E}^{B(t-\xi_\iota-2\varsigma)^\beta}_{-\varsigma}C_\iota)(\xi)\\ &= \frac{1}{\Gamma(1-\beta)}\int_{-\varsigma}^{\xi}(\xi-t)^{-\beta}(EC_\iota)'dt\\ &= B\mathbb{E}^{B(\xi-\xi_\iota-3\varsigma)^\beta}_{-\varsigma}C_\iota.\end{aligned}$$

(ii) For $\xi_\iota \in (0, \xi-(k-1)\varsigma]$, we have

$$\mathbb{E}^{B(\xi-\xi_\iota-2\varsigma)^\beta}_{-\varsigma}C_\iota = \sum_{m=0}^{k-1} B^m \frac{(\xi-\xi_\iota-m\varsigma)^{m\beta}}{\Gamma(m\beta+1)}C_\iota. \tag{10}$$

By Definition 3, Lemma 1 and Equation (10), one has

$$\begin{aligned}&({}^{RL}\mathbb{D}^{\beta}_{-\varsigma^+}\mathbb{E}^{B(t-\xi_\iota-2\varsigma)^\beta}_{-\varsigma}C_\iota)(\xi)\\ =\ & ({}^{C}\mathbb{D}^{\beta}_{-\varsigma^+}\mathbb{E}^{B(t-\xi_\iota-2\varsigma)^\beta}_{-\varsigma}C_\iota)(\xi)\\ =\ & \frac{B}{\Gamma(1-\beta)\Gamma(\beta)}\int_{\xi_\iota+\varsigma}^{\xi}(\xi-t)^{-\beta}(t-\xi_\iota-\varsigma)^{\beta-1}C_\iota dt\\ &+\frac{B^2}{\Gamma(1-\beta)\Gamma(2\beta)}\int_{\xi_\iota+2\varsigma}^{\xi}(\xi-t)^{-\beta}(t-\xi_\iota-2\varsigma)^{2\beta-1}C_\iota dt\\ &\cdots+\frac{B^{k-1}}{\Gamma(1-\beta)\Gamma((k-1)\beta)}\int_{\xi_\iota+(k-1)\varsigma}^{\xi}(\xi-t)^{-\beta}(t-\xi_\iota-(k-1)\varsigma)^{(k-1)\beta-1}C_\iota dt\\ =\ & B\left(EC_\iota + B^2\frac{(\xi-\xi_\iota-2\varsigma)^\beta}{\Gamma(\beta+1)}C_\iota+\cdots+B^{k-1}\frac{(\xi-\xi_\iota-(k-1)\varsigma)^{(k-2)\beta}}{\Gamma((k-2)\beta+1)}C_\iota\right)\\ =\ & B\sum_{m=0}^{k-2}B^m\frac{(\xi-\xi_\iota-(m+1)\varsigma)^{m\beta}}{\Gamma(m\beta+1)}C_\iota\\ =\ & B\mathbb{E}^{B(\xi-\xi_\iota-3\varsigma)^\beta}_{-\varsigma}C_\iota.\end{aligned}$$

(iii) For $\xi_\iota \in (\xi-(n+1)\varsigma, \xi-n\varsigma]$, $n=2,\cdots,k-2$, we have

$$\mathbb{E}^{B(\xi-\xi_\iota-2\varsigma)^\beta}_{-\varsigma}C_\iota = \sum_{m=0}^{n} B^m \frac{(\xi-\xi_\iota-m\varsigma)^{m\beta}}{\Gamma(m\beta+1)}C_\iota. \tag{11}$$

By Definition 3, Lemma 1 and Equation (11), one has

$$\begin{aligned}&({}^{RL}\mathbb{D}^{\beta}_{-\varsigma^+}\mathbb{E}^{B(t-\xi_\iota-2\varsigma)^\beta}_{-\varsigma}C_\iota)(\xi)\\ =\ & ({}^{C}\mathbb{D}^{\beta}_{-\varsigma^+}\mathbb{E}^{B(t-\xi_\iota-2\varsigma)^\beta}_{-\varsigma}C_\iota)(\xi)\\ =\ & \frac{1}{\Gamma(1-\beta)}\left(\int_{\xi_\iota+\varsigma}^{\xi_\iota+2\varsigma}(\xi-t)^{-\beta}B\frac{\beta(t-\xi_\iota-\varsigma)^{\beta-1}}{\Gamma(\beta+1)}C_\iota dt+\right.\\ &\left.\cdots+\int_{\xi_\iota+n\varsigma}^{\xi}(\xi-t)^{-\beta}\sum_{m=0}^{n}B^m\frac{m\beta(t-\xi_\iota-m\varsigma)^{m\beta-1}}{\Gamma(m\beta+1)}C_\iota dt\right)\\ =\ & \frac{B}{\Gamma(1-\beta)\Gamma(\beta)}\left(\int_{\xi_\iota+\varsigma}^{\xi}(\xi-t)^{-\beta}(t-\xi_\iota-\varsigma)^{\beta-1}C_\iota dt\right.\\ &+\frac{B^2}{\Gamma(1-\beta)\Gamma(2\beta)}\int_{\xi_\iota+2\varsigma}^{\xi}(\xi-t)^{-\beta}(t-\xi_\iota-2\varsigma)^{2\beta-1}C_\iota dt\\ &\left.\cdots+\frac{B^n}{\Gamma(1-\beta)\Gamma(n\beta)}\int_{\xi_\iota+n\varsigma}^{\xi}(\xi-t)^{-\beta}(t-\xi_\iota-n\varsigma)^{n\beta-1}C_\iota dt\right)\end{aligned}$$

$$\begin{aligned}
&= B\left(EC_\imath + B\frac{(\xi-\xi_\imath-2\varsigma)^\beta}{\Gamma(\beta+1)}C_\imath + \cdots + B^{n-1}\frac{(\xi-\xi_\imath-(n-1)\varsigma-\varsigma)^{(n-1)\beta}}{\Gamma((n-1)\beta+1)}C_\imath\right)\\
&= B\sum_{m=0}^{n-1} B^m\frac{(\xi-\varsigma-\xi_\imath-m\varsigma)^{m\beta}}{\Gamma(m\beta+1)}C_\imath\\
&= B\mathbb{E}_{-\varsigma}^{B(\xi-\xi_\imath-3\varsigma)^\beta}C_\imath.
\end{aligned}$$

The proof is finished. □

Theorem 2. *The impulsive delayed Mittag–Leffler-type vector function $Q_{-\varsigma,\beta}(\cdot)$ is the fundamental solution of* (3).

Proof. By Definition 3 and Lemma 1, one has

$$\begin{aligned}
\left({}^{RL}\mathbb{D}^\beta_{-\varsigma^+}\sum_{0<\xi_\imath<\xi}\mathbb{E}_{-\varsigma}^{B(t-\xi_\imath-2\varsigma)^\beta}C_\imath\right)(\xi) &= \left({}^{C}\mathbb{D}^\beta_{-\varsigma^+}\sum_{0<\xi_\imath<\xi}\mathbb{E}_{-\varsigma}^{B(t-\xi_\imath-2\varsigma)^\beta}C_\imath\right)(\xi)\\
&= \frac{1}{\Gamma(1-\beta)}\int_{-\varsigma}^{\xi}(\xi-t)^{-\beta}\sum_{0<\xi_\imath<\xi}(\mathbb{E}_{-\varsigma}^{B(t-\xi_\imath-2\varsigma)^\beta})'C_\imath dt\\
&= \left(\sum_{0<\xi_\imath<\xi}{}^{C}\mathbb{D}^\beta_{-\varsigma^+}\mathbb{E}_{-\varsigma}^{B(t-\xi_\imath-2\varsigma)^\beta}C_\imath\right)(\xi)\\
&= B\sum_{0<\xi_\imath<\xi}\mathbb{E}_{-\varsigma}^{B(\xi-\xi_\imath-3\varsigma)^\beta}C_\imath.
\end{aligned}$$

Let $\xi_\imath \in (0,\xi)$ and $\imath = 1,2,\cdots,p(T,0)$; we will prove $Q_{-\varsigma,\beta}(\xi_\imath^+) = Q_{-\varsigma,\beta}(\xi_\imath^-) + C_\imath$.

$$\begin{aligned}
Q_{-\varsigma,\beta}(\xi_\imath^+) &= \sum_{k=1}^{\imath}\mathbb{E}_{-\varsigma}^{B(\xi_\imath^+-\xi_k-2\varsigma)^\beta}C_k\\
&= \sum_{k=1}^{\imath-1}\mathbb{E}_{-\varsigma}^{B(\xi_\imath^--\xi_k-2\varsigma)^\beta}C_k + C_\imath,\ \xi_\imath^+\in(\xi_\imath,\xi_{\imath+1}],\\
Q_{-\varsigma,\beta}(\xi_\imath^-) &= \sum_{k=1}^{\imath-1}\mathbb{E}_{-\varsigma}^{B(\xi_\imath^--\xi_k-2\varsigma)^\beta}C_k,\ \xi_\imath^-\in(\xi_{\imath-1},\xi_\imath],
\end{aligned}$$

which implies that $Q_{-\varsigma,\beta}(\xi_\imath^+) = Q_{-\varsigma,\beta}(\xi_\imath^-) + C_\imath$. The proof is complete. □

Theorem 3. *The solution $v \in PC(\Omega,\mathbb{R}^n)\cap PC([-\varsigma,T],\mathbb{R}^n)$ of* (3) *has the form*

$$v(\xi) = e_{-\varsigma,\beta}^{B\xi^\beta}\varpi(-\varsigma) + \int_{-\varsigma}^{0} e_{-\varsigma,\beta}^{B(\xi-\varsigma-s)^\beta}({}^{RL}\mathbb{D}^\beta_{-\varsigma^+}\varpi)(s)ds + \sum_{0<\xi_\imath<\xi}\mathbb{E}_{-\varsigma}^{B(\xi-\xi_\imath-2\varsigma)^\beta}C_\imath,$$

where either $\Omega = ((k-1)\varsigma, k\varsigma]$ for $0<\beta<\frac{1}{k+1}$ or $\Omega = [(k-1)\varsigma, k\varsigma]$ for $\beta \geq \frac{1}{k+1}$.

Proof. The proof of this theorem is analogous to ([22], Theorem 3.2).

The general solution of (3) that satisfies $v(\xi) = \varpi(\xi)$, $-\varsigma \leq \xi \leq 0$ has the following form

$$v(\xi) = e_{-\varsigma,\beta}^{B\xi^\beta}c + \int_{-\varsigma}^{0} e_{-\varsigma,\beta}^{B(\xi-\varsigma-s)^\beta}y(s)ds + Q_{-\varsigma,\beta}(\xi),\ 0\leq\xi\leq T. \quad (12)$$

where c is an unknown vector and $y \in C([-\varsigma, T], \mathbb{R}^n)$ is an unknown function. We choose a c satisfying $(\mathbb{I}^{1-\beta}_{-\varsigma^+} z)(-\varsigma^+) = \varpi(-\varsigma)$; then, one has

$$e^{B\xi^\beta}_{-\varsigma,\beta} c + \int_{-\varsigma}^{0} e^{B(\xi-\varsigma-s)^\beta}_{-\varsigma,\beta} y(s)ds = \varpi(\xi), \ \ -\varsigma \le \xi \le 0.$$

By (6), let $\xi = -\varsigma$, and we obtain $e^{B(-2\varsigma-s)^\beta}_{-\varsigma,\beta} = \Theta$ with $-\varsigma \le s \le 0$. For $-\varsigma \le \xi \le 0$, we have

$$\begin{aligned}
\varpi(-\varsigma) &= (\mathbb{I}^{1-\beta}_{-\varsigma^+} v)(-\varsigma^+) \\
&= \lim_{\xi \to -\varsigma^+} (\mathbb{I}^{1-\beta}_{-\varsigma^+} v)(\xi) \\
&= \lim_{\xi \to -\varsigma^+} \left(\frac{1}{\Gamma(1-\beta)} \int_{-\varsigma}^{\xi} (\xi - t)^{-\beta} e^{Bt^\beta}_{-\varsigma,\beta} c dt \right) \\
&= \lim_{\xi \to -\varsigma^+} \frac{c}{\Gamma(1-\beta)\Gamma(\beta)} \int_{-\varsigma}^{\xi} (\xi - t)^{-\beta} (t+\varsigma)^{\beta-1} dt \\
&= \lim_{\xi \to -\varsigma^+} c = c,
\end{aligned}$$

which implies that

$$v(\xi) = e^{B\xi^\beta}_{-\varsigma,\beta} \varpi(-\varsigma) + \int_{-\varsigma}^{0} e^{B(\xi-\varsigma-s)^\beta}_{-\varsigma,\beta} y(s)ds + Q_{-\varsigma,\beta}(\xi).$$

For any $-\varsigma \le \xi \le 0$, one has

$$e^{B(\xi-\varsigma-s)^\beta}_{-\varsigma,\beta} = \begin{cases} \Theta, \ \ \xi \le s \le 0, \\ E\dfrac{(\xi - s)^{\beta-1}}{\Gamma(\beta)}, \ \ -\varsigma \le s \le \xi. \end{cases}$$

Thus, for any $-\varsigma \le \xi \le 0$, we have

$$\varpi(\xi) = \frac{(\xi+\varsigma)^{\beta-1}}{\Gamma(\beta)} \varpi(-\varsigma) + \int_{-\varsigma}^{\xi} \frac{(\xi - s)^{\beta-1}}{\Gamma(\beta)} y(s)ds. \tag{13}$$

Using Riemann–Liouville fractional differentiation on both sides of (13), we have

$$\begin{aligned}
({}^{RL}\mathbb{D}^{\beta}_{-\varsigma^+} \varpi)(\xi) &= \frac{1}{\Gamma(1-\beta)} \frac{d}{d\xi} \int_{-\varsigma}^{\xi} (\xi - t)^{-\beta} \bigg(\frac{(t+\varsigma)^{\beta-1}}{\Gamma(\beta)} \varpi(-\varsigma) \\
&\quad + \int_{-\varsigma}^{t} \frac{(t-s)^{\beta-1}}{\Gamma(\beta)} y(s)ds \bigg) dt \\
&= \frac{1}{\Gamma(1-\beta)\Gamma(\beta)} \frac{d}{d\xi} \int_{-\varsigma}^{\xi} y(s) \left(\int_{s}^{\xi} (\xi - t)^{-\beta} (t-s)^{\beta-1} dt \right) ds \\
&= \frac{d}{d\xi} \int_{-\varsigma}^{\xi} y(s)ds \\
&= y(\xi).
\end{aligned}$$

For any $\xi \in [0, T]$ and $\xi_\iota \in (0, \xi)$, we have

$$\begin{aligned} v(\xi_\iota^+) &= e_{-\varsigma,\beta}^{B(\xi_\iota^+)^\beta}\varpi(-\varsigma) + \int_{-\varsigma}^{0} e_{-\varsigma,\beta}^{B(\xi_\iota^+-\varsigma-s)^\beta}({}^{RL}\mathbb{D}_{-\varsigma^+}^{\beta}\varpi)(s)ds + \sum_{k=1}^{\iota}\mathbb{E}_{-\varsigma}^{B(\xi_\iota^+-\xi_k-2\varsigma)^\beta}C_k \\ &= e_{-\varsigma,\beta}^{B(\xi_\iota^-)^\beta}\varpi(-\varsigma) + \int_{-\varsigma}^{0} e_{-\varsigma,\beta}^{B(\xi_\iota^--\varsigma-s)^\beta}({}^{RL}\mathbb{D}_{-\varsigma^+}^{\beta}\varpi)(s)ds + \sum_{k=1}^{\iota-1}\mathbb{E}_{-\varsigma}^{B(\xi_\iota-\xi_k-2\varsigma)^\beta}C_k + C_\iota \\ &= v(\xi_\iota^-) + C_\iota. \end{aligned}$$

This proof is complete. □

Theorem 4. *The solution $\widetilde{v} \in C((0,T],\mathbb{R}^n)$ of (1) with $\widetilde{v}(\xi) \equiv \mathbf{0} = (0,0,\cdots,0)^\top, -\varsigma \le \xi \le 0$ can be written as*

$$\widetilde{v}(\xi) = \int_{-\varsigma}^{\xi} e_{-\varsigma,\beta}^{B(\xi-\varsigma-t)^\beta} g(t)dt.$$

Proof. The proof of this theorem is analogous to ([22], Theorem 3.3). □

Next, combined with Theorems 3 and 4, the solution of (4) can be obtained.

Theorem 5. *The solution $v \in PC(\Omega,\mathbb{R}^n) \cap PC([-\varsigma,T],\mathbb{R}^n)$ of (4) has the form*

$$\begin{aligned} v(\xi) &= e_{-\varsigma,\beta}^{B\xi^\beta}\varpi(-\varsigma) + \int_{-\varsigma}^{0} e_{-\varsigma,\beta}^{B(\xi-\varsigma-s)^\beta}({}^{RL}\mathbb{D}_{-\varsigma^+}^{\beta}\varpi)(s)ds + \sum_{0<\xi_\iota<\xi}\mathbb{E}_{-\varsigma}^{B(\xi-\xi_\iota-2\varsigma)^\beta}C_\iota \\ &\quad + \int_{-\varsigma}^{\xi} e_{-\varsigma,\beta}^{B(\xi-\varsigma-t)^\beta} g(t)dt. \end{aligned}$$

Proof. Equation (4) can be decomposed into (1) and (3) (where (1) satisfies $\widetilde{v}(\xi) \equiv \mathbf{0}$, $-\varsigma \le \xi \le 0$); thus, the solution of (4) can be manifested as $v(\xi) = v_0(\xi) + \widetilde{v}(\xi)$, where $v_0(\xi)$ is a solution of (3) and $\widetilde{v}(\xi)$ is a solution of (1) satisfying the zero initial condition. □

4. FTS of (4)

Now, we will give the results of FTS.

$[H_1]$ $M = \sup_{-\varsigma\le s\le 0} \|({}^{RL}\mathbb{D}_{-\varsigma^+}^{\beta}\varpi)(s)\| < \infty$.

$[H_2]$ $0 < N = (\int_{-\varsigma}^{0} \|({}^{RL}\mathbb{D}_{-\varsigma^+}^{\beta}\varpi)(s)\|^q ds)^{\frac{1}{q}} < \infty$, $\frac{1}{q} = 1 - \frac{1}{p}$, $p > 1$.

$[H_3]$ $\exists \kappa \in L^q([-\varsigma,T],\mathbb{R}^+)$, $\frac{1}{q} = 1 - \frac{1}{p}$, $p > 1$ such that $\|g(\xi)\| \le \kappa(\xi)$ for $\xi \in [-\varsigma, T]$ and $\psi(\xi) := \left(\int_{-\varsigma}^{\xi} \kappa(t)^q dt\right)^{\frac{1}{q}} < \infty$.

For every $\xi \in ((k-1)\varsigma, k\varsigma]$ and $k = 1, 2, \cdots k^*$, we define

$$\Psi_1(\xi) = \begin{cases} (\xi-(k-1)\varsigma)^{\beta+\gamma-1}E_{\beta,\beta}(\|B\|(\xi-(k-1)\varsigma)^\beta), \; 0<\beta<\dfrac{1}{k+1}, \\ (\xi-(k-1)\varsigma)^{\gamma}\displaystyle\sum_{m=0}^{k}\|B\|^m\frac{(\xi-(m-1)\varsigma)^{(m+1)\beta-1}}{\Gamma(m\beta+\beta)}, \; \dfrac{1}{k+1}\le\beta<\dfrac{1}{2}, \\ \xi^{\beta+\gamma-1}E_{\beta,\beta}(\|B\|\xi^\beta), \; \beta\ge\dfrac{1}{2}, \end{cases}$$

and

$$\Psi_2(\xi) = \sum_{m=0}^{k} \frac{\|B\|^m}{\Gamma((m+1)\beta+1)}(\xi-(m-1)\varsigma)^{(m+1)\beta} - \sum_{m=1}^{k} \frac{\|B\|^{m-1}}{\Gamma(m\beta+1)}(\xi-(m-1)\varsigma)^{m\beta},$$

$$\Psi_3(\xi) = \sum_{m=0}^{k} \frac{\|B\|^m(\xi-(m-1)\varsigma)^{(m+1)\beta}}{\Gamma((m+1)\beta+1)},$$

$$\Psi_4(\xi) = \sum_{m=0}^{k} \left(\frac{\|B\|^m}{\Gamma(m\beta+\beta)} \frac{(\xi-(m-1)\varsigma)^{(m+1)\beta-1-\frac{1}{p}}}{(p(m+1)\beta-p+1)^{\frac{1}{p}}} \right).$$

Theorem 6. *Suppose that $\beta+\gamma-1>0$ and $[H_1]$ holds. If*

$$\Psi_1(\xi)\delta + (\xi-(k-1)\varsigma)^\gamma \Big(M\Psi_2(\xi) + \sum_{0<\xi_\iota<\xi} E_{\beta,1}(\|B\|(\xi-\xi_\iota-2\varsigma)^\beta)\|C_\iota\| + \|g\|_C \Psi_3(\xi) \Big) < \eta, \tag{14}$$

then (4) *is finite-time stable with regard to* $\{0, J, \varsigma, \delta, \eta\}$.

Proof. By Lemmas 2, 3 and 5, we have

$$\begin{aligned}
& \|(\xi-(k-1)\varsigma)^\gamma v(\xi)\| \\
\leq\ & \|(\xi-(k-1)\varsigma)^\gamma e_{-\varsigma,\beta}^{B\xi^\beta}\|\|\omega(-\varsigma)\| \\
& +(\xi-(k-1)\varsigma)^\gamma \int_{-\varsigma}^{0} \|e_{-\varsigma,\beta}^{B(\xi-\varsigma-s)^\beta}\|\|({}^{RL}\mathbb{D}^\beta_{-\varsigma^+}\omega)(s)\|ds \\
& +(\xi-(k-1)\varsigma)^\gamma \sum_{0<\xi_\iota<\xi} \|\mathbb{E}_{-\varsigma}^{B(\xi-\xi_\iota-2\varsigma)^\beta}\|\|C_\iota\| \\
& +(\xi-(k-1)\varsigma)^\gamma \int_{-\varsigma}^{\xi} \|e_{-\varsigma,\beta}^{B(\xi-\varsigma-t)^\beta}\|\|g(t)\|dt \\
\leq\ & \Psi_1(\xi)\delta + (\xi-(k-1)\varsigma)^\gamma M\Psi_2(\xi) \\
& +(\xi-(k-1)\varsigma)^\gamma \sum_{0<\xi_\iota<\xi} E_{\beta,1}(\|B\|(\xi-\xi_\iota-2\varsigma)^\beta)\|C_\iota\| \\
& +(\xi-(k-1)\varsigma)^\gamma \|g\|_C \sum_{m=0}^{k} \frac{\|B\|^m}{\Gamma((m+1)\beta)} \int_{-\varsigma}^{\xi-m\varsigma} (\xi-m\varsigma-t)^{(m+1)\beta-1}dt \\
\leq\ & \Psi_1(\xi)\delta + (\xi-(k-1)\varsigma)^\gamma \Big(M\Psi_2(\xi) \\
& + \sum_{0<\xi_\iota<\xi} E_{\beta,1}(\|B\|(\xi-\xi_\iota-2\varsigma)^\beta)\|C_\iota\| + \|g\|_C\Psi_3(\xi) \Big) \\
<\ & \eta.
\end{aligned}$$

This proof is complete. □

Theorem 7. *Suppose that* $\beta > \max\{1-\gamma,\ 1-\frac{1}{p}\}$ *and* $[H_2]$ *and* $[H_3]$ *hold. If*

$$\Psi_1(\xi)\delta + (\xi-(k-1)\varsigma)^\gamma\Big(\Psi_4(\xi)N + \Psi_4(\xi)\psi(\xi) + \sum_{0<\xi_\iota<\xi} E_{\beta,1}(\|B\|(\xi-\xi_\iota-2\varsigma)^\beta)\|C_\iota\|\Big) < \eta, \tag{15}$$

then (4) *is finite-time stable with regard to* $\{0, J, \varsigma, \delta, \eta\}$.

Proof. By Lemmas 2 and 4, we have

$$\begin{aligned}
&\|(\xi-(k-1)\varsigma)^\gamma v(\xi)\| \\
\leq\ &\|(\xi-(k-1)\varsigma)^\gamma e^{B\xi^\beta}_{-\varsigma,\beta}\|\|\varpi(-\varsigma)\| \\
&+(\xi-(k-1)\varsigma)^\gamma\int_{-\varsigma}^{0}\|e^{B(\xi-\varsigma-s)^\beta}_{-\varsigma,\beta}\|\|({}^{RL}\mathbb{D}^\beta_{-\varsigma^+}\varpi)(s)\|ds \\
&+(\xi-(k-1)\varsigma)^\gamma\sum_{0<\xi_\iota<\xi}\|\mathbb{E}^{B(\xi-\xi_\iota-2\varsigma)^\beta}_{-\varsigma}\|\|C_\iota\| \\
&+(\xi-(k-1)\varsigma)^\gamma\int_{-\varsigma}^{\xi}\|e^{B(\xi-\varsigma-t)^\beta}_{-\varsigma,\beta}\|\|g(t)\|dt \\
\leq\ &\Psi_1(\xi)\delta + (\xi-(k-1)\varsigma)^\gamma\Big(\Psi_4(\xi)N + \sum_{0<\xi_\iota<\xi}E_{\beta,1}(\|B\|(\xi-\xi_\iota-2\varsigma)^\beta)\|C_\iota\| \\
&+\sum_{m=0}^{k}\frac{\|B\|^m}{\Gamma((m+1)\beta)}\int_{-\varsigma}^{\xi-m\varsigma}(\xi-m\varsigma-t)^{(m+1)\beta-1}\kappa(t)dt\Big) \\
\leq\ &\Psi_1(\xi)\delta + (\xi-(k-1)\varsigma)^\gamma\Big(\Psi_4(\xi)N + \sum_{0<\xi_\iota<\xi}E_{\beta,1}(\|B\|(\xi-\xi_\iota-2\varsigma)^\beta)\|C_\iota\| \\
&+\sum_{m=0}^{k}\frac{\|B\|^m}{\Gamma((m+1)\beta)}\Big(\int_{-\varsigma}^{\xi-m\varsigma}(\xi-m\varsigma-t)^{p((m+1)\beta-1)}dt\Big)^{\frac{1}{p}}\Big(\int_{-\varsigma}^{\xi}\kappa(t)^q dt\Big)^{\frac{1}{q}}\Big) \\
\leq\ &\Psi_1(\xi)\delta + (\xi-(k-1)\varsigma)^\gamma\Big(\Psi_4(\xi)N \\
&+\sum_{0<\xi_\iota<\xi}E_{\beta,1}(\|B\|(\xi-\xi_\iota-2\varsigma)^\beta)\|C_\iota\| + \Psi_4(\xi)\psi(\xi)\Big) \\
<\ &\eta.
\end{aligned}$$

This proof is complete. □

Theorem 8. *Suppose that* $\beta > \max\{\frac{1}{2},\ 1-\gamma\}$ *and* $[H_1]$ *holds. If*

$$\begin{aligned}
&\Psi_1(\xi)\delta + M\varsigma\xi^{\gamma+\beta-1}E_{\beta,\beta}(\|B\|\xi^\beta) \\
&\quad+\xi^\gamma\sum_{0<\xi_\iota<\xi}E_{\beta,1}(\|B\|(\xi-\xi_\iota-2\varsigma)^\beta)\|C_\iota\| + \xi^\gamma\|g\|_C\Psi_3(\xi) < \eta,
\end{aligned} \tag{16}$$

then (4) *is finite-time stable with regard to* $\{0, J, \varsigma, \delta, \eta\}$.

Proof. By Lemmas 2 and 5, we have

$$
\begin{aligned}
& \|(\xi-(k-1)\varsigma)^{\gamma}v(\xi)\| \\
\leq\ & \|(\xi-(k-1)\varsigma)^{\gamma}e^{B\xi^{\beta}}_{-\varsigma,\beta}\|\|\varpi(-\varsigma)\| \\
& +(\xi-(k-1)\varsigma)^{\gamma}\int_{-\varsigma}^{0}\|e^{B(\xi-\varsigma-s)^{\beta}}_{-\varsigma,\beta}\|\|({}^{RL}\mathbb{D}^{\beta}_{-\varsigma^{+}}\varpi)(s)\|ds \\
& +(\xi-(k-1)\varsigma)^{\gamma}\sum_{0<\xi_{\imath}<\xi}\|\mathbb{E}^{B(\xi-\xi_{\imath}-2\varsigma)^{\beta}}_{-\varsigma}\|\|C_{\imath}\| \\
& +(\xi-(k-1)\varsigma)^{\gamma}\int_{-\varsigma}^{\xi}\|e^{B(\xi-\varsigma-t)^{\beta}}_{-\varsigma,\beta}\|\|g(t)\|dt \\
\leq\ & \Psi_1(\xi)\delta+\xi^{\gamma}\Bigg(\sum_{m=0}^{k}\frac{\|B\|^{m}\varsigma^{(m+1)\beta-1}}{\Gamma(m\beta+\beta)}\int_{-\varsigma}^{0}\|{}^{RL}\mathbb{D}^{\beta}_{-\varsigma^{+}}\varpi)(s)\|ds \\
& +\sum_{0<\xi_{\imath}<\xi}E_{\beta,1}(\|B\|(\xi-\xi_{\imath}-2\varsigma)^{\beta})\|C_{\imath}\|+\|g\|_{C}\int_{-\varsigma}^{\xi}\|e^{B(\xi-\varsigma-t)^{\beta}}_{-\varsigma,\beta}\|dt\Bigg) \\
\leq\ & \Psi_1(\xi)\delta+M\varsigma\xi^{\gamma+\beta-1}E_{\beta,\beta}(\|B\|\xi^{\beta}) \\
& +\xi^{\gamma}\sum_{0<\xi_{\imath}<\xi}E_{\beta,1}(\|B\|(\xi-\xi_{\imath}-2\varsigma)^{\beta})\|C_{\imath}\|+\xi^{\gamma}\|g\|_{C}\Psi_3(\xi) \\
<\ & \eta.
\end{aligned}
$$

This proof is complete. □

Theorem 9. *Suppose that* $\beta>\max\{\frac{1}{2},\,1-\gamma,\,1-\frac{1}{p}\}$ *and* $[H_1]$ *and* $[H_3]$ *hold. If*

$$
\begin{aligned}
& \Psi_1(\xi)\delta+\xi^{\gamma}\sum_{0<\xi_{\imath}<\xi}E_{\beta,1}(\|B\|(\xi-\xi_{\imath}-2\varsigma)^{\beta})\|C_{\imath}\| \\
& +E_{\beta,\beta}(\|B\|\xi^{\beta})\left(M\varsigma\xi^{\gamma+\beta-1}+\xi^{\gamma}\psi(\xi)\frac{(\xi+\varsigma)^{\beta-1+\frac{1}{p}}}{(p(\beta-1)+1)^{\frac{1}{p}}}\right)<\eta,
\end{aligned}
\tag{17}
$$

then (4) *is finite-time stable with regard to* $\{0,J,\varsigma,\delta,\eta\}$.

Proof. By Lemmas 2 and 5, we have

$$
\begin{aligned}
& \|(\xi-(k-1)\varsigma)^{\gamma}v(\xi)\| \\
\leq\ & \|(\xi-(k-1)\varsigma)^{\gamma}e^{B\xi^{\beta}}_{-\varsigma,\beta}\|\|\varpi(-\varsigma)\| \\
& +(\xi-(k-1)\varsigma)^{\gamma}\int_{-\varsigma}^{0}\|e^{B(\xi-\varsigma-s)^{\beta}}_{-\varsigma,\beta}\|\|({}^{RL}\mathbb{D}^{\beta}_{-\varsigma^{+}}\varpi)(s)\|ds \\
& +(\xi-(k-1)\varsigma)^{\gamma}\sum_{0<\xi_{\imath}<\xi}\|\mathbb{E}^{B(\xi-\xi_{\imath}-2\varsigma)^{\beta}}_{-\varsigma}\|\|C_{\imath}\| \\
& +(\xi-(k-1)\varsigma)^{\gamma}\int_{-\varsigma}^{\xi}\|e^{B(\xi-\varsigma-t)^{\beta}}_{-\varsigma,\beta}\|\|g(t)\|dt \\
\leq\ & \Psi_1(\xi)\delta+\xi^{\gamma}\Bigg(\sum_{m=0}^{k}\frac{\|B\|^{m}\varsigma^{(m+1)\beta-1}}{\Gamma(m\beta+\beta)}\int_{-\varsigma}^{0}\|{}^{RL}\mathbb{D}^{\beta}_{-\varsigma^{+}}\varpi)(s)\|ds \\
& +\sum_{0<\xi_{\imath}<\xi}E_{\beta,1}(\|B\|(\xi-\xi_{\imath}-2\varsigma)^{\beta})\|C_{\imath}\| \\
& +\sum_{m=0}^{k}\frac{\|B\|^{m}}{\Gamma(m\beta+\beta)}\int_{-\varsigma}^{\xi-m\varsigma}(\xi-m\varsigma-t)^{(m+1)\beta-1}\kappa(t)dt\Bigg)
\end{aligned}
$$

$$
\begin{aligned}
&\le \Psi_1(\xi)\delta + \xi^{\gamma}\Bigg(M\varsigma\xi^{\beta-1}E_{\beta,\beta}(\|B\|\xi^{\beta}) + \sum_{0<\xi_\imath<\xi} E_{\beta,1}(\|B\|(\xi-\xi_\imath-2\varsigma)^{\beta})\|C_\imath\| \\
&\quad + \sum_{m=0}^{k}\frac{\|B\|^m\xi^{m\beta}}{\Gamma(m\beta+\beta)}\int_{\varsigma}^{\xi}(\xi-t)^{\beta-1}\kappa(t)dt\Bigg) \\
&\le \Psi_1(\xi)\delta + \xi^{\gamma}\Bigg(M\varsigma\xi^{\beta-1}E_{\beta,\beta}(\|B\|\xi^{\beta}) + \sum_{0<\xi_\imath<\xi} E_{\beta,1}(\|B\|(\xi-\xi_\imath-2\varsigma)^{\beta})\|C_\imath\| \\
&\quad + E_{\beta,\beta}(\|B\|\xi^{\beta})\Big(\int_{-\varsigma}^{\xi}(\xi-t)^{p(\beta-1)}dt\Big)^{\frac{1}{p}}\Big(\int_{-\varsigma}^{\xi}\kappa(t)^q dt\Big)^{\frac{1}{q}} \\
&\le \Psi_1(\xi)\delta + \xi^{\gamma}\sum_{0<\xi_\imath<\xi} E_{\beta,1}(\|B\|(\xi-\xi_\imath-2\varsigma)^{\beta})\|C_\imath\| \\
&\quad + E_{\beta,\beta}(\|B\|\xi^{\beta})\Bigg(M\varsigma\xi^{\gamma+\beta-1} + \xi^{\gamma}\psi(\xi)\frac{(\xi+\varsigma)^{\beta-1+\frac{1}{p}}}{(p(\beta-1)+1)^{\frac{1}{p}}}\Bigg) \\
&< \eta.
\end{aligned}
$$

This proof is complete. □

5. Example

Example 1. *Let $\beta = 0.6$, $\varsigma = 0.3$, $k^* = 3$, $\xi_1 = 0.2$ and $\xi_2 = 0.5$. Consider*

$$
\begin{cases}
({}^{RL}\mathbb{D}^{\beta}_{-0.3^+}v)(\xi) = Bv(\xi-0.3) + g(\xi),\ \xi \neq \xi_\imath,\ \xi \in (0, 0.9], \\
v(\xi_\imath^+) = v(\xi_\imath^-) + C_\imath,\ \xi = \xi_\imath,\ \imath = 1,2, \\
\varpi(\xi) = (\xi+0.3, 0.1(\xi+0.3))^{\top},\ -0.3 < \xi \le 0, \\
(\mathbb{I}^{0.4}_{-0.3^+}v)(-0.3^+) = \varpi(-0.3) = (0,0)^{\top},
\end{cases}
\tag{18}
$$

where

$$
v(x) = \begin{pmatrix} v_1(\xi) \\ v_2(\xi) \end{pmatrix},\ B = \begin{pmatrix} 0.1 & 0.1 \\ 0.3 & 0.5 \end{pmatrix},\ C_\imath = \begin{pmatrix} \frac{\imath}{10} \\ \frac{\imath}{20} \end{pmatrix},\ g(\xi) = \begin{pmatrix} \xi \\ \xi^2 \end{pmatrix}.
\tag{19}
$$

By Theorem 5, for any $\xi \in [-0.3, 0.9]$, one has

$$
\begin{aligned}
v(\xi) &= e^{B\xi^{0.6}}_{-0.3,0.6}\varpi(-0.3) + \int_{-0.3}^{0} e^{B(\xi-0.3-s)^{0.6}}_{-0.3,0.6}({}^{RL}\mathbb{D}^{0.6}_{-0.3^+}\varpi)(s)ds \\
&\quad + \sum_{0<\xi_\imath<\xi}\mathbb{E}^{B(\xi-\xi_\imath-0.6)^{0.6}}_{-0.3}C_\imath + \int_{-0.3}^{\xi} e^{B(\xi-0.3-t)^{0.6}}_{-0.3,0.6}g(t)dt,
\end{aligned}
$$

where

$$
e^{B\xi^{0.6}}_{-0.3,0.6} = \begin{cases}
E\dfrac{(\xi+0.3)^{-0.4}}{\Gamma(0.6)} + B\dfrac{\xi^{0.2}}{\Gamma(1.2)},\ \xi \in (0, 0.3], \\
E\dfrac{(\xi+0.3)^{-0.4}}{\Gamma(0.6)} + B\dfrac{\xi^{0.2}}{\Gamma(1.2)} + B^2\dfrac{(\xi-0.3)^{0.8}}{\Gamma(1.8)},\ \xi \in (0.3, 0.6], \\
E\dfrac{(\xi+0.3)^{-0.4}}{\Gamma(0.6)} + B\dfrac{\xi^{0.2}}{\Gamma(1.2)} + B^2\dfrac{(\xi-0.3)^{0.8}}{\Gamma(1.8)} + B^3\dfrac{(\xi-0.6)^{1.4}}{\Gamma(2.4)},\ \xi \in (0.6, 0.9],
\end{cases}
$$

and

$$\sum_{s<\xi_\iota<\xi} \mathbb{E}_{-0.3}^{B(\xi-\xi_\iota-0.6)^{0.6}} C_\iota = \begin{cases} \begin{pmatrix} 0 \\ 0 \end{pmatrix}, \ \xi \in [0, 0.2], \\ \begin{pmatrix} \frac{1}{10} \\ \frac{1}{20} \end{pmatrix}, \ \xi \in (0.2, 0.5], \\ \left(E + B\frac{(\xi-0.5)^{0.6}}{\Gamma(1.6)}\right)\begin{pmatrix} \frac{1}{10} \\ \frac{1}{20} \end{pmatrix} + \begin{pmatrix} \frac{2}{10} \\ \frac{2}{20} \end{pmatrix}, \ \xi \in (0.5, 0.8], \\ \left(E + B\frac{(\xi-0.5)^{0.6}}{\Gamma(1.6)} + B^2\frac{(\xi-0.8)^{1.2}}{\Gamma(2.2)}\right)\begin{pmatrix} \frac{1}{10} \\ \frac{1}{20} \end{pmatrix} \\ + \left(E + B\frac{(\xi-0.8)^{0.6}}{\Gamma(1.6)}\right)\begin{pmatrix} \frac{2}{10} \\ \frac{2}{20} \end{pmatrix}, \ \xi \in [0.8, 0.9]. \end{cases}$$

Set $p = 2$, $q = 2$ and $\gamma = 0.5$. We can obtain that $\|B\| = 0.6$, $\|g\|_C = 1.71$, $M = 0.7659$, $N = 0.4195$, $\psi(0.9) = 0.9105$. Next, $\Phi_1(0.9) = 1.8211$, $\Phi_2(0.9) = 0.4479$, $\Phi_3(0.9) = 1.8181$, $\Phi_4(0.9) = 1.6056$. Choosing $\delta = 0.331$, we present the FTS results of (18) in Table 1.

By Definition 8, we find an appropriate η, ensuring that $\|z\|_{C_\gamma}$ in (18) is no more than η on J. So, through numerical simulation, we can use the explicit solution of (10) to find a suitable $\eta = 1.770$ for a fixed $T = 0.9$ (see Figure 1). Furthermore, by verifying the conditions in Theorems 6, 7, 8, 9 for $[-0.3, 0.9]$, compared with the values of η in Table 1, we can choose a better value of $\eta = 2.03$.

Table 1. FTS results of (18) with $T = 0.9$.

Theorem	$\|\varpi\|_C$	β	T	δ	$\|z\|_{C_\gamma}$	η	FTS
6	0.33	0.6	0.9	0.331	2.7398	2.75	Yes
7	0.33	0.6	0.9	0.331	2.0187	2.03 (optimal)	Yes
8	0.33	0.6	0.9	0.331	4.3801	4.38	Yes
9	0.33	0.6	0.9	0.331	5.0680	5.07	Yes

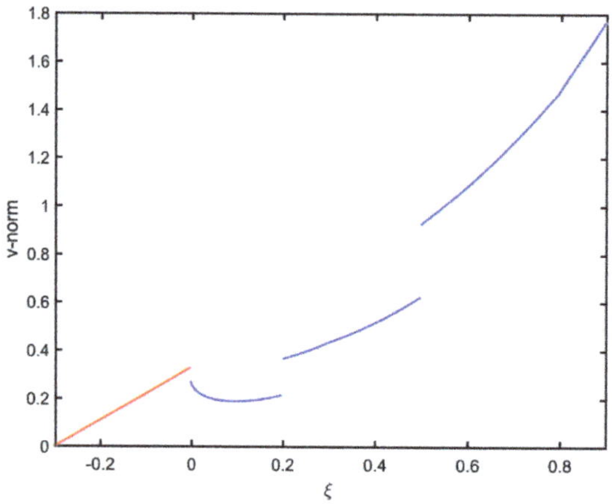

Figure 1. $\|(\xi - 0.3(k-1))^{0.5} v(\xi)\|$ of (18) with $T = 0.9$, $k = 0, 1, 2, 3$.

Example 2. *Let $\beta = 0.7$, $\varsigma = 0.2$, $k^* = 3$, $\xi_1 = 0.2$ and $\xi_2 = 0.5$. Consider*

$$\begin{cases} ({}^{RL}\mathbb{D}^{\beta}_{-0.2^+} v)(\xi) = Bv(\xi - 0.2) + g(\xi),\ \xi \neq \xi_\imath,\ \xi \in (0, 0.6], \\ v(\xi_\imath^+) = v(\xi_\imath^-) + C_\imath,\ \xi = \xi_\imath,\ \imath = 1, 2, \\ \varpi(\xi) = (\xi + 0.2, (\xi + 0.2)^2)^\top,\ -0.2 < \xi \leq 0, \\ (\mathbb{I}^{0.3}_{-0.2^+} v)(-0.2^+) = \varpi(-0.2) = (0, 0)^\top, \end{cases} \tag{20}$$

where

$$v(x) = \begin{pmatrix} v_1(\xi) \\ v_2(\xi) \end{pmatrix},\ B = \begin{pmatrix} 0.1 & 0.1 \\ 0.3 & 0.5 \end{pmatrix},\ C_\imath = \begin{pmatrix} \frac{\imath}{10} \\ \frac{\imath}{20} \end{pmatrix},\ g(\xi) = \begin{pmatrix} \xi \\ \xi^2 \end{pmatrix}. \tag{21}$$

By Theorem 5, for any $\xi \in [-0.2, 0.6]$, one has

$$\begin{aligned} v(\xi) &= e^{B\xi^{0.7}}_{-0.2,0.7}\varpi(-0.2) + \int_{-0.2}^{0} e^{B(\xi-0.2-s)^{0.7}}_{-0.2,0.7} ({}^{RL}\mathbb{D}^{0.7}_{-0.2^+}\varpi)(s)ds \\ &\quad + \sum_{0<\xi_\imath<\xi} \mathbb{E}^{B(\xi-\xi_\imath-0.4)^{0.7}}_{-0.2} C_\imath + \int_{-0.2}^{\xi} e^{B(\xi-0.2-t)^{0.7}}_{-0.2,0.7} g(t)dt, \end{aligned}$$

where

$$e^{B\xi^{0.7}}_{-0.2,0.7} = \begin{cases} E\dfrac{(\xi+0.2)^{-0.3}}{\Gamma(0.7)} + B\dfrac{\xi^{0.4}}{\Gamma(1.4)},\ \xi \in (0, 0.2], \\ E\dfrac{(\xi+0.2)^{-0.3}}{\Gamma(0.7)} + B\dfrac{\xi^{0.4}}{\Gamma(1.4)} + B^2\dfrac{(\xi-0.2)^{1.1}}{\Gamma(2.1)},\ \xi \in (0.2, 0.4], \\ E\dfrac{(\xi+0.2)^{-0.3}}{\Gamma(0.7)} + B\dfrac{\xi^{0.4}}{\Gamma(1.4)} + B^2\dfrac{(\xi-0.2)^{1.1}}{\Gamma(2.1)} + B^3\dfrac{(\xi-0.4)^{1.8}}{\Gamma(2.8)},\ \xi \in (0.4, 0.6], \end{cases}$$

and

$$\sum_{s<\xi_\imath<\xi} \mathbb{E}^{B(\xi-\xi_\imath-0.7)^{0.7}}_{-0.2} C_\imath = \begin{cases} \begin{pmatrix} 0 \\ 0 \end{pmatrix},\ \xi \in [0, 0.2], \\ \begin{pmatrix} \frac{1}{10} \\ \frac{1}{20} \end{pmatrix},\ \xi \in (0.2, 0.4], \\ \left(E + B\dfrac{(\xi-0.4)^{0.7}}{\Gamma(1.7)}\right)\begin{pmatrix} \frac{1}{10} \\ \frac{1}{20} \end{pmatrix},\ \xi \in (0.4, 0.5], \\ \left(E + B\dfrac{(\xi-0.4)^{0.7}}{\Gamma(1.7)}\right)\begin{pmatrix} \frac{1}{10} \\ \frac{1}{20} \end{pmatrix} + \begin{pmatrix} \frac{2}{10} \\ \frac{2}{20} \end{pmatrix},\ \xi \in [0.5, 0.6]. \end{cases}$$

Set $p = 2$, $q = 2$ and $\gamma = 0.5$. We can get $\|B\| = 0.6$, $\|g\|_C = 0.96$, $M = 0.8991$, $N = 0.2587$, $\psi(0.6) = 0.4574$. Next, $\Phi_1(0.6) = 1.3245$, $\Phi_2(0.6) = 0.2929$, $\Phi_3(0.6) = 1.2021$, $\Phi_4(0.6) = 2.1050$. Choosing $\delta = 0.241$, we present the FTS results of (20) in Table 2.

Like Example 1, we can choose a suitable $\eta = 1.037$ for a fixed $T = 0.6$ (see Figure 2). Furthermore, compared with the values of η in Table 2, we can choose a better value of $\eta = 1.07$.

Table 2. FTS results of (20) with $T = 0.6$.

Theorem	$\|\varpi\|_C$	β	T	δ	$\|z\|_{C_\gamma}$	η	FTS
6	0.24	0.7	0.6	0.241	1.0661	1.07 (optimal)	Yes
7	0.24	0.7	0.6	0.241	1.1064	1.17	Yes
8	0.24	0.7	0.6	0.241	1.6471	1.65	Yes
9	0.24	0.7	0.6	0.241	1.3502	1.36	Yes

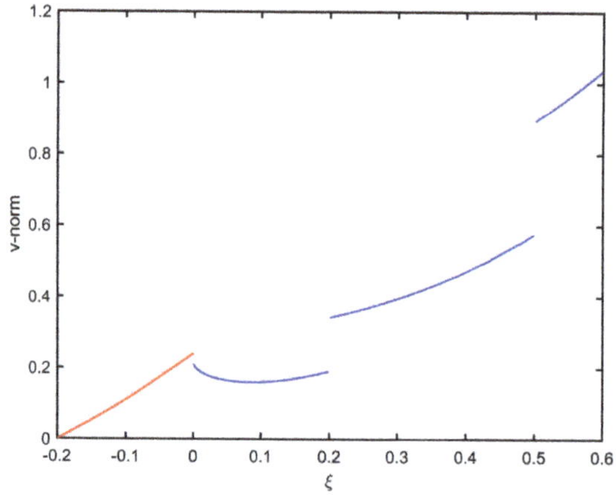

Figure 2. $\|(\xi - 0.2(k-1))^{0.5}v(\xi)\|$ of (20) with $T = 0.6, k = 0,1,2,3$.

Example 3. *Let* $\beta = 0.6$, $\varsigma = 0.2$, $k^* = 3$, $\xi_1 = 0.2$ *and* $\xi_2 = 0.5$. *Consider*

$$\begin{cases} ({}^{RL}\mathbb{D}^{\beta}_{-0.2^+}v)(\xi) = Bv(\xi - 0.2) + g(\xi),\ \xi \neq \xi_\imath,\ \xi \in (0, 0.6], \\ v(\xi_\imath^+) = v(\xi_\imath^-) + C_\imath,\ \xi = \xi_\imath,\ \imath = 1, 2, \\ \varpi(\xi) = (\xi + 0.2, (\xi + 0.2)^2)^\top,\ -0.2 < \xi \leq 0, \\ (\mathbb{I}^{0.3}_{-0.2^+}v)(-0.2^+) = \varpi(-0.2) = (0, 0)^\top, \end{cases} \tag{22}$$

where

$$v(x) = \begin{pmatrix} v_1(\xi) \\ v_2(\xi) \end{pmatrix},\ B = \begin{pmatrix} 0.1 & 0.1 \\ 0.3 & 0.5 \end{pmatrix},\ C_\imath = \begin{pmatrix} \frac{\imath}{10} \\ \frac{\imath}{20} \end{pmatrix},\ g(\xi) = \begin{pmatrix} \xi \\ \xi^2 \end{pmatrix}. \tag{23}$$

By Theorem 5, for any $\xi \in [-0.2, 0.6]$, one has

$$\begin{aligned} v(\xi) \ &= \ e^{B\xi^{0.6}}_{-0.2,0.6}\varpi(-0.2) + \int_{-0.2}^{0} e^{B(\xi-0.2-s)^{0.6}}_{-0.2,0.6}({}^{RL}\mathbb{D}^{0.6}_{-0.2^+}\varpi)(s)ds \\ &\quad + \sum_{0<\xi_\imath<\xi} \mathbb{E}^{B(\xi-\xi_\imath-0.4)^{0.6}}_{-0.2} C_\imath + \int_{-0.2}^{\xi} e^{B(\xi-0.2-t)^{0.6}}_{-0.2,0.6} g(t)dt, \end{aligned}$$

Set $p = 2$, $q = 2$ and $\gamma = 0.5$. We can get $\|B\| = 0.6$, $\|g\|_C = 0.96$, $M = 0.7612$, $N = 0.2663$, $\psi(0.6) = 0.4574$. Next, $\Phi_1(0.6) = 1.3834$, $\Phi_2(0.6) = 0.2998$, $\Phi_3(0.6) = 1.3167$, $\Phi_4(0.6) = 2.6823$. Choose $\delta = 0.241$, we give the FTS results of (22) in Table 3.

Like Example 2, we can choose a suitable $\eta = 0.900$ for a fixed $T = 0.6$ (see Figure 3). Furthermore, compared with the values of η in Table 3, we can choose a better value $\eta = 1.12$.

Comparing Example 1, Example 2 and Example 3, we find the following: When the order is the same, the time delay is different, and when the time delay is the same, the order is different, and the system is finite-time stable.

Table 3. FTS results of (22) with $T = 0.6$.

Theorem	$\|\varpi\|_C$	β	T	δ	$\|z\|_{C_\gamma}$	η	FTS
6	0.24	0.6	0.6	0.241	1.1198	1.12 (optimal)	Yes
7	0.24	0.6	0.6	0.241	1.4095	1.41	Yes
8	0.24	0.6	0.6	0.241	1.7294	1.73	Yes
9	0.24	0.6	0.6	0.241	1.8641	1.87	Yes

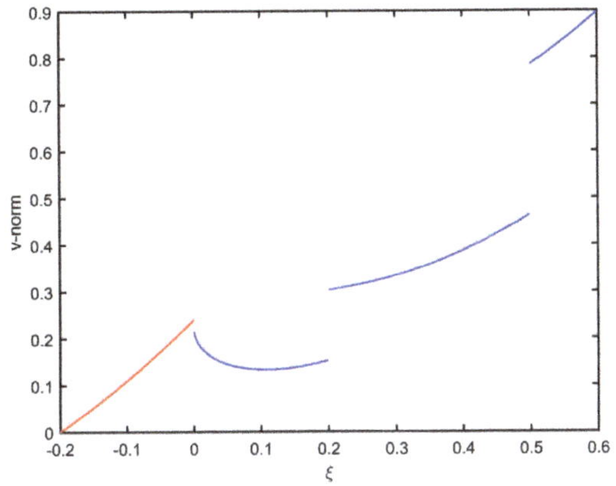

Figure 3. $\|(\xi - 0.2(k-1))^{0.5}v(\xi)\|$ of (22) with $T = 0.6, k = 0, 1, 2, 3$.

6. Conclusions

In this study, we introduce the Mittag–Leffler-type vector function with an impulsive delay, and give the explicit solution of the Riemann–Liouville fractional differential equation using the constant variation method. On this basis, by scaling the base solution matrix and the integral, we verify that the system is finite-time stable. Finally, the results are verified by four examples under different conditions. In the future, we may continue to study the other properties of the system, including stability or controllability. Due to the importance of impulsive differential equations, we believe that the results obtained by us will arouse the interest of many readers.

Author Contributions: Conceptualization, T.X. and M.L.; methodology, T.X.; validation, T.X. and M.L.; writing—original draft preparation, T.X.; writing—review and editing, M.L.; funding acquisition, M.L. All authors have read and agreed to the published version of the manuscript.

Funding: This research was funded by the National Natural Science Foundation of China (12201148) and Guizhou Provincial Science and Technology Projects (No. QKHJC-ZK[2022]YB069).

Institutional Review Board Statement: Not applicable.

Data Availability Statement: Data are contained within the article.

Conflicts of Interest: The authors declare no conflict of interest.

References

1. Hilfer, R. *Application of Fractional Calculus in Physics*; World Scientific: Singapore, 2001.
2. Kilbas, A.; Srivastava, H.; Trujillo, J. *Theory and Applications of Fractional Differential Equations*; Elsevier: Amsterdam, The Netherlands, 2006.
3. Sabatier, J.; Agrawal, O.; Machado, J. *Advances in Fractional Calculus*; Springer: Berlin/Heidelberg, Germany, 2007.
4. Stone, L.; Shulgin, B.; Agur, Z. Theoretical examination of the pulse vaccination policy in the SIR epidemic model. *Math. Comput. Model.* **2000**, *31*, 207–215. [CrossRef]
5. Wei, W.; Xiang, X.; Peng, Y. Nonlinear impulsive integro-differential equations of mixed type and optimal controls. *Optimization* **2006**, *55*, 141–156. [CrossRef]
6. Zhao, Z.; Chen, L.; Song, X. Impulsive vaccination of SEIR epidemic model with time delay and nonlinear incidence rate. *Math. Comput. Simul.* **2008**, *79*, 500–510. [CrossRef]
7. Cao, W.; Pan, T. Dynamics of an impulsive stochastic SIR epidemic model with saturated incidence rate. *J. Appl. Anal.* **2020**, *10*, 1396–1415. [CrossRef] [PubMed]
8. Wang, Y.; Tian, Y.; Li, X. Global exponential synchronization of interval neural networks with mixed delays via delayed impulsive control. *Neurocomputing* **2021**, *420*, 290–298. [CrossRef]
9. Wu, G.; Baleanu, D.; Huang, L. Novel Mittag–Leffler stability of linear fractional delay difference equations with impulse. *Appl. Math. Lett.* **2018**, *82*, 71–78. [CrossRef]

10. Li, M.; Wang, J. Exploring delayed Mittag–Leffler type matrix functions to study finite time stability of fractional delay differential equations. *Appl. Math. Comput.* **2018**, *324*, 254–265. [CrossRef]
11. You, Z.; Wang, J. Stability of impulsive delay differential equations. *J. Appl. Math. Comput.* **2018**, *56*, 253–268. [CrossRef]
12. Chen, C.; Li, M. Existence and ulam type stability for impulsive fractional differential systems with pure delay. *Fractal Fract.* **2022**, *6*, 742. [CrossRef]
13. Liu, L.; Dong, Q.; Li, G. Exact solutions and finite time stability for higher fractional-order differential equations with pure delay. *Math. Methods Appl. Sci.* **2023**, *46*, 2334–2353. [CrossRef]
14. Tian, M.; Luo, D. Existence and Finite-Time Stability Results for Impulsive Caputo-Type Fractional Stochastic Differential Equations with Time Delays. *Math. Slovaca* **2023**, *73*, 387–406. [CrossRef]
15. Lazarević, M. Finite time stability analysis of PD^{α} fractional control of robotic time-delay systems. *Mech. Res. Commun.* **2006**, *33*, 269–279.
16. Lazarević, M.; Spasić, A. Finite-time stability analysis of fractional order time-delay system: Gronwall's approach. *Mech. Res. Commun.* **2009**, *49*, 475–481.
17. Wu, R.; Lu, Y.; Chen, L. Finite-time stability of fractional delayed neural networks. *Neurocomputing* **2015**, *149*, 700–707. [CrossRef]
18. Li, M.; Wang, J. Finite time stability and relative controllability of Riemann Liouville fractional delay differential equations. *Math. Methods Appl. Sci.* **2019**, *42*, 6607–6623. [CrossRef]
19. Rakkiyappan, R.; Velmurugan, G; Cao, J. Finite-time stability analysis of fractional-order complex-valued memristor-based neural networks with time delays. *Nonlinear Dyn.* **2014**, *78*, 2823–2836. [CrossRef]
20. Hei, X.; Wu, R. Finite-time stability of impulsive fractional-order systems with time-delay. *Appl. Math. Model.* **2016**, *40*, 4285–4290. [CrossRef]
21. Wu, G.; Baleanu, D.; Zeng, S. Finite-time stability of discrete fractional delay systems: Gronwall inequality and stability criterion. *Commun. Nonlinear Sci. Numer. Simul.* **2018**, *57*, 299–308. [CrossRef]
22. Li, M.; Wang, J. Representation of solution of a Riemann–Liouville fractional differential equation with pure delay. *Appl. Math. Lett.* **2018**, *85*, 118–124. [CrossRef]

axioms

MDPI

Article

New Summation and Integral Representations for 2-Variable (p, q)-Hermite Polynomials

Nusrat Raza [1], Mohammed Fadel [2] and Wei-Shih Du [3,*]

[1] Mathematics Section, Women's College, Aligarh Muslim University, Aligarh 202002, India; nusrat.wc@amu.ac.in or nraza.maths@gmail.com
[2] Department of Mathematics, Lahej University, Lahej 73560, Yemen; muhammad.fadl.edu.s@aden-univ.net or mohdfadel80@gmail.com
[3] Department of Mathematics, National Kaohsiung Normal University, Kaohsiung 82444, Taiwan
* Correspondence: wsdu@mail.nknu.edu.tw

Abstract: In this paper, we introduce and study new features for 2-variable (p,q)-Hermite polynomials, such as the (p,q)-diffusion equation, (p,q)-differential formula and integral representations. In addition, we establish some summation models and their (p,q)-derivatives. Certain parting remarks and nontrivial examples are also provided.

Keywords: (p,q)-calculus; 2-variable (p,q)-Hermite polynomials; shift operator for polynomials; (p,q)-differential equation summation formulas; integral representations

MSC: 11B83; 33C10; 33E20

1. Introduction

Applications of the (p,q)-calculus can be found in other disciplines including quantum mechanics, statistical physics and number theory. In particular, it has been used to study the quantum group $SU_{p,q}(2)$, which is a deformation of the Lie group $SU(2)$ and has applications in quantum field theory. In fact, all the (p,q)-calculus results decrease into the corresponding results to the q-calculus when $p = 1$. Similar (p,q)-calculus results additionally decrease to the corresponding outcomes of ordinary calculus when $p = 1$ and $q \to 1$. Therefore the (p,q)-calculus is a real generalization of the q-calculus that allows for non-commutative calculus. It has been used to define (p,q)-analogues of various special functions and polynomials and has applications in many areas of mathematics and physics. Recently, (p,q)-calculus got attention from the researchers of various fields of mathematics and physics. Presented and thoroughly investigated are the (p,q)-analogues of several conventional special functions, including the Hermite polynomials, Bernoulli polynomials, Euler polynomials, Beta function, Gamma function, generalized bivariate (p,q)-Bernoulli–Fibonacci polynomials and generalized bivariate (p,q)-Bernoulli–Lucas polynomials, family of (p,q)-hybrid polynomials and (p,q)-sine and (p,q)-cosine Fubini polynomials; for more details, we refer the readers to [1–9] and references therein.

Hermite polynomials are certain of the greatest significant and historical orthogonal special functions from classical times, and they have been used extensively. It is the collection of differential equation solutions with an oscillator of harmonics that match the Schrödinger equation in quantum mechanics. These polynomials are very important for considering classical boundary-value problems in parabolic regions with parabolic coordinates. Hermite polynomials are also found in the field of signal processing as Hermitian wavelets in the wavelet transform analysis probability, combinatorics as a manifestation of an Appell series observing the umbral calculus, and numerical computation. The range of applications whose mathematical description is based on polynomials is very wide in approximation theory. For further information, the interested reader may consult the research papers [10–17].

Hermite polynomials are the series solutions of Hermite differential equations. Recall that the classical Hermite polynomials $H_n(x)$ (see, e.g., [18]) are defined by means of the following generating function

$$e^{2xt-t^2} = \sum_{n=0}^{\infty} H_n(x)\frac{t^n}{n!}$$

and the series definition was stated as follows:

$$H_n(x) = n!\sum_{k=0}^{[n/2]} \frac{(-1)^k}{k!(n-2k)!}(2x)^{n-2k}.$$

Many authors have worked on its generalization in various directions of the famous Hermitian polynomials. The 2-variable Hermite polynomials $H_n(x,y)$ (see [19]) are defined by means of the following generating function

$$e^{xt+yt^2} = \sum_{n=0}^{\infty} H_n(x,y)\frac{t^n}{n!}$$

and the series definition was stated as follows:

$$H_n(x,y) = n!\sum_{k=0}^{[n/2]} \frac{1}{k!(n-2k)!}x^{n-2k}y^k \qquad \text{for } y \neq 0,$$

and

$$H_n(x,0) = x^n.$$

It is known that these polynomials satisfy the following parabolic equation (Heat equation) (see [10,20–22]):

$$\frac{\partial^2 z}{\partial x^2} = \frac{\partial z}{\partial y},$$

which is called the diffusion equation of the 2-variable Hermite polynomials $H_n(x,y)$ (see [22]). In 2021, Raza, Fadel, Nisar and Zakarya [5] introduced and studied the 2-variable (p,q)-Hermite polynomials $H_{n,p,q}(x,y)$. They used the following generating function to generate 2-variable (p,q)-Hermite polynomials $H_{n,p,q}(x,y)$:

$$e_{p,q}(xt)\, e_{p,q}(yt^2) = \sum_{n=0}^{\infty} H_{n,p,q}(x,y)\frac{t^n}{[n]_{p,q}!} \tag{1}$$

and series definition was stated as follows:

$$H_{n,p,q}(x,y) = [n]_{p,q}!\sum_{k=0}^{[n/2]} \frac{(x)_{p,q}^{n-2k}(y)_{p,q}^{k}}{[n-2k]_{p,q}![k]_{p,q}!}. \tag{2}$$

Some important properties and relations for the 2-variable (p,q)-Hermite polynomials $H_{n,p,q}(x,y)$ were established; for more details, we refer the readers to [5].

In this work, we devote our attention to investigate new various features of 2-variable (p,q)-Hermite polynomials and introduce some new ones. The features of 2-variable (p,q)-Hermite polynomials, such as differential equations, integral and summation representations are studied and established in Sections 3 and 4. Finally, in Section 5, we will conclude this paper by highlighting some significant research directions that could be studied in the future.

2. Preliminaries

In this section, we recall some basic definitions, notations and known results, which will be used and discussed further in this paper. The (p,q)-number $[\alpha]_{p,q}$ [23] is specified as

$$[\alpha]_{p,q} = \frac{p^\alpha - q^\alpha}{p-q} \qquad \text{for } 0<q<p\leq 1 \text{ and } \alpha\in\mathbb{N}.$$

Presented is the value of the (p,q)-factorial [23]:

$$[m]_{p,q}! = \begin{cases} \prod_{r=1}^{m}[r]_{p,q}, & m\in\mathbb{N},\\ 1, & m=0. \end{cases}$$

The (p,q)-binomial coefficients [23] is defined by

$$\begin{bmatrix} n \\ k \end{bmatrix}_{p,q} = \frac{[n]_{p,q}!}{[n-k]_{p,q}![k]_{p,q}!} \qquad \text{for } k=0,1,\ldots,n,$$

which for $p=1$ and $q\to 1$, gives the following usual binomial coefficients [18]

$$\begin{bmatrix} n \\ k \end{bmatrix} = \frac{[n]!}{[n-k]![k]!} \qquad \text{for } k=0,1,\ldots,n.$$

The raising (p,q)-power [1] is defined by

$$(x\oplus a)^n_{p,q} = \sum_{m=0}^{n} \begin{bmatrix} n \\ m \end{bmatrix}_{p,q} p^{\binom{m}{2}} q^{\binom{n-m}{2}} x^m a^{n-m}. \tag{3}$$

In particular, when $a=0$, Equation (3) yields

$$(x)^n_{p,q} = p^{\binom{n}{2}} x^n. \tag{4}$$

From the above equation, it is straightforward to prove that

$$(bx)^n_{p,q} = b^n (x)^n_{p,q}.$$

In q-calculus, there are two (p,q)-exponential functions, designated by $e_{p,q}(x)$ and $E_{p,q}(x)$, that have been described as [1]:

$$e_{p,q}(x) = \sum_{n=0}^{\infty} p^{\binom{n}{2}} \frac{x^n}{[n]_{p,q}!} \tag{5}$$

and

$$E_{p,q}(x) = \sum_{n=0}^{\infty} q^{\binom{n}{2}} \frac{x^n}{[n]_{p,q}!}, \tag{6}$$

alternatively. The following relationship between $e_{p,q}(x)$ and $E_{p,q}(x)$ is known (see [1]):

$$e_{p,q}(x)E_{p,q}(-x) = 1. \tag{7}$$

In [24], a function f has a specific formula to describe its (p,q)-derivative with respect to x is given by

$$D_{p,q,x}f(x) = \begin{cases} \frac{f(px)-f(qx)}{(p-q)x}, & x\neq 0,\\ f'(0), & x=0. \end{cases}$$

More specifically, we have

$$D_{p,q,x}(f(x)g(x)) = f(px)D_{p,q,x}g(x) + g(qx)D_{p,q,x}(f(x)),$$

$$D_{p,q,x}x^n = [n]_{p,q}x^{n-1},$$

$$D_{p,q,x}e_{p,q}(\alpha x) = \alpha e_{p,q}(\alpha px)$$

and

$$D_{p,q,x}E_{p,q}(\alpha x) = \alpha E_{p,q}(\alpha qx).$$

The following are the derivatives of the (p,q)-exponential functions that correspond to the mth order (see [24]):

$$D^m_{p,q,x}e_{p,q}(\alpha x) = \alpha^n p^{\binom{m}{2}} e_{p,q}(\alpha p^m x) \qquad \text{for } m \geq 1 \tag{8}$$

and

$$D^m_{p,q,x}E_{p,q}(\alpha x) = \alpha^m q^{\binom{m}{2}} e_{p,q}(\alpha q^m x) \qquad \text{for } m \geq 1.$$

where symbol $D^m_{p,q,x}$ indicated the mth (p,q)-derivative with regard to x.

Moreover, an expression (p,q) integral for f is provided via [24]:

$$\int_0^a f(x)d_{p,q}x = (p-q)a\sum_{n=0}^{\infty}\frac{p^n}{q^{n+1}} f\left(\frac{p^n}{q^{n+1}}a\right) \qquad \text{for } \left|\frac{p}{q}\right| < 1. \tag{9}$$

From Equation (9), it is clear that

$$\int_a^b \Big(f(x)d_{p,q}x + g(x)d_{p,q}x\Big) = \int_a^b f(x)d_{p,q}x + \int_a^b g(x)d_{p,q}x. \tag{10}$$

Given is the (p,q)-definite integral of the (p,q)-derivative of a function f (see [24]):

$$\int_a^b D_{p,q}f(x)d_{p,q}x = f(b) - f(a). \tag{11}$$

In [5], the (p,q)-partial derivative of formula in terms of x and y is given by

$$D_{p,q,x}H_{n,p,q}(x,y) = [n]_{p,q}H_{n-1,p,q}(px,y), \qquad n \geq 1 \tag{12}$$

and

$$D_{p,q,y}\Big(H_{n,p,q}(x,y)\Big) = [n]_{p,q}[n-1]_{p,q}H_{n-2,p,q}(x,py), \qquad n \geq 2, \tag{13}$$

alternatively. According to [5], the pure recurrence relation for $H_{n,p,q}(x,y)$ is as described below:

$$\begin{aligned} &H_{n+1,p,q}(x,y) \\ &= xH_{n,p,q}(px,p^2y) + [n]_{p,q}y\Big(pH_{n-1,p,q}(qx,p^2y) + qH_{n-1,p,q}(qx,pqy)\Big) = 0 \quad \text{for } n \geq 1. \end{aligned} \tag{14}$$

The shift operators $L_{a,x}$ and $L_{a,y}$ for any (p,q)-function of two variables $f(x,y)$ are defined as [5]:

$$L_{a,x}f(x,y) = f(ax,y) \tag{15}$$

and

$$L_{a,y}f(x,y) = f(x,ay),$$

where a is a constant. From Equation (15), the shift operator $L_{a,x}$ satisfy the following properties:

$$L_{a,x}L_{b,x}f(x,y) = f(abx,y) = L_{ab,x}f(x,y). \tag{16}$$

In particular, for $a = b$, we have

$$L_{a^2,x}f(x,y) = f(a^2x,y) = L_{a,x}L_{a,x}f(x,y) = L^2_{a,x}f(x,y). \tag{17}$$

Since $L_{a,x}^{-1}$ is the reverse of the operator $L_{a,x}$, that is $L_{a,x}^{-1}\, L_{a,x} = I$, which I is an identity operator that produces $If(x,y) = f(x,y)$. Then, from Equation (15), we have

$$L_{a,x}^{-1} f(ax,y) = f(x,y).$$

Replacing ax by x in the above equation, we acquire

$$L_{a,x}^{-1}\, f(x,y) = f\left(\frac{1}{a}x, y\right) = f(a^{-1}x, y),$$

which on using Equation (15), gives

$$L_{a,x}^{-1}\, f(x,y) = L_{a^{-1},x}\, f(x,y).$$

Using induction method, Equations (16) and (17), gives

$$L_{a^r,x} f(x,y) = L_{a,x}^{r} f(x,y) \quad \text{for } r \in \mathbb{Z}.$$

In a similar way, it has been demonstrated that $L_{a,y}$ has the characteristics that follow:

$$L_{ab,y} f(x,y) = L_{a,y} L_{b,y} f(x,y)$$

and

$$L_{a^r,y} f(x,y) = L_{a,y}^{r} f(x,y) \quad \text{for } r \in \mathbb{Z}.$$

3. New Properties of 2-Variable (p,q)-Hermite Polynomials

During this part, we establish some features about 2-variable (p,q)-Hermite polynomials such as differential equations and integral representations. Further, from Equation (2), it can be easily verified that

$$H_{n,p,q}(ax, a^2y) = a^n H_{n,p,q}(x,y), \tag{18}$$

wherein a has a fixed value.

Applying the 2nd order (p,q)-partial derivative of both the sides of Equation (1) with respect to x, then using Equation (8) for $m = 2$, we get

$$pt^2 e_{p,q}(pxt) e_{p,q}(yt^2) = \sum_{n=0}^{\infty} D_{p,q,x}^2 H_{n,p,q}(x,y) \frac{t^n}{[n]_{p,q}!}.$$

Again, applying the Equation (1) on the left part of previous equation, provides us

$$p \sum_{n=2}^{\infty} H_{n-2,p,q}(p^2x, y, z) \frac{t^n}{[n-2]_{p,q}!} = \sum_{n=0}^{\infty} D_{p,q,x}^2 H_{n,p,q}(x,y) \frac{t^n}{[n]_{p,q}!}.$$

Therefore, when the corresponding values of t from each aspect are compared, we obtain

$$D_{p,q,x}^2 H_{n,p,q}(x,y) = [n]_{p,q}[n-1]_{p,q} p\, H_{n-2,p,q}(p^2x, y) \qquad (n \geq 2). \tag{19}$$

In the context of Equations (13), (18) and (19) it is easy to verify that the 2V(p,q)HP $H_{n,p,q}(x,y)$ satisfy the following (p,q)-partial differential equation :

$$D_{p,q,x}^2 H_{n,p,q}(x, p^3y) = p\, D_{p,q,y} H_{n,p,q}(p^2x, p^2y), H_{n,p,q}(x, p^3y), \quad H_{n,p,q}(x,0) = (x)_{p,q}^n. \tag{20}$$

Equation (20), is called the (p,q)-analogue of diffusion equation, which for $p = 1$, gives the for the q-analogue of diffusion equation for 2-variable q-Hermite polynomials $H_{n,q}(x,y)$ [5]. Further, for $p = 1, q \to 1^-$, gives the classical diffusion equation for 2-variable Hermite polynomials $H_n(x,y)$ (see [10,22]).

Example 1. *The following correlations of (p,q)-diffusion equations for 2-variable (p,q)-Hermite polynomials can be obtained immediately by applying* (20):

$$D^2_{1,2/3,x}H_{2,1,2/3}(x,y) - D_{1,2/3,y}H_{2,1,2/3}(x,y) = 0,$$
$$D^2_{2/3,3/5,x}H_{2,2/3,3/5}(x,8/27y) - 2/3\, D_{2/3,3/5,y}H_{2,2/3,3/5}(4/9x,4/9y) = 0,$$
$$D^2_{3/4,4/5,x}H_{3,3/4,4/5}(x,16/64y) - 3/4\, D_{3/4,4/5,y}H_{3,3/4,4/5}(9/16x,9/16y) = 0.$$

Afterwards, we will demonstrate the next outcome:

Theorem 1. *The subsequent (p,q)-differential equation for (p,q)-Hermite polynomials of 2-variables holds true:*

$$yL^{-2}_{p,x}\, L_{q,x}\left(1+\left(\frac{q}{p}\right)^{\frac{n}{2}} L_{\sqrt{\frac{p}{q}},x}\right)H''_{n,p,q}(x,y) + pxH'_{n,p,q}(x,y) - [n]_{p,q}\, p^{2-n}L_{p,x}H_{n,p,q}(x,y) = 0, \tag{21}$$

in which $L_{.,x}$ represents the shift operator described in (15).

Proof. Substituting n by $(n-1)$ into the expression (14) and after using Equation (18) in the resulting formula, we arrive at

$$\begin{aligned} &H_{n,p,q}(x,y) - xp^{n-1}H_{n-1,p,q}(x,y) \\ &\quad - [n-1]_{p,q}y\left(p^{n-1}H_{n-2,p,q}\left(\frac{q}{p}x,y\right) + q^{n-1}H_{n-2,p,q}\left(x,\frac{p}{q}y\right)\right) = 0, \quad n \geq 2. \end{aligned} \tag{22}$$

From Equation (15), we possess

$$H_{n-2,p,q}\left(\frac{q}{p}x,y\right) = L_{\frac{q}{p^3},x}H_{n-2,p,q}(p^2x,y). \tag{23}$$

Moreover, from Equations (15) and (18), we obtain

$$H_{n-2,p,q}\left(x,\frac{p}{q}y\right) = \left(\sqrt{\frac{p}{q}}\right)^{n-2} L_{\frac{\sqrt{q}}{p^2\sqrt{p}},x}H_{n-2,p,q}\left(p^2x,y\right). \tag{24}$$

Using Equations (15), (23) and (24) in Equation (22), we get

$$\begin{aligned} &H_{n,p,q}(x,y) - xp^{n-1}L_{p^{-1},x}H_{n-1,p,q}(px,y) - [n-1]_{p,q}y\Big(p^{n-1}L_{\frac{q}{p^3},x} \\ &\qquad + q^{n-1}\left(\sqrt{\frac{p}{q}}\right)^{n-2} L_{\sqrt{\frac{q}{p}}p^{-2},x}\Big)H_{n-2,p,q}(p^2x,y) = 0, \quad n \geq 2. \end{aligned} \tag{25}$$

Now, using Equation (12) in Equation (25) and denoting $D_{p,q,x}H_{n,p,q}(x,y)$ by $H'_{n,p,q}(x,y)$, we get

$$\begin{aligned} &H_{n,p,q}(x,y) - \frac{xp^{n-1}}{[n]_{p,q}}\, L_{p^{-1},x}\, H'_{n,p,q}(x,y) - \frac{y}{p[n]_{p,q}}\Big(p^{n-1}L_{p^{-3}q,x} \\ &\qquad + \frac{q^n}{p}\left(\sqrt{\frac{p}{q}}\right)^{n} L_{p^{\frac{-5}{2}}q^{\frac{-1}{2}},x}\Big)H''_{n,p,q}(x,y) = 0, \end{aligned}$$

or, equivalently,

$$yL_{p,x}^{-3}\left(p^n L_{q,x} + q^n \left(\sqrt{\frac{p}{q}}\right)^n L_{\sqrt{pq},x}\right) H''_{n,p,q}(x,y)$$
$$+ xp^{n+1} L_{p,x}^{-1} H'_{n,p,q}(x,y) - p^2[n]_{p,q} H_{n,p,q}(x,y) = 0.$$

It, with additional simplifying, leads to the claim (21). □

Example 2. *The following correlations of (p,q)-differential equations for 2-variable (p,q)-Hermite polynomials can be obtained immediately by applying* (21):

$$yL_{p,x}^{-2} L_{q,x}\left(1 + L_{\sqrt{\frac{p}{q}},x}\right) H''_{0,p,q}(x,y) = p^2 L_{p,x} H_{0,p,q}(x,y) - pxH'_{0,p,q}(x,y),$$

$$yL_{p,x}^{-2} L_{q,x}\left(1 + \left(\frac{q}{p}\right)^{\frac{1}{2}} L_{\sqrt{\frac{p}{q}},x}\right) H''_{1,p,q}(x,y) = [1]_{p,q}\, pL_{p,x} H_{1,p,q}(x,y) - pxH'_{1,p,q}(x,y),$$

$$yL_{p,x}^{-2} L_{q,x}\left(1 + \left(\frac{q}{p}\right) L_{\sqrt{\frac{p}{q}},x}\right) H''_{2,p,q}(x,y) = [2]_{p,q}\, L_{p,x} H_{2,p,q}(x,y) - pxH'_{2,p,q}(x,y),$$

$$yL_{p,x}^{-2} L_{q,x}\left(1 + \left(\frac{q}{p}\right)^{\frac{3}{2}} L_{\sqrt{\frac{p}{q}},x}\right) H''_{3,p,q}(x,y) = [3]_{p,q}\, p^{-1} L_{p,x} H_{3,p,q}(x,y) - pxH'_{3,p,q}(x,y),$$

$$yL_{p,x}^{-2} L_{q,x}\left(1 + \left(\frac{q}{p}\right)^{2} L_{\sqrt{\frac{p}{q}},x}\right) H''_{4,p,q}(x,y) = [4]_{p,q}\, p^{-2} L_{p,x} H_{4,p,q}(x,y) - pxH'_{4,p,q}(x,y),$$

$$yL_{p,x}^{-2} L_{q,x}\left(1 + \left(\frac{q}{p}\right)^{\frac{5}{2}} L_{\sqrt{\frac{p}{q}},x}\right) H''_{5,p,q}(x,y) = [5]_{p,q}\, p^{-3} L_{p,x} H_{5,p,q}(x,y) - pxH'_{5,p,q}(x,y).$$

We then derive the integral representations about 2-variable (p,q)-Hermite polynomials $H_{n,p,q}(x,y)$ in the following manner:

Theorem 2. *The definite (p,q)-integral of $H_{n,p,q}(x,y)$ with regard to x is as follows:*

$$\int_a^b H_{n,p,q}(x,y) d_{p,q}x = p\frac{H_{n+1,p,q}\left(\frac{b}{p},y\right) - H_{n+1,p,q}\left(\frac{a}{p},y\right)}{[n+1]_{p,q}}. \tag{26}$$

Proof. Using Equation (12), we get

$$\int_a^b H_{n,p,q}(x,y) d_{p,q}x = \frac{p}{[n+1]_{p,q}} \int_a^b D_{p,q,x} H_{n+1,p,q}\left(\frac{x}{p},y\right) d_{p,q}x,$$

which yields the assertion (26) when applying Equation (11) on the right hand side. □

Following that, we determine the subsequent outcome:

Theorem 3. *The definite (p,q)-integral of $H_{n,p,q}(x,y)$ with respect to y is as follows:*

$$\int_c^d H_{n,p,q}(x,y) d_{p,q}y = p\frac{H_{n+2,p,q}\left(x,\frac{d}{p}\right) - H_{n+2,p,q}\left(x,\frac{c}{p}\right)}{[n+1]_{p,q}[n+2]_{p,q}}. \tag{27}$$

Proof. Using Equation (13), we get

$$\int_a^b H_{n,p,q}(x,y)d_{p,q}y = \frac{p}{[n+1]_{p,q}[n+2]_{p,q}} \int_a^b D_{p,q,y}H_{n+2,p,q}\left(x,\frac{y}{p}\right)d_{p,q}y,$$

This, when applied to Equation (11) on the right side, yields assertion (27). □

We can obtain the following result in light of Theorems 2 and 3:

Corollary 1. *The formula that follows is the double (p,q)-integration of $H_{n,p,q}(x,y)$:*

$$\int_c^d \int_a^b H_{n,p,q}(x,y)d_{p,q}x\, d_{p,q}y$$
$$= \frac{[n]_{p,q}!p^2}{[n+3]_{p,q}!}\left(H_{n+3,p,q}\left(\frac{b}{p},\frac{d}{p}\right) + H_{n+3,p,q}\left(\frac{a}{p},\frac{c}{p}\right) - H_{n+3,p,q}\left(\frac{b}{p},\frac{c}{p}\right) - H_{n+3,p,q}\left(\frac{a}{p},\frac{d}{p}\right)\right). \quad (28)$$

Proof. Integrating Equation (26) with regard to y by finding the limit through c through d and utilizing Equation (10), that we get

$$\int_c^d \int_a^b H_{n,p,q}(x,y)d_{p,q}x\, d_{p,q}y$$
$$= \frac{p}{[n+1]_{p,q}}\left(\int_c^d H_{n+1,p,q}\left(\frac{b}{p},y\right)d_{p,q}y - \int_c^d H_{n+1,p,q}\left(\frac{a}{p},y\right)d_{p,q}y\right),$$

Hence, according to Equation (27), provides

$$\int_c^d \int_a^b H_{n,p,q}(x,y)d_{p,q}x\, d_{p,q}y$$
$$= \frac{p^2}{[n+1]_{p,q}[n+2]_{p,q}[n+3]_{p,q}}\left(H_{n+3,p,q}\left(\frac{b}{p},\frac{d}{p}\right) + H_{n+3,p,q}\left(\frac{a}{p},\frac{c}{p}\right) - H_{n+3,p,q}\left(\frac{b}{p},\frac{c}{p}\right) - H_{n+3,p,q}\left(\frac{a}{p}\right)\right). \quad (29)$$

From Equation (29), we obtain the assertion (28). □

4. New Summation Models for $H_{n,p,q}(x,y)$ and (p,q)-Derivatives

In this section, we will create some summation models for the (p,q)-Hermite polynomials $H_{n,p,q}(x,y)$ and their (p,q)-derivatives. First, we get several summation models for 2V(p,q)HP by employing the generating function of $H_{n,p,q}(x,y)$ and the identities (5) and (7). The summing models for (p,q)-Hermite polynomials of 2-variables are the ones that follow:

Theorem 4. *The summation models for (p,q)-Hermite polynomials of 2-variables are given below:*

$$\sum_{r=0}^{[n/2]} \frac{q^{\binom{r}{2}}(-y)^r H_{n-2r,p,q}(x,y)}{[r]_{p,q}![n-2r]_{p,q}!} = \frac{p^{\binom{n}{2}}x^n}{[n]_{p,q}!}. \quad (30)$$

(1) If $n = 2m$ ($m \in \mathbb{N}$), then

$$\sum_{r=0}^{2m} \frac{q^{\binom{r}{2}}(-x)^r H_{2m-r,p,q}(x,y)}{[r]_{p,q}![2m-r]_{p,q}!} = \frac{p^{\binom{m}{2}}y^m}{[m]_{p,q}!}. \quad (31)$$

(2) If $n = 2m+1$ ($m \in \mathbb{N} \cup \{0\}$), then

$$\sum_{r=0}^{2m+1} \frac{q^{\binom{r}{2}}(-x)^r H_{2m+1-r,p,q}(x,y)}{[r]_{p,q}![2m+1-r]_{p,q}!} = 0. \quad (32)$$

Proof. In the context of the Equation (7), it is clear

$$e_{p,q}(xt)\, e_{p,q}(yt^2)E_{p,q}(-yt^2) = e_{p,q}(xt),$$

which on using Equations (1), (5) and (6) gives

$$\sum_{n=0}^{\infty} H_{n,p,q}(x,y)\frac{t^n}{[n]_{p,q}!}\sum_{r=0}^{\infty}\frac{q^{\binom{r}{2}}(-y)^r t^{2r}}{[r]_{p,q}!} = \sum_{n=0}^{\infty}\frac{p^{\binom{n}{2}}x^n t^n}{[n]_{p,q}!},$$

or, equivalently,

$$\sum_{n=0}^{\infty}\sum_{r=0}^{\infty}\frac{H_{n,p,q}(x,y)q^{\binom{r}{2}}(-y)^r\, t^{n+2r}}{[n]_{p,q}![r]_{p,q}!} = \sum_{n=0}^{\infty}\frac{p^{\binom{n}{2}}x^n t^n}{[n]_{p,q}!},$$

which after utilizing the subsequent series arrangement method as in [18]:

$$\sum_{n=0}^{\infty}\sum_{m=0}^{\infty} A(m,n) = \sum_{n=0}^{\infty}\sum_{m=0}^{[n/2]} A(m,n-2m),$$

we get

$$\sum_{n=0}^{\infty}\sum_{k=0}^{[n/2]}\frac{H_{n-2r,p,q}(x,y)q^{\binom{r}{2}}(-y)^r\, t^n}{[n-2r]_{p,q}![r]_{p,q}!} = \sum_{n=0}^{\infty}\frac{p^{\binom{n}{2}}x^n t^n}{[n]_{p,q}!}.$$

Therefore, when the corresponding values of t from each side are compared, yields the assertion (30).

Once more, utilizing Formula (7), the result is

$$E_{p,q}(-xt)\, e_{p,q}(xt)e_{p,q}(yt^2) = e_{p,q}(yt^2).$$

Utilizing Formulas (1), (5) and (6) in the above equation, we receive

$$\sum_{n=0}^{\infty}\sum_{r=0}^{\infty}\frac{q^{\binom{r}{2}}(-x)^r H_{n,p,q}(x,y)\, t^{n+r}}{[n]_{p,q}![r]_{p,q}!} = \sum_{n=0}^{\infty}\frac{p^{\binom{n}{2}}y^n t^{2n}}{[n]_{p,q}!},$$

which after utilizing the subsequent series arrangement method as in [18]:

$$\sum_{n=0}^{\infty}\sum_{k=0}^{\infty} A(k,n) = \sum_{n=0}^{\infty}\sum_{k=0}^{n} A(k,n-k),$$

gives

$$\sum_{n=0}^{\infty}\sum_{r=0}^{n}\frac{q^{\binom{r}{2}}(-x)^r H_{n-r,p,q}(x,y)t^n}{[r]_{p,q}![n-r]_{p,q}!} = \sum_{n=0}^{\infty}\frac{p^{\binom{n}{2}}y^n t^{2n}}{[n]_{p,q}!}. \tag{33}$$

When each of the even as well as odd values of t from each side of Equation (33), are compared, we get the assertions (31) and (32). The proof is completed. □

Remark 1. *It is worth mentioning that the corresponding expression of the summation models, provided in Equation* (32)*, is as outlined below:*

$$\sum_{r=0}^{2m}\frac{q^{\binom{r}{2}}(-x)^r H_{2m+1-r,p,q}(x,y)}{[r]_{p,q}![2m+1-r]_{p,q}!} = \frac{q^{\binom{2m+1}{2}}x^{2m+1}}{[2m+1]_{p,q}!}. \tag{34}$$

We derive the subsequent summation models for the (p,q)-derivative of $H_{n,p,q}(x,y)$ from Theorem 1 and Remark 1:

Corollary 2. *The following summation models hold*

$$\sum_{r=0}^{[n/2]} \frac{q^{\binom{r}{2}}(-p^2y)^r D_{p,q,x} H_{n+1-2r,p,q}(x,p^2y)}{[r]_{p,q}![n+1-2r]_{p,q}!} = \frac{(px)^n_{p,q}}{[n]_{p,q}!}, \tag{35}$$

$$\sum_{r=0}^{2m} \frac{q^{\binom{r}{2}}(-px)^r D_{p,q,x} H_{2m+1-r,p,q}(x,p^2y)}{[r]_{p,q}![2m+1-r]_{p,q}!} = \frac{(p^2y)^m_{p,q}}{[m]_{p,q}!} \tag{36}$$

and

$$\sum_{r=0}^{2m} \frac{q^{\binom{r}{2}}(-px)^r D_{p,q,x} H_{2m+2-r,p,q}(x,p^2y)}{[r]_{p,q}![2m+2-r]_{p,q}!} = \frac{q^{\binom{2m+1}{2}}(px)^{2m+1}}{[2m+1]_{p,q}!}. \tag{37}$$

Proof. Using Equation (12), we get

$$D_{p,q,x} H_{n+1-2r,p,q}(x,p^2y) = [n+1-2r]_{p,q} H_{n-2r,p,q}(px,p^2y),$$

which on using Equation (18) and simplifying, gives

$$H_{n-2r,p,q}(x,y) = \frac{D_{p,q,x} H_{n+1-2r,p,q}(x,p^2y)}{p^{n-2r}[n+1-2r]_{p,q}}. \tag{38}$$

Using Equation (38) in Equation (30), we get the assertion (35). Similarly, using Equations (12) and (18), we get

$$H_{2m-r,p,q}(x,y) = \frac{D_{p,q,x} H_{2m+1-r,p,q}(x,p^2y)}{p^{2m-r}[2m+1-r]_{p,q}}. \tag{39}$$

We acquire the claim (36) by combining Equations (4) and (39) in Equation (31). We can deduce from Equation (39) that

$$H_{2m+1-r,p,q}(x,y) = \frac{D_{p,q,x} H_{2m+2-r,p,q}(x,p^2y)}{p^{2m+1-r}[2m+2-r]_{p,q}}. \tag{40}$$

Using Equation (40) in Equation (34), we get the assertion (37). □

Remark 2. *The subsequent alternatives are obtained by applying Equation* (18) *to the right-side of Equations* (36) *and* (37)*:*

$$\sum_{r=0}^{2m} \frac{q^{\binom{r}{2}}(-x)^r D_{p,q,x} H_{2m+1-r,p,q}(\frac{x}{p},y)}{[r]_{p,q}![2m+1-r]_{p,q}!} = \frac{(y)^m_{p,q}}{p[m]_{p,q}!}$$

and

$$\sum_{r=0}^{2m} \frac{q^{\binom{r}{2}}(-x)^r D_{p,q,x} H_{2m+2-r,p,q}(\frac{x}{p},y)}{[r]_{p,q}![2m+1-r]_{p,q}!} = \frac{q^{\binom{2m+1}{2}}(x)^{2m+1}}{[2m+1]_{p,q}!},$$

respectively.

Likewise, we obtain the subsequent summation expressions for (p,q)-derivative of 2V(p,q)HP $H_{n,p,q}(x,y)$ with regard to y utilising Equations (13) and (18) in Equations (30), (31) and (34):

Corollary 3. *The summation models for the (p,q)-derivative of $H_{n,p,q}(x,y)$ are listed below:*

$$\sum_{r=0}^{[n/2]} \frac{q^{\binom{r}{2}}(-p^2y)^r D_{p,q,y} H_{n-2r+2,p,q}(px,py)}{[r]_{p,q}![n-2r+2]_{p,q}!} = \frac{(px)^n_{p,q}}{[n]_{p,q}!},$$

$$\sum_{r=0}^{2m} \frac{q^{\binom{r}{2}}\left(-\sqrt{p}x\right)^r D_{p,q,y} H_{2m+2-r,p,q}\left(\sqrt{p}x, y\right)}{[r]_{p,q}![2m+2-r]_{p,q}!} = \frac{(py)^m_{p,q}}{[m]_{p,q}!}$$

and

$$\sum_{r=0}^{2m} \frac{q^{\binom{r}{2}}\left(-\sqrt{p}x\right)^r D_{p,q,y} H_{2m+3-r,p,q}\left(\sqrt{p}x, y\right)}{[r]_{p,q}![2m+3-r]_{p,q}!} = \frac{q^{\binom{2m+1}{2}}\left(\sqrt{p}x\right)^{2m+1}}{[2m+1]_{p,q}!}.$$

Example 3. *The following correlations of (p,q)-summation models for 2-variable (p,q)-Hermite polynomials can be obtained immediately by applying* (30) *and* (35)*:*

$$\frac{H_{4,p,q}(x,y)}{[4]_{p,q}!} - \frac{yH_{2,p,q}(x,y)}{[2]_{p,q}!} + \frac{qy^2}{[2]_{p,q}!} = \frac{p^6x^4}{[4]_{p,q}!},$$

$$\frac{D_{p,q,x}H_{5,p,q}(x,p^2y)}{[5]_{p,q}!} - \frac{p^2yD_{p,q,x}H_{3,p,q}(x,p^2y)}{[3]_{p,q}!} + \frac{p^4y^2D_{p,q,x}H_{1,p,q}(x,p^2y)}{[2]_{p,q}!} = \frac{(px)^4_{p,q}}{[4]_{p,q}!},$$

5. Recommendations for Future Research

We conclude this article by highlighting some important research directions that could be considered in the future.

Since in (p,q)-calculus, we have two types of exponential functions, we exploit this opportunity to introduce some other kinds of 2-variable(p,q)-Hermite polynomials. In view of the following identity (see [25,26]):

$$e_{p,q}(a)\ E_{p,q}(b) = \sum_{n=0}^{\infty} \frac{(a \oplus b)^n_{p,q}}{[n]_{p,q}!}, \tag{41}$$

we have

$$e_{p,q}(xt)\ E_{p,q}(yt^2) = \sum_{n=0}^{\infty} \frac{(xt \oplus yt^2)^n_{p,q}}{[n]_{p,q}!}, \tag{42}$$

We now create another form of the two-variable (p,q)-Hermite polynomials $\mathcal{H}_{n,p,q}(x,y)$ in the following manner:

$$e_{p,q}(xt)\ E_{p,q}(yt^2) = \sum_{n=0}^{\infty} \mathcal{H}_{n,p,q}(x,y)\frac{t^n}{[n]_{p,q}!}. \tag{43}$$

Using Equation (41) in Equation (43), we get

$$\sum_{n=0}^{\infty} \frac{(xt \oplus yt^2)^n_{p,q}}{[n]_{p,q}!} = \sum_{n=0}^{\infty} \mathcal{H}_{n,p,q}(x,y)\frac{t^n}{[n]_{p,q}!}. \tag{44}$$

Using Equation (3) and the subsequent series rearrangement technique (see [18]), the left side of Equation (44) is expanded as as follows:

$$\sum_{n=0}^{\infty}\sum_{k=0}^{n} A(n-k,k) = \sum_{n=0}^{\infty}\sum_{k=0}^{[n/2]} A(n-2k,k)$$

and then comparing the equal powers of t from the both sides of the resultant equation, gives the following series definition of 2V$(p,q)\mathcal{H}$P $\mathcal{H}_{n,p,q}(x,y)$:

$$\mathcal{H}_{n,p,q}(x,y) = [n]_{p,q}! \sum_{k=0}^{[n/2]} \frac{x^k (y)^{n-2k}_{p,q} q^{\binom{k}{2}}}{[n-2k]_{p,q}![k]_{p,q}!}.$$

Applying the (p,q)-partial derivative of each side of Equation (43) with regard to x, then once more using Equation (43), then comparing the equal values of t of each of the sides of the resulting equation, we receive

$$D_{p,q,x}\mathcal{H}_{n,p,q}(x,y) = [n]_{p,q}\mathcal{H}_{n-1,p,q}(px,y) \quad \text{for } n \geq 1.$$

Likewise, taking the (p,q)-partial derivative of each side of Equation (43) with respect to y, then done once again using Equation (43) and matching the identical values of t from the two sides of the resulting equation, we obtain

$$D_{p,q,y}\Big(\mathcal{H}_{n,p,q}(x,y)\Big) = [n]_{p,q}[n-1]_{p,q}\mathcal{H}_{n-2,p,q}(x,qy) \quad \text{for } n \geq 1.$$

We believe that the above newly discovered results will help us obtain new results such as recurrence relations, (p,q)-differential equation, summation formulas and integral representations related to other kinds of 2-variable (p,q)-Hermite polynomials in future studies.

6. Conclusions

In this paper, we establish new various features of 2-variable (p,q)-Hermite polynomials, such as diffusion equation, differential equations, integral and summation representations as follows:

- **(p,q)-Diffusion equation** (see Equation (20)):

$$D^2_{p,q,x}H_{n,p,q}(x,p^3y) = p\, D_{p,q,y}H_{n,p,q}(p^2x,p^2y).$$

- **(p,q)-Differential equation** (see Theorem 1):
The subsequent (p,q)-differential equation for (p,q)-Hermite polynomials of 2-variables holds true:

$$yL^{-2}_{p,x}\, L_{q,x}\left(1+\left(\frac{q}{p}\right)^{\frac{n}{2}} L_{\sqrt{\frac{p}{q}},x}\right)H''_{n,p,q}(x,y) + pxH'_{n,p,q}(x,y) - [n]_{p,q}\, p^{2-n}L_{p,x}H_{n,p,q}(x,y) = 0,$$

in which $L_{.,x}$ represents the shift operator described in (15).

- **Integral representations** (see Theorems 2 and 3):
(i) The definite (p,q)-integral of $H_{n,p,q}(x,y)$ with regard to x is as follows:

$$\int_a^b H_{n,p,q}(x,y)d_{p,q}x = p\frac{H_{n+1,p,q}\left(\frac{b}{p},y\right) - H_{n+1,p,q}\left(\frac{a}{p},y\right)}{[n+1]_{p,q}}.$$

(ii) The definite (p,q)-integral of $H_{n,p,q}(x,y)$ with respect to y is as follows:

$$\int_c^d H_{n,p,q}(x,y)d_{p,q}y = p\frac{H_{n+2,p,q}\left(x,\frac{d}{p}\right) - H_{n+2,p,q}\left(x,\frac{c}{p}\right)}{[n+1]_{p,q}[n+2]_{p,q}}.$$

- **Summation representations** (see Theorem 4):
The summation models for (p,q)-Hermite polynomials of 2-variables are given below:

$$\sum_{r=0}^{[n/2]}\frac{q^{\binom{r}{2}}(-y)^r H_{n-2r,p,q}(x,y)}{[r]_{p,q}![n-2r]_{p,q}!} = \frac{p^{\binom{n}{2}}x^n}{[n]_{p,q}!}.$$

(1) If $n = 2m$ $(m \in \mathbb{N})$, then

$$\sum_{r=0}^{2m} \frac{q^{\binom{r}{2}}(-x)^r H_{2m-r,p,q}(x,y)}{[r]_{p,q}![2m-r]_{p,q}!} = \frac{p^{\binom{m}{2}} y^m}{[m]_{p,q}!}.$$

(2) If $n = 2m+1$ $(m \in \mathbb{N} \cup \{0\})$, then

$$\sum_{r=0}^{2m+1} \frac{q^{\binom{r}{2}}(-x)^r H_{2m+1-r,p,q}(x,y)}{[r]_{p,q}![2m+1-r]_{p,q}!} = 0.$$

As applications, some new features for 2-variable (p,q)-Hermite polynomials are presented in Sections 3 and 4.

Author Contributions: Writing—original draft, N.R., M.F. and W.-S.D.; writing—review and editing, N.R., M.F. and W.-S.D. All authors have read and agreed to the published version of the manuscript.

Funding: Wei-Shih Du is partially supported by Grant No. NSTC 112-2115-M-017-002 of the National Science and Technology Council of the Republic of China.

Institutional Review Board Statement: Not applicable.

Informed Consent Statement: Not applicable.

Data Availability Statement: No new data were created or analyzed in this study. Data sharing is not applicable to this article.

Acknowledgments: The authors wish to express their sincere thanks to the anonymous referees for their valuable suggestions and comments.

Conflicts of Interest: The authors declare no conflict of interest.

References

1. Duran, U.; Acikgoz, M.; Araci, S. On (p,q)-Bernoulli, (p,q)-Euler and (p,q)-Genocchi Polynomials. *J. Comput. Theor. Nanosci.* **2016**, *13*, 7833–7846. [CrossRef]
2. Guan, H.; Khan, W.A.; Kızılateş, C. On Generalized Bivariate (p,q)-Bernoulli-Fibonacci Polynomials and Generalized Bivariate (p,q)-Bernoulli-Lucas Polynomials. *Symmetry* **2023**, *15*, 943. [CrossRef]
3. Husain, S.; Saddam; Khan, N.; Usman, T.; Junesang, C. The (p,q)-sine and (p,q)-cosine polynomials and their associated (p,q)-polynomials. *Analysis* **2024**, *44*, 47–65. [CrossRef]
4. Khan, W.A.; Muhiuddin, G.; Duran, U.; Al-Kadi, D. On (p,q)-Sine and (p,q)-Cosine Fubini Polynomials. *Symmetry* **2022**, *14*, 572. [CrossRef]
5. Raza, N.; Fadel, M.; Nisar, K.S.; Zakarya, M. On 2-variable q-Hermite polynomials. *AIMS Math.* **2021**, *8*, 8705–8727. [CrossRef]
6. Sadjang, P.N. On the (p,q)-Gamma and the (p,q)-Beta functions. *arXiv* **2015**, arXiv:1506.07394.
7. Sadjang, P.N. On (p,q)-Appell Polynomials. *arXiv* **2017**, arXiv:1712.01324.
8. Sadjang, P.N. On the Fundamental Theorem of (p,q)-Calculus and Some (p,q)-Taylor Formulas. *Results Math.* **2018**, *73*, 39. [CrossRef]
9. Yasmin, G.; Muhyi, A. On a family of (p,q)-hybrid polynomials. *Kragujev. J. Math.* **2021**, *45*, 409–426. [CrossRef]
10. Babusci, D.; Dattoli; Giuseppe, L.; Licciardi, S.; Sabia, E. *Mathematical Methods for Physicists*; World Scientific Publishing Co. Pte. Ltd.: Hackensack, NJ, USA, 2020.
11. Dattoli, G.; Torre, A. Symmetric q-Bessel functions. *Adv. Differ. Equ.* **1996**, *51*, 153–167.
12. Dattoli, G.; Torre, A. q-Bessel functions: The point of view of the generating function method. *Rend. Di Mat. E Delle Sue Applicazioni. Ser. VII* **1997**, *7*, 329–345.
13. Milovanović, G.V.; Vijay, G.; Neha, M. (p,q)-Beta functions and applications in approximation. *Boletín De La Soc. Matemática Mex.* **2018**, *24*, 219–237. [CrossRef]
14. José L., L.; Nico M., T. Approximations of orthogonal polynomials in terms of Hermite polynomials. *Abstr. Appl. Anal.* **1999**, *6*, 131–146.
15. Mursaleen, M.; Ansari, K.J.; Khan, A. On (p,q)-analogue of Bernstein operators. *Appl. Math. Comput.* **2015**, *266*, 874–882. [CrossRef]
16. Salih, Y.; Müge, A.; Mehmet, S. A collocation method using Hermite polynomials for approximate solution of pantograph equations. *J. Frankl. Inst.* **2011**, *6*, 1128–1139.

17. Soontharanon, J.; Sitthiwirattham, T. Existence results of nonlocal Robin boundary value problems for fractional (p, q)-integrodifference equations. *Adv. Differ. Equ.* **2020**, *2020*, 1–17. [CrossRef]
18. Andrews, L.C. *Special Functions of Mathematics for Engineers*, 2nd ed.; McGraw-Hill, Inc.: New York, NY, USA, 1992.
19. Appell, P.; De Fériet, J.K. *Fonctions Hypergéométriques et Hypersphériques: Polynomes d'Hermite*; Gauthier-Villars: Paris, France, 1926.
20. Cesarano, C. Hermite polynomials and some generalizations on the heat equations. *Int. J. Syst. Appl. Eng. Dev.* **2014**, *8*, 193–197.
21. Dattoli, G.; Roberto, G.; Licciardi, S. Hermite, Higher order Hermite, Laguerre type polynomials and Burgers like equations. *J. Comput. Appl. Math.* **2024**, *445*, 115821. [CrossRef]
22. Widder, D.V. *The Heat Equation*; Academic Press: Cambridge, MA, USA, 1976; Volume 67.
23. Chakrabarti, R.; Jagannathan, R. A (p, q)-oscillator realization of two-parameter quantum algebras. *J. Phys. Math. Gen.* **1991**, *24*, L711–L718. [CrossRef]
24. Burban, I.M.; Klimyk, A.U. (P, Q)-differentiation, (P, Q)-integration and (P, Q)-hypergeometric functions related to quantum groups. *Integral Transform. Spec. Funct.* **1994**, 2, 15–36. [CrossRef]
25. Duran, U.; Acikgoz, M.; Esi, A.; Araci, S. A note on the (p, q)-Hermite polynomials. *Appl. Math. Inf. Sci.* **2018**, *12*, 227–231. [CrossRef]
26. Duran, U.; Acikgoz, M.; Araci, S. A Study on Some New Results Arising from (p, q)-Calculus. *TWMS J. Pure Appl. Math.* **2020**, *11*, 57–71.

axiomS

MDPI

Article

Existence of Solutions: Investigating Fredholm Integral Equations via a Fixed-Point Theorem

Faruk Özger [1,*], Merve Temizer Ersoy [2] and Zeynep Ödemiş Özger [3]

1 Department of Computer Engineering, Igdır University, 76000 Igdır, Turkey
2 Faculty of Engineering, Department of Software Engineering, Istanbul Topkapi University, 34662 Istanbul, Turkey; mervetemizerersoy@topkapi.edu.tr
3 Department of Software Engineering, Igdır University, 76000 Igdır, Turkey; zynp.odemis@gmail.com
* Correspondence: farukozger@gmail.com

Abstract: Integral equations, which are defined as "the equation containing an unknown function under the integral sign", have many applications of real-world problems. The second type of Fredholm integral equations is generally used in radiation transfer theory, kinetic theory of gases, and neutron transfer theory. A special case of these equations, known as the quadratic Chandrasekhar integral equation, given by $x(s) = 1 + \lambda x(s) \int_0^1 \frac{s}{t+s} x(t)dt$, can be very often encountered in many applications, where x is the function to be determined, λ is a parameter, and $t, s \in [0,1]$. In this paper, using a fixed-point theorem, the existence conditions for the solution of Fredholm integral equations of the form $\chi(l) = \varrho(l) + \chi(l) \int_p^q k(l,z)(V\chi)(z)dz$ are investigated in the space $C_\omega[p,q]$, where χ is the unknown function to be determined, V is a given operator, and ϱ, k are two given functions. Moreover, certain important applications demonstrating the applicability of the existence theorem presented in this paper are provided.

Keywords: Fredholm integral equations; quadratic Chandrasekhar integral equation; Hölder space, tempered modulus of continuity; the space $C_\omega(X)$; fixed-point theorem

MSC: 45G10; 45B05; 47H10

1. Introduction

Fredholm integral equations are a class of integral equations named after the Swedish mathematician Erik Ivar Fredholm. These equations are of the form

$$\phi(x) = f(x) + \lambda \int_a^b K(x,t)\phi(t)dt,$$

where $\phi(x)$ is the unknown function to be determined, $f(x)$ is a given function, $K(x,t)$ is the kernel function, and λ is a parameter, often referred to as the Fredholm parameter.

Fredholm integral equations arise in various areas of mathematics and physics, including potential theory, signal processing, and quantum mechanics. They represent a wide range of problems where an unknown function is defined in terms of its integral over some interval or domain.

One of the key aspects of Fredholm integral equations is the study of their solvability and properties of their solutions. Depending on the properties of the kernel function $K(x,t)$ and the interval of integration, solutions to Fredholm integral equations may exhibit different behaviors, including uniqueness, existence, and convergence properties.

Fredholm integral equations have been extensively studied, and various numerical and analytical methods have been developed to solve them. These methods include—but are not limited to—Fredholm's alternative, Green's functions, eigenfunction expansions, and numerical quadrature techniques.

Overall, Fredholm integral equations play a significant role in mathematical analysis and have applications in diverse fields, making them an essential topic of study in both pure and applied mathematics.

Fractional integral and differential equations are becoming increasingly vital for modeling real-world scenarios in physics, mechanics, and related fields. They provide a powerful framework for describing complex phenomena that traditional integer-order calculus struggles to capture adequately.

Quadratic integral equations are a specific class of integral equations where the unknown function appears squared within the integral. They are represented by equations of the form

$$\phi(x) = f(x) + \lambda \int_a^b K(x,t)\phi(t)^2 dt.$$

These equations arise in various fields of science and engineering, particularly in problems where phenomena exhibit quadratic dependencies. Examples include nonlinear wave propagation, population dynamics, and certain types of chemical reaction kinetics.

The study of quadratic integral equations involves investigating the existence, uniqueness, and certain properties of their solutions. Analytical techniques such as iteration methods, Fredholm alternative, and fixed-point theorems are often employed. Numerical methods may also be used for practical solutions.

Understanding quadratic integral equations is crucial for modeling nonlinear phenomena accurately and finding solutions to a wide range of problems in diverse scientific and engineering applications.

Quadratic integral equations, in particular, have significant applications in fields like radiative transfer, neutron transport, and kinetic theory of gases. They arise naturally in these contexts and have been extensively studied for their existence properties and solution behavior.

Recent developments in fractional calculus, including Riemann–Liouville, Caputo, and Hadamard approaches, have further enriched our understanding and application of these equations. Researchers have been exploring various types of quadratic integral equations and extending their study to fractional versions like Urysohn type, Erdélyi–Kober type, and Hadamard types.

The existence, local attractivity, and stability of solutions to these fractional quadratic integral equations are crucial aspects of the research. Additionally, recent works have focused on studying the solvability of quadratic integral equations of Fredholm type in spaces of functions satisfying specific continuity conditions, such as the Hölder condition. These investigations contribute to both theoretical understanding and practical applications of these equations in diverse fields [1–25].

Moreover, the mathematical description of many processes in engineering, biological and physical sciences give rise to quadratic integral equations. For instance, research in radiative transfer theory and in kinetic theory of gases leads to the quadratic integral equation (see [15,16]).

$$x(t) = 1 + tx(t) \int_0^1 \frac{\Phi(\tau)}{t+\tau} x(\tau) d\tau,$$

Furthermore, some articles using simulant techniques have been applied to vibrations in thermoelasticity and a micropolar porous body [21,22]. That is, these articles are applied to a micropolar porous body, including voidage time derivative among the independent constitutive variables.

Quadratic integral equations are frequently applicable in neutron transport, radiative transfer and traffic theories and in kinetic theory of gases [16–18]. Particularly, the Chandrasekhar-type quadratic integral equation, which is defined as

$$x(s) = 1 + \lambda x(s) \int_0^1 \frac{s}{t+s} x(t) dt,$$

can be very frequently encountered in many applications [16].

Moreover, certain biology and queuing theory research problems lead to the following nonlinear integral equation [20]:

$$y(t) = f(t) + \frac{y(t)}{\Gamma(\alpha)} \int_0^t \frac{u(\tau, y(\tau))}{(t-\tau)^{1-\alpha}} d\tau, \ t \in [0,T], \alpha \in (0,1].$$

The aim of current paper is to prove an existence theorem for the nonlinear quadratic integral equation of the following form in the space $C_\omega[p,q]$, where ω is a modulus of continuity (see Section 2):

$$\chi(l) = \varrho(l) + \chi(l) \int_p^q k(l,z)(V\chi)(z)dz, \tag{1}$$

where V is a given operator and ϱ, k THE GAP BEFORE k IS REMOVED are two given functions.

By using a sufficient condition for the relative compactness in the space of functions with moduli of continuity and the classical Schauder fixed-point theorem, we derive a new existence result (see Theorem 4).

In Section 2, general definitions and theorems are given. The third section provides the main result of the paper and shows that there is at least one solution of the investigated equation. In the last section, two applications are given to support our main result.

2. Preliminaries

Let us give the notations, definitions and theorems that we will use in the paper .

Definition 1 ([8]). *A nondecreasing function $\omega : \mathbb{R}_+ \to \mathbb{R}_+$ is said to be a modulus of continuity if $\omega(0) = 0$ and $\omega(\epsilon) > 0$ for $\epsilon > 0$.*

The space of continuous functions on $[p,q]$ with the sup norm

$$\|\chi\|_\infty = \sup\{|\chi(l)| : l \in [p,q]\}$$

is denoted by $C[p,q]$ for $\chi \in C[p,q]$. Let $([p,q],d)$ be a given bounded metric space and $C_\omega[p,q]$ be the set of all real functions defined on $[p,q]$ such that their growths are tempered by the modulus of continuity ω with respect to d. A function $\chi = \chi(l)$ is in the set $C_\omega[p,q]$ if there exists a constant $H > 0$ satisfying

$$|\chi(l) - \chi(m)| \leqslant H\omega(d(l,m)) \tag{2}$$

for all $l, m \in [p,q]$. Also, $C_\omega[p,q]$ is a linear subspace of $C[p,q]$.

The least possible constant H_χ^ω for which the inequality (2) is satisfied is given as

$$H_\chi^\omega = \sup\left\{ \frac{|\chi(l) - \chi(m)|}{\omega(d(l,m))} : l, m \in [p,q], l \neq m \right\}, \tag{3}$$

where $\chi \in C_\omega[p,q]$.

The norm on the space $C_\omega[p,q]$ is

$$\|\chi\|_\omega = |\chi(p)| + \sup\left\{ \frac{|\chi(l) - \chi(m)|}{\omega(d(l,m))} : l, m \in [p,q], l \neq m \right\} \tag{4}$$

for $\chi \in C_\omega[p,q]$. By (3) and (4), we can write

$$\|\chi\|_\omega = |\chi(p)| + H_\chi^\omega.$$

The space $C_\omega[p,q]$ depends on the metric d and continuity modulus ω.

If we take $d(l,m) = |l-m|$ and $\omega(\varepsilon) = \varepsilon^\alpha$ for $0 < \alpha < 1$, the space $C_\omega[p,q]$ becomes the space $H_\alpha[p,q]$ (i.e., Hölder Space). In [8], the authors proved that $(C_\omega[p,q], \|\cdot\|_\omega)$ is a Banach space.

Lemma 1 ([25]). *The following relation is satisfied for each $\chi \in C_\omega[p,q]$:*

$$\|\chi\|_\infty \leqslant \max\{1, \omega(diam[p,q])\}\|\chi\|_\omega,$$

where $diam[p,q]$ denotes the diameter of the metric space $[p,q]$.

Lemma 2 ([25]). *The following relation is satisfied for each $\chi \in C_\omega[p,q]$. Suppose that $\omega_2(d(l,m)) \leqslant L\omega_1(d(l,m))$ for all $l,m \in [p,q]$, where $L > 0$. Then*

$$C_{\omega_2}[p,q] \subset C_{\omega_1}[p,q] \subset C[p,q].$$

Furthermore, the following expression is satisfied for any $\chi \in C_{\omega_2}[p,q]$:

$$\|\chi\|_{\omega_1} \leqslant \max\{1, L\}\|\chi\|_{\omega_2}.$$

Remark 1 ([25]). *Let $\lim_{\varepsilon\to 0} \frac{\omega_2(\varepsilon)}{\omega_1(\varepsilon)} = 0$ then, there exists a number $M > 0$ satisfying*

$$\omega_2(d(l,m)) \leqslant M\omega_1(d(l,m))$$

for all $l,m \in [p,q]$ and so imbedding relations in Lemma 2 and the inequality

$$\|\chi\|_{\omega_1} \leqslant \max\{1, M\}\|\chi\|_{\omega_2}.$$

also hold for any $\chi \in C_{\omega_2}[p,q]$.

Theorem 1 (Theorem 5 in [8]). *Let (X,d) be a compact metric space and*

$$\lim_{\varepsilon\to 0} \frac{\omega_2(\varepsilon)}{\omega_1(\varepsilon)} = 0,$$

where ω_1, ω_2 are moduli of continuity being continuous at zero. Then, if A is a bounded subset of the space $C_{\omega_2}(X)$, the set A is relatively compact in the space $C_{\omega_1}(X)$.

Theorem 2 ([25]). *Let $\lim_{\varepsilon\to 0} \frac{\omega_2(\varepsilon)}{\omega_1(\varepsilon)} = 0$. Then the set $B_r^{\omega_2} \in C_{\omega_1}[p,q]$ given by $B_r^{\omega_2} = \left\{\chi \in C_{\omega_2}[p,q] : \|\chi\|_{\omega_2} \leqslant r\right\}$ is compact.*

Theorem 3 (Schauder's fixed-point theorem [23]). *Let $T : \Omega \to \Omega$ be a continuous mapping, where Ω is a nonempty, compact and convex subset of a Banach space $(X, \|\cdot\|)$, then T has at least one fixed point in Ω.*

3. Existence Theorem

In this part, we provide sufficient conditions that guarantee the Equation (1) has at least one solution in $C_{\omega_1}[p,q]$.

Let $([p,q],d)$ be a compact metric space and

$$\lim_{\varepsilon\to 0} \frac{\omega_2(\varepsilon)}{\omega_1(\varepsilon)} = 0,$$

where ω_1, ω_2 are moduli of continuity being continuous at zero. We use the hypotheses presented below:

(i) $\varrho \in C_{\omega_2}[p,q]$,

(ii) The continuous function $k : [p,q] \times [p,q] \to \mathbb{R}$ satisfies the tempered by the modulus of continuity with respect to the first variable, that is, there exists a constant k_{ω_2} such that

$$|k(l,z) - k(m,z)| \leqslant k_{\omega_2}\omega_2(d(l,m))$$

for any $l, m, z \in [p,q]$.

(iii) Let $V : C_{\omega_2}[p,q] \to C[p,q]$ be a continuous operator on $C_{\omega_2}[p,q]$ with respect to norm $\|.\|_{\omega_1}$ and $f : \mathbb{R}^+ \to \mathbb{R}^+$ be a non-decreasing function, the following inequality is satisfied for each $\chi \in C_{\omega_2}[p,q]$:

$$\|V\chi\|_\infty \leqslant f(\|\chi\|_{\omega_2}).$$

(iv) There exists a positive solution $r = r_0$ of the inequality

$$\overline{P} + [\eta_2 K + K + \eta_2 k_{\omega_2}(q-p)]f(r)r \leqslant r,$$

where $\overline{P}$, K and η_2 are the constants such that $\|\varrho\|_{\omega_2} \leqslant \overline{P}$,

$$\sup\left\{\int_p^q |k(l,z)|dz : l \in [p,q]\right\} \leqslant K$$

and

$$\eta_2 = \max\{1, \omega_2(\text{diam}[p,q])\}.$$

Theorem 4. *The Equation (1) has at least one solution belonging to the space $C_{\omega_1}[p,q]$ under the assumptions (i)–(iv).*

Proof. We set the operator $\Lambda \in C_{\omega_2}[p,q]$ as follows:

$$(\Lambda\chi)(l) = \varrho(l) + \chi(l)\int_p^q k(l,z)(V\chi)(z)dz, \; l \in [p,q].$$

We first show that Λ transforms the space $C_{\omega_2}[p,q]$ into itself. For arbitrarily fixed $\chi \in C_{\omega_2}[p,q]$ and $l, m \in [p,q]$, taking into account the assumptions, we obtain that

$$\begin{aligned}(\Lambda\chi)(l) - (\Lambda\chi)(m) &= \varrho(l) + \chi(l)\int_p^q k(l,z)(V\chi)(z)dz \\ &\quad -\varrho(m) - \chi(m)\int_p^q k(m,z)(V\chi)(z)dz \\ &= \varrho(l) - \varrho(m) + [\chi(l) - \chi(m)]\int_p^q k(l,z)(V\chi)(z)dz \\ &\quad +\chi(m)\int_p^q [k(l,z) - k(m,z)](V\chi)(z)dz\end{aligned}$$

which implies that

$$
\begin{aligned}
&\frac{|(\Lambda\chi)(l)-(\Lambda\chi)(m)|}{\omega_2(d(l,m))} \\
\leqslant\ & \frac{|\varrho(l)-\varrho(m)|}{\omega_2(d(l,m))}+\frac{|\chi(l)-\chi(m)|}{\omega_2(d(l,m))}\int_p^q |k(l,z)||(V\chi)(z)|dz \\
&+|\chi(m)|\int_p^q \frac{|k(l,z)-k(m,z)|}{\omega_2(d(l,m))}|(V\chi)(z)|dz \\
\leqslant\ & \frac{|\varrho(l)-\varrho(m)|}{\omega_2(d(l,m))}+\frac{|\chi(l)-\chi(m)|}{\omega_2(d(l,m))}\|V\chi\|_\infty\int_p^q |k(l,z)|dz \\
&+\|\chi\|_\infty\|V\chi\|_\infty\int_p^q \frac{k_{\omega_2}\omega_2(d(l,m))}{\omega_2(d(l,m))}dz \\
\leqslant\ & H_\varrho^{\omega_2}+H_\chi^{\omega_2}\|V\chi\|_\infty K+\|\chi\|_\infty\|V\chi\|_\infty k_{\omega_2}(q-p) \qquad (5)
\end{aligned}
$$

for all $l,m\in[p,q]$ and $l\neq m$. By using the fact that $H_\chi^\omega\leqslant\|\chi\|_\omega$ and Lemma 1, we infer from (5) that

$$
\begin{aligned}
\frac{|(\Lambda\chi)(l)-(\Lambda\chi)(m)|}{\omega_2(d(l,m))} \leqslant\ & H_\varrho^{\omega_2}+\|V\chi\|_\infty\|\chi\|_{\omega_2}K \\
&+\eta_2\|V\chi\|_\infty\|\chi\|_{\omega_2}k_{\omega_2}(q-p) \\
\leqslant\ & H_\varrho^{\omega_2}+f\left(\|\chi\|_{\omega_2}\right)\|\chi\|_{\omega_2}K \\
&+f\left(\|\chi\|_{\omega_2}\right)\eta_2\|\chi\|_{\omega_2}k_{\omega_2}(q-p), \qquad (6)
\end{aligned}
$$

where

$$\eta_2=\max\{1,\omega_2(\mathrm{diam}[p,q])\}.$$

From (6), we have $\Lambda\chi\in C_{\omega_2}[p,q]$. This proves that the operator Λ maps the space $C_{\omega_2}[p,q]$ into itself.

Also, we derive that

$$
\begin{aligned}
|(\Lambda\chi)(p)| =\ & \left|\varrho(p)+\chi(p)\int_p^q k(p,z)(V\chi)(z)dz\right| \\
\leqslant\ & |\varrho(p)|+|\chi(p)|\int_p^q |k(p,z)||(V\chi)(z)|dz \\
\leqslant\ & |\varrho(p)|+\|\chi\|_\infty\|V\chi\|_\infty K \\
\leqslant\ & |\varrho(p)|+(\max\{1,\omega_2(\mathrm{diam}[p,q])\})\|\chi\|_{\omega_2}\|V\chi\|_\infty K \\
\leqslant\ & |\varrho(p)|+\eta_2\|\chi\|_{\omega_2}f\left(\|\chi\|_{\omega_2}\right)K. \qquad (7)
\end{aligned}
$$

By using definition of the norm $\|\Lambda\chi\|_{\omega_2}$, (6) and (7), we can write

$$
\begin{aligned}
\|\Lambda\chi\|_{\omega_2} =\ & |(\Lambda\chi)(p)|+\sup\left\{\frac{|(\Lambda\chi)(l)-(\Lambda\chi)(m)|}{\omega_2(d(l,m))}:l,m\in[p,q],l\neq m\right\} \\
\leqslant\ & |\varrho(p)|+f\left(\|\chi\|_{\omega_2}\right)\eta_2\|\chi\|_{\omega_2}K \\
&+H_\varrho^{\omega_2}+f\left(\|\chi\|_{\omega_2}\right)\|\chi\|_{\omega_2}K \\
&+f\left(\|\chi\|_{\omega_2}\right)\eta_2\|\chi\|_{\omega_2}k_{\omega_2}(q-p) \\
\leqslant\ & \|\varrho\|_{\omega_2}+[\eta_2K+K+\eta_2k_{\omega_2}(q-p)]f\left(\|\chi\|_{\omega_2}\right)\|\chi\|_{\omega_2} \qquad (8)
\end{aligned}
$$

for any $\chi \in C_{\omega_2}[p,q]$. So, if we take χ in $B_{r_0}^{\omega_2}$ then by (8) and the assumption (iv) we get the following inequality:

$$\|\Lambda\chi\|_{\omega_2} \leqslant \overline{P} + [\eta_2 K + K + \eta_2 k_{\omega_2}(q-p)]f(r_0)r_0 \leqslant r_0.$$

So $\Lambda\chi \in B_{r_0}^{\omega_2}$. Thus, Λ transforms the ball

$$B_{r_0}^{\omega_2} = \{\chi \in C_{\omega_2}[p,q] : \|\chi\|_{\omega_2} \leqslant r_0\}$$

into itself. That is, $\Lambda : B_{r_0}^{\omega_2} \to B_{r_0}^{\omega_2}$. Next, we will show that the operator Λ is continuous on $B_{r_0}^{\omega_2}$ with respect to norm $\|\cdot\|_{\omega_1}$. To carry this out, we fix $\psi \in B_{r_0}^{\omega_2}$ and an arbitrary $\varepsilon > 0$. Since the operator $V : C_{\omega_2}[p,q] \to C[p,q]$ is continuous on $C_{\omega_2}[p,q]$ with respect to norm $\|.\|_{\omega_1}$, there is a positive number δ such that the estimate

$$\|V\chi - V\psi\|_\infty < \frac{\varepsilon}{2(KL + L(q-p)\eta_2 k_{\omega_2} + K\eta_2)r_0}$$

is satisfied for all $\chi \in B_{r_0}^{\omega_2}$, where $\|\chi - \psi\|_{\omega_1} < \delta$, where δ is a number satisfying the following inequality:

$$0 < \delta < \frac{\varepsilon}{2(K + \eta_1 L(q-p)k_{\omega_2} + K\eta_1)f(r_0)},$$

where

$$\max\{1, \omega_1(\mathrm{diam}[p,q])\} = \eta_1.$$

By using the equality

$$\begin{aligned}
& (\Lambda\chi)(l) - (\Lambda\psi)(l) - ((\Lambda\chi)(m) - (\Lambda\psi)(m)) \\
= \; & \chi(l)\int_p^q k(l,z)(V\chi)(z)dz - \psi(l)\int_p^q k(l,z)(V\psi)(z)dz \\
& -\chi(m)\int_p^q k(m,z)(V\chi)(z)dz + \psi(m)\int_p^q k(m,z)(V\psi)(z)dz \\
= \; & [\chi(l) - \psi(l)]\int_p^q k(l,z)(V\chi)(z)dz + \psi(l)\int_p^q k(l,z)[(V\chi)(z) - (V\psi)(z)]dz \\
& -[\chi(m) - \psi(m)]\int_p^q k(m,z)(V\chi)(z)dz - \psi(m)\int_p^q k(m,z)[(V\chi)(z) - (V\psi)(z)]dz \\
= \; & \{[\chi(l) - \psi(l)] - [\chi(m) - \psi(m)]\}\int_p^q k(l,z)(V\chi)(z)dz \\
& +[\chi(m) - \psi(m)]\int_p^q [k(l,z) - k(m,z)](V\chi)(z)dz \\
& +[\psi(l) - \psi(m)]\int_p^q k(l,z)[(V\chi)(z) - (V\psi)(z)]dz \\
& +\psi(m)\int_p^q [k(l,z) - k(m,z)][(V\chi)(z) - (V\psi)(z)]dz,
\end{aligned}$$

we obtain that

$$
\begin{aligned}
&\frac{|[(\Lambda\chi)(l)-(\Lambda\psi)(l)]-[(\Lambda\chi)(m)-(\Lambda\psi)(m)]|}{\omega_1(d(l,m))}\\
\leqslant\ & \frac{1}{\omega_1(d(l,m))}|[\chi(l)-\psi(l)]-[\chi(m)-\psi(m)]|\left|\int_p^q k(l,z)(V\chi)(z)dz\right|\\
&+\frac{1}{\omega_1(d(l,m))}|\chi(m)-\psi(m)|\left|\int_p^q [k(l,z)-k(m,z)](V\chi)(z)dz\right|\\
&+\frac{1}{\omega_1(d(l,m))}\left|[\psi(l)-\psi(m)]\int_p^q k(l,z)[(V\chi)(z)-(V\psi)(z)]dz\right|\\
&+\frac{1}{\omega_1(d(l,m))}\left|\psi(m)\int_p^q [k(l,z)-k(m,z)][(V\chi)(z)-(V\psi)(z)]dz\right|
\end{aligned}
$$

which yields that

$$
\begin{aligned}
&\frac{|[(\Lambda\chi)(l)-(\Lambda\psi)(l)]-[(\Lambda\chi)(m)-(\Lambda\psi)(m)]|}{\omega_1(d(l,m))}\\
\leqslant\ & \frac{|[\chi(l)-\psi(l)]-[\chi(m)-\psi(m)]|}{\omega_1(d(l,m))}\|V\chi\|_\infty\int_p^q |k(l,z)|dz\\
&+\|\chi-\psi\|_\omega\|V\chi\|_\omega\int_p^q \frac{|k(l,z)-k(m,z)|}{\omega_1(d(l,m))}dz\\
&+\frac{|\psi(l)-\psi(m)|}{\omega_1(d(l,m))}\left|\int_p^q k(l,z)[(V\chi)(z)-(V\psi)(z)]dz\right|\\
&+|\psi(m)|\left|\int_p^q \frac{k(l,z)-k(m,z)}{\omega_1(d(l,m))}[(V\chi)(z)-(V\psi)(z)]dz\right|\\
\leqslant\ & H^{\omega_1}_{\chi-\psi}\|V\chi\|_\infty K+\eta_1\|\chi-\psi\|_{\omega_1}\|V\chi\|_\infty\int_p^q \frac{|k(l,z)-k(m,z)|}{\omega_1(d(l,m))}dz\\
&+\frac{|\psi(l)-\psi(m)|}{\omega_1(d(l,m))}\int_p^q |k(l,z)||(V\chi)(z)-(V\psi)(z)|dz\\
&+|\psi(m)|\int_p^q \frac{|k(l,z)-k(m,z)|}{\omega_1(d(l,m))}|(V\chi)(z)-(V\psi)(z)|dz
\end{aligned}
\tag{9}
$$

for all $l,m\in[p,q]$ with $l\neq m$. The estimates

$$\|\chi\|_\infty\leqslant\max\{1,\omega_2(\mathrm{diam}[p,q])\}\|\chi\|_{\omega_2}$$

and

$$H^\omega_\chi\leqslant\|\chi\|_\omega$$

hold from Lemma 1 and definition of the norm $\|\chi\|_\omega$. By (9), we derive the following estimate:

$$
\begin{aligned}
&\frac{|[(\Lambda\chi)(l)-(\Lambda\psi)(l)]-[(\Lambda\chi)(m)-(\Lambda\psi)(m)]|}{\omega_1(d(l,m))}\\
\leqslant\ & K\|V\chi\|_\infty H^{\omega_1}_{\chi-\psi}+\eta_1\|\chi-\psi\|_{\omega_1}\|V\chi\|_\infty\int_p^q \frac{k_{\omega_2}\omega_2(d(l,m))}{\omega_1(d(l,m))}dz\\
&+\frac{|\psi(l)-\psi(m)|}{\omega_2(d(l,m))}\frac{\omega_2(d(l,m))}{\omega_1(d(l,m))}\int_p^q |k(l,z)||(V\chi)(z)-(V\psi)(z)|dz\\
&+|\psi(m)|\int_p^q \frac{k_{\omega_2}\omega_2(d(l,m))}{\omega_1(d(l,m))}|(V\chi)(z)-(V\psi)(z)|dz\\
\leqslant\ & K\|V\chi\|_\infty\|\chi-\psi\|_{\omega_1}+\eta_1L(q-p)k_{\omega_2}\|V\chi\|_\infty\|\chi-\psi\|_{\omega_1}\\
&+KLH^{\omega_2}_\psi\|V\chi-V\psi\|_\infty+L(q-p)k_{\omega_2}\|\psi\|_\infty\|V\chi-V\psi\|_\infty,
\end{aligned}
\tag{10}
$$

Then, by the assumption (*iii*), Lemma 1 and (10), we obtain the following inequality:

$$\begin{aligned}
&\frac{|[(\Lambda\chi)(l)-(\Lambda\psi)(l)]-[(\Lambda\chi)(m)-(\Lambda\psi)(m)]|}{\omega_1(d(l,m))}\\
\leqslant\;& Kf\left(\|\chi\|_{\omega_2}\right)\|\chi-\psi\|_{\omega_1}+\eta_1 L(q-p)k_{\omega_2}f\left(\|\chi\|_{\omega_2}\right)\|\chi-\psi\|_{\omega_1}\\
&+KL\|\psi\|_{\omega_2}\|V\chi-V\psi\|_\infty+L(q-p)\eta_2 k_{\omega_2}\|\psi\|_{\omega_2}\|V\chi-V\psi\|_\infty\\
\leqslant\;& Kf(r_0)\delta+\eta_1 L(q-p)k_{\omega_2}f(r_0)\delta+KLr_0\|V\chi-V\psi\|_\infty\\
&+L(q-p)\eta_2 k_{\omega_2}r_0\|V\chi-V\psi\|_\infty.
\end{aligned}\tag{11}$$

On the other hand,

$$\begin{aligned}
(\Lambda\chi)(p)-(\Lambda\psi)(p) &= \chi(p)\int_p^q k(p,z)(V\chi)(z)dz\\
&\quad-\psi(p)\int_p^q k(p,z)(V\psi)(z)dz\\
&= \chi(p)\int_p^q k(p,z)[(V\chi)(z)-(V\psi)(z)]dz\\
&\quad+[\chi(p)-\psi(p)]\int_p^q k(p,z)(V\psi)(z)dz
\end{aligned}$$

and hence

$$\begin{aligned}
&|(\Lambda\chi)(p)-(\Lambda\psi)(p)|\\
\leqslant\;& |\chi(p)|\int_p^q |k(p,z)||(V\chi)(z)-(V\psi)(z)|dz\\
&+|\chi(p)-\psi(p)|\int_p^q |k(p,z)||(V\psi)(z)|dz\\
\leqslant\;& K\|\chi\|_\infty\|V\chi-V\psi\|_\infty+K\|V\psi\|_\infty\|\chi-\psi\|_\infty\\
\leqslant\;& K\|\chi\|_{\omega_2}\eta_2\|V\chi-V\psi\|_\infty+K\|V\psi\|_\infty\eta_1\|\chi-\psi\|_{\omega_1}\\
\leqslant\;& K\eta_2\|\chi\|_{\omega_2}\|V\chi-V\psi\|_\infty+K\eta_1 f(\|\psi\|_{\omega_2})\|\chi-\psi\|_{\omega_1}\\
\leqslant\;& K\eta_2 r_0\|V\chi-V\psi\|_\infty+K\eta_1 f(r_0)\delta.
\end{aligned}\tag{12}$$

From (11) and (12), it follows that

$$\begin{aligned}
&\|\Lambda\chi-\Lambda\psi\|_{\omega_1}\\
=\;& |(\Lambda\chi)(p)-(\Lambda\psi)(p)|+H^{\omega_1}_{\Lambda\chi-\Lambda\psi}\\
=\;& |(\Lambda\chi)(p)-(\Lambda\psi)(p)|\\
&+\sup\left\{\frac{|[(\Lambda\chi)(l)-(\Lambda\psi)(l)]-[(\Lambda\chi)(m)-(\Lambda\psi)(m)]|}{\omega_1(d(l,m))}:l,m\in[p,q],l\neq m\right\}\\
\leqslant\;& (K+\eta_1 L(q-p)k_{\omega_2}+K\eta_1)f(r_0)\delta\\
&+(KL+L(q-p)\eta_2 k_{\omega_2}+K\eta_2)r_0\|V\chi-V\psi\|_\infty\\
<\;& \frac{\varepsilon}{2}+\frac{\varepsilon}{2}=\varepsilon.
\end{aligned}$$

Therefore, the operator Λ is continuous at the point $\chi\in B^{\omega_2}_{r_0}$. We conclude that Λ is continuous on $B^{\omega_2}_{r_0}$ with respect to the norm $\|\cdot\|_{\omega_1}$. By Theorem 2, $B^{\omega_2}_{r_0}$ is compact in $C_{\omega_1}[p,q]$ and through Schauder fixed-point theorem proof is completed. □

4. Applications

In this section, we employed the regularization method combined with some of the proper well-known techniques to handle the Fredholm integral equations. Our approach has demonstrated reliability in tackling these challenging problems. To further illustrate the effectiveness of our method, we present two numerical applications that corroborate our fundamental theorem. Through these applications, we aim to reinforce our findings and foster a deeper, more abstract comprehension of the topic.

Application 1. Let n and $\hat{n}$ be two non-negative constants and $l \in [0,1]$. Consider the integral equation given below:

$$\chi(l) = \sqrt[3]{n\sin(\pi l) + \hat{n}} + \chi(l)\int_0^1 \sqrt[5]{5l^2 + z}\sqrt{|\chi(z)|}\,dz. \tag{13}$$

Also, define the operator V as $(V\chi)(z) = \sqrt{|\chi(z)|}$ for all $l, z \in [0,1]$ and set $\varrho(l) = \sqrt[3]{n\sin(\pi l) + \hat{n}}$, $k(l,z) = \sqrt[5]{5l^2 + z}$.

Additionally we choose $\omega_2(\varepsilon) = \varepsilon^{\frac{1}{3}}$, $\omega_1(\varepsilon) = \varepsilon^{\alpha}$ such that $0 < \alpha < 1/3$ and $d(l,m) = |l - m|$. Since the function $h(l) = \sqrt[3]{l}$ is concave for $h : \mathbb{R}^+ \to \mathbb{R}^+$, this function is subadditive from Lemma 4.4 in [24]. Moreover, if we take into account $|\sin\chi - \sin\psi| \leqslant |\chi - \psi|$ for $\chi, \psi \in \mathbb{R}$, we have

$$\begin{aligned} |\varrho(l) - \varrho(m)| &= \left|\sqrt[3]{n\sin\pi l + \hat{n}} - \sqrt[3]{n\sin\pi m + \hat{n}}\right| \\ &\leqslant \sqrt[3]{|n(\sin\pi l - \sin\pi m)|} \\ &\leqslant \sqrt[3]{n\pi}|l - m|^{\frac{1}{3}}. \end{aligned}$$

Thus,

$$\begin{aligned} \|\varrho\|_{\omega_2} &= |\varrho(0)| + \sup\left\{\frac{|\varrho(l) - \varrho(m)|}{\omega_2(d(l,m))} : l, m \in [0,1], l \neq m\right\} \\ &= \left|\sqrt[3]{\hat{n}}\right| + \sup\left\{\frac{|\varrho(l) - \varrho(m)|}{|l - m|^{\frac{1}{3}}} : l, m \in [0,1], l \neq m\right\} \\ &\leqslant \left|\sqrt[3]{\hat{n}}\right| + \sup\left\{\frac{\sqrt[3]{n\pi}|l - m|^{\frac{1}{3}}}{|l - m|^{\frac{1}{3}}} : l, m \in [0,1], l \neq m\right\} \\ &\leqslant \sqrt[3]{\hat{n}} + \sqrt[3]{n\pi} = \overline{P} \end{aligned}$$

which means that the condition (i) of Theorem 4 is fulfilled.

Further, we have

$$\begin{aligned} |k(l,z) - k(m,z)| &= \left|\sqrt[5]{5l^2 + z} - \sqrt[5]{5m^2 + z}\right| \\ &\leqslant \sqrt[5]{|5l^2 - 5m^2|} \\ &\leqslant \sqrt[5]{10}|l - m|^{\frac{1}{5}} \end{aligned}$$

for all $l, m \in [0,1]$. The condition (ii) of Theorem 4 holds with $k_{\omega_2} = \sqrt[5]{10}$, $d(l,m) = |l - m|$ and $\omega_2(d(l,m)) = |l - m|^{1/5}$.

Since

$$\begin{aligned} \sup\left\{\int_0^1 |k(l,z)|dz : l \in [0,1]\right\} &= \sup\left\{\int_0^1 \left|\sqrt[5]{5l^2 + z}\right|dz : l \in [0,1]\right\} \\ &= \frac{5}{6}(5l^2 + z)^{6/5}\Big|_0^1 \\ &\leqslant \frac{5}{6}(6\sqrt[5]{6} - 5\sqrt[5]{5}), \end{aligned}$$

the constant K can be taken as $K = \frac{5}{6}(6\sqrt[5]{6} - 5\sqrt[5]{5})$.

Since
$$\eta_2 = \max\{1, \omega_2(\mathrm{diam}[0,1])\} = \max\left\{1, 1^{\frac{1}{5}}\right\} = 1,$$
we have
$$|(V\chi)(z)| = \sqrt{|\chi(z)|} \leqslant \sqrt{\|\chi\|_\infty} \leqslant \sqrt{\eta_2\|\chi\|_{\omega_2}} = \sqrt{\|\chi\|_{\omega_2}} \tag{14}$$
for all $\chi \in C_{\omega_2}[0,1]$ and $z \in [0,1]$. (14) yields that
$$\|V\chi\|_\infty \leqslant \sqrt{\|\chi\|_{\omega_2}}$$
for all $\chi \in C_{\omega_2}[0,1]$. Therefore, V is an operator from $C_{\omega_2}[0,1]$ into $C[0,1]$ and we can choose the function $f : \mathbb{R}^+ \to \mathbb{R}^+$ as $f(\chi) = \sqrt{\chi}$. This function is non-decreasing and verifies the assumption (iii).

Now, we prove that V is continuous on $C_{\omega_2}[0,1]$ with $\|.\|_{\omega_1}$. Let $\psi \in C_{\omega_2}[0,1]$ and $\varepsilon > 0$. Also, let $\chi \in C_{\omega_2}[0,1]$ be an arbitrary function satisfying $\|\chi - \psi\|_{\omega_1} < \delta$ such that $0 < \delta \leqslant \varepsilon^2$.

The inequality
$$|(V\chi)(z) - (V\psi)(z)| = \sqrt{|\chi(z) - \psi(z)|} \leqslant \sqrt{\|\chi - \psi\|_\infty} \leqslant \sqrt{\eta_1\|\chi - \psi\|_{\omega_1}}$$
holds for all $\chi, \psi \in C_{\omega_2}[0,1]$ and $z \in [0,1]$. Since
$$\eta_1 = \max\{1, \omega_1(\mathrm{diam}[0,1])\} = \max\{1, 1^\alpha\} = 1,$$
we have
$$\|V\chi - V\psi\|_\infty \leqslant \sqrt{\|\chi - \psi\|_{\omega_1}}$$
for all $\chi, \psi \in C_{\omega_2}[0,1]$.

Hence, V is continuous at the point $\psi \in C_{\omega_2}[0,1]$ with $\|.\|_{\omega_1}$ since ψ is arbitrarily selected.
$$\overline{P} + [\eta_2 K + K + \eta_2 k_{\omega_2}(q-p)]f(r)r \leqslant r$$
is equivalent to
$$\sqrt[3]{\hat{n}} + \sqrt[3]{n\pi} + \left[\frac{5}{3}\left(6\sqrt[5]{6} - 5\sqrt[5]{5}\right) + \sqrt[5]{10}(1-0)\right]r\sqrt{r} \leqslant r. \tag{15}$$

If we take the constants n and $\hat{n}$ as suitable, then there exists a positive number r_0 satisfying (15). For instance, if we select $n = 0$ and $\hat{n} = 0$, then (15) holds for $r = r_0 \in (0, 0.0517272]$.

Therefore, we show the existence of the solution for Equation (13) in the space $C_{\omega_1}[0,1]$ via Theorem 4.

Application 2. Consider the following quadratic integral equation:
$$\chi(l) = \frac{1}{100}\sqrt{\arctan(l-1)} + \chi(l)\int_1^e \frac{\sqrt[3]{\ln l + \ln z}}{z}\sin\chi(z)dz, \tag{16}$$
where $l, z \in [1, e]$.

Set $\varrho(l) = \frac{1}{100}\sqrt{\arctan(l-1)}$, $k(l,z) = \frac{\sqrt[3]{\ln l + \ln z}}{z}$, $(V\chi)(z) = \sin\chi(z)$ and $\omega_2(\varepsilon) = \varepsilon^{\frac{1}{3}}$, $\omega_1(\varepsilon) = \varepsilon^\alpha$ for $0 < \alpha < 1/3$, $d(l,m) = |\ln l - \ln m|$.

Since the function $h : \mathbb{R}^+ \to \mathbb{R}^+$ defined by $h(\chi) = \sqrt{\chi}$ is concave and $h(0) = 0$, this function is subadditive from Remark 4.5 in [24] ref IS CHANGED AS cite. If we consider $|\arctan \chi - \arctan \psi| \leqslant |\chi - \psi|$ for $\chi, \psi \in \mathbb{R}$, we can write

$$\begin{aligned} |\varrho(l) - \varrho(m)| &= \left| \frac{1}{100}\sqrt{\arctan(l-1)} - \frac{1}{100}\sqrt{\arctan(m-1)} \right| \\ &\leqslant \frac{1}{100}\sqrt{|\arctan(l-1) - \arctan(m-1)|} \\ &\leqslant \frac{1}{100}\sqrt{|l-m|} \end{aligned}$$

for all $l, m \in [1, e]$.

Let $l < m$, so there is $\xi \in (l, m)$ satisfying

$$|\ln l - \ln m| = \frac{1}{\xi}|l - m|$$

which yields that

$$|\ln l - \ln m| \geqslant \frac{1}{e}|l - m|$$

and hence

$$\frac{1}{|\ln l - \ln m|^{\frac{1}{3}}} \leqslant \frac{\sqrt[3]{e}}{|l - m|^{\frac{1}{3}}}$$

for all $l, m \in [1, e]$ and $l \neq m$.

Since

$$\begin{aligned} \|\varrho\|_{\omega_2} &= |\varrho(1)| + \sup\left\{ \frac{|\varrho(l) - \varrho(m)|}{\omega_2(d(l,m))} : l, m \in [1,e], l \neq m \right\} \\ &= \sup\left\{ \frac{|\varrho(l) - \varrho(m)|}{|\ln l - \ln m|^{\frac{1}{3}}} : l, m \in [1,e], l \neq m \right\} \\ &\leqslant \frac{\sqrt[3]{e}}{100} \sup\left\{ |l - m|^{\frac{1}{6}} : l, m \in [1,e], l \neq m \right\} \\ &\leqslant \frac{1}{50} = \overline{P}, \end{aligned}$$

assumption (i) of Theorem 4 is satisfied.

Further, we have

$$\begin{aligned} |k(l,z) - k(m,z)| &= \frac{1}{z}\left| \sqrt[3]{\ln l + \ln z} - \sqrt[3]{\ln m + \ln z} \right| \\ &\leqslant \frac{1}{z}\sqrt[3]{|\ln l - \ln m|} \\ &\leqslant |\ln l - \ln m|^{\frac{1}{3}} \\ &= \omega_2(d(l,m)) \end{aligned}$$

for all $l, m, z \in [1, e]$. Condition (ii) of Theorem 4 holds with the constant $k_{\omega_2} = 1$.

Also,

$$\begin{aligned} \sup\left\{ \int_1^e |k(l,z)| dz : l \in [1,e] \right\} &= \sup\left\{ \int_1^e \left| \frac{\sqrt[3]{\ln l + \ln z}}{z} \right| dz : l \in [1,e] \right\} \\ &\leqslant \int_1^e \frac{\sqrt[3]{1 + \ln z}}{z} dz \\ &= \frac{3}{4}\left(\sqrt[3]{16} - 1 \right). \end{aligned}$$

So the constant K can be taken as $\frac{3}{4}\left(\sqrt[3]{16}-1\right)$.

Since
$$\eta_2 = \max\{1, \omega_2(\text{diam}[1,e])\} = \max\left\{1, (\ln e - \ln 1)^{\frac{1}{3}}\right\} = 1,$$
the estimate
$$|(V\chi)(z)| = |\sin \chi(z)| \leqslant |\chi(z)| \leqslant \|\chi\|_\infty \leqslant \eta_2 \|\chi\|_{\omega_2} = \|\chi\|_{\omega_2}$$
holds for all $\chi \in C_{\omega_2}[1,e]$ and $z \in [1,e]$, and hence
$$\|V\chi\|_\infty = \sup_{z\in[0,1]} |(V\chi)(z)| \leqslant \|\chi\|_{\omega_2}.$$

Therefore, V is an operator from $C_{\omega_2}[1,e]$ into $C[1,e]$, and we can take the function $f : \mathbb{R}^+ \to \mathbb{R}^+$ as $f(\chi) = \chi$. It is obvious that the function f is non-decreasing and satisfies assumption (iv).

Now, we show that the operator V is continuous on $C_{\omega_2}[1,e]$ with $\|.\|_{\omega_1}$. Let $\psi \in C_{\omega_2}[1,e]$ be arbitrarily selected, $\varepsilon > 0$ and $\chi \in C_{\omega_2}[1,e]$ be an arbitrary function, and inequality $\|\chi - \psi\|_{\omega_1} < \delta$ be satisfied such that $0 < \delta \leqslant \varepsilon$.

Then, for arbitrary $l, m \in [1,e]$, we obtain
$$|\sin \chi(z) - \sin \psi(z)| \leqslant |\chi(z) - \psi(z)| \leqslant \|\chi - \psi\|_\infty \leqslant \eta_1 \|\chi - \psi\|_{\omega_1} = \|\chi - \psi\|_{\omega_1},$$
where
$$\eta_1 = \max\{1, \omega_1(\text{diam}[1,e])\} = \max\{1, (\ln e - \ln 1)^\alpha\} = 1.$$

Thus,
$$\|V\chi - V\psi\|_\infty = \sup_{z\in[0,1]} |\sin \chi(z) - \sin \psi(z)| \leqslant \|\chi - \psi\|_{\omega_1}$$
which implies
$$\|V\chi - V\psi\|_\infty < \delta \leqslant \varepsilon$$
is satisfied for all $\chi \in C_{\omega_2}[1,e]$. This proves that the operator V is continuous at the point $\psi \in C_{\omega_2}[1,e]$, and it is continuous on $C_{\omega_2}[1,e]$ with $\|.\|_{\omega_1}$ because ψ is arbitrarily selected.

Hypothesis (iv) of Theorem 4
$$\overline{P} + [\eta_2 K + K + \eta_2 k_{\omega_2}(q-p)] f(r) r \leqslant r$$
is equivalent to
$$\frac{1}{50} + \left[\frac{3}{2}\left(\sqrt[3]{16}-1\right) + (e-1)\right] r^2 \leqslant r. \tag{17}$$
The number r_0 chosen as $r_0 \in [0.0219212, 0.228201]$ satisfies inequality (17).

Therefore, we show the existence of solution for Equation (16) in the space $C_{\omega_1}[1,e]$ via Theorem 4.

5. Conclusions

In this paper, using a fixed-point theorem, the existence conditions for the solution of Fredholm integral equations of the form
$$\chi(l) = \varrho(l) + \chi(l) \int_p^q k(l,z)(V\chi)(z)dz$$
are investigated in the space $C_\omega[p,q]$. The main theorem is based on a useful technique. It is clear that this theorem is more general than many equations considered so far. By using a sufficient condition for the relative compactness in the space of functions with tempered moduli of continuity (see Theorem 2) and the classical Schauder fixed-point

theorem, we derive a new existence result (see Theorem 4). Fredholm integral equations are used in various scientific and engineering disciplines to model phenomena like heat transfer, population dynamics, and signal processing. The established results in this paper could be applied to problems in these fields where existence of solutions is crucial for model validity. The existence theorems provide a theoretical foundation for developing numerical methods to solve Fredholm integral equations. By guaranteeing the existence of a solution, these results can help guide the development of more robust and efficient numerical algorithms.

Author Contributions: Methodology and writing—original draft preparation: F.Ö., M.T.E., and Z.Ö.Ö. All authors have read and agreed to the published version of the manuscript.

Funding: The authors did not receive support from any organization for the submitted work.

Data Availability Statement: All data generated or analyzed during this study are included in this published article.

Conflicts of Interest: All authors certify that they have no affiliations with or involvement in any organization or entity with any financial interest or non-financial interest in the subject matter or materials discussed in this manuscript.

References

1. Baleanu, D.; Machado, J.A.T.; Luo, A.C.-J. *Fractional Dynamics and Control*; Springer: Berlin/Heidelberg, Germany, 2012.
2. Kilbas, A.A.; Srivastava, H.M.; Trujillo, J.J. *Theory and Applications of Fractional Differential Equations*, North-Holland Mathematics Studies; Elsevier Science B. V.: Amsterdam, The Netherland, 2006; Volume 204.
3. Lakshmikantham, V.; Leela, S.; Devi, J.V. *Theory of Fractional Dynamic Systems*; Cambridge Scientific Publishers: Cambridge, UK, 2009.
4. Miller, K.S.; Ross, B. *An Introduction to the Fractional Calculus and Differential Equations*; John Wiley: New York, NY, USA, 1993.
5. Podlubny, I. *Fractional Differential Equations*; Academic Press: San Diego, CA, USA, 1999.
6. Tarasov, V.E. *Fractional Dynamics: Application of Fractional Calculus to Dynamics of Particles, Fields and Media*; HEP; Springer: Berlin/Heidelberg, Germany, 2010.
7. Srivastava, H.M.; Deep, A.; Abbas S.; Hazarika, B. Solvability for a class of generalized functional-integral equations by means of Petryshyn's fixed point theorem. *J. Nonlinear Convex Anal.* **2021**, *22*, 2715–2737.
8. Banaś, J.; Nalepa, R. On the space of functions with growths tempered by a modulus of continuity and its applications. *J. Funct. Spaces Appl.* **2013**, *2013*, 820437. [CrossRef]
9. O'Regan, D. Existence theory for nonlinear Volterra integrodifferential and integral equations. *Nonlinear Anal.* **1998**, *31*, 317–341.
10. Banaś, J.; Rzepka, B. On existence and asymptotic stability of solutions of a nonlinear integral equation. *J. Math. Anal. Appl.* **2003**, *284*, 165–173. [CrossRef]
11. Argyros, I.K. Quadratic equations and applications to Chandrasekhars and related equations. *Bull. Austral. Math. Soc.* **1985**, *32*, 275–292. [CrossRef]
12. Freed, A.D.; Diethelm, K.; Luchko, Y. *Fractional-Order Viscoelasticity (FOV): Constitutive Developments Using the Fractional Calculus: First Annual Report*; Technical Memorandum, TM-2002-211914; NASA Glenn Research Center: Cleveland, OH, USA, 2002.
13. Agarwal, R.P.; O'Regan, D. *Infinite Interval Problems for Differential, Difference and Integral Equations*; Kluwer Academic Publishers: Dordrecht, The Netherlands, 2001.
14. Agarwal, R.P.; O'Regan, D.; Wong, P.J.Y. *Positive Solutions of Differential, Difference and Integral Equations*; Kluwer Academic Publishers: Dordrecht, The Netherlands, 1991.
15. Chandrasekhar, S. *Radiative Transfer*; Oxford University Press: London, UK, 1950.
16. Hu, S.; Khavani, M.; Zhuang, W. Integral equations arising in the kinetic theory of gases. *J. Appl. Anal.* **1989**, *34*, 261–266. [CrossRef]
17. Kelly, C.T. Approximation of solutions of some quadratic integral equations in transport theory. *J. Int. Eq.* **1982**, *4*, 221–237.
18. Argyros, I.K. On a class of quadratic integral equations with perturbation. *Funct. Approx. Comment. Math.* **1992**, *20*, 51–63.
19. Okrasinska-Plociniczak, H.; Plociniczak, L.; Rocha, J.; Sadarangani, K. Solvability in Hölder spaces of an integral equation which models dynamics of the capillary rise. *J. Math. Anal. Appl.* **2020**, *490*, 124237. [CrossRef]
20. Deimling, K. *Nonlinear Functional Analysis*; Springer: Berlin, Germany, 1985.
21. Marin, M. An approach of a heat-flux dependent theory for micropolar porous media. *Meccanica* **2016**, *51*, 1127–1133. [CrossRef]
22. Marin, M. Some estimates on vibrations in thermoelasticity of dipolar bodies. *J. Vib. Control* **2010**, *16*, 33–47. [CrossRef]
23. Toledano, J.M.A.; Benavides, T.D.; Acedo, G.L. *Measures of Noncompactness in Metric Fixed Point Theory*; Birkhauser: Basel, Switzerland, 1997.

24. Caballero, J.; Abdalla Darwish, M.; Sadarangani, K. Solvability of a quadratic integral equation of Fredholm type in Hölder spaces. *Electron. J. Differ. Equ.* **2014**, *2014*, 1–10. [CrossRef]
25. Peng, S.; Wang, J.; Chen, F. A Quadratic integral equations in the space of functions with tempered moduli of continuity. *J. Appl. Math. Inform.* **2015**, *33*, 351–363. [CrossRef]

MDPI AG
Grosspeteranlage 5
4052 Basel
Switzerland
Tel.: +41 61 683 77 34

Axioms Editorial Office
E-mail: axioms@mdpi.com
www.mdpi.com/journal/axioms

www.ingramcontent.com/pod-product-compliance
Lightning Source LLC
Chambersburg PA
CBHW061613210926
51850CB00009B/2305